Praise for

Hungry Heart

"Haven't we all wondered exactly how the many-splendored Jennifer Weiner became so many-splendored? This candid, poignant, and very funny memoir tells all, and I'm confident other readers will be as fascinated and moved by it as I was."

—Curtis Sittenfeld, *New York Times* bestselling author of *Eligible*

"You'll laugh, you'll cry, you'll want to read it again."

—*TheSkimm*

"The bestselling mastermind behind characters such as Cannie Shapiro bares her soul in a series of essays about family, writing, and body image. Weiner's first journey into nonfiction, this aptly titled memoir chronicles her childhood and adult life with a dose of wit. Like the protagonists of her novels, Weiner's voice is relatable and poignant as she shares the struggles that shaped the woman she is today."

—*Library Journal*

"In her new memoir, Weiner turns her understanding eye on her most compelling character yet—herself—and reveals the story behind some of her most beloved books. You'll laugh, you'll cry—and in true Jen style, there's a happy ending."

—*Good Housekeeping*

"Weiner lays her heart bare in this memoir, which is insightful and affecting and affirms exactly why she is so popular—she is gifted in the ability to write honestly and easily. In one essay, she talks about how reading Nora Ephron is 'more like sitting down for coffee with a friend than listening to a capital-A Author deliver pronouncements from on high.' The same can be said here, in spades."

—Booklist

"An unflinching look at Weiner's own experiences that will make you realize why she writes so persuasively about her characters' complicated issues: she's faced them herself. With the chatty, disarming frankness of a best friend, she tackles tough subjects . . . and mines her life for comic gold, too—and throws in some parenting advice and body-image pep talks for good measure."

—Entertainment Weekly

"A beautifully heartfelt new memoir. Her honesty, charm, and buoyant spirit come through on every page of this hilarious, wise, putting-it-all-out-there book."

—BookPage

"Just as warm and funny as you'd imagine . . . In *Hungry Heart* Weiner takes on marriage, love, parenthood, and that one summer that she was called 'the fat Jennifer' with grace, humor, and intelligence."

—PopSugar

"This memoir mirrors what we already know about Jennifer Weiner—from her Twitter commentary, from her books, from her public feuds on behalf of female authors. The through-line between #Franzenfreude and *The Bachelor* live-tweets is one very simple message: women's stories deserve to be told, in all their messy, wondrous glory. Jennifer Weiner is sharing her story, and maybe by reading hers, you'll find yourself feeling a little less alone."

—Bustle

"Funny, fierce, feisty!"

—Glamour

"Like her enormously popular commercial fiction, from its very first page this memoir will enthusiastically reach out to female readers and swiftly draw them close."

—*Publishers Weekly* (starred review)

"These essays investigate what it means to live as a woman today, navigating these labels and roles and how they all fit together."

—*Allure*

"With candor, wit, and insight, Jennifer Weiner writes beautifully about her darkest struggles and brightest triumphs, about growing up and getting on with it, about gaining and losing, about herself and also—ultimately—about all of us. I was spellbound by *Hungry Heart* from the first page to the last."

—Cheryl Strayed, *New York Times* bestselling author of *Wild*

"Fans of the *Good in Bed* author, rejoice! The prolific novelist spares no (or at least very few) details from her life in this generous memoir. From her struggles growing up as a bookish, overweight nerd to her fight for equality at Princeton's famed eating clubs to coping with being abandoned by her father to motherhood and beyond, Weiner pulls back the curtain on the experiences that have given her the material for her bestselling books. Weiner, who has fiercely defended the 'chick-lit' genre, continues to prove that there is a place for women's stories and they deserve to be told."

—*Real Simple*

"In this funny, brave, and bold book she tells the whole truth, and nothing but. It's her ups and downs and ups and downs, from which she got back up from again and again."

—Amy Poehler's Smart Girls

BOOKS BY JENNIFER WEINER

FICTION

Good in Bed

In Her Shoes

Little Earthquakes

Goodnight Nobody

The Guy Not Taken

Certain Girls

Best Friends Forever

Fly Away Home

Then Came You

The Next Best Thing

All Fall Down

Who Do You Love

FOR YOUNG READERS

The Littlest Bigfoot

hungry *heart*

ADVENTURES IN LIFE, LOVE,
AND WRITING

jennifer *Weiner*

WASHINGTON SQUARE PRESS

—

ATRIA

New York   London   Toronto   Sydney   New Delhi

An Imprint of Simon & Schuster, Inc.
1230 Avenue of the Americas
New York, NY 10020

First Washington Square Press/Atria Paperback edition June 2017

WASHINGTON SQUARE PRESS/**ATRIA** PAPERBACK and colophon are trademarks of Simon & Schuster, Inc.

For information about special discounts for bulk purchases, please contact Simon & Schuster Special Sales at 1-866-506-1949 or business@simonandschuster.com.

The Simon & Schuster Speakers Bureau can bring authors to your live event. For more information or to book an event, contact the Simon & Schuster Speakers Bureau at 1-866-248-3049 or visit our website at www.simonspeakers.com.

Manufactured in the United States of America

10 9 8 7 6 5 4 3

Library of Congress Cataloging-in-Publication Control Number: 2016022112

ISBN 978-1-4767-2340-2
ISBN 978-1-4767-2342-6 (pbk)
ISBN 978-1-4767-2344-0 (ebook)

For my family

"I wrote my way out."

—"HURRICANE," *HAMILTON*

Contents

Hungry Heart

The other day, I was walking from the hair salon to pick up my eight-year-old after school. It was a beautiful February afternoon, unseasonably sunny and springlike, with a sweet breeze rummaging in the tree branches that were just starting to bud.

Also, my hair looked spectacular.

I was feeling really good. I'd put in a solid morning writing; then I'd done a spinning class, where, according to the computerized rankings that I obsessively checked, I hadn't finished last. I was wearing my favorite jeans, which are dark-rinsed, straight-legged, stretchy and forgiving, and the Eileen Fisher cashmere sweater that I'd snagged for 70 percent off at the cash-only sale. With my UGG boots on my feet and my purse, with its furry purse-charm, slung over my shoulder, I strode confidently down Lombard Street, feeling like I was on top of things, like this was a day when I had it all figured out.

And then I fell.

My toe must have caught a crack in the pavement as I hurried to cross Twenty-Fifth Street before the light changed. I felt myself leave the ground, saw my arms flailing, then heard myself shout in pain after I smacked down on the pavement, landing on my knees and the heels of my hands. This was not a cute stumble, not the dainty little stutter-step you'd see in a ZZ Top video right before the band launched into a paean to the high-heel-wearing, miniskirted heroine's legs. This was a full-on pratfall, a wind-knocked-out-of-you, flat-out, oh-my-God, people-running-over-to-see-if-you're-okay face-plant.

I think I lay there whimpering for a minute before I hauled myself to my feet, assured my fellow pedestrians that I was fine, staggered through the school gate, and inspected the damage. There was dirt and grit and gravel ground into my palms. My jeans were torn. Both of my knees were bruised and bleeding.

"Mommy, are you okay?" asked Phoebe moments later when she came out of the classroom and found me holding a paper napkin to my knee.

"Yeah, I'll be fine," I muttered. I limped outside, where we waited for an Uber—no way was I walking home in this condition—and I realized that this was not just a trip, not just a stumble; it was a metaphor for my life, maybe for every woman's life.

You fall, you get hurt, you get up again.

Last summer, the *New York Times* wrote a profile of the author Judy Blume, in which she described herself and her work. "I'm a storyteller—you know what I mean—an inventor of people," Blume said. "And their relationships. It's not that I love the words—that's not the kind of writer I am. So I'm not"—she made a furious scribbling motion with her right hand—"I'm not a great writer. But maybe I'm a really good storyteller."

I don't think I've ever identified so completely with a description, or the way it plays into the seemingly endless debate over what qualifies as literature. I, too, am a storyteller; I, too, eschew the furious-scribbling-motion kind of writing. I care about language and structure and pace, but I care about plot and characters more. I know I'm not the kind of writer who wins prizes and a place on the ninth-grade summer reading list, the kind of writer who gets called "great." And, lucky me, if I was ever in danger of forgetting precisely where on the literary food chain I reside, there are people lined up on the Internet to remind me.

But "great writer" was never my ambition . . . and I suspect was never within the realm of possibility. I believe that, through education and inclination, through temperament and history, all authors grow up to be a particular kind of writer, to tell a specific type of story. We could no more change the kind of work we do—the voice in which we write, the characters that call to us—than we could our own blood type.

I am the proud and happy writer of popular fiction, and I would never argue that it matters as much as the award-winning, breathtaking, life-changing meditations on love and humanity and the Way We Live Now. I would also note that critics still stumble over the gender divide, where a man's dissection of a marriage or a family is seen as important and literary, whereas a woman's book about the same topic is dismissed as precious and jewel-like, domestic and small. Double standards persist, and in general, men's books are still perceived as more meaningful, more important, more desirable. Last summer, a writer for the feminist website *Jezebel* revealed that querying six literary agents under a male name netted her five responses (including three requests to see the manuscript) within twenty-four hours, while the exact same letter, sent fifty times under her own name, had gotten a total of just two invitations to send her manuscript. "The judgments about my work that had seemed as solid as the walls of my house had turned out to be meaningless," she wrote. "My novel wasn't the problem, it was me—Catherine."

Clearly, there is progress to be made in terms of how we regard women's work . . . and being the one who points out the problem does not earn you the Miss Congeniality sash. Particularly when your insistence on fair play and a level playing field is interpreted as a form of delusion about the kind of books you write and the kind of attention you deserve.

She thinks she's as good as Jonathan Franzen, my critics sneer. *She thinks her stuff belongs in the* New Yorker. Not true! As a lifelong reader of both literary and popular fiction, I am completely equipped to tell the difference, and I know what belongs where. What I believe is that popular fiction by and for women deserves the same regard as popular fiction by and for men. I believe that if the *New York Times* is going to review mysteries and thrillers and science fiction, it should also review romance—which remains by far the bestselling genre of all literature—and everything that comes under the catch-all umbrella of "commercial women's fiction." Maybe books like mine won't win the National Book Award, but that doesn't mean they don't matter at all. Nor does it mean that the women who read them deserve to be ignored or erased. Women's stories matter, the stories we write, the stories we read—the big-deal winners of literary prizes, and Harlequin romances, and documentaries, and soap operas, and PBS investigations, and Lifetime movies of the week. *Women's stories matter.* They tell us who we are, they give us places to explore our problems, to try on identities and imagine happy endings. They entertain us, they divert us, they comfort us when we're lonely or alone. Women's stories matter. And women matter, too.

• • •

You fall down. You get hurt. You get up again.

In my own life, I can trace the ups and downs, the things that have gone spectacularly wrong, and the things that have gone right beyond any imagining. There has been heartache. There has been embarrassment. There was that time I had to read about my father's scrotum in the newspaper. (Fear not; we'll get there.)

But I've realized my childhood dream of becoming a published author and a contributing writer for the *New York Times*. I have a beautiful home in a city I love, and friends who've stood by me, and a wonderful, loving, crazy family that's come with me for the ride.

I've lived through a divorce and a miscarriage. I've seen my books become successful in a way few books do. I've taken stands, and taken heat, and—I hope—seen the world change, a little bit, because I spoke up.

I had a father who left me. I have girls whom I will never leave. I had a marriage end. I have a man I hope will love me forever.

You fall down. You get hurt. You get up again.

These are stories about hunger, that thing that women are taught to ignore or endure. They're about wanting something from a world that instructs women that appetites are unattractive, that we should never push, should never demand, and should never, ever raise our voices. But we all want something from the world—love, approval, a boyfriend, a partner, a sense of belonging, a way of doing some good. We all desire, we all yearn, we all dream that if only I had this or lost that, if I could live in that house, marry that man, get that promotion, lose those thirty pounds, then my life would be perfect. As we get older we all learn that there isn't a finish line . . . or maybe there is, but it keeps moving. It's a rare moment where we look around, sigh with satisfaction, pull our spouse or kids or pets or parents closer, and say, *This is perfect*, or *Now I have everything*. Wanting is the human condition. It's what led us to invent fire and the wheel and Instagram. There's nothing wrong with desire, but just like every self-help book, bumper sticker, and issue of *O* magazine insists, it's not the destination that matters, but the journey; not the summit but the climb.

I know I'll never get every single thing I dreamed of. I'll never be thin. I'll never win a Pulitzer or even, probably, the pie-baking contest at the Agriculture Fair in Truro every August (because I think the judges are biased against summer people, but that's another story). I will never get a do-over on my first marriage, or on my older daughter's infancy; I'll never get to not be divorced. I will never give birth again, and neither of my births were what I'd hoped for. I'll never get my father back; never get to ask him why he left and whether he was sorry and whether he ever found what he was looking for. But, dammit, I got this far, and I got some stories along the way, and maybe that was the point, the point of the whole thing, the point all along.

I know how lucky I am for this simple reason: I remember being six years old and telling anyone who asked that I wanted to be a writer. And now here I am—I got to be the thing I wanted to be when I grew up. How many people get to say that? (Besides every fireman and ballerina.)

I knew I wanted to write, and I knew what kind of writer I wanted to be and who I was there for. To the extent that there was choice involved, I wanted to write novels for the girls like me, the ones who never got to see themselves on TV or in the movies, the ones who learned to flip quickly past the fashion spreads in *Elle* and *Vogue* because nothing in those pictures would ever fit, the ones who learned to turn away from mirrors and hurry past their reflections and instantly unfocus their eyes when confronted with their own image. I wanted to say to those girls and women, *I see you. You matter.* I wanted to give them stories like life rafts, or cozy blankets on cold nights, or a friend who'd sit next to you and tell you that whatever was happening, it was going to be okay. I wanted to tell them what I wish someone had told me when I was young and my own father said that no one would want me, that I'd never be worth much: to hang on and believe in yourself and fight for your own happy ending. I wanted to tell them that you can find friends who become like your sisters, that you can build a family that will cherish and support you, that you can find partners who will see your beauty, that you can find work that you love, that you can make a place for yourself in the world.

These are my stories about hunger and satisfaction, about falling down and getting up and moving on. They're stories about learning, slowly but surely, that the grace isn't in the happily-ever-after but in the fall, and the pain, the bruised knees and bloody palms, and then the sheepish scramble back onto your feet.

And now here they are for you.

The Outsiders

They fuck you up, your mum and dad.

It is a truth universally acknowledged among writers that an unhappy childhood is the greatest gift a parent can provide. What's less discussed is how many of us would return that gift, if only we could.

Philip Larkin's "This Be the Verse" is everyone's go-to poem, universally beloved because it's universally true. There's no one who doesn't feel wronged by her parents; no one who, when the time comes and if she's honest, can't imagine that she'll cause her own children pain.

But when I think about my parents, the poem that comes to mind is "I Go Back to May 1937," by Sharon Olds. The poem begins with the narrator watching her parents, who are young and beautiful, in college, as they fall in love:

> *They are about to graduate, they are about to get married*
> *they are kids, they are dumb, all they know is they are*
> *innocent, they would never hurt anybody.*

But then they do.

I want to go up to them and say Stop,
don't do it—she's the wrong woman,
he's the wrong man, you are going to do things
you cannot imagine you would ever do,
you are going to do bad things to children
you are going to suffer in ways you have not heard of,
you are going to want to die.

Stop. Don't do it. She's the wrong woman. He's the wrong man.
My parents met in college, and the story of how was always one of my favorites.

It is, I imagine, a beautiful, crisp fall morning in Ann Arbor, Michigan, in September 1961. Coeds are streaming through campus, carrying their books, pushing their bicycles. It's bicycle registration day, and everyone who's got a bike has to sign it up.

My mother—blond and blue-eyed, five foot eight, a tennis and basketball and field hockey standout, broad-shouldered and big-handed and strong—is waiting in line with her blue Schwinn ten-speed. My father—barrel-chested, short and stocky, with curly black hair, deep-set dark brown eyes, an aggressive beak of a nose, and thick horn-rimmed plastic glasses—is walking along a glass-lined corridor called the Fishbowl. He looks down and spots my mother.

"All of the other girls were crouching down, or lying on their backs, trying to see the number underneath the seat," he would tell me and my sister and my brothers as we sat, enthralled. "And your mom just lifted her bike over her head." He would demonstrate, lifting one arm up as fast as if he were holding feathers, and smile with nostalgic approval.

He must have imagined that she was some Nordic goddess, a shiksa, the ultimate forbidden fruit for a Jewish boy who'd gone to an Orthodox yeshiva all through elementary school, and fed himself canned foods on paper plates because his parents refused to keep kosher. He must have been disappointed to learn not only that Frances Lynn Frumin was Jewish, but that his family and hers were practically neighbors, and that his father and her uncle had been friends, and their mothers played mah-jongg together.

My mother's father, Herman, came to America when he was twelve, sailing to Ellis Island from a shtetl that Google tells me is called Krychyl's'k, in the Ukraine. His parents had left him in the old country with his maternal grandparents while they got settled and, eventually, had another son, an English-speaking American boy who must have been bewildering to my grandfather when he finally arrived. He was smart enough for college, and he'd dreamed of law school, but the Great Depression changed his plans. He finished high school, stayed in college for a year, and went to work, eventually in the furniture business, starting off with an assistant and a cart, going to apartments where there'd been a death or a divorce to make an offer on the furniture. My Nanna finished high school, spent a summer learning to be a key-punch operator, but couldn't find a job and went to work at Kresge's, a five-and-dime on the corner, where she managed a counter of yarn and thread and notions.

Faye met her future husband when she was sixteen. For New Year's in 1931, Nanna was supposed to have gone to Grand Rapids to meet a boy, spending the week with her aunt and uncle and New Year's Eve with him, but a snowstorm kept her in Detroit. Her best friend Edith's boyfriend, Leonard, said, "I have a fella— he's very nice and very shy, and will you go?" Nanna went. "Your grandfather was the handsomest man there. Dressed beautifully. I told him I'd go with him, but that I wouldn't go seriously. I said, 'I'm not getting serious until I'm twenty-one.'" She kept her word, dating other people, living first in Detroit with her older sister Sophie and Sophie's husband, Max, then moving in with her parents, who'd gone to Flint after the bakery in Detroit where her father worked had closed and he'd been offered a job there. "Herman always came to visit. Every Sunday. I knew I was going to marry him." When she was twenty-one, she did.

They honeymooned in Atlantic City, making the trip by car and bringing Nanna's little brother Freddy, who'd never seen the ocean, along for the ride. Then they settled in Detroit and eventually had two daughters, my aunt Marlene, born in 1941, and my mother, Frances, who arrived two years later.

Marlene was the good girl: blond, feminine, an academic standout who skipped a grade and finished college at nineteen. Frances sounds like a precursor to my sister, Molly, with a twist of my older daughter, Lucy—willful and smart and stubborn, determined to get her way and willing to throw terrible tantrums to make it happen.

"Oh, yes, she was a handful," says Nanna, her voice clear and vibrant on the phone. Nanna celebrated her hundredth birthday six months ago. Her mind is still sharp, and her memories of her younger daughter still make her sound both rueful and amused.

"She was the exact opposite of Marlene. She was fun but hard to handle. She wanted her way, and that was it!"

Fran's lackey and worshipful sycophant was her cousin Sharon, Nanna's brother's daughter. Freddy had come home from the war with a Purple Heart and courted and married Ruth, a war widow with a young daughter. He'd adopted Sharon, who was a year younger than my mother and who, according to Nanna, would have done anything for Fran's approval.

"Your mother would tell Sharon, 'We're going fishing. But you have to get up early to get the fish.' So Sharon would get up at four in the morning, and we'd hear her in the kitchen, making Frances her cheese sandwiches . . . and then your mother would make her go outside and dig the worms!"

Fran loved lemon meringue pie and taking big biographies

out of the library. She hated to clean. "She never hung anything up. Not one thing. It was all either on her bed or on the floor. I wouldn't clean in there, and I told Margie, the girl who cleaned for us, not to go in there either. I said, 'She knows where everything is.' And then," Nanna says, pausing dramatically for the punch line, "at camp she got a blue ribbon for the neatest bunk. I never got over it. A blue ribbon!"

Nanna's favorite Fran story unfolded in New York. Nanna and Pappa had gone on vacation with Freddy and Ruth and Sharon and Marlene and a seven- or eight-year-old Fran. "We stayed at the Waldorf, and money wasn't that great back then. They wanted dessert, and I said, 'We'll order a piece of pie for every two people, and we'll share.' Well, your mother wouldn't have it. She wanted her own slice! Sharon said, 'I won't have any. Frances can have mine.' She was so crazy about Frances that she'd let her have anything. But your mother insisted. She had to have her own piece. So we got her her own piece."

Girls weren't allowed to wear pants to school back then. Fran didn't care. "I can't tell you how many times I got called to school to come in and talk about her—about her clothes, or that she was annoying people. I'd tell them, 'I'm sorry, I can't do a thing about it. She refuses to wear a dress.'" She and Pappa considered private school, "but that didn't appeal at all. There was nothing we could do but get her through to college."

Now that I have girls myself—one of them a tomboy who'd rather have her nails pulled out than have her hair blown dry, who'd rather give up her iPhone than put on a dress—I can imagine what my mother must have been like, the fights over clothes and shoes and hair, the negotiations and threats and bribes. In the Fran and Sharon stories, I hear echoes of my daughters—willful, stubborn Lucy, demanding to have things her way, and sweet, placating Phoebe, saying, in her piping little voice, "It is okay. She can have mine." I can imagine how Nanna must have decided when to fight and when she'd just let little Franny ride off on her bike, dressed in a checked shirt and cowgirl boots and pants.

When my mother was seven, her parents decided that she was old enough to spend her summers at Camp Tanuga, a sleep-away camp in northern Michigan. My mother loved camp—loved the freedom, loved the outdoors, loved paddling a canoe and learning to play tennis. She and her sister went for ten summers, each going from camper to counselor. Marlene eventually met her husband there.

At Mumford High in Detroit, Fran was a three-sport athlete, and ran for student council with the slogan "NO B.S.*," in big letters, with an asterisk below attached to the words "BETTER SECRETARY," in smaller type. She followed Marlene to the University of Michigan, where, if she'd been like most girls, she would have been expected to find a husband and to choose between the two available, acceptable careers—teacher or nurse.

My father's childhood was more complicated. His father, Abe, was a contractor, an enormous, jovial man who weighed three hundred pounds when he died at age fifty-three. Abe loved a party, loved to play cards, and had a sharp sense of humor. Visiting a potential client's house, he'd survey the kitchen or bathroom they wanted renovated, discuss his proposal and his price, then smile. "Sound good?" he'd ask . . . and, when the homeowner would politely agree, he'd say, "Then let's get started," and lift a sledgehammer over his shoulder, bringing it down to smash a bathtub or a countertop, thus ensuring that he, and not another contractor, would be hired to fix the damage and do the job. I wonder about that story a lot; about the way that my dad looked when he told it. What message were we supposed to take? What moral were we meant to draw from his smirk, his raised eyebrows, his pleased expression? When we grew up, would we be rewarded for sliding around the rules like that?

His mother, like my mother's mom, had been born with the

name Fanny, and again, like my mom's mom, had changed it to Faye. She was Canadian, and one of my father's earliest memories was learning the roster of American presidents, helping her study for the citizenship test. Faye was always well dressed and proper, her hair sprayed and set in a bouffant, in lipstick and crisp dresses with narrow leather belts. She liked things tidy and quiet and clean, but she'd married a man who liked noise and tumult, liquor and cigarettes, a man who chose to be out of the house a lot, leaving her alone with her children. For adult companionship, she had her husband's two sisters, Ann and Alice, who both eventually ended up institutionalized—Ann for schizophrenia and manic spending sprees, Alice for intransigent depression. They were both given electroshock therapy and, at one point, they were both in the same facility, where Alice refused to speak to Ann, even when they were wheeled past each other on their way to the treatment room.

Like my mother, my father had a single sibling, a sister, nine years younger, named Renay, spelled phonetically to ensure it would always be pronounced correctly. When Larry was left in charge of his sister, he'd roll her up so tightly in a quilt that she couldn't move, then abandon her. Or he'd tell her that John Beresford Tipton, the titular star of *The Millionaire*, had stopped by while she was in the bathroom, and that he'd had a check, but when my dad said Renay was unavailable, he'd headed off to another little girl's house.

Like my mom, my father went to public elementary schools, but then he attended an Orthodox yeshiva after school, traveling from his suburb to Detroit's old Jewish neighborhood because, he said, the yeshiva bus stopped on his corner, and so his parents put him on it. It was a strange way to grow up, trying to observe the dietary laws and religious rituals that his parents had abandoned. His only friends were his cousins. Ann and Alice had both given their sons the same name, although one was Allen and the other was Allyn, always called "Zissl," which was his middle name. For his ninth birthday, my father used to tell us, his parents bought him a bicycle . . . only he wasn't allowed to ride it. Too dangerous. Besides, his mother was already thinking about medical school, and surgeons had to protect their hands. My father was allowed to go visit his bike, to look at it in the window of the hardware store, but not ride it, not once. Not ever.

He, too, attended Mumford High, but never met my mom, until he spied her that morning from the Fishbowl and vowed that she would be his.

So he orchestrated an introduction and invited my mom to come over and watch Adlai Stevenson discussing the Cuban Missile Crisis.

Larry ushered Fran into a slovenly off-campus apartment. ("Socks," my mother recalls. "I remember dirty black socks. Everywhere.") He served her canned Franco-American SpaghettiOs and regaled her with his thoughts on politics. Somehow, all of this led to a second date, and then they became a casual couple for a few months. The romance sputtered after my dad invited my mother to celebrate New Year's Eve at a fancy restaurant. He ordered lobster, the most expensive and, coincidentally, the least kosher thing on the menu, and spent the night throwing up in the bathroom.

"We broke up after that," my mother reports. But six months later, my dad was back, standing at her off-campus apartment door, with a cigar clenched between his teeth. "Want to go to the track?" he asked. She went. They were married in June 1967, the big, fancy synagogue wedding and sit-down dinner that my mom didn't want. "Just send me an invitation, and I'll show up," my mother told her mother . . . and that is exactly what she did.

So Frannie Frumin became Fran Weiner, and my father became Captain Weiner. The two of them drove cross-country from Detroit to Louisiana, and my father reported for duty at Fort

Polk, hoping desperately not to be sent to Vietnam. They lived in an army-issued trailer, in a town that still hosted the occasional Klan rally. On the night of March 27, 1970, Fran went into labor, and Larry, a physician, freaked out. Arriving at the base hospital, he tried to open a locked door, refusing to give up, insisting that he knew the way in, that his door was the right one, even when my mother toted the suitcase she'd packed around to the back, found the correct, unlocked door, checked herself in, and gave birth the next morning.

They named me Jennifer Agnes—Jennifer, because they liked the song "Jennifer Juniper" and, isolated as they were, had no idea how popular the name was becoming; Agnes was in memory of Abe, my father's father, and because they'd seen an Italian movie where one of the characters was a prostitute named Agnesia.

I was, according to Fran, an easy baby, relaxed and good-natured and given to spending my early morning hours staring quietly at my mobile or my hand. I was the kind of baby who left her parents with the impression that they were excellent, competent nurturers who could easily handle additions to their family. God laughed. Fifteen months later, they had my sister, Molly, who was born faceup and screaming, and has not stopped screaming since.

When my father was discharged from the army, my mom says that they never thought of going back to Michigan. They were ready to see the country, to live somewhere different, to be on their own, unlike their sisters, who both ended up moving blocks away from their parents and the houses where they'd grown up.

My father had offers to finish his training in psychiatry in New York City, in Washington, DC, in Boston, and in Connecticut, at the Institute of Living in West Hartford. As my parents drove over Avon Mountain, with a toddler and a newborn asleep in their car seats, Simsbury, Connecticut, must have looked idyllic, like a movie set: sweet, sleepy, small-town New England. There were farms with red barns and fields like green and gold squares of a patchwork quilt. The First Church of Christ stood at the corner of Hopmeadow Street and Firetown Road, its white spires bright against the blue sky. There was a five-and-dime called Leader's, and an ice-cream shop called A. C. Peterson's, and a grocery store called Fitzgerald's where both of my brothers would eventually work, bagging groceries after school. There were ponds where you could swim in the summer or skate in the winter, a recreation complex with pools and courts for tennis and paddleball. The public high school had a crew team that rowed on the Farmington River, and students at Ethel Walker, a private girls' boarding school, rode and jumped their horses in a vast, rolling meadow across the street from their tidy brick campus.

Simsbury was eight hundred miles and completely different from Michigan. Simsbury was unfamiliar, un-Jewish, unlike any place they'd lived before. It had an outstanding public school system, and you could get much more house for your money than in neighboring West Hartford, where there were two synagogues and a Jewish Community Center.

Maybe they thought it would be exciting, a challenge, a fresh start. Maybe they didn't think about being outsiders, or how their kids would grow up in a religious minority . . . or, if they did, maybe they believed that a childhood spent on the margins would teach us resilience. Maybe they just saw how beautiful the town looked, dozing in the light of early summer, and didn't think of anything at all.

With my mother's parents' help, Fran and Larry bought a three-bedroom, single-story ranch house at 9 Simsbury Manor Drive, in a part of town called Weatogue, near the base of Talcott Mountain. There were families with kids our age across the street. Our next-door neighbors had an aboveground pool, where we learned to swim. In our backyard, a cherry tree bloomed exuberantly pink in the spring and grew tart glossy-red fruit in the summer.

My siblings and I grew up in a house full of books. The living-room wall was lined with plank-and-cinder-block shelves that sagged beneath the weight of my father's medical textbooks and hefty biographies, the books by Jewish authors—Saul Bellow, Philip Roth, Isaac Bashevis Singer—that he and my mother both liked, the novels and contemporary fiction that my mother read for the two book clubs she would eventually join. The two of them were readers, too, of books and magazines and the two papers—three on Sundays—that we got. They wanted to raise kids who were readers, too, which meant limiting television to a scant hour a day of PBS (with occasional dips into network programming for *Mutual of Omaha's Wild Kingdom*) and throwing their library wide open. The rule was that any child could take any book off the shelf and read it, provided we could give an explanation of the story to Mom or Dad.

In the mornings, my father would put on suits and ties and shiny shoes and go off to work. My mother supervised us, or sent us out to play, or left me alone to read. She'd give us sandwiches for lunch and baked chicken or pasta or steak for dinner, with a scoop of ice cream or three Oreos for dessert. At night, after dinner, my father was the one who clipped our fingernails, lifting each child onto his lap, his hands steady around the tiny manicure scissors, and he was the one who read us our bedtime stories. We'd lie next to him, tucked into my parents' big bed, and my father would read *Grimm's Fairy Tales* or *Where the Sidewalk Ends* or *The Red Balloon*. He found abridged versions of Shakespeare and the *Aeneid*, and collections of classic poems for children. Sometimes he'd make tapes of himself reading "The Charge of the Light Brigade" or "Barbara Frietchie," and I'd interrupt the poem to ask a pressing question. "Daddy, will you make us French toast tomorrow?" "Sure," came my father's deep, soothing voice. "Sure."

I must have sensed even then that he was quirky, that he had a strange sense of humor, that there was a darkness about him, that he was different from the other dads. He was fastidious about his clothes, and particular about his car, a silver 1976 Corvette with a maroon leather interior—he didn't like us touching it, or even, it seemed, looking at it for too long. He hated to socialize, and, sometimes, if my mother had invited people over for a dinner party, he'd hide in the closet, once stomping on a bag of potato chips, like a six-year-old throwing a tantrum, to communicate his pique. But he could be funny, too, growing his beard out every October and dressing like Fidel Castro, with his army jacket inside out, his pants tucked into his boots, and a cigar between his teeth. For an anniversary, he found a cement sculpture of a boar and left it in the shower with a note for my mom: "Fifteen years and it's never been boring." I don't remember cruelty. That came later. When I was a little girl, five and six and seven, what I remember was how much he loved me, how he was kind and gentle and endlessly patient, how he made me feel safe, how he praised me for asking good questions or reading big words; how, when we asked him to tell us a story, he never refused.

Molly and I and eventually Jake, who was born in 1973, went to nursery school at the Jewish Community Center in West Hartford three mornings a week. While we painted at easels, wearing our father's cast-off button-downs as smocks, or ate grapes and graham crackers, or napped, my mother swam in the JCC's Olympic-size pool, and would come get us with her hair still wet, smelling of chlorine.

Back then, I had a button nose and wavy light brown hair. I was cute in a way I've never been since. Molly and I had matching pigtails, and, while my mother's fashion sense could best be described as "not naked," our grandparents sent us the occasional ensemble, like our complementary T-shirts—mine said KISS ME and Molly's said HUG ME.

We lived two blocks from Latimer Lane Elementary School, a new, modern brick building that housed kindergarten through sixth grade. Living that close to the school made me a "walker," which meant—as unthinkable as it seems now—that when I was five years old and ready for kindergarten, I was allowed to walk, by myself, down Simsbury Manor Drive, then along two blocks of busy Mountain View Road, and across the street to school. I would set off in the mornings, spending the next four hours with Miss Burdick, who'd let me read quietly in a corner—*Black Beauty* or the Bobbsey Twins, *Anne of Green Gables* or the Encyclopedia Brown mysteries—while my classmates colored or practiced writing their letters and numbers, and then I would walk home in time for lunch.

Simsbury was one of the first school districts in the state to offer gifted classes, mandatory enrichment for kids whose IQs were over a certain level. When I was five, my father walked with me to Latimer Lane on a Saturday and, bent over to look me in the eye, gravely informed me that I would be taking an important test, and that I should do my best. For the next few hours, I sat in a guidance counselor's office, re-creating patterns with black-and-white blocks, reciting back series of numbers and, at the tester's instruction, drawing a picture of a person. My subject was my father, of course, with his curly beard and his tie and his glasses, and I remember that I kept asking for the paper back, to add another detail—the knot of the tie, his ears, a shoelace. I wanted to make it clear to whoever was grading the test that this was someone of great importance, someone specific and special—my father.

I don't know what my score was, but it was good enough to get me tagged as "gifted." My teachers would give me extra work, sending me home with math word problems, or more challenging addition and subtraction. Mrs. Palen, my first-grade teacher, would let me stay in from recess and write poems, or stories. I preferred reading and writing in the empty classroom to running around a playground in the company of my peers.

When I was eight years old, we moved across town, into a four-bedroom Colonial on Harvest Hill Road where I'd live until I left for college. My mother was pregnant again, and my father was doing well enough to buy a house with a two-car garage and an inground swimming pool in the backyard so that, in the summertime, my mom could swim laps at home, and we could have pool parties, where Fran would serve barbecued chicken or steak at wooden picnic tables on the deck.

Our new neighborhood, West Simsbury, was fancier than our old one. Everything was bigger—the lawns, the houses, the rooms themselves. The bedroom that I'd share with Molly had wall-to-wall white carpeting, cream-colored wallpaper with a pattern of strawberry vines, twin beds, matching white dressers, and a white bookcase in the center with a foldout desk that neither one of us used. My favorite reading spot was on my belly, on the floor between the beds. Molly's favorite activity was jumping from bed to bed, chanting, "The quick brown fox jumps OVER the lazy dog, the quick brown fox jumps OVER the lazy dog." I would ignore her, as my mother had instructed, until I couldn't take it anymore, and I'd thrust my fist in the air, catching Molly mid-jump in the belly, sending her crashing down on top of me.

With our new home came a new school. Where Latimer Lane was bright and airy, Belden was a hulking brownstone that seemed to huddle away from the street and glower at pedestrians in the shade. At one time it had been the district's high school, so it was enormous, with endless staircases, echoing bathrooms, and cavernous classrooms that seemed ill suited for little kids. Belden combined its second and third grade into one class, so there were dozens of kids to meet. Amy Smallwood had a loud voice and black hair and big teeth; Christie Kellerman, even at eight, was cool and beautiful, blond and blue-eyed, with feathered hair and a thin navy-blue ribbon around the neck of her pale blue button-down. Brendan Flaherty was squinty and flat-faced and freckled, a boy who couldn't see a ponytail without yanking it, or pass a water fountain without jamming his thumb over the spigot.

One warm fall morning my first week at Belden, Brendan cornered me in the playground. "You're Jewish," he said.

I lifted my chin. "Yes."

Brendan glared at me. "You killed Jesus."

I was shocked. I knew that being Jewish meant that my family celebrated different holidays, that our prayers were in a different language, that we went to synagogue instead of church and celebrated Chanukah, not Christmas. But this was the first time I'd been insulted for my religion, the first time I'd ever connected being Jewish with doing something wrong. And as for Jesus, my mother had explained that Jews believed he was "a great teacher," but not the Messiah, which left me with the vague impression that Jesus was like Miss Burdick or Mrs. Palen, that He'd taught kids like me, maybe in a neighboring district or a different school. I might not have been clear on where He worked, but I was positive no one I knew was responsible for His demise.

Tears prickled the backs of my eyes. "I didn't kill anyone!"

Brendan shrugged. "Probably your parents did."

I hit him in the nose. He bled. We both cried, and we both got in trouble. That was the beginning of my unhappy time in Simsbury, which would stretch out for the better part of the next decade.

Ultimately, religion was the least of my problems. Simsbury was a place where good looks mattered, and the preppy aesthetic ruled. With my wardrobe of hand-me-downs from Aunt Marlene's daughter Rachel and clearance items from Marshalls, with my big nose and dark skin, my Semitic features, and eventually, my ungainly body, I was neither pretty nor preppy. I took up space. I made noise. I was smart and mouthy, cracking jokes my classmates didn't get, trying out my new vocabulary words in conversation, even if I wasn't sure I was pronouncing them right. I wanted friends desperately, but I couldn't understand how the thing that pleased my father the most—my intelligence—could make other kids hate me. So I'd thrust my hand in the air every time I knew an answer, and I would casually drop references to Freud or Isaac Asimov into conversations in the cafeteria, or say things like "Kelly! Have you no couth!" to an undoubtedly befuddled classmate at the bus stop.

On Girl Scout hiking trips, I'd spend my time talking to the troop leader. At away games, the soccer coach would have to assign one of her daughters to be my roommate, because no girl ever volunteered. On the bus to and from school, I would sit by myself; on the playground, during recess, I'd be by myself. After school, I would sometimes join the neighborhood pack that included my siblings and the kids who lived nearby, and I would always have a book to keep me company, but I never had a real friend, a friend who was just mine.

Simsbury, and the people who lived there, looked like an Abercrombie & Fitch ad. I looked like a Lane Bryant outtake that had wandered onto the set. My sister was petite and adorable, my brothers were athletic and handsome, all of them were well liked, but I was large and weird and unlucky. Other kids could, for example, get away with a quick nose-pick, or discreetly pulling their underwear out of their butt crack after it had ridden up during chorus. Not me. I always ended up picking my wedgie in full view of Christie Kellerman, who'd laugh, and point, and call her friends over to join in the mockery.

I'm not sure my parents knew about my social ineptitude or how lonely I was. If they'd known, I'm not sure what they would have done; whether they would have tried to fix it. My guess is that they would have left it alone, saying, *This will give you empathy, and stories to tell*, or *Someday this pain will be useful to you*. It was a different time . . . and, soon enough, my parents would be locked in their own battles, their own misery, and my father wouldn't be a father to us anymore.

In the Sharon Olds poem, the narrator imagines pulling the

paper dolls apart, setting her parents on different paths, away from each other. Of course she doesn't, no more than any of us can or would.

> *. . . I want to live. I*
> *take them up like the male and female*
> *paper dolls and bang them together*
> *at the hips, like chips of flint, as if to*
> *strike sparks from them, I say*
> *Do what you are going to do, and I will tell about it.*

It would be years and years before I could tell about it, before I could take the raw material of all that hurt and embarrassment and spin it into fiction, but even at five or six or seven, I was already taking steps in the right direction. I was always writing—back then, it was poems about the wind and spring flowers, or short stories about lost balloons. With my teachers' encouragement, I would submit the poems to children's magazines. One summer day when I was eight or nine, I went to get the mail for my mother, who was probably expecting a new issue of the *New Yorker*, and was surprised to find an envelope with my name—JENNY WEINER—typed on the front. Inside was a check for twenty-five dollars and a letter, on stationery with a letterhead on top, informing me that my poem "The Sunny Day" was going to be published.

I can remember everything (except strangely the name of the magazine)—the feeling of the envelope in my hands, the slap of my bare feet on the burning pavement as I ran across the street and through the front yard, then the house, and up to the pool, the way my heart jumped when I saw my name, typed out, all official looking, my mother's delight when I told her. For days I walked around, wrapped in my own invisible robe of happiness. Someone had paid me—had given me money—for words that I'd written! Other people would read those words and would see what I'd wanted them to see and feel the way I'd wanted my words to make them feel!

It was one of the best days I'd ever had, and even though it would be years before anyone else paid me for a piece of writing, I'd been set on the path. Storytelling—taking readers into a place you'd created, just with marks on a page—that was a kind of magic. If I could figure out how to make that magic my life's work, I would be the luckiest girl in the world.

I wrote whenever I could . . . but my encouraging first-grade teacher gave way to a less indulgent second-grade teacher, who made it clear that I was an aggravation, mostly because I had the bad habit of reading in between words during spelling quizzes, pulling my book out of my desk and into my lap as soon as I'd scribbled down the answer. Mrs. Brooks accused me of cheating; I told her that I was just bored because of her "interminable pauses." My parents were called in, the principal was consulted, and, together, they all decided that I'd skip third grade. Because, really, what better to do with the chunky, mouthy, socially inept eight-year-old than move her into a different school with strange classmates a year older than she is?

The trend of skipping grades stopped once educators realized that they were creating a generation of social cripples. By then it was too late for me. On my first day of fourth grade, it felt like everyone took turns telling me that I'd gotten off the bus at the wrong school. "No, I'm supposed to be here," I kept saying. It seemed like my classmates didn't believe me . . . or that, if they did, they didn't want it to be true.

Luckily, my new school had a dedicated gifted teacher. Every day, I'd skip social studies and science and go to Mrs. Ciabotti's little classroom, with its glass walls that looked out into the hall (all those missed classes are the reason that I can't read a map, name the states or their capitals, or explain photosynthesis or why the sky is blue).

Mrs. Ciabotti was a trim woman with iron-gray hair and bright blue eyes. She wore shirtwaist dresses, pink lipstick, and glasses, and she treated education like an all-you-can-eat buffet, where the five of us—me, Louise, Peter, Philip, and Derek, who'd also skipped third grade—were allowed to fill our plates by ourselves, sampling whatever we wanted, gorging on our favorites.

In her classroom, we'd go on deep-dives into the environment or history or human biology. In fifth grade, I won a local science fair with a scale model of the human nervous system, complete with electrical circuits that lit up if viewers followed the taped narration and pulled the switches at the right times. Mrs. Ciabotti would let me spend entire afternoons with a book and a dictionary and a stack of blank paper, working on poems and pieces of stories. She even arranged for one of the high school English teachers to make the trip to Central once a week and read my poetry, which he would do with gravity and care, questioning me about word choice and tone, assigning me Walt Whitman and T. S. Eliot poems to read.

In sixth grade, I wrote a play that the entire grade performed. I took nascent stabs at writing novels that I kept in notebooks and never showed anyone. By the time I made it through the crucible of Henry James Junior High and into Simsbury High, I was writing speculative fiction loosely based on my own life and heavily influenced by Stephen King. (What if the weird, silent diners at the restaurant where our heroine buses tables were actually vampires? What if it turned out that the administrators at the high school our heroine attends were secretly sacrificing and eating students, as a way to stay eternally young?)

I wrote and I watched, telling myself that things would get better and paying attention all the time. I watched other kids and tried to figure out what made me different. Was it their clothes, their expressions, their hair? Was it the TV shows they talked about, the songs they sang, the way they stood with their hands in their pockets and their JanSport backpacks dangling from just one shoulder? How did some girls know, without being told, which boys to talk to and which to avoid? Why was Andrea Freeh, who was very heavy, popular with girls and boys, while Monica Levy, who was just slightly chunky, was derided as fat, with no friends at all?

As hard as I tried to crack the code, or to arm myself with its signifiers—a French braid, ribboned barrettes, an ABBA cassette—I never got it right. Everything would always be the tiniest bit off—too tight, or the wrong brand, or the right brand but the wrong color, or the right color but the wrong cut. I'd save up for Nikes and finally buy a pair and arrive in homeroom only to find out that, at some point during spring break, all the girls in junior high had decided that Tretorns were now the thing; or I'd ask for an alligator shirt and my mom would find an Izod-style shirt at Marshalls, a shirt that would look right until you noticed that the animal on the breast pocket was a tiger instead of an alligator, or that there wasn't any animal at all.

With adolescence came my growth spurt, which was actually spurts, plural, because it was as if each part of my anatomy decided to embark upon the journey to adulthood at a different time. When I was twelve, my nose and my breasts took off, sprinting for the finish line while the rest of my face and body were much slower out of the gate. In junior high I had a mouth full of braces and a Dorothy Hamill–style wedge haircut. I had wide hips and broad shoulders and double-D-sized breasts that I was constantly trying to hide in baggy shirts and boxy sweaters that only made me look bigger. Nothing worked—not my hair or my clothes, not the makeup I didn't own and wouldn't have known how to apply if I'd had it. In every picture that exists from that era, I'm hiding behind someone or something—a parent, a tree, my hands.

The older I got, the more things at home changed. The more outspoken and contrary the four of us became, the more my father shut down, swinging between sullen silences, absences, and terrifying, violent eruptions of rage. He'd always had high standards for everything, including appearances, and if you didn't meet them, he was not likely to give you a comforting hug and tell you he'd help you do better next time. If I got a ninety-nine on the math quiz, he'd ask what happened to the other point, and if I brought home anything less than an A, he'd thunder, "You want to be a secretary? Because that's all you're good for." When he got angry, he'd yank whatever paperback I was reading out of my hands and tear it into chunks. When I'd ask if a shirt or new dress looked nice, he would eye me slowly up and down, then say, "No."

My mom loved us, but she was busy and distracted. She had four kids and a life of her own—she took classes, in slow pursuit of the master's degree she finally finished when I was in college; she read books for her two book clubs. At 9 Simsbury Manor, she turned our basement into a darkroom and became a competent photographer; at 13 Harvest Hill Road, she and a friend launched a mail-order spice business that they ran from our dining-room table. At both houses, she swam a mile every single day. As we got old enough to take care of ourselves, she adopted an attitude that could be kindly described as benign neglect. "I'm not refereeing," she'd frequently say when we came to her with our disputes and tales of the injustices, or sometimes, our bruises and bloody wounds. We fought violently, with teeth and nails and kicks and punches. Hair was pulled, names were called, blood was drawn. Jake called me fat. I called Jake a male chauvinist pig. We took turns locking poor Joe in the basement, where, we'd told him, a fifth brother named Josh had been buried. This went on until my father left and we united against a common enemy.

Back then, I didn't understand that what was happening in my house was not happening in everyone's house at night, when the doors were shut and the blinds were drawn. It took me just as long to sort out my physical self—how to dress in a way that flattered my shape, how to do my hair and makeup (or pay professionals to do it), how to be in a body, in the world. It took time before I could take all that pain and use it; transform all that loneliness and isolation and shame into stories.

But eventually it happened. I went to college, I fell in love, I got a job and found friends and read hundreds of wonderful books. Then wrote my own . . . and the grown-up versions of the girls who were so cruel to me in elementary school and junior high started coming to my readings. In California and New York and San Francisco and Rhode Island, at synagogues and schools and bookstore bathrooms, they appear. They find me on Facebook, they message me on Twitter. They look into my eyes, they reach for my hands, they name one of my heroines—the lonely, smart-mouthed, fat reporter in *Good in Bed*; the lonely, sarcastic, plus-size lawyer in *In Her Shoes*; the girls without boyfriends, the girls without girlfriends, the girls whose parents were too wrapped up in their own misery to see them or help them, and they say, *That was me, too.*

Part of me doesn't believe them. Part of me is angry, still. Part of me wants to say, *Where were you in seventh grade, when I'd put my books down on a table in the cafeteria, a table where five other girls had hung their purses from their chairs, and I'd go and get my iceberg lettuce and chickpeas and bacon bits that were not bacon and tasted like gravel on a Styrofoam plate, and when I came back to the table all five purses had disappeared and the girls were sitting somewhere else? Where were you when I was being laughed at, where were you when I was being ignored, where were you during all those bus rides when I sat by myself, all those recesses, years of recess, when I stayed inside because I knew that if I went out I wouldn't have anyone to play with?*

But I don't do it . . . not any more than Sharon Olds tore up those paper dolls. I smile. I squeeze their hands. I remember that one of the girls who left me alone in the cafeteria in junior high had a mustache, and not a faint, barely noticeable one, either, and that another queen bee spent half of high school hospitalized for anorexia, that even the ones whose lives looked, or look, perfect have suffered, will suffer, are suffering now.

Maybe I was lucky, after all. Maybe the damaged ones, the broken ones, the outcasts and outsiders end up survivors, and successful, and with empathy as their superpower, an extra-sensitivity to other people's pain, and the ability to spin their own sorrow into something useful. Maybe my parents and Simsbury and all those hard, lonely years did me a favor.

Because now I have stories to tell.

. . . and Then There Was Nora

My mother and my Nanna have a handful of anecdotes about me that they never get tired of telling. One of their favorites dates back to 1980, when I was ten years old and spending my summer at Camp Shalom.

"You got off the bus," my mother begins.

". . . and you were reading your book," Nanna continues. "Walking down the stairs and off the bus and reading the entire time."

"And you got off the bus, and you were barefoot! And we asked, 'Jenny, where are your shoes?'"

"And you just shrugged," Nanna continues. "You'd managed to lose your shoes." The two of them finish the story in harmony: "But you'd never lose your book."

When you're sad and lonely where you are, it only makes sense that you'd do whatever you could to get someplace else. That was what books were for—my lifeline, my oxygen when I was underwater, my escape. They gave me other worlds that I could inhabit, characters into whose skin I could slip. In book-world, I wasn't chunky or clumsy, the girl whose overlarge vocabulary was the equivalent of a "kick me" sign taped to my back, the girl with the ugly face, the weird clothes, the complete lack of friends. I was Nancy Drew, zipping around in her roadster, solving mysteries, or Anne of Green Gables, finding her "bosom friend," or Laura Ingalls, standing in the door of my little house on the prairie and watching Indians on horseback file solemnly by, or Meg Murry, bravely searching the universe for my missing father.

Books were a series of magic carpets, each one with the power to deliver me to another, better place. That was all I wanted—to be brave and beautiful and admired and beloved, to be somewhere other than my hometown, where no one—not my teachers, not my rabbi, not my Girl Scout leader, and definitely not my parents—seemed to notice that I was being eaten alive.

My father set the hook. Every night when I was four, he began reading me and my sister a chapter of Nancy Drew, ending each session with a cliffhanger. One afternoon, after school, only one chapter away from solving *The Secret of the Old Clock*, Molly and I couldn't stand it anymore. We snuck the book out of my parents' bedroom, where it had been waiting on the nightstand, and took it down to the basement playroom, which was the kids' domain. The playroom was carpeted, equipped with Legos and wooden blocks, a three-note Playskool xylophone, an old couch, and an orange-and-white Fisher-Price record player that we could use to play records from *The Jungle Book* or *Free to Be . . . You and Me*. Molly and I sat down, side by side, our backs against the fake-wood paneling, and I opened *The Secret of the Old Clock* to my father's bookmark, one slim wedge of pages from the book's conclusion.

At first, the words looked like cuneiform, random slashes and squiggles. I took a deep breath. There was a story in there, I just had to figure out how to get to it. Molly peered down at the page, then up at my face. "No?" she said.

I kept staring. I knew my letters. I knew which sound each letter made, and most of the sounds in combination. I could recognize dozens of words by sight; I'd been following along with my father for weeks. "N-a-n-c-y" was "Nancy." "Look-ed" was "looked." "Nancy look-ed. Nancy looked at her friends."

Molly clapped her hands with delight as the cuneiform became letters, and the letters became sounds, and the sounds became words, and the words turned into a story. I started to read, first painfully slowly, sounding out each syllable, then gaining confidence and fluency until, with my head aching and my eyes burning, we got to the end of the chapter, to the detective's arrival and the bad guy's arrest and Nancy's joyful reunion with her father. Molly went racing up the stairs, out of the basement and into the kitchen, which always smelled faintly of garlic, probably because Fran kept a desiccating Hebrew National salami hanging from a nail in the doorway, shouting, "Jenny can read!" I was almost five, and the doors of the world had swung open. My imaginary life, the one that sometimes felt more real to me than the real world, had finally begun.

I started my career as a reader with my father's medical textbooks—mostly because there were pictures of naked people in them. I was curious about boys and, other than glimpses of my brothers in the bathtub, I hadn't seen much. Each hardcover had thick, glossy pages that smelled of formaldehyde, and each was crowded with tiny type and vivid color pictures—"Plate 1," "Plate 2"—of various horrific rashes and lesions and tumors. I paged through the book, enthralled and horrified, until I came to pictures of a naked little boy with a black bar over his eyes and, due to some kind of pituitary tumor, the secondary sex characteristics of a grown man. I slammed the book shut at my first glimpse of the boy, and the words ("penis," "testicles"), looking around anxiously to see if anyone was watching. When it was clear that no one was, I opened the book again and stared until my curiosity was satisfied. What I remember most was not his body hair or the adult heft and size of what he had between his legs, but how his belly curved outward, and the way he stood, slightly pigeon-toed, like every little boy I knew.

My next stop was my mother's novels. I dipped into *The Bell Jar*, but had barely made it past the title page and my explanation that it was "by a very sad lady named Saliva Plath," when my mother decided I'd have to wait a few years. She wasn't so quick with a book called *Widow*, by Lynn Caine, about a woman whose husband dies of explicitly described colorectal cancer. That book gave me nightmares, as well as a lingering habit of inspecting the contents of the toilet bowl after I'd used it, certain that I'd see traces of blood and discover that I, too, was dying. I didn't think anything between two covers could be quite as vivid or disturbing. Then I discovered Erica Jong's *How to Save Your Own Life*, with its scene about a couple having uninhibited sex during the woman's menstrual period. When you're eight years old and you've read about a man chewing on a woman's used tampon, it gives you a slightly skewed sense of the grown-up world. You start to see it as an odd, not entirely safe place, full of weird corners, strange angles, bad behavior. The adults I was meeting in books felt like oversize children, children who could (and did) have sex, but did not seem any wiser or more reasoned than the kids I knew.

I read voraciously, indiscriminately, gulping down anything that held my interest. My parents' books were supplemented by the ones I'd borrow from my classrooms, and from my school library, and visits to the Simsbury Free Library, which had been built in 1890, a Colonial Revival–style building with a pillared entryway and imposing windows, three stories high, with a basement for the children's section. I'd go at least once a week and come back with a brown paper grocery bag full of books— picture books, chapter books, poetry, biographies of presidents and inventors, enough to carry me through a week.

The library was just a few blocks from Belden Elementary, and maybe a mile away from Central Elementary, where I went for fourth through sixth grade. There was a path through the woods, from Central down to Belden. From there, you could follow the sidewalk down to the library. I was allowed to make the trip after school, as long as I promised to stay on the sidewalks. I would walk or skip, sometimes humming to myself, enjoying my freedom. Being at the library felt like spending time in some eccentric aunt's book-crammed house. The periodicals and nonfiction were on the first floor, fiction was on the second, and there was a young adult section in the small, cramped attic—two rooms, a few tables, the spicy smell of ink and old paper, walls lined with bookshelves, and spinning wire stands of paperbacks stuck wherever there was space.

I read *The Citadel* by A. J. Cronin, and *A Child's History of the World* by V. M. Hillyer. I devoured Judy Blume's work, especially the library's single, dog-eared, passed-around copy of *Forever . . .* that made the rounds through the Henry James cafeteria and would fall open immediately to the sex scenes. When I was twelve, I found Stephen King's short-story collection *Night Shift* in the library—this was the paperback with the eyeball-covered hand on its front cover—and made the mistake of reading it during a babysitting gig after the kids were asleep. It left me so terrified that I sprinted the entire length of the street back home.

I read for entertainment and I read for knowledge and for previews of coming attractions. (Boys! Sex! Babies! Divorce! Feminist awakenings! And that was just the first three chapters of *The Women's Room.*) I read *Ancient Evenings* and *The Persian Boy* and *Lace*, by Shirley Conran, a racy book about three best friends and the sexual adventures they had in boarding school, a book that spawned an eventual miniseries that I wasn't allowed to see. I read Isaac Bashevis Singer and *Portnoy's Complaint*, which gave me an excellent reason to eschew liver on the rare occasions that my mother prepared it. My neighbor Rosanne McFarland's mom was into Harlequins, and I would take three or four home and read them, one after the other, and fall asleep dreaming of the prince who would someday come, in the guise of a lonely cowboy or a widowed surgeon or a wounded war hero whom I'd patiently nurse back to health.

I read kids' books, too, Shel Silverstein and the All-of-a-Kind Family, all the Ramona and Beezus books, the Great Brain and Encyclopedia Brown and Roald Dahl—first everything he wrote for children, then the grotesque and twisty stories he wrote for adults. I had a taste for the dark stuff, and there was plenty of it to find. My father had given me a hardcover book, a collection of short stories called something like *Eerie Tales*. There were classics like "The Tell-Tale Heart" and "The Most Dangerous Game," and one of Dahl's lesser-known stories, "Man from the South." In that one, a hard-core gambler staying at a luxury resort overhears a soldier casually bragging about the excellence of his cigarette lighter. In his accented, sibilant English, the gambler proposes a bet: If the soldier can strike a flame ten times in a row, he'll give him a brand-new Cadillac. If he fails, he'll collect the man's little finger. The soldier accepts, even though his girlfriend begs him not to. As a crowd gathers, and as our narrator is recruited to count each flick, the soldier thumbs the wheel of the lighter and sparks a flame once . . . twice . . . three times. I think he gets all the way to nine before the gambler's wife storms into the room, grabbing her husband and shaking him, berating him in some foreign language. While the gambler stands, shame-faced, his wife explains to the stunned crowd that the Cadillac wasn't even the man's to bet with. It was hers. "I took everything," she said. "It took me a long, long time, but I got it all in the end." When the unnamed narrator shakes the wife's hand, he notices that it feels very strange . . . then he looks down and sees that she has only her index finger and her thumb.

That was a long way from *Charlie and the Chocolate Factory*. Except that book, too, had a kind of underlying savagery that I, and presumably other children readers, accepted without question. In the books I loved, people were poor, teachers were cruel, fathers lost their jobs, parents died and their children were adopted by horrible, hateful great-aunts who were horrible and hateful just because they disliked children. In one of the Great Brain books, a Jewish merchant starves to death because the Mormons in town don't patronize his business and he's too proud to let them know that he can no longer buy food. The *Grimm's Fairy Tales* that my father read from wasn't the redacted, Disneyfied collection of stories, with wasp-waisted, doe-eyed girls drifting about and singing "A Dream Is a Wish Your Heart Makes" while mice and little birds made their beds. In my version, Cinderella's stepsisters hacked off their heels and sliced away their toes to try to cram their bloody feet into the glass slipper—and then they had their eyes pecked out by Cinderella's loyal bird companions after they'd failed. When the miller's daughter guessed Rumpelstiltskin's name, he flew into a rage that ended only after he tore himself in half, and when the Little Mermaid got her prince and her legs and what was between them, not only did she lose her voice, but with every step she took she felt like she was walking on knives.

This all confirmed my understanding of how things worked. Other kids were mean. They would hate you if you wore the wrong clothes, if you celebrated the wrong holidays, if you looked or sounded different, and the grown-ups either didn't see or didn't care.

This vision of the world also fit in with what I saw at home, where all of us tiptoed over the thin ice that lay atop the roiling black water of my father's temper. Anything could set him off—a wet towel on the floor, a bicycle dumped on its side in the garage instead of parked neatly, a smart mouth, a scrape or bump, real or imagined, of his new Corvette, this one a red 1984 version. In the garage at Harvest Hill Road, he strung old couch cushions together, forming a makeshift bumper that encircled the car. He loved his Corvette unconditionally. As for the rest of us, he loved us when we performed—when Jake scored goals for his soccer team, when I got perfect scores on my tests. When we'd fail to meet his expectations—when we misbehaved or broke the rules or, worst of all, when we embarrassed him—he'd be cold and scornful, dismissive and cruel, the opposite of the gentle, loving father who'd read us stories every night when we were little.

When I was ten, I tried out for and made our town's travel soccer team, much to my parents' astonishment, and my own. I wasn't a very good player—not fast, not coordinated, definitely not liked by my teammates—but I must have had a very good day at the tryouts. At a home game, when I was playing fullback, an opponent fired a shot at the goal. I intercepted it and tried to kick it forward, but the ball spun and bounced backward off my ankle, past our goalie, and into the goal.

"She scored for the WRONG TEAM!" I heard one of my teammates say. People were laughing. Our coach was shaking her head. On the sidelines, my father was staring, not at me, but through me, as if I'd suddenly become invisible. In the car, on the way home, I cried and said, "I want to quit the team." He stared straight ahead and said, "Maybe you should."

If he'd been that way all the time, I would have known to avoid him. But sometimes he'd be the father I remembered, the one who'd encouraged me to read, the one who'd say tersely, "Proud of you" when I brought home those good grades, or who'd introduce me to his secretary and his colleagues and beam as he said, "This is Jenny, my oldest."

There was no predictability, no way of knowing which father you'd get, a suburban version of "The Lady, or the Tiger?" Every night we'd hear the garage door go up and listen to the Corvette rumble to a stop. The door to the house from the garage would open. He'd set down his briefcase and stand there in the hallway. His suit and tie would be as pristine as they'd been when he'd left, shoes polished to a high gloss, watch and wedding ring shining, and the five of us—my mother in the kitchen, the kids upstairs or in the family room watching *The Electric Company*— would hold our breath. Would he smile, dance into the kitchen, reach for my mother and enfold her in a hug? Or would there be a chilly silence as he swept us with his gaze, his expression stony, his posture defeated, like a man who'd expected to check into a five-star hotel and instead found himself in a squalid shack full of kids and noise and mess?

Home made no sense. Books were much better, even the ones that affirmed the world's darkness . . . but some of the ones I loved the best offered not confirmation but the fantasy of escape.

When I was twelve, I found Judith Krantz's sex-and-shopping sagas and became an instant devotee of her stories about beautiful movie stars and the dashing descendants of Russian czars who loved them (*Princess Daisy*), or three generations of stunning models-turned-businesswomen and the famous artist who loved them (*Mistral's Daughter*). In Krantz's world, being unhappy in high school meant only that, within a chapter or two, you'd start taking flying lessons, and fall in love with your older, dashing war-hero instructor . . . and being overweight and unlovely meant only that transformation was imminent.

My favorite Judith Krantz book, then and now, is *Scruples*, a fable of an ugly duckling who blossoms into a beautiful, extremely wealthy, and sexually satisfied swan. For the unenlightened, *Scruples*, and its sequel, *Scruples Two*, tells the story of Wilhelmina Hunnenwell Winthrop Ikehorn Orsini Elliot, always called Billy, who grew up heavy and lonely, shunned by her wealthy Bostonian peers in a way that felt, to me, devastatingly familiar. I had soccer-team humiliation; Billy had dance class, where, in a fit of nerves and shame, she threw up on herself, and her all-wrong shiny blue satin dress. My physician father could be mean and cold; Billy's research-scientist father barely knew she existed. Both of us ate to stuff the pain down, and for the pleasure food gave us, neither of us could connect with our classmates. After high school, Billy gathered her courage and a small inheritance from an eccentric aunt and went to Paris. There she perfected her French and dropped ninety pounds (you know it's fiction when a girl goes to Paris and loses weight). She had unsatisfying sex with her first boyfriend, figured out how to have satisfying sex all by herself, and returned to America to begin her conquest of the world, driven by, among other things, a desire to show up all those snotty Boston girls who'd shunned her.

I'd been entertained, even engrossed by leading ladies before, but Billy felt personal. I saw myself when I read about Billy in her boarding-school kitchen, gobbling bowls of Cream of Wheat topped with butter and brown sugar. I identified completely with her descriptions of how it felt when you know people are talking about you, laughing behind your back. More than that, I recognized Billy's drive, her desire to prove to the world that she mattered. I read, turning the pages breathlessly, on my single bed, in my no-brand jeans and too-tight shirts, smelling like Designer Knockoff Versace, as Billy shed her weight and acquired a chic Parisian wardrobe, a secretarial degree, a loyal best friend, and a handsome, much-older billionaire husband, who died with convenient alacrity, leaving Billy still young, newly single, extremely wealthy, and perfectly positioned to take over the world.

I wanted to be Billy. I didn't have Billy's discipline, her willingness to subsist on poached fish and steamed vegetables, to eschew chocolate by pretending it was poop. Was a happy ending possible if you didn't get thin? Could you reap Billy Ikehorn Orsini–level rewards even if you stayed a size fourteen, even if you couldn't find a single prom dress to zip up over your bosom, even if all of the popular boys in your high school class were short and skinny, cute instead of handsome, and you felt like the Jewish Jolly Green Giant on the rare occasions you ever stood anywhere near them?

All of Krantz's heroines were slim and lovely. Judy Blume never wrote a plus-size protagonist—Blubber, you'll remember, was not the hero of the story, which was told from the perspective of one of her reluctant tormentors. Nancy Drew and Trixie Belden were both blessed with quick wit and fast metabolisms. Ayla, the heroine of the Clan of the Cave Bear saga, sounded like a supermodel when Jean Auel described her long, smoothly muscled legs, her tumble of white-blond hair and wide blue eyes. Even Meg Murry from *A Wrinkle in Time* turned out to be beautiful when she took her glasses off. Nobody had cellulite or belly rolls or stretch marks or size-ten feet; nobody wore a triple-D brassiere made with enough underwire to fashion a set of handcuffs. Everyone's hair was thick and shiny, not thin and limp and impossible to style; everyone had symmetrical features, not a giant nose stuck between two squinty, close-set eyes, and a chin that was already showing a tendency toward doubling.

Thank God for Susan Isaacs. Specifically, thank God for *Almost Paradise*, one of my mother's book-club picks, which I found the summer I was fifteen. The heroine was another lonely girl with a dead mother and a distant father, only in the case of poor Jane Heissenhuber, her father remarried disastrously to a would-be queen of Cincinnati society who realized, too late, that her husband was a nobody who would never be a somebody. Unfashionably tall, with lashings of long, dark hair, heavy hips, and wide thighs, Jane found love and power and fortune and fame, and never dieted herself to a size any smaller than a ten.

Still, a movie star married her, and the public embraced her, and, when it was time for her to conquer her demons and deal with the trauma of her past, her weight was a nonissue, and her regular body didn't hold her back. Instead, they made her a relatable Everywoman, and a television star in her own right. Jane was my beacon, my writing on the wall. Here was a character, and an author, who told me, *You can dream up a happy ending, and you can get it without losing half your body weight first.*

And then there was Nora. I found Fran's paperback version of Nora Ephron's *Crazy Salad and Scribble Scribble: Some Things About Women* and *Notes on Media* in the family-room shelves. The book had a light blue cover filled with a cornucopia of clay renderings in the shapes of a naked female figure, a telephone with a sign reading WOMEN, and a can of vaginal deodorant up front. I savored every essay—Nora's take on the Pillsbury Bake-Off; on the folly of trying to get your vagina to smell like a bouquet of meadow flowers (and the people whose job it was to sniff women's crotches and evaluate the product's effectiveness); on her own imperfect body and persistent flat-chestedness.

More than the topics, Ephron's voice captivated me. It was conversational, not writerly, more like hearing my mom talking with her friends than listening to a capital-A Author deliver pronouncements from on high. In my sophomore-year honors English class we were plowing through Mark Twain and Nathaniel Hawthorne, Henry James and Edith Wharton, American literature's greatest hits. I knew how literature sounded, I knew the subjects that significant authors considered worthwhile (sin, redemption, suburban ennui, sledding accidents). I didn't know that real writing could feature things Ephron discussed—breasts and vaginas and recipes for desserts; private parts and personal lives, shame and doubt and heartache. I didn't know a writer could sound like she did; could write in such an intimate and honest manner, a way that felt not only specifically female but specifically Jewish. This, I thought, was what I wanted for myself. Judith Krantz's novels were aspirational fairy tales, delicious and diverting but not ultimately attainable. Nora Ephron's essays were authentic, tough and tender all at once.

Nora got her start as a journalist, and I imagined a similar future for myself. I wanted to write about women, and how women decided how, and who, they wanted to be in the world. I wanted to write with Ephron's specificity, her eye for detail and her sense of what mattered: bras that pinched, parents too busy working and feuding and having nervous breakdowns to give their children what they needed, and who'd excuse their lapses with a tossed-off "everything is copy," and why men always thought it was any available female's job to locate and deliver food (I'll never forget Ephron's riff in *Heartburn* where her narrative stand-in, the cookbook author and betrayed wife Rachel Samstat, recounts her husband asking, "Do you think butter would be good with this?" as he held up a piece of plain, dry toast).

Reading gave me a framework, a way forward, a way out. And if Nora was my beacon, Adrienne Rich gave me a map. When I read "Diving into the Wreck," I glimpsed how stories could be simultaneously rescue and escape.

> *I came to explore the wreck.*
> *The words are purposes.*
> *The words are maps.*
> *I came to see the damage that was done*
> *and the treasures that prevail.*
> *I stroke the beam of my lamp*
> *slowly along the flank*
> *of something more permanent*
> *than fish or weed*

the thing I came for:
the wreck and not the story of the wreck
the thing itself and not the myth
the drowned face always staring
toward the sun
the evidence of damage
worn by salt and sway into this threadbare beauty
the ribs of the disaster
curving their assertion
among the tentative haunters.

That was how it could work—you'd go down as deep as you had to; you would face "not the story of the wreck" but "the thing itself"; and you'd swim back up to the surface with your arms full of tales to tell, and one of them would be the story of your own escape.

Road Trip

My parents had renounced Michigan, building their lives and their family in New England . . . but, much like the Mafia, Michigan kept pulling them back in. At least once a year and sometimes twice, they'd load us into the maroon and cream Chevrolet Suburban with its three rows of seats and double gas tanks and drive back to their ancestral home, where their entire extended families—parents, siblings, nieces and nephews and cousins—continued to reside.

My mom was afraid of flying, but, even if she hadn't been, four kids made air travel prohibitively expensive. So for Thanksgiving or the winter holidays or Passover, we'd pile into the car—two adults, four kids, one elderly, rheumy-eyed poodle, and one CB radio into which my father, in dark prescription sunglasses, a plaid shirt and jeans belted beneath his belly and hanging loosely over his flat behind, would mutter a convincing "Breaker one-nine." Our suitcases would be stacked into a strap-on black canvas ziggurat mounted to the top of the car. My parents would be up front; my sister, my brothers Jake and Joe, who'd arrived in

1978, and the dog would arrange themselves in the back rows; and I'd be in the way-back, behind the third row of seats, lying on top of a pile of suitcases with my book.

My parents never stopped for meals, as much as we begged for Big Macs and chicken nuggets. Instead, my mom would serve a version of the school lunches the four of us suffered through until we were old enough to prepare our own food, or use part of our allowance to buy hot lunch.

The day before we left, Fran would gather frozen bagels, sliced turkey breast, apples and cut-up carrots and celery, the cans of Coke my father drank, bottles of unflavored seltzer that the rest of us would share, and a dozen peeled hard-boiled eggs. All of this went into a plastic Playmate cooler, along with the ice packs that were kept in the freezer between trips. I can remember that cooler the way you remember the face of an old friend, or maybe the first guy who broke your heart. Red with white handles and a crosshatched red lid, no matter how carefully we washed it, the cooler carried the permanent sulfurous stink of the hard-boiled eggs, and it would sit there, smugly mocking us as we drove past each highway exit's signs for McDonald's and Burger King.

When we were little, the trips were exciting. Going anywhere was exciting, and going to Michigan, where we'd be fussed over and spoiled, where grandparents would take us out to restaurants for lunch and aunts and uncles would take us bowling or to the movies, was one of the highlights of the year.

But first we had to get there. The mood in the car was one of barely restrained violence. We would tiptoe around my father's temper while still doing the normal amount of pinching and slapping and squabbling among ourselves. I had books, which I'd read until I got carsick, and Fran would have gone to the library and made tapes of old radio plays, *The Lone Ranger* and *The Shadow*. We'd listen, and when even the adventures of the Lone

Ranger and Tonto's efforts to head off the ambush at Medicine Rock couldn't entertain, Fran would plug a portable black-and-white television set into the car's cigarette lighter. For maybe an hour of the sixteen-hour trip, the antenna could pull in a strong enough signal to watch a snatch of the news, or a *Star Trek* rerun.

Eventually, though, the temptation to start trouble would become too strong. One of us would lift the lid of the metal ashtray built into the car's armrest and let it snap back into place with an unmistakable and soul-satisfying *click*.

Behind the wheel, my father's shoulders would tense. "Who's flicking the goddamn ashtrays?" was the typical opening salvo. None of us would answer. There'd be silence, except for whatever was on the radio or the tape deck. Then, just as my father would loosen his grip on the wheel, another *click* would come, as Joe or Jake or Molly or I couldn't resist. "GODDAMNIT," he would yell, jerking the car into the breakdown lane and squealing to a halt, "WHO IS FLICKING THE GODDAMN ASH-TRAYS?" He would threaten to Turn This Car Around Right Now if the culprit failed to come clean, and my mother, in between soothing murmurs of "Larry," would try to appease us by flinging handfuls of sugary cereal into the backseats (I'm sure she actually passed back the box, but in my memory she's tossing handfuls of flakes or Os at us, like we're ducks in a pond).

The journey usually started on a Friday afternoon, the day school let out for Thanksgiving or spring break. We'd get off the bus and into the car, drive for eight hours, get a hotel room when we neared the Canadian border, and sleep, my father and the boys in one bed, my mother, snoring, in the bed with me and Molly.

Between gas-station stops and bathroom breaks, it would be late afternoon on Saturday when we pulled into my grandparents' driveway and piled out of the car. By then, we were messy, be-draggled, bed-headed, and road-weary, covered with stray bits of Count Chocula, surrounded by the stink of the hard-boiled eggs.

Kids and dog would charge into my grandparents' tastefully decorated, immaculately clean, child-free house. Our first stop was the glass dishes kept full of Brach's candy, which we'd empty. My brothers would race up and down the halls, around the living room and back again, while I'd endure hugs and kisses, then sprawl on the couch, sniffing the air for the smell of dinner. "*Vildechayas*," my Nanna would mutter. Not affectionately. Compared with my aunt Marlene's four kids, who lived two blocks away, we probably did resemble wild animals, bad-mannered, free-ranging monsters who'd never been taught how to behave or dress or brush their hair.

My parents would set up their base camp at Nanna and Pappa's house, and farm the rest of us out. One girl would be dispatched to my father's mother house, to lounge on silk sheets, swim in a bathtub the size of a small pool, with its own three-step staircase and a mosaic frieze on the wall, and play Crazy Eights late into the night with Grandma Faye, who seemed to never sleep. Another kid would go to the Gurvitzes—my father's cousin Linda, her husband, Alan, and their kids, Eric and Michelle, who were around our ages. There was a pinball machine in the dining room, which worked even without quarters, and Eric and Michelle each had their own bedroom. Michelle's room was painted light blue with a rainbow circling the walls. Above her desk was a corkboard lined with certificates of academic achievement. Inside of it was a shoebox full of neatly written love letters from a boy in her class. "He's just a friend," she would say nonchalantly, as if every girl had a boy who was crushing on her. Linda, who was bighearted and kind, would let her kids stay home from school when we visited. We'd go bowling or to the movies or out to lunch, commonplace weekend activities for the Michigan cousins, but special treats for us.

You could stay with my father's sister, Aunt Renay, and her husband and their son, Evan, whose basement housed a child-

size train that you could actually ride on, or you could stay with
the Schwartzes, my mother's sister, Marlene, her husband, Richard, and their four children, the youngest of whom was a year
older than me. Their kids' bathroom had a laundry chute with a
metal door, and a passage that ran from the bathroom all the way
down to the basement, and was an object of endless fascination
for all four of us. (Could a kid fit down that chute? Had anyone
tried?) Rachel, the youngest, was the only girl, and her bedroom
had an entire wall of closets with mirrored doors, which con-
tained a perfect wardrobe. Every oxford and Izod that I'd ever
dreamed of owning, every Benetton or Esprit ensemble, seemed
to live in that closet.

One night we'd all gather for a dinner of takeout sandwiches
at Grandma Faye's. Her house had a curtain made of blue glass
beads that hung between the dining room and the kitchen. One
of our favorite things to do was to walk back and forth through
the beads, letting them brush our hair and face and hands, as
Grandma Faye watched in consternation and tried to shoo us
toward the deli platters. We would drink Vernors, a kind of
soda that you could get only in the Midwest, and eat Sanders
Bumpy Cake, a devil's food cake with ridges of marshmallow
topping draped in dark chocolate. Nanna would bake rugelach,
twists of sweet pastry wrapped around chopped nuts and jam
(or raisins, which I hated). We'd order in Little Caesar's pizza
(which was not yet a national chain) and go out to eat at the
Stage Deli, where I'd get a mushroom omelet and rye toast, the
exact same thing every time, but I'd order it only after reading
slowly through each item on the menu to make sure there wasn't
something else I'd prefer.

Restaurants were big deals for the four of us. At home, on
the rare occasions when we went out to eat, my mother would
announce that two or three entrees would be plenty for the four
of us. Then she'd decide what those entrees would be. Then she'd

order them herself. "If you're still hungry, you can get more later," she'd say, when we'd protest that whatever she'd picked wouldn't be enough. Needless to say, "later" never came, and we'd all go home hungry. In Michigan, though, each kid could order his or her own meal—sometimes with side dishes! And drinks! And dessert!

Michigan was fun, with going out to eat, or bowling, or to the matinees, hanging around the fringes of the dinner parties and listening to the grown-ups gossip, but with each visit, there were also certain obligations. Visiting the sick, my mother told us, was a mitzvah—a blessing—and our trips to Michigan would also always include a visit to whatever senior center, assisted-care facility, or hospital bed housed whichever aged relatives were unwell. When I was little, my father's grandmother lived in a nursing home, and I must have wandered off past an open door, where I saw a woman sitting in the wheelchair by her bed, with her thin hair drawn into a bun and a knitted afghan on her lap. "Little girl . . . little girl," she called.

I went inside. When I was close enough, she grabbed my hands in both of hers, with a surprisingly strong grip, and started to call me Sarah. "Why don't you ever come to see me?" she asked. "The doctors are killing me! They're killing me!"

"I have to go," I whispered, looking around desperately for my mom and dad or a nurse to free me. I could see the tops of two legs underneath the afghan, but only one foot on the wheelchair's footrest. Her hands felt like a bundle of bones loosely wrapped in skin, and were mottled with age spots and ropy blue veins. The room was warm and smelled like chicken soup, mothballs, and pee. I tried to pull away, but the woman gripped harder, her cracked voice rising, calling me Sarah, demanding to know why I'd put her there, why I was letting the doctors kill her. I was old enough to know, by then, that fairy tales were just made up and witches weren't real, but in that moment, with her fingers locked around my hands, I thought she was going to pull me into her lap, right up against her, and do something terrible that might have involved cannibalism.

I pulled. She clung. I think we were both crying by the time someone finally pried the woman's hands off mine and got me out of her room and back to my parents, who I don't think had even noticed I was gone. For the rest of my childhood, I hated those visits; hated the smell of those places, the way one parent or the other would put a hand on the small of my back, steering me toward the couch or the chair or the bed, making me speak to whichever relative was in it; the way I was always convinced that someone was going to grab me and not let go, only the next time it happened no one would notice and no one would save me.

By the time I was a teenager, though, the visits tipped from terror to comic relief.

"Now, Marty's been a little depressed," Fran began one year, leading Molly and me up a driveway on a frosty winter night. "Oh, and remember, he had another stroke."

"Hold up, Fran," Molly would say, but by then Fran had her finger on the doorbell. In we would go, to watch poor Marty talking out of half his mouth, shuffling around the kitchen to make tea, boiling water and gathering mugs with an arm that hung by his side, then sitting on the couch and crying.

"That was grim," Molly observed when we were back in the car on our way to the next visit.

Fran pretended not to hear her. "Next stop! Now, Louise just got out of the hospital."

"What was she in the hospital for?" I asked.

"Diabetes. They had to amputate. Don't stare."

In we went, to a living room that had been emptied of all furniture, with a hospital bed in the center, and a woman, with a sheet draped over the space where her leg used to be, lying on top of it.

"Hello!" said my mom, her voice too bright and too loud, making a sweeping gesture toward me and Molly, who'd been hanging back against the wall. "Look who came to see you!"

On our way back to the car, Molly shook her head as Fran muttered to herself, consulting the directions she'd scribbled on a pad. "Now, the doctors think this round of shock treatments finally did the trick . . ."

Molly stopped, hands on her hips, boots planted in the frosty grass. "Fran," she demanded, "how are we even related to these people?"

As eager as I always was to go to Michigan, that was how reluctant I was to return to my life back home. When I was a girl, it meant the resumption of classes after vacation, the end of special treats and shopping trips, restaurant meals and soda with desserts, grandmothers who'd lavish me with kisses and let me stay up late. When I was older—twelve and thirteen and fourteen—I'd go home knowing that I'd failed again, failed to find favor with my attractive, popular cousins just as I had with the attractive, popular kids in Simsbury. All of them, Michelle and Eric, Rachel and Ronnie, were always nice enough, but I could tell that even in their hand-me-downs I was an impostor, a geeky pretender to the cool-kid throne whose friendlessness they could smell. Every year I daydreamed that we'd come out of the Windsor Tunnel, out of Canada, back into America again, and I would somehow be made new. I'd go back to Simsbury with a mysterious new smile, carrying myself like a girl with a secret, a girl who'd been kissed, a girl who knew she was beloved and beautiful.

This never happened.

We would make the return trip in one day, leaving before seven to reach Simsbury by midnight. Driving into the early-morning light, I would lie on my side in the way-back, on top of the suitcases and the cases of Vernors my parents brought home, as far away from the cooler and its smell as I could manage. I'd have a book open on my chest and I'd stare at the car's ceiling, spangled with light, then dappled with shadow, then dark as we plunged into the tunnel, and wonder if it would always be like this.

Fat Jennifer in the Promised Land

Simsbury was miserable. Michigan changed nothing, but I knew I'd get a chance to turn my social life around during the six-week tour of Israel that I'd take the summer between my sophomore and junior years. There, I would be with kids from other towns, kids who did not know my sad social history, kids who would maybe be my friends.

By then I was not just longing for acceptance—someone to talk with in the cafeteria, someone to call up on a weekend and invite to the Westfarms Mall to look at jewelry at Claire's or clothes at the Gap. Acceptance was too mundane. I wanted it all—the gold medal, the blue ribbon, the brass ring. I wanted to be POPULAR.

I thought that I could do it. I had a plan. Hadn't I spent the last few years studying, with a Talmudic scholar's attention to detail, the princesses of my class, the Missys and the Courtneys, the Rachels and the Kims? In my imagination, where I conducted endless rehearsals, I could imitate their intonations, the tosses of their spiral perms, the pauses between their "likes" and "you knows"; I'd memorized the trill of their giggles and the cut and dye of their jeans and the way their braces glistened in the late-afternoon sunshine that streamed in through the window during Mr. Cohen's honors biology. I knew what they wore, the TV shows they liked, the bands whose T-shirts they sported the weekend after their concerts at the Hartford Civic Center (the Grateful Dead, Rush). I'd show up in Jerusalem and, armed with my encyclopedic, meticulously gleaned knowledge of All Things Teenage Girl, circa 1985, infiltrate the top social tier of the West Hartford girls—West Hartford being the mostly Jewish suburb from which the largest contingent of Teen Tourers would come. Once my position was secure, my Simsbury sisters would be sorry they'd ignored me . . . and I would rub their noses in their failure to accept me, just like post-makeover Sandy in the final scene of *Grease*, in black Lycra and leather, twirling the toe of her stiletto on a lit cigarette.

Cigarettes, as it turned out, were where my troubles began. Our group of thirty or so Jewish teenagers, rising high school juniors just like me, began its journey early in the morning at the West Hartford JCC. On the bus to LaGuardia, kids were still half-asleep, and the ones from my synagogue had arranged themselves in their usual groupings (Kara with Ronnie; Andi with Lisa; Alison Landis, who spat when she talked, with Lori Morganstern, who was overweight; me by myself). At LaGuardia, our counselors distributed tickets to the El Al flight to Jerusalem. "Who wants a seat in the smoking section?" our jaded old (he might have been all of thirty-five) Israeli guide, Eitan, asked. Hands shot up in the air, and I watched in astonishment as my would-be peers hustled to the back of the plane, pulling packs of Marlboro Lights from the pockets of jean jackets as they went.

They smoked? Didn't they know smoking was bad? Didn't they remember that picture of the rotted lung tissue the police officer had displayed during a fifth-grade "D.A.R.E." lecture, alongside an ancient suitcase full of fingerprint-smeared plastic

Baggies stuffed full of fake "goofballs" and "'ludes" and "Black Beauties" and some dusty-looking, weedy "Mary Jane"?

Oh, well. I supposed I could have tried to buy a pack of cigarettes of my own, or asked to bum one from one of the West Hartford girls, but I hated the way smoke smelled, and I'd never even tried a puff, and figured that if I started smoking for the first time on the plane I'd just disgrace myself. I opened my James Michener novel, found a window seat, and resolved to wait.

The Teen Tour was divided into two three-week segments. We'd spend the first three weeks on a kibbutz, living with, and like, Israeli teenagers. We'd have jobs, like our Israeli counterparts, but also free time to socialize and swim. For the last three weeks, we would sightsee, visiting the Western Wall in Jerusalem, swimming in the Dead Sea, climbing Masada, visiting Tel Aviv and Eilat.

Somehow, I'd been assigned to a room with two of the West Hartford princesses, plus a Simsbury classmate, a not-too-popular girl who'd treated me with more indifference than disdain. I'd identified Debbie, one of the West Hartford girls, as a potential friend. She seemed friendly and easygoing, with a ready, rolling laugh, merry blue eyes, and curly brown hair. Instead of the preppy clothes that most of my classmates sported, she had her own style, which involved feathered earrings, woven rope bracelets, and a jacket with the Grateful Dead's rainbow-colored dancing teddy bears embroidered on the back. She'd been to six Dead shows, and she smoked, but she wasn't aggressive about it, and if she didn't seem especially smart, with a vocabulary heavy on the "wows" and "whoas," at least she didn't seem mean.

We spent our first morning in the Promised Land complaining about jet lag and unpacking. I set out my Nikes where everyone would see them, right by the door. I'd bought them myself. My parents had given me half the cash, and I'd earned the rest myself. Starting when I was fourteen, I'd work through the summer, five or six hours a day, picking strawberries and green beans at Rosedale Farms on East Weatogue Street, or babysitting on Friday and Saturday nights. I'd bought them in May, but I'd kept them in their box, pristine and untouched, in preparation for the trip. Then I'd devoted the rest of the spring to convincing my mother to let me shave my legs. ("Up to you," she'd finally said, cutting off my pestering with a shrug. "But once you start, it's just going to grow back.")

I adjusted my sneakers, admiring the white swoosh's gleam. "Oh, I hope I didn't forget my razor," I announced, loud enough so my three roommates could hear me, as we all got into our swimsuits. (Bikinis! They were wearing bikinis!) The plain navy-blue tank suit that I'd bought at Bob's looked impossibly dowdy. And then, when I emerged from the bathroom stall and saw where my three roommates' gazes had gone, as if their eyeballs had been magnetized, I realized with a sick feeling that while I'd been concentrating on my calves, I hadn't considered that there were other places I should also have been shaving. My mother's bathing suits all had skirts and, honestly, while I'd put in many late-night hours exploring the territory below my waist, very little of that exploration had involved looking. I ducked into the bathroom with my razor and a bar of soap, but succeeded mostly in mauling myself while leaving swaths of the offending hair behind.

Strike one.

By the second day, we had our work assignments. We woke up at five in the morning to make our way sleepily to the communal dining hall and breakfast on rye bread, cucumbers, tomatoes, and Nutella. After breakfast half the girls headed to a combine that drove up and down the rows of the kibbutz's tomato fields. Instead of simply plucking tomatoes from the vines, the machine uprooted the plants entirely, sucked them out of the ground, and spat them, with their dusty roots still wrapped around clumps of dirt, onto a conveyor belt that ran down the center of the combine. Our job was to stand at the conveyor belt and separate tomatoes from vines and dirt, as the machine rumbled up and down the rows and lumbered around corners.

Our first morning as kibbutzniks, all three of my roommates and I showed up for work. The next morning, Debbie lay in bed, moaning that she had cramps. By the third day, both of my other roommates had joined her . . . and, somehow, all three of them, along with the majority of girls on the trip, managed to not only sync their menstrual cycles, but also have their period for the next three weeks. Each morning, they would lie in bed in agony, unable to work, then miraculously they'd recover by pool-time every afternoon. Meanwhile, I hadn't gotten my period yet, and didn't think I'd be able to fake menstruation convincingly—I would do or say something that would give me away as a pretender. I'd also had jobs for two summers by then, and I knew how many thousands of dollars my parents had paid for the trip. Even though I was pretty sure that the kibbutz's bottom line wouldn't be affected one way or another by my failure to show up and sort tomatoes, I was still too much of a good girl to bail. So every morning I trudged off to the fields. By noon, when it had gotten too hot to work, I would have dirt everywhere— underneath my nails, in the folds of my ears, in my eyelashes and eyebrows. I could taste dirt when I swallowed, feel grains of it under my eyelids when I blinked. At night, when I'd brush my teeth in the communal bathroom, I'd rinse my mouth and spit out toothpaste foam and dirt.

On Day Four, Debbie left her journal open on her desk. We were all supposed to keep journals, making nightly entries about how inspiring it was to be in our ancestral homeland, or how impressed we were by our Israeli counterparts, who were all tanned and fit, who all spoke heavily accented if perfectly understandable English, and who seemed much more adult than we were. Heart beating hard, I leaned in for a peek. "Jennifer W. is annoying everyone," Debbie had written.

I rocked back on my heels. My skin felt icy. My eyes stung. How? How was I annoying everyone? I was barely talking to anyone! Silence was part of my plan. I had figured out, through close study of my peers, *Seventeen* magazine's advice columns, and a handbook from the 1950s called *How to Be Popular* that I'd checked out of the library, that talking was surely one of my mistakes. People didn't want to hear what you had to say, they didn't want to laugh at your jokes (years later, I was amused to find this nugget repackaged in a popular dating manual called *The Rules*, which instructed that if a guy wanted to be amused, he'd stay home and watch Letterman). The secret, I knew, was to listen—to smile, to nod, to say "That sounds awful," or "That must have been great," to be a kind of friendly mirror, offering people the best possible versions of themselves. Laughing and listening, those were my watchwords, and I'd tried, I really had, but somehow, bits of my old, noxious personality must have seeped out, in things I'd said or not said, or in my clothes or my shoes or maybe even how I stood or sat or swam in the big, overchlorinated pool.

It was like my difference was written on my skin, in ink that everyone could read but me, or it was a smell that surrounded me, no matter how hard I tried to scrub it off. People, even strangers, needed to spend only ten minutes in my presence to know that I was a loser, a misfit, a freak.

It wasn't just that I was smart. Stacey Goldblum was smart. Laurie Weiss was smart. But Stacey was quiet, with large breasts and an adorable stammer, and Laurie was freckled and laconic and sporty. The two of them had friends. Boys liked them. Nobody liked me. Not even the kids who had a reputation for being nice—Lindsay Gross, who was small and squat and freckly, and had such terrible breath that it smelled like she'd eaten trash; Dana Blum, who was much heavier than I was; Rob Teitelbaum, whose mother had died when we were in junior high and was known for his moody silences and his kindness to Lindsay and to Dana—not even those kids were nice to me.

"Put the book down," said Eitan, our fearless leader . . . except I knew that if I did, not only would I be lonely, but I'd be bored, too. James Michener kept me company as we piled onto, and off, our charter bus with the high-backed seats covered in garish blue-and-red-print fabric, making our way through the Land of Milk and Honey, which struck me as an unlovely scrap of overbaked, cactus-studded wasteland. Eitan didn't have any other advice for me. I doubt he was being paid enough to try to figure out what was going on, or to find me more amenable roommates, or to offer me tips for survival. He'd shepherded thirty spoiled suburbanites through Israel the summer before; he'd be herding another thirty the next summer. If I was miserable, well, I wouldn't be miserable on his watch for long . . . and, unlike my Israeli counterparts, it was unlikely that my woes would ever include gunfire.

I wanted to go home. As much as I'd looked forward to the trip, as much as I had hated Simsbury and been desperate to leave, that was exactly how much I was longing to return. At least at home I knew precisely who'd be awful to me, and what flavor the awfulness would take. Israel was a constant buffet of unpleasant surprises; new people being mean in new ways and different languages. But even if I could have faked injury or illness and gotten myself on a plane back to Connecticut, my parents weren't there. They'd taken my siblings on a trip across the country that summer, leaving the house empty and my grandparents in Michigan as my emergency contact.

I was on my own.

I tried to sound brave in the letters I'd write to my parents, at night, on thin sheets of airmail stationery, letters they wouldn't get until days after my return. I'd sit cross-legged on my bed in my empty room while my peers were outside, on the poured-concrete porch, smoking. I'd tell them about the tomato combine

and the pool and whichever historically important sights we'd
been bused to that week. I wrote about everything that we were
doing, and didn't let on that I was doing all of it alone. I didn't
tell them what had happened with Randy Gutman, a handsome
boy whose shiny white smile and smooth tanned skin and crisp
dark hair made him look like a young Erik Estrada, who'd approached me one day on the bus.

Randy hooked his arms into the metal luggage rack over-
head. His T-shirt stretched tight against his chest as he looked
down at me. "Is this seat taken?" he asked, gesturing toward the
eternally empty spot beside me. He had dimples when he smiled,
deep dents in his honey-colored skin. I smiled up at him help-
lessly. "It's all yours," I said, which sounded, to my ears, like the
kind of thing a girl in a movie would say.

His grin widened as he moved away instead, his body swaying with the movement of the bus, like he was surfing, I thought.
A minute later, Donnie Kaplan plopped down glumly beside me.
Donnie was tall and had a horrible case of cystic acne that had
turned his face into a red, lumpy wasteland studded with black-
heads and whiteheads and the occasional rivulet of pus. Zits by
themselves did not spell social isolation, but Donnie had gotten
a boner on the diving board one of our first days at the pool, thus
ensuring that he'd be the only person to spend the six-week trip
even lower in the group's estimation than I was. Of course he
didn't acknowledge me, and I didn't speak to him. We each knew
that proximity to each other could only make things worse.

I didn't tell my parents about that, or about the time, a few
days later, when I'd overheard Randy talking with a few of the
other boys, Ethan and Caleb and Matt. I heard my name . . .
or, rather, I heard the name "Jennifer," of whom there were five
on the trip. "Oh, no," Randy said, holding each of his hands approximately three feet away from his hips, "not the fat one."

I wasn't fat. I look at pictures of my fifteen-year-old self now,
thirty years later, and it makes me want to cry that other kids

said that, and that I believed them. I was larger than the Kims and the Staceys, who were living on cigarettes and, in a few cases, sticking their fingers down their throats even after our vegetable-heavy meals, but I was a three-season athlete who followed up crew and cross-country ski practices with five-mile bike rides home (this was what you did when you had a mother who'd announced that you were too old to be picked up and dropped off). I was big and busty, but I was fit and strong. Of course, in the wake of that comment I felt as if I must have looked like the love child of Jabba the Hutt and Moby Dick after a month at the all-u-can-eat buffet. I don't think I wore shorts for the rest of the trip, exchanging anything remotely revealing for the long-sleeved shirt and long skirt we'd been told to pack for visits to religious sites and shrines. For the duration of the trip I never went swimming again.

My chief tormentor—of course I had one—was a girl named Ronni. Ronni wasn't one of the prettier girls—those girls mostly left me alone, too secure in their own beauty and, when we went to Jerusalem, in the attention of the young Israeli soldiers to waste their time picking on me. Ronni had tiny, close-set pale blue eyes, a generous scoop of a nose (soon to be surgically reduced), big, feathered dirty-blond hair, and an even bigger mouth. Ronni was wide-hipped and flat-chested, a condition she camouflaged by tying a succession of fringed scarves around the hips of her swimsuits. When anyone said or did something stupid in her presence, her watery little eyes would widen, and she'd cock her head, looking like a blond pigeon that had just plucked a bit of trash from an especially fetid crack in the sidewalk. Ronni's particular genius—and, as I've been unable to find her on Facebook, I can only wonder whether she found a way to translate it into a career—was sensing weakness among her peers and pointing it out to others. She lived to humiliate me. In high school, I was going by Jen or Jennifer, but the kids who'd known me since elementary school, a few of whom were on the trip, still called me Jenny, like my siblings and my parents did. Ronni's nasal bray turned the pet name into the vilest insult. "Oh, JEN-NEE," she'd singsong when she'd catch sight of me. I'd hunch my shoulders, duck my head, try to ignore her, try to make myself less visible, less embarrassing, less there.

In Jerusalem, where we spent the last week of the trip, we joined up with the hundreds of other American kids on dozens of other trips. Our group was staying near kids from suburban New York, and among them was a boy named Ralph. Ralph liked me. Ralph did not realize that I was uncool. Ralph was cute, in a kind of lunky, no-necked high-school-wrestler way . . . but as you may have surmised, Ralph was not especially smart. (Although, in retrospect, maybe he was actually a genius who'd managed to take me in with one beady-eyed, heavy-lidded assessing glance and realize that I was so lonely that I'd do just about anything for companionship, of the male or female variety.)

Ralph and I shared a single "date," during which I clutched his meaty palm as we walked through the cobbled streets of the Old City of Jerusalem, and then, in a bar in the shadow of the Dome of the Rock, tried to order a drink (Israel has no drinking age, but I'm still fairly certain that the vodka and soda I asked for was Sprite and Sprite).

If the trip had been a movie, Ralph would have been sweet and sensitive; he would have been funny and kind, and we would have stayed up all night talking about art and books and music and dreams, and made plans to meet up the next summer (actually, if it had been a movie, Randy-who-looked-like-Erik-Estrada would have fallen for me). But Ralph could barely string six words together, and communicated mostly through gestures and grunts, and by pulling me into shadowed corners or abandoned dorm rooms and putting his heavy hands on various parts of my body where they lay there like hot water bottles or the poultices I'd read about in *Little House on the Prairie*. Everywhere he touched me, I was convinced that I was jiggling beneath his fingers; that he could feel ripples and wobbles and discrete bumps of cellulite. He must have thought I was a prude because I kept grabbing his hands and squirming away, or trying to distract him with my own explorations of his body, which felt like a hot, damp slab of rock underneath a Mamaroneck Wrestling Team T-shirt.

Somehow Ronni got wind of our night together. "Hey, JEN-nee, how's your BOY-friend?" she would call when she saw me, to the general amusement of the rest of the kids. I went from using my journal to write lies about how I'd wept at the Western Wall and been incredibly moved by the sunrise from the top of Masada to scribbling down the truth: how I'd left the group dur-ing our free weekend in Jerusalem and thought about not going back, how I had climbed up Mount Masada and watched the sun come up alone. Finally I just used it to count the weeks, then the days, then the hours, until we'd get on the plane back home. I told myself that all of these kids, the Ronnis and the Randys and the Debbies, would peak in high school; that they'd burn through the best years of their lives before they turned eighteen, and that they'd see me someday on TV collecting some literary award or on the red carpet for the premiere of the movie that I'd written, and turn to their drab and ordinary spouses and shriek, "I knew her!" On our bus rides to Ein Gedi or Yad Vashem, and, finally, on the airplane ride back home, I'd construct elabo-rate daydreams, about how Ronni, her pear shape swollen after childbirth, her dishwater hair dingy and her teeth reverted to their original state after twenty years without braces, would be walking in New York City when she'd see me—how she'd grab my hands, gushing to her husband or her kids about how she'd known me, back in the day, and how I'd smile with a practiced, distant politeness, then give my own version of her pigeon head-cock and say, "Sorry, have we met?"

On the bus from LaGuardia back to West Hartford, I sat by myself, as close to the door as I could get. I hadn't even tried to find a seatmate, hadn't even flinched when my fellow travelers walked past me without making eye contact and everyone paired up but me. I was done trying, done pretending to be someone I wasn't, done trying to fit in. When the bus doors creaked open, there was a crowd of parents assembled on the curb, dads in polo shirts and mothers with sunglasses shoved up into their highlighted hair, all of them eager to see their children after six weeks away. My parents weren't there. They were still out west, finishing up their cross-country trip, and had made plans for me to get a ride home with my former babysitter, then stay with neighbors until they got back.

I was first off the bus. I remember a woman's hands reaching for me: painted nails, a gold watch, a diamond ring. Everyone was hugging everyone, it turned out, and maybe she thought she'd generously welcome the first girl off the bus with an embrace.

"Don't fucking touch me!" I snarled.

I remembered the look of shock on her face, the way her lipsticked mouth fell open, and how it sent an icy thrill right through me. I'd never been the aggressor, never been mean like that, never been rude, hardly ever said "fuck" out loud, and absolutely never said it to a grown-up . . . but the chances were good that one of the kids who'd made my life so awful for the past month and a half was her son or her daughter and thus her responsibility. She'd raised a monster. Fuck her.

I shoved through the crowd, collected the one piece of my luggage that El Al hadn't managed to lose, and found my sitter, Carrie.

"Did you have fun?" she asked, putting her parents' car in reverse, flicking on WTIC, her tone letting me know she didn't really care one way or another.

"Fine," I said. "It was fine." She drove us back over the mountain, back to Simsbury, and I fished the house key out from underneath a rock by the front step and let myself inside. The house was empty. Instead of reporting directly to the neighbors who'd agreed to keep me overnight, I unpacked and took a long shower. Naked, I looked at myself in the mirror, standing front, then sideways, inspecting my tanned face and arms, the shocking white of my breasts and belly, and I stood on the scale in my parents' bathroom long enough to see a number lower than I'd ever see again in my life. *Fat Jennifer*, I thought. Fuck them.

Then I got a garbage bag from the laundry room, where my mother kept them, and went to my bedroom, and scooped up every copy of *Seventeen* magazine that I'd kept stacked next to my bed, and threw them all away. Whatever I'd learned, whatever I'd done, whatever I'd shaved, saved for, or convinced my parents to buy me, it hadn't been enough. It would never be enough. I would never be enough.

I called the McDanielses and thanked them for offering to host me, and told them I'd be fine at home by myself.

"Really?" said Mrs. McDaniels, sounding dubious but harried. There were five McDaniels kids, four around the age of me and my siblings, and a toddler.

"Really," I said. That night I slept in an empty house, in the guest room, spread out in the queen-size bed. It felt like the first night of my adult life, the beginning of a new epoch, the Era of Not Giving a Fuck.

Two weeks later, junior year began. For once, I didn't pester my mother about Guess jeans and Ocean Pacific tops, or beg her to take me to the Limited. I wore a pair of hot-pink overalls and a white T-shirt and pink high-top Chuck Taylors—trendy enough for 1985, but not necessarily what the other girls would be wearing. I didn't care. I rode my bike to the high school, locked it in the rack, and walked inside, for once not worrying about how I looked or who was or was not saying hello to me, or who was noticing that I was or was not being greeted. I was friendly but not trying too hard in classes. At lunch, I sat down with my crew teammates, and paid more attention to my meal than to who was sitting where or who was talking to whom.

And then, suddenly, people were talking to me. They were laughing at my jokes, which were as cruel as all the things the Israel-trip kids had said about me ("Do you know that Libby Lessner's breath is so bad it smells like her braces are made of rotten seaweed?"), they were asking my opinion, they were admiring my sneakers. Just like that, I had friends.

Maybe it was because I was thinner, because the Middle Eastern sunshine had tanned my skin and put golden highlights in my hair. Maybe the six-week trip had been the equivalent of a stint in a blast oven, where my personality was baked into something more pleasant. But what I think happened is that I gave up. I stopped trying to be popular or quieter; I stopped trying to be cuter or more fashionable. I wasn't biting my tongue to prevent the weird jokes from escaping, or modeling my hairstyle on one girl, my clothes on another, and taking care to let my backpack dangle from one strap. I wore my backpack over both shoulders; I wore clothes I liked; I kept my hair cut short, shaved at the back of my neck, in a kind of modified, Molly Ringwald–esque crop that wouldn't look too bad even in the absence of a blow-dryer and hot rollers and a curling iron. I was done trying to be anyone except who I was, and if nobody liked me, if I didn't find my people until college or graduate school or ever, well, then, I'd manage. I'd hung on for six weeks, all by myself, halfway around the world. I could do it in high school; could do it, if I had to, for the rest of my life. I was going to stop saving up my money to buy the Tretorn sneakers or the Benetton sweaters the popular girls wore, because I'd worn them, and it hadn't made a difference. I was going to stop lying about the music that I liked and boys I was crushing on with the hope that I'd sound more palatable and mainstream, because that hadn't worked. I was going to wear my high-top sneakers with everything from jeans to overalls to a white eyelet lace-trimmed skirt and a pale-pink henley top. (It was the 1980s. That was almost a thing.)

It turned out that there were people—not the princesses or the soccer stars, but smart, quirky, funny people, some of whom had just started to come into their own, too—who liked me. They wouldn't laugh when I told them that I liked Broadway musical soundtracks and I hated the Grateful Dead; they would laugh when, after Meredith Markson stumbled through reading out loud in science class, I'd turn to her and ask, slowly and loudly, "HOW ARE YOU ENJOYING YOUR TIME IN OUR COUNTRY?" or when I described a skinny blond boy in a black Lycra one-piece ski racing outfit as looking like a sperm. (I suspect that my teenage years have a lot in common with the episode of *30 Rock* when Liz Lemon goes to her high school reunion, complaining that nobody was nice to her and learning that, in fact, she wasn't nice to anyone.)

Still, people wanted to sit with me on the bus when the crew team went to Worcester or Middletown for meets, or when the cross-country ski team went to Vermont for races. Suddenly I had invitations to parties on the weekends, at kids' houses where the parents weren't home, where there was drinking (drinking!) and smoking and people making out in the bedrooms. I had people to giggle with over Jell-O shots and invite me to sleep over or go to the mall or drive to the movies with on Fridays. I had—very briefly—a boyfriend when I was a junior, and even after he dumped me for one of my teammates, I didn't feel like such an outcast.

My last two years of high school weren't perfect, but they were infinitely better than my previous nine years in public school had been. Because I was younger than my classmates, I didn't turn sixteen and get my license until the tail end of my junior year. I rode my bike to school and to crew practice, to my babysitting assignments and my after-school and weekend job busing tables and waitressing at Hop Brook Tavern. I had a look that I put together from thrift-store finds and Marshalls purchases, a budget wardrobe that let me spend my money on books and concert tickets—books I wanted to read, bands I wanted to hear. I learned that I could make people laugh, and that if not everyone got me or my humor, that was fine, because, someday, maybe, there'd be enough people in the world who would.

Admissions

McCosh 50 was one of the largest lecture halls at Princeton University. With its sloping hardwood floors and wooden desks bolted in place, you could imagine it looking the same fifty or a hundred years earlier, when Princeton had been a male-only bastion for the wealthy white sons of privileged East Coast professionals, doctors and lawyers, ministers and politicians. That night in November 1989, every seat was taken, and there were people standing in rows near the back, craning to see the stage.

Up front, beneath the bright lights, there were two wooden tables with a single podium between them. At one table was Russel H. "Cap" Beatie Jr., Princeton class of 1959 and the lawyer for Tiger Inn, one of Princeton's eating clubs, the university's substitution for fraternities and sororities, where upperclassmen ate their meals and socialized. Sitting next to him was Mike Palermo, class of 1990, the current president of what its denizens called the Glorious Tiger Inn. At the other end was Sally Frank, class of 1980, who, as an undergraduate, had filed a lawsuit against the all-male clubs, charging that, as part of the university, they could not legally discriminate against female students. And next to Sally Frank was me.

The room looked enormous, and it seemed to be expanding with every breath I took. So did my thighs. I could feel my heart hammering, feel my palms sweat, as I heard the people in the crowd murmuring and laughing and settling into their seats. *This is what you wanted*, I told myself. I'd wanted a stage, I'd wanted a microphone, I'd wanted a challenge and a place to find my voice. But, in that moment, on that stage, with what looked like half the student body in front of me, I didn't want any of it at all.

My parents—my mom in particular—had raised me to be a liberal, a Democrat, and a feminist. From the time I was old enough to understand politics, I was taught that the Republicans were the party of the rich and the Democrats stood up for the workers and the poor. One of the first things I can remember is my parents leaning toward our television set, watching the Watergate hearings . . . and then my father lifting me into the seat of a metal grocery cart, his beard tickling the top of my head as he reached over me to put a newspaper into the basket and saying, "We have a new president now."

My parents kept up with politics—through newspapers and magazines, and the constant background hum of NPR. When the four of us begged for music in the car, instead of Top 40, we'd get Pete Seeger protest songs and Holly Near love songs (foreshadowing!) and the Rude Girls' rendition of old labor movement and antiwar songs like "Mothers, Daughters, Wives" and the lesbian ballad "The Girl in the Red Velvet Dress" (MORE FORESHADOWING!). My mother lived her feminist beliefs, that clothes and makeup weren't important, opinions and actions were. Her outfits were functional and activity-specific—bathing suits for swimming, tennis clothes for her weekly game, sneakers every place she could get away with them, and for when she went back to work as a teacher, loose-fitting, all-cotton, elastic-waist skirts and cropped pants paired with tunics in colors that were not necessarily complementary. Fran kept her hair short, in a version of the same cut for what's now fifty years and counting. Her dangly, beaded earrings were her only vanity. She didn't own a tube of lipstick or a pair of high-heeled shoes. Instead of purses, she preferred to keep her wallet and her keys, her folded-up *New York Times* crossword puzzles, her hairbrush, and, if we were going on a trip, her jar of generic peanut butter and loaf of white bread in one of a series of canvas tote bags that were the premiums for her gifts to the local public-radio station.

Being a young feminist in New England meant you grew up knowing about the Seven Sisters, the all-female counterpart to the Ivy League. From the time I'd started considering college, I had wanted to go to Smith, in nearby Northampton, Massachusetts. Madeleine L'Engle, who wrote *A Wrinkle in Time*, went to Smith. Sylvia Plath went to Smith. Gloria Steinem went to Smith. Betty Friedan, author of *The Feminine Mystique*, went to Smith, along with the activist, law professor, and antiporn activist Catharine MacKinnon, and the journalist Molly Ivins. (So did Nancy Davis, who became Nancy Reagan, and Barbara Pierce, who became Barbara Bush. I tried not to dwell.) In the days before the Ivy League opened its doors to female students, women's colleges produced the most brilliant women in the world, and I wanted to join their ranks. I imagined that I'd combine my love of reading and writing and my interest in politics and feminism and become a speechwriter, the way Susan Isaacs had, or that maybe I'd write magazine articles and novels and screenplays, like Isaacs and like Nora Ephron.

My grades were good. My writing samples were solid. But what was better—what made me stand out from all the other smart girls who could write—was the spot I'd held for two years on the varsity crew team, which meant that I was a recruitment-worthy rower.

For the uninitiated, crew involves sitting on a sliding seat in a super-lightweight boat made of wafer-thin fiberglass, with an oar in your hand, pulling on those oars as hard as possible for a distance of three miles (in the fall season) or 1,500 meters (in the spring). Crew turned out to be the perfect sport for me, because you don't have to be coordinated (I wasn't) or speedy (I wasn't) or a quick thinker who could memorize plays and come up with strategies under pressure (I couldn't). All you had to be was strong, with a certain amount of endurance, and the kind of mulish temperament that lent itself to sitting in a boat, staring at the back, and the backside, of the girl in front of you, yanking on your oar in time with your teammates, going backward, through a body of water, while a coxswain, the ideally very small, light person who sat at the front and steered the boat, called out the cadence and screamed exhortations through a megaphone or microphone. My performance was only enhanced by the fact that, by senior year, our varsity coxswain was my sister, Molly, who was incredibly profane, and whose voice I heard, it seemed, from the moment I woke up with her in the twin bed six feet to my left until the moment I fell asleep, typically with Molly still talking. My brothers had their own bedrooms, due to some retrograde notion on my allegedly progressive parents' part about which gender required privacy. I was condemned to nights of Molly, who talked incessantly, usually while I was trying to read. ("Jenny, do you think Tim Cavanaugh likes me? Jenny, if we asked Mom to get us a curling iron, she probably would, if we paid for half of it and we told her it was for both of us. You didn't spend your babysitting money yet, did you? Did you? Jenny? Jenny? JENNY, ARE YOU LISTENING TO ME?")

Molly was fifteen months younger than I was, petite, and charming, with a cap of shiny, permed dark brown curls and a natural sense of style. In the time-honored fashion of little sisters everywhere, Molly drove me crazy. She'd take my best clothes out of my half of the closet—the Esprit vest that Nanna had bought me in Michigan, the cranberry wool Benetton sweater that I'd saved for—and wear them to school, hiding them under her jacket so I wouldn't notice at the bus stop. If she happened to cross my path at school during the day, she'd turn on her heel and run, usually with me chasing after her, and a teacher calling after us, announcing that there was no running in the hallways. She eavesdropped on my phone calls; she found everything I hid, whether it was my diary or a copy of Anaïs Nin's *Little Birds*, and she'd usually let me know she'd located what I'd tried to hide by doing dramatic readings out loud. She was six inches shorter and many pounds lighter than I was, attractive to boys and maddeningly indifferent to food. At dinner, even if it was her favorite meatloaf, peas, and mashed potatoes, she'd leave most of her meal just sitting on the plate, while I'd wolf down my portion, then seconds, and then eye her leftovers hungrily.

If I found my niche as a rower, Molly found hers as a coxswain. "PULL on those OARS, you fat BEASTS!" she would yell, or she'd count out the cadence of a racing start: "Half stroke, half, three-quarters, full slide, power ten. ONE! TWO! THREE! FOUR!" I'd pull as hard as I could, then even harder, perhaps imagining that if I pushed with my feet and I pulled on the handle with all my might, I'd actually be able to escape from the eternal sound of my sister.

As it turns out, I pulled that oar hard enough to make the junior-varsity eight my sophomore year, and the first boat—the top of the crew food chain—as a junior. By 1985, I was stronger than 85 percent of the other girls who submitted to the Junior National tryouts. The tryout, held at Yale's gym, consisted of a five-thousand-meter "piece" on an ergometer, an indoor rowing machine/torture device that replicated the motion of rowing, measuring strength and time. During my piece, I spent the last eight hundred meters feeling like my lungs and legs were all on fire, the last two hundred meters convinced that I was going to puke and pass out, and the final hundred meters convinced I was going to die. Then there were bench rows. For two minutes, you'd lie facedown on a weight bench, yanking a forty-pound barbell up and banging it into the bottom of the bench as many times as you could.

I trained hard, and luck was on my side. My athletic prowess reached its peak my junior year of high school, the precise moment that college coaches were paying attention. There were only a handful of high schools on the East Coast that even had crew teams, and almost all of them were prep schools. Being an accomplished rower who wasn't a legacy and who hadn't attended Andover or Exeter meant that, even as a girl from an affluent Connecticut suburb with upper-middle-class parents, I was practically an affirmative-action candidate.

So there I was, with my solid grades, my stellar verbal SAT score, my significantly less impressive math SAT score, and my rowing prowess. Seven Sisters, here I come!

I visited Smith's campus the September of my senior year in high school, and it was everything I'd thought it would be: ivy-covered Gothic buildings, a lake ringed by weeping willows, smart, intense-looking young women walking in pairs or groups through quads strewn with gold and crimson leaves, gorgeous old dormitories and a quaint small town with a homey little bookstore and a coffee shop. Smith had all kinds of charming traditions, from Friday teas to "mountain day," where the dean would pick an especially lovely day in autumn and ring a bell to cancel classes. I loved it there, and thought that I'd fit right in.

I also had a sense—a small, nagging feeling at first that grew as my senior year progressed—that Smith would be an easy place for me, and not easy in a good way. I was politically liberal; so were most of the people at Smith. I was a feminist, and feminism was woven into the fabric of Smith's very existence. Everyone would be like me . . . but was that a good thing?

There was also an issue with my father. My dad, who was in and out of the house (and his marriage) by then, was less than enthusiastic about my chosen institution. Not because it was a women's college, he took pains to make clear, but because it was a college. A university, he argued, would give me a better education—it would have more resources, more facilities, more opportunities to learn different things . . . and, if he was going to be the one paying, then he wanted to be the one who'd ultimately decide. At least, that's the case he made in public, although now I wonder if he was actually less worried about my education than my sexuality (EXTRA FORESHADOWING!).

I ended up applying to five schools, which was an average number back then—you'd have one or two safety schools, one or two "reaches," and a place or two that you were pretty sure you'd get into. I got into Smith and Mount Holyoke early action. Cornell rejected me (their admissions department did send a very nice note about how, if I went somewhere else and did better at math, I should definitely consider trying to transfer). I got into Penn . . . and I got into Princeton, where I'd applied because it struck me, during my visit, as a kind of anti-Smith. Not that it wasn't lovely—it was. It looked, in fact, like Smith to the next power, with the same kind of gracious, ivy-draped, history-drenched buildings, only more of them, bigger and grander. The slate sidewalks were wider, the grass of the quads was greener, everything was so picturesque and so perfect that I wondered if the university employed set dressers, who'd show up on autumnal mornings when prospective students were visiting to light the marble buildings to their best advantage, to groom the ivy and strew the paths with just the right color and combination of leaves and arrange for attractive, well-dressed, diverse extras to wander around, chatting or studying or singing a cappella underneath the arches.

Princeton's crew teams practiced and raced on a man-made lake commissioned and named after Andrew Carnegie. The 1887 boathouse was a mansion, cream with dark red trim. Enormous as it was, it was stuffed to the rafters, crammed with top-of-the-line Vespoli quads and fours and eight-man shells stacked in rows, and an adjoining structure that housed indoor rowing tanks.

Princeton had beauty and resources and history, a distinguished alumni body, and some of the best writers in the world as faculty. I would page through the glossy admissions brochure, admiring the pictures, memorizing the names and the pedigrees of the professors: John McPhee, Toni Morrison, Joyce Carol Oates. Nor did these luminaries just sit around in their endowed-chair offices and host the occasional graduate-student seminar. They taught undergraduates, even freshmen.

All of that was appealing. So was the cachet of being able to say you went to Princeton—to the *Ivy League*, my father would intone, his low voice lingering over the syllables, his eyes solemn behind his glasses. That was a very big deal in Simsbury, and an even bigger deal to my midwestern parents, who'd both gotten perfectly solid educations at a state school but who, like many converts, became their religion's most zealous advocates.

I was torn. The part of me that had dreamed about Smith still wanted to go there. High school had been such a struggle— to find my people, to finally feel a degree of comfort in who I was and how I looked and how I saw the world sounded amazing. I wasn't sure I was ready to start that struggle all over again, and I knew, or at least sensed, that at Princeton, I'd have to. Princeton had been the last of the Ivies to admit women and it still had the feeling of being the most southern, old-fashioned, least progressive of the eight institutions. Smith's purpose was to educate women. At Princeton, women had spent the eighteen years since coeducation fighting for everything, from getting more tenured females on the faculty to convincing the administration to put locks on the dormitory doors.

Smith would be like spending four years in a bathtub—warm and comforting, unquestionably safe and maybe the tiniest bit confining. Princeton would be like jumping into a plunge pool—icy and bracing and uncomfortable. But I thought that Princeton, unlike Smith, was a place where feminism mattered, where there was still work to be done, as opposed to a place so progressive and evolved that there was no longer anything to be progressive or evolved about.

I showed up in New Jersey in September of 1987. My dorm room was on the second floor of Campbell Hall, in Mathey College, one of the five residential colleges where all the freshmen—or "first-year students," as some of the more enlightened among us tried to remember to say—were housed. Mathey and Rockefeller were the two oldest, and grandest, Gothic dormitories and dining halls, with high, arched ceilings and pristine, perfectly maintained lawns and plantings. My college was beautiful, and my suite itself was lovely, with two small bedrooms, each with a set of bunk beds, and a spacious common room, with hardwood floors, and a working fireplace, and a built-in window seat in front of a set of leaded windows overlooking the quad. I guessed that Campbell Hall could be the nicest place I would live in for years, until I really got my career off the ground, and I wasn't wrong.

I had three roommates. The first, who was there when I arrived, was a chic young woman with high cheekbones and almond-shaped eyes named Lesedi, from South Africa by way of Connecticut, where her father was a college professor. Next to join us was a first-generation Chinese-American girl named Anita who was from Boston. She had a shiny blunt-cut bob, and a boyfriend in Canada* who made her mixtapes. Our fourth roommate was a science star, a Presidential Medal of Honor winner, a tiny, sprightly blonde named Cole. All of my new roommates were thin and attractive. Anita and Cole were cute; Lesedi, with her swaying walk, lovely face, and elegant, narrow-hipped body, and the designer wardrobe that had won her "best dressed" honors at her prep school in New Hampshire, was beautiful.

I pressed my lips together as I stowed my brother's borrowed hockey bag underneath my bunk bed and started to set up the stereo that had been my high school graduation gift. *Hello, Inadequacy, my old friend.* It had taken me two years to shake the echo of Fat Jennifer, to believe that I looked just fine, that I looked the way I was supposed to. Living side by side by side with these three—not to mention the girls in the suite next to us, an all-American ice hockey player and a tiny, freckled girl named Cindy who had the same bullying attitude, and even the same beady-eyed head tilt as my Israeli traveling companion Ronni—it was going to be hard not to feel like crap.

I was bracing for misery when there was a knock on the door, and a tall, broad-shouldered blond girl, whose face was flushed with either heat or dismay, stepped inside and shut the door behind her.

"Oh my God," she said. "I was carrying my stuff upstairs—I'm on the third floor, right above you—and I say to my mom, 'It must be a hundred degrees out,' and this voice from the top bunk says . . ." She pinched her nostrils to imitate a nasal little-girl's drone. "Fahrenheit or Celsius?"

Anita and Cole and I started laughing. Lesedi smiled politely, then drifted back to her room. Soon the sounds of Eric B. &

---

* The rare boy/girlfriend in Canada who was actually in existence.

Rakim floated out from underneath her door. Lesedi, it turned out, had arrived on campus a week ahead of the rest of us, in order to attend a special seminar for minority students, and seemed to have decided that she'd made all the friends she needed and had no reason to be anything more than coolly pleasant to her roommates. Sarah, which turned out to be the blond girl's name, became my first real Princeton friend, one of the only other young women on that campus full of sleek, smart, sophisticated beauties who didn't scare me and make me feel like a fraud.

Up to that point, I'd felt inadequate about any number of things in my life. But I'd never once worried about being stupid. Turns out there was a first time for everything, and the longer the first semester went on, whether I was standing in line to register for classes, or serving breakfast in the grand, high-ceilinged dining hall, or sitting in my Italian 101 class, which met at nine in the morning ("Genoveffa," my professor said, a frown pursing his full lips, as he assigned me my Italian moniker. "Ees not—*come si dice?*—such a beautiful name. Ees name of Cinderella's stepsister, *in Italia*")—the less qualified I felt to be there.

You wanted a challenge, I reminded myself as I'd struggle to memorize Italian vocabulary or to follow along during the field trips in my Geology 201 class, affectionately known as Rocks for Jocks. The academics weren't easy, but it was more just the way the place felt, how Princeton managed to take Simsbury's physical beauty, and the loveliness of its inhabitants, and elevate it to a degree that I'd never imagined possible, and then add sophistication on top. My classmates were the sons and daughters of senators or Fortune 500 CEOs, NPR anchors, soap-opera stars, and even Middle Eastern potentates. Brooke Shields, the model-turned-actress, had graduated the spring before I'd arrived. Wendy Kopp, whose senior thesis gave the world Teach for America, was the year ahead of me; Senator Ted Cruz, who was a champion debater, was the year behind. A significant proportion of the student body had attended private school or boarding school, which meant that, instead of their first experience with independent living, Princeton just meant a new set of dorms.

I felt like a country mouse, wide-eyed and wrong-footed, doing things like mispronouncing "heinous" in front of a snickering classmate or failing to apply for creative writing classes my first semester because the information on how to do so was published in the *Daily Princetonian* and I hadn't gotten a subscription.

Then there was food.

I'd never been skinny, but I'd always been fit in high school, with my weight kept under relative control by three-hour-a-day, three-seasons-a-year practices. I was rowing, I was running, I was skiing, cross-country and downhill, and working out on the ergometer in the off-season, and riding my ten-speed bike everywhere. When my mother put dinner on the table, there'd be enough breaded baked chicken or meatloaf or pasta for everyone to have seconds, but not thirds.

But in college, there was food everywhere. The dining halls served eggs and bacon and English muffins and French toast every morning; soups and salads and at least two different entrees at lunch and dinner, and desserts at both meals, plus soft ice-cream dispensers and bottomless bins of the sugary cereals I was used to seeing maybe twice a year. At least once a week the dining hall would serve a dessert called Crazy Cake, which was a half-cake/half-pudding hybrid served in towering, dense squares. Every Monday, the International Student Union hosted a four-dollar lunch where you'd get a paper plate that sagged under the weight of rice and gravy and curried chicken and salad, and at least once a month, the dining halls would throw a fancy dinner with a steamship roast of beef that was the size of a small child, and a man in a white toque and a white chef's jacket to carve off as much as you wanted.

There were no limits in the dining hall, where the food never ran out. In addition to meals, there was the student center, which served bagels and muffins and other starchy, carb-laden treats around the clock. And there were study breaks. Just about every day, some team or group or club or cause that was recruiting would invite freshmen to attend a speech or a meeting in the common room, luring us with greasy wedges of thin-crust pizza or Thomas Sweet ice cream, homemade and meltingly rich. For ten dollars—eight if you'd clipped a coupon from the *Daily Princetonian*—you could get a one-topping pizza delivered right to your room, and, for twice that, you could splurge on pan-fried pork dumplings and General Tso's chicken—a novelty for a girl who'd grown up in a town with zero delivery options. There were bags of mint Milanos from the U Store, and candy bars and sugar-laced bottles of Snapple. You could get drunk (or, in my case, just act like you were drunk) and have an excuse to stuff your face with Wawa hot dogs and squishy-soft salted pretzels in the wee small hours of the morning, and then show up for breakfast, where there'd be apple Danish and pancakes and sausage and quiche.

I did not handle this new bounty well. I ate because I was hungry; I ate because the food was there and it tasted good; I ate because I was lonely and homesick, anxious about my ability to do the work and insecure about the way I looked on a campus full of beautiful people. By October, any pair of pants without an elastic waistband was getting tight. By November, when it was cold enough to require sweaters, my arms were looking disturbingly sausage-y in my cardigans. Worse, at practice, I could feel the dubious eyes of the women's freshman coach upon me.

I knew that I had to lose weight, except I really had no idea how. I hadn't grown up in a house with a dieting mother—the only evidence of attempted weight loss I ever saw was a dusty, long-past-its-expiration-date tub of SlimFast in the back of the pantry. Signing up for Weight Watchers felt unimaginably embarrassing. I'd try to exert my willpower, day by day, or even meal by meal. I'd sit with Jamie Desjardin, a women's studies major from Berkeley with spiky brown hair who'd whisk mustard and soy sauce in a cup to make salad dressing. Listening to the *tink, tink, tink* of the tines of her metal fork against the glass, dousing my own iceberg lettuce and chickpeas in the ugly tan sauce, I'd think, *I can do this.* Then Jamie would head off to class and I would slink to the automated ice-cream dispenser, squirting a cereal-bowlful of chocolate.

I had, I knew, other options. Any girl who visited the bathroom after mealtime knew what those options were, when you'd glance toward the bottom of a row of stalls and see pairs of feet turned the wrong way, or you'd smell bile in the air, or see the grim-faced janitors toting mops and buckets and plungers down to the bathroom every other day, to clear the toilets, and sometimes the showers, of vomit. I gave bulimia a few halfhearted attempts, but I hated throwing up so much that I knew I'd never be able to make it work as a long-term plan.

Looking back, I can see that I was lucky that I didn't end up with a drinking problem or an eating disorder, lucky that all I got was fat. But fat was enough to, essentially, get me kicked off the crew team. "You need to lose a lot of weight," the freshman coach explained to me as he looked across the dining-room table (probably after I'd finished my second plateful of whatever stir-fry or meatloaf they were serving). It was spring break by then, everyone else had gone home, and I'd elected to stick it out on campus and do two-a-day workouts with my soon-to-be former teammates. The coach ordered "seat races," where two boats race against each other with one rower in, say, each boat's third seat, and then just those two rowers would switch. Every boat I was in lost every race. I made it back to my dorm room before I started to cry, and I made it through the season—even though it was clear that the coach would have been very happy if I'd left—and then I was done with crew forever.

I knew, and had probably known for a while, that I wasn't going to be a college athlete. The practices were harrowing, five-hundred-meter sprints or five-thousand-meter marathons, repeated over and over, on the water or in the tanks or on rowing machines, in all weather, in the spring or fall, workouts that would leave your lungs burning and your hands blistered, your back aching, and your arms so sore that you'd be too weak to wash your hair. On top of the work you'd do on the water, there were weights to be lifted, miles to be run, all in the company of girls with first names like Lasseter and Montgomery, who summered on Nantucket and had all been to Europe and dated blandly handsome boys who'd gone to Exeter or Choate.

I hadn't made friends among my fellow rowers. My people were the pale, black-wearing Goth girls and the long-haired, poetry-reading boys who were trying to be vegetarian or gay, or trying even harder (and, in only one case I remember, succeeding) to have threesomes; they were the Monty Python–quoting nerds from New Jersey, girls from Alaska and Montana who joked that they'd gotten in for being "g.d.," which stood for "geographically desirable." My friends joined the Wildcats after the Tiger Lilies, the oldest and most prestigious of the female a cappella groups, turned them down, and played club rugby or intramural Ultimate Frisbee after they'd been cut by, or gotten fed up with the rigors of, the field hockey or soccer team. My people weren't averse to spending a Saturday night drinking tea and playing board games along with the born-again Christians, who also eschewed booze-filled parties.

Sophomore year, after an unhappy summer at home, I came back to campus not a pound thinner, and with a raging case of impostor syndrome. Without crew, I believed, there was no way I'd have gotten into Princeton . . . so I tried as hard as I could to prove that, academically, I did belong there, and to leave the place better than I'd found it. There were plenty of causes to choose from—divestment, CIA recruiting on campus, abortion rights (then, as now, under attack)—and it didn't take me long to settle on the one that would be mine.

When I'd been looking at colleges, I knew I hadn't wanted a school with a big Greek life. I'd seen *Animal House* and *Revenge of the Nerds* multiple times apiece. I knew that I probably wouldn't cut it as a sorority girl—not unless my chosen institution had a chapter of Omega Mu—and I didn't want my social life for the next four years to center around beer-soaked bacchanals in run-down mansions.*

Princeton did not, officially, have fraternities or sororities. What it had instead were eating clubs—a row of mansions, just across the street from the center of campus, where members ate and partied.

---

* A few words here about the Mus, the sorority sisters in *Revenge of the Nerds*. The movie is one of my favorites, and it is both hugely entertaining and hugely problematic (the scene where Lewis basically tricks the pretty sorority girl Betty Childs into letting him go down on her by disguising himself as her football-hero boyfriend? We have a phrase for that, pal, and that phrase is *date rape*). Then there were the Omega Mus, the sister sorority to the socially outcast Tri-Lams, heavy and unattractive women whose looks were played for laughs. On the one hand, the portrayal of the ladies of Omega Mu confirmed everything I'd learned about how the world treats fat women, and confirmed my worst fears about how college boys would treat me. The nerds are so nerdy that the only girls who will come to their party are the fatties! The Mus—pronounced "Moos," of course—are so hideous that of course the BMOC frat taunts them by releasing a herd of greased pigs at the Lambda Lambda Lambda bash! However, the Mus gave me the all-too-rare chance to see women who looked like me on-screen. And the scene where Dudley "Booger" Dawson is blissfully dancing with, and squeezing on, the big behind of one of the Mus left me with the teensiest flicker of hope. Even if it was clear, when one of the Mus cut in on her sister, and Booger, with his eyes still shut, instantly began squeezing *her* butt, that he, and the movie, saw the larger ladies as completely interchangeable and nothing more than objectified body parts. Plus, the Mus, "clappin' along" during the Nerds' big performance, looked pretty damn good. And one of the Nerds ended up with a Mu as a girlfriend. Not one of the fat ones, but they were in love, and she didn't get the classic movie makeover, or pull off her glasses and emerge as a babe— she just stayed nerdy. Message: someone needs to do a feminist update of *Revenge of the Nerds*, and it absolutely must include Curtis Armstrong's cry of "You Mus sure know how to party!"

There were twelve clubs in the late 1980s, each with its own character. Terrace, a stucco-and-timber mansion on Washington Street, around the corner from Prospect Avenue and the more respectable clubs, was for Princeton's artsy undergrads, the English and architecture majors, the actors and the dancers and students identifying, or experimenting with identifying, as gay. Terrace looked fancy until you got close enough to see that it was a mess inside. The food was delicious, but the public rooms smelled like ashtrays and mop water. The carpets were worn, the lawn was patchy, the windows had hairline cracks, and the walls were scuffed and stained with cigarette smoke.

Around the corner, on Prospect Avenue, there was Tower Club, affectionately known as the "tool shed," where the Woodrow Wilson School majors, future politicians and government types, congregated, and Quadrangle, or Quad, for the engineering students. Cottage and Cap and Gown were the "bicker" clubs for Princeton's prettiest people and its best athletes, the clubs you had to rush, like a fraternity, to get in. Charter and Colonial were where the kids who'd been rejected, or "hosed," during bicker, ended up. Ivy, one of the remaining all-male clubs, had been immortalized by F. Scott Fitzgerald as "detached and breathlessly aristocratic." There, waiters in tuxedoes served dinner, and women weren't allowed inside without a male escort. Tiger Inn, or T.I., was Ivy's raucous, party-hearty little brother, which could be counted on to send kids to the hospital with alcohol poisoning a few times each semester. T.I. was for the jocks and the serious drinkers, a place where, in addition to Beer Pong and Quarters, you could play Trees and Trolls. The game was not complicated: the tall guys ("trees") would line up on one side of the room; the shorter guys ("trolls") would assemble on the other, and, at a signal, they'd charge at each other, screaming.

Back in 1980, Sally Frank had taken on the all-male clubs

in court for gender discrimination. If women pay the same tuition, why shouldn't they have the same opportunities? Why shouldn't all of Princeton, not just parts of it, be available? Frank filed a lawsuit, which, seven years later, was still wending its way through the system. When I got to campus, conventional wisdom seemed to be that only a handful of hairy-legged, strident, shouty feminists cared about the two clubs' exclusionary policies. Most women figured they got into the all-male clubs on Friday and Saturday nights, at parties, when it mattered.

The all-male clubs were allowed to persist in their all-maleness because, technically, they were not an official part of the university. Practically, though, it was clear that the clubs were essential to Princeton's life. The university depended on the clubs to feed its upperclassmen; precepts and study groups and concerts all were occasionally held there. Maybe my classmates didn't care, as long as there were some clubs that would consider them, but I found the sexism galling. Why did men get eleven choices, and we had only nine? Goddamnit, what if I wanted to play Trees and Trolls . . . or, more pertinently, what if I'd wanted to belong to F. Scott Fitzgerald's old eating club, or rub shoulders with Frank Deford or James Baker, both Ivy members who presumably might come back for reunion and meet a promising young writer in search of advice or employment? The truth was, I had no interest in bickering, in trying to get into a fancy club that I couldn't afford and from which I'd surely be rejected . . . but why did certain clubs get to make that choice for me? Besides that, taking up arms against the eating clubs was, unlike a seat race, or a battle with my own body, a war that I might win, a place to use my words and make my parents proud.

In Mathey's shared computer lab, I wrote op-eds that made my case (after a pair of male Mathey residents found what I'd written on the hard drive and read it out loud, in cruel falsetto, I took pains to delete my drafts and began petitioning my parents for my own computer). I wrote speeches and op-eds and letters to the editors of various campus publications. I made posters and made up chants ("Two, four, six, eight, why won't you coeducate?"). I made friends with a girl named Melissa Hardin, a willowy classmate who'd grown up on Park Avenue in New York City. ("Was that your prom?" I asked, spotting a photograph of her in a fancy white dress in a silver frame on her bedside table. Melissa's dorm room had a bedside table, draped in a floral fabric that coordinated with her bedspread, and her pictures were in frames, not tacked to her walls. "No," she said, sounding a little shamefaced, "that was my debut.") We led a demonstration during bicker, and while a steady stream of khaki-and-oxford-shirt-clad male classmates streamed by us and into the club's front doors, we walked in a circle on the sidewalk outside (public space, Sally Frank—who was by then a lawyer—had assured us), brandishing our picket signs and chanting. My friend Sarah, whose father had been a member of T.I., walked with us. I wasn't sure whether she did it because she cared or because she cared about me, but either way, I appreciated having her there, with her MY DAD JOINED T.I.—WHY CAN'T I? poster.

Which brought me to that November night at McCosh. In my lace-up brown ankle boots, elastic-waist olive-green skirt, and black turtleneck from the Gap, in front of a standing-room-only crowd of six hundred students, professors, and administrators, I delivered the speech that I'd written out by hand and practiced in front of the full-length mirror Fun-Takked to the door of my single dorm room in Henry Hall. Women were at Princeton, for better or worse. It was time for us to be at the same Princeton as our classmates, a Princeton where all the doors were open.

Some of the audience members applauded. A few of the rowdier guys hissed. A few more groaned when T.I.'s lawyer clumsily defended the eating club's members as broad-minded and inclusive because, a few years back, they'd elected a "big black guy" as their president. Sally Frank leaned over and whispered that I had to clap for him, no matter how offensive I found his remarks. There was no victor declared that night. The next day's story in the *Daily Princetonian* didn't quote a single line of my speech. But I walked home, through that grand, ivied campus, for once, feeling like a winner, feeling like no one could tell me that I didn't belong.

By spring, the issue of coeducation wasn't just the concern of a tiny clique of radicals. Undergrads and graduate students, staff and administrators and alums were showing up and speaking out. Melissa and I organized a rally in front of Robertson Hall. For weeks leading up to the event, professors would teach wearing pro-coed buttons that we'd had made. On the night of the rally, Sally Frank spoke to the crowd, along with the university's vice president, Thomas Wright, class of 1962, a lean, tweedy, perfectly correct man and a onetime member of Ivy, who denounced his club's practices. Still, it was a sophomore, Hillary Hodges, speaking on behalf of sixty sophomore women who'd petitioned to bicker at the clubs, who was probably the most convincing when she said, "Let us join. . . . We want to help you pay for your beer!" Two weeks after the rally, the undergraduate membership of both remaining all-male clubs voted to admit women. Later that spring, the Supreme Court declined to hear the appeal that Tiger Inn's legal team had pushed for on the grounds that the club's membership should be able to choose, instead of being forced, to accept women.

After that vote—which I'm still proud of—I wrote letters to the *Daily Princetonian*, opinion pieces for the *Nassau Weekly*, and columns for the monthly *Princeton Progressive*, where, thanks to a course on ancient Greek drama, I had the best pseudonym ever: Liz Sistrata. I sang Mozart pieces with the Glee Club and organized buses for pro-choice demonstrations in Washington. I worked fifteen hours a week, first at the dining halls and then as a waitress at one of the eating clubs, and still found time to stay, nominally, with my older hometown boyfriend while nursing a dead-end crush on a senior classics major named Jon Sender, whose thesis included the unforgettable line "Sacrificial pig in tow" (it sounds better in Greek).

At the *Nassau Weekly*, Princeton's news, culture, and opinion magazine, I became a staff writer, then a senior writer, then an opinion editor, and spent long Tuesday nights on the top floor of Aaron Burr Hall with a pot of glue and an X-Acto knife, printing out stories from the paper's Mac Classic, then cutting and pasting copy and headlines that would be driven to the printer in Trenton, then distributed on Thursday mornings.

On weekends, when the rest of the campus got drunk on Prospect Avenue, I would disappear into one of the subterranean levels of Firestone Library, sometimes with a cup from Thomas Sweet ice cream, chocolate chocolate chip topped with bittersweet hot fudge. I would sit with a book, spooning my treat into my mouth faster and faster, until my tongue, then my lips, then my entire face went numb, until I couldn't feel anything but the sweetness and the cold and how hard my heart would beat when all that sugar hit my veins. Sometimes I'd study, or I'd lose myself in a novel. I would tell myself that I wasn't lonely, and wouldn't even think of the shame that was underneath the loneliness and how I felt like a failure and a fraud. *This will get better*, I would think.

A college story: I remember one night sitting on the saggy porch at 2 Dickinson Street, the vegetarian co-op called Two D where I took my meals my senior year, not because I was a vegetarian, but because it was the least expensive option, a few hundred dollars a semester versus the thousands that even Terrace cost. The porch, with rotting boards and flaking paint, was lined with cast-off couches and battered armchairs, and I was passionately making the case for equality with an Ivy member nicknamed Trip, a fellow who had a first name that sounded like a last name, and a Roman numeral at the end of his actual last name, and who seemed more bemused than irritated. "Membership has its privileges," he kept saying, as if repeating a credit-card slogan could change my mind. I'd argue that merely being born with the right kind of genitalia over another shouldn't be the qualifying criteria for anything. "Princeton discriminates," he said. "It discriminates against dumb people." I rolled my eyes, thinking that right there before me was a walking, talking example that such discrimination did not always apply.

"You need a brain to do the work at Princeton. So tell me," I said, winding up for the grand slam, "exactly what's going on in your eating club that requires a penis?"

Zing! I stood on the porch, flushed with triumph, until one of the Two D denizens, a girl with creamy skin and straight, gleaming blond hair, pulled me aside and whispered, "Your fly is down."

Princeton.

Inadequacy and impostor syndrome are painful. They're also great motivators. I worked my ass off in college, eschewing parties and flirtations and late-night, dope-and-booze-fueled bullshit sessions about What It All Means in favor of work and work and more work. I didn't drink. I never once skipped class—not after the morning freshman year when, bored in an anthropology lecture, I'd calculated how much each class cost, dividing the tuition check by the number of times each course met each semester. I don't remember what the exact number was, but it was high enough to convince me not to skip a single lecture or preceptorial. Rather than settle for the required four classes, most semesters, I took five. I was determined to wring every possible advantage out of my expensive education, studying with every star professor who'd have me, learning as much about every subject as I could, taking on extra projects for extra credit, turning my senior thesis in early. I was a girl in a hurry, a girl in an extra-large black cotton Gap dress and black tights and knockoff Doc Martens from Payless, with her books in the same purple backpack she'd bought in high school, long hair pulled into a velvet scrunchie, head down, race-walking to the library. I was eager to get my degree and let it start opening the doors I'd been promised it would unlock, eager to stop costing money and start earning it, eager to begin to find my feet, and start to find my place in the world.

Worth

On our way home from visiting colleges in the fall of 1986, my mother told me that my father was leaving. We were at the Vince Lombardi Service Area on the New Jersey Turnpike, where we'd stopped to get gas. I don't remember what we were wearing, how she looked or even exactly what she said, but I remember how it smelled—like fried chicken and disinfectant—and how the other people had their travel faces on, the blank looks people wear when they know they're not going to be seeing coworkers or bumping into neighbors or spouses or children.

"He might be gone by the time we get back," she said. I was shocked, even though there had been clues. The cross-country trip they'd taken the summer I was in Israel had gone disastrously, culminating with my mom getting out of the car and walking in a breakdown lane in Utah while my father drove behind her, muttering, "This trip has come to a grinding halt." When they came home, there had been fights, conducted in whispers, late at night. Sometimes my father didn't come home at all, and worse than both the fights and the absences were the nights when he'd stood out front with the light on, underneath the window of the bedroom I shared with my sister, smoking.

The light kept me from sleeping. The smoke was even worse. It curled through the window screen, the acrid stink filling first our bedroom, then the hallway, then the whole upstairs. "Turn off the light, please!" I'd call, and he'd snarl something back at me, something about how it was his house and unless I cared to pay the mortgage he could do whatever he wanted. My youngest brother would cry. He was just seven, mid-indoctrination about the Evils of Smoking; he'd been shown the pictures of necrotic tissue and people dying of lung cancer. "Please don't smoke!" Joe would beg him. I don't remember what my father said back.

By the time my mother and I got home, I was ready for him to be gone. I was already planning how I'd frame this new stage of my life, what I would tell my friends, and whether I would, or would not, accept their sympathy. Should I be strong and stoic? Weepy and broken?

When we pulled down the pebbled driveway, though, his red Corvette was still in the garage, and my father was in the bedroom, with a suitcase open on the bed, pairing black socks and then folding them into bundles. He'd started wearing a pinkie ring the year before, a heavy Roman coin set in gold, and I remember that it gleamed in the light as he reached past my mother and shut the door.

The first time my father filed for bankruptcy was in 1988, when I was eighteen and home for my first summer from college. This was two years after he'd left with the words "I don't want you to think of me as a father. Think of me as more of an uncle."

We got the message. He was lighting out for the territories, to have adventures, to find the fun he'd been denied. We were all familiar with his complaint, how he'd say, "I never got to have a childhood," how he'd remind us of the presidents he'd memorized as a kid; how he'd been pushed to excel, to achieve, since he was old enough to read. He'd grown up laboring under the expectation that not only would he be the first in his family to attend college, but he'd also get an advanced degree and be a professional, a doctor or a lawyer, securing his spot in respectable upper-middle-class America. My father's parents, my mother's parents, everyone in the generation of Jews who had lived through the Holocaust knew that almost anything of worth could be taken from you—your home, your jewelry, your heirlooms—but no one could ever take your education.

My father wasn't a traditionally handsome man. His face was dominated by his nose, his curly black beard covered pock-marked, pale skin, and his most common expression was a skeptical scowl . . . but, resplendent in the tailored suits and glossy silk ties that he wore for work, with his slim leather briefcase at his side and his reputation as one of the best child psychiatrists in Hartford, he had a certain allure, especially to all the single ladies, the educators and the social workers and doctors and lawyers he met on the job.

By the summer of 1988, as far as my siblings and my mother were concerned, my father existed as a collage of red-bordered envelopes, creditors' calls, and our own conversations and guesses. We didn't see him, didn't even know where he was living, but we could trace his movements through the bills and come-ons that kept arriving in our mailbox: invitations to join frequent-visitor clubs at hotels in Saratoga and casinos in Atlantic City, postcards from jewelry stores and art galleries thanking him for his business. My parents weren't officially divorced then, just separated, so there were no legal orders in place for alimony and child support . . . just what my father had promised: *Of course I'll take care of you.*

But he didn't. Small stuff—clothes, groceries, gifts for birth-day parties—went on my mother's credit card. Big things meant panic. When our refrigerator gave out, my mom had to ask her mom for money to replace it. My father went off and got to have the life he'd wanted, the fun he'd missed, travel and glamour and glamorous traveling companions. We got the bills. It was as if, like his long-dead contractor father, he'd hefted his own sledge-hammer and sent it smashing down, but instead of shattering a countertop or a tiled floor, what he broke was our life; the illu-sion of us as a happy, normal family, the idea that he'd loved us or valued us enough to stick around.

The creditors' letters came first, sounding as if someone had translated the text from English into some obscure language with a spiky and difficult grammar, and then translated it back again.

"Your obligations to this creditor are seriously delinquent."

"This letter will serve as formal demand for payment of amounts owed to my client."

"Please be advised," they would say, and *"We are confident that you would like to resolve this matter now."*

As things progressed and no payments arrived, the letters' tone would shift, becoming first passive-aggressive, then sim-ply aggressive. *"Frankly, we would like to know if you intend to pay this,"* wrote American Express Travel. *"If your answer is 'yes,' please fill in the space below, and we will both feel better. But do it now! Courtesy costs so little: means so much."*

Eventually, the niceties would be abandoned, and the mis-sives would be written in shouty caps-lock: "YOUR FAILURE TO RESPOND TO OUR PREVIOUS REQUESTS HAS CONSTRAINED US TO REFER YOUR ACCOUNT TO OUR LEGAL DEPARTMENT FOR REVIEW. IF IT IS

DETERMINED THAT YOU ARE A CANDIDATE FOR
LEGAL PROCEDURES TO RECOVER THE AMOUNT
DUE, YOU MAY BE REQUIRED TO PAY ALL COLLEC-
TION COSTS TOGETHER WITH ANY INTEREST, AS
ALLOWED BY CONTRACT OR LAW. TO AVOID THIS
UNPLEASANT OCCURRENCE, UPON RECEIPT OF
THIS NOTICE, PLEASE CONTACT THIS OFFICE
TOLL-FREE."

My father owed money to American Express and Citibank
and Barclays, to the mechanic who cared for his cars and the garage that housed them, to a storage facility and to the car-phone
company and a half dozen department stores. Instead of paying
the bills he filed for bankruptcy, hiring lawyers to represent him.
He didn't pay them, either, and eventually their firms would send
collection letters of their own.

The letters didn't work. They couldn't—my father wasn't
there to receive them, we didn't know where to send them, and if
we had known where to contact our father, we would have probably asked him to take care of his obligations to us before paying
anyone else.

By that summer, the phone calls began, starting at seven in the
morning, ending at ten or even eleven o'clock at night, sometimes after I'd fallen asleep. The white kitchen phone, bolted to
the wall above the desk where my mother kept her address book
and paid the bills, would ring, or the cordless phone we'd carry
to the pool, or into the family room, would shrill.

"Is Doctor Weener there?" or "Let me speak to your father,"
the voice on the other end of the line would say, mispronouncing
our last name with malicious, sneering glee. Sometimes the voices
belonged to men, and sometimes to women, but that tone—
nagging, exhausted, bossy, aggrieved—was always the same.

"He isn't here," I—or my brother Jake, or my sister, Molly, would respond. "He doesn't live here anymore."

That summer, we would say those words over and over and over again—*we don't know where he is, he doesn't live here anymore.* It felt like punishment; like being forced over and over to admit our own failings.

"This is the number I have for him," the voice would say. Or "I know he's there." Or sometimes "I'm going to call your neighbors." There'd be a pause, a rustling of pages. "I'm calling the Chamberlains, and asking if his car's in the driveway." The Chamberlains, whose children were teenagers and young adults, lived next door, and rarely even said hello; the Efkins, an older couple with no kids, were our other next-door neighbors, and were friendly. The creditors' failure to pronounce "Efkin" correctly was one of the many things we tried to laugh about that summer. "Eefkin!" Joe would say, shaking his head. "Eefkin!" "Efkin" wasn't a hard name, which meant that the creditors were dummies, not as smart as we were, not as smart as my father, either, or they'd be able to track him down.

He's not here, we would say. *No, we don't have another number. No, we don't know where he is.*

"No, no, I don't want to talk to *you*," one of the collectors, this one male, yelled at me when I answered the phone at ten-thirty p.m. I was going to tell him off for calling that late, to tell him that some of us were trying to sleep because some of us had jobs, but he started in on me first. "Put your father on the phone."

"He isn't here," I said again, my voice high and stubborn, and the man made a rude noise and hung up.

"You're lying," one of the agents said to my brother Joe, who was eleven at the time. "Didn't anyone teach you that it's wrong to lie?" Joe hung up the phone and, tight-lipped, white-faced, walked out of the family room, up the stairs, and into his bedroom and locked his door. He didn't leave for eighteen hours, not even after we knocked and told him that he hadn't done anything wrong, that this would all, somehow, be fine.

Thanks to the women's studies course I'd taken my freshman spring, I came home that summer determined to reject the gendered norms of the workplace. No traditionally female, pink-collar ghetto for me, no taking care of children or waitressing or answering some man's phone. Instead, I took a job at a landscaping company, a move that would both destabilize the patriarchy and possibly result in noticeable weight loss and a killer tan.

From seven in the morning until four in the afternoon, in my bright yellow T-shirt, khaki pants, a baseball cap, and steel-toed work boots, I pushed a giant power mower across the wide, sloping lawns of the companies whose corporate offices lined the Berlin Turnpike. I drove the truck, filled the mowers' tanks with gas, gulped quarts of Gatorade and ice water from the cooler in the back of the truck as the temperature rose past ninety every afternoon. My palms blistered from the vibrating metal handle of the mower. I did, indeed, get very tan but did not, alas, get thin. I saved every paycheck, forty hours a week times seven dollars an hour, knowing I'd need the money to pay for shoes and clothes and textbooks, which were frighteningly expensive.

Molly, who was starting her senior year of high school in September, scooped ice cream at Friendly's on Route 44. This was ironic, given that my sister was then, and still remains, only selectively friendly. That summer, she served up some truly disturbing Cone Head sundaes to the children of happier families, whose dinners weren't interrupted by the blast of the telephone, the beep and hiss of the answering machine.

Joe went away to sleepaway camp for two weeks, the longest respite my mother could afford, and Jake caddied at a country club, carrying golf bags, making small talk with the fathers of his friends who belonged there. *How's your dad?* they'd ask, and Jake, the most socially adroit of the four of us, had figured out how to say *He's fine* in a way that precluded additional questions.

My mother had gone back to work a few years previously, after Joe had started school full-time. Like the rest of us, she had summers off. She swam. If she was home, she was in the water, churning out endless laps of the crawl, back and forth like a metronome, punctuating the still summer air with the splash of her stroking arm coming down, the flap of her swim skirt as she flipped. You couldn't hear the phone underwater. Even if you could, you'd never have to be the one to answer.

"Is Mister Weener there?" At some point, my father had stopped being a *doctor*. "No, honey, I don't want to talk to you," they'd say over and over again when I'd give my explanation, when I'd ask if I could help them instead. "Put your father on the phone."

When September came, I couldn't get back to school fast enough. My boyfriend, the older brother of a high school friend whom I'd been dating for two years, drove me to campus, and I stood in line to register for classes and collect the keys to my dorm room. When I got to the front, the woman peered at the ledger in front of her, then looked up at me, then left to have a whispered conversation with her supervisor before directing me to the bursar's office. Registration was at one end of campus. The bursar's office, where I'd never been, was all the way at the other. I walked uphill, along the slate paths, under the leafy green trees, head bent, listening to my classmates greeting one another, exchanging hugs and backslaps and asking how the summer had been. *Oh, we were in the Hamptons . . . I was in Italy, with my parents . . . San Francisco, with my dad, such a bore.* My hands were still callused. I kept them in my pockets and presented myself to a smiling woman behind a desk, who directed me upstairs to an

unsmiling man in an office, who told me that I wouldn't be allowed to attend classes, because no one had sent a tuition check.
"Do you know how to reach your father?" I remember him asking. His office was flooded with late-morning light that made
the floorboards glow like honey. His desk had spindly wooden
legs, and his ebony-painted chair had the university's crest on
the headrest, picked out in gold paint. Ivy edged along the panes
of his window overlooking the quad. I shook my head, reciting
the lines I'd said all summer. *We don't have another number for
him. We don't know where he lives.* I wondered if I could go home,
get my landscaping job back, rake leaves until it got cold, then
learn how to run a snowblower and a plow. I'd get friends to send
me the curriculum and the reading lists; I'd be an autodidact, and
write my first novel before I turned twenty-five, and I'd sell it for
a seven-figure advance, and wouldn't the school, and my father,
be sorry then?

I'd never thought much about money before that summer and
fall. My father was a successful physician; my mom worked as
a substitute teacher, but was mostly home with us. When I was
growing up, we'd never once gotten a call from a creditor; I'd
never seen a bill marked LAST NOTICE in the mail. Money—for
trips to Michigan or Florida, for a pair of used skis or hockey
skates from Play It Again Sports, for school supplies, for pets
and vets and doctor's visits—had always been there, the way
there was water when you turned on a tap, or heat when you
adjusted the thermostat, a steady, reliable presence. Even if my
parents were loath to spring for the designer clothes I'd craved
as a teen, we'd never not had money, and I'd never given much
thought to my relationship with it, or how much it could matter.
That fall—maybe even that moment, in the bursar's office—was
when I decided that I was going to be rich; that I'd earn myself,

somehow, a big, giant pile of cash. I didn't lust for things, didn't imagine myself draped in diamonds, wrapped in furs, or opening the doors of my mansion to the cameras of *Lifestyles of the Rich and Famous.* I wanted security. I never wanted to get pulled out of another line, or receive a single red-bordered envelope in my mailbox, or feel that sense of dread and misery when the phone rang. I wanted to never worry, to never feel attacked or insecure, worthless or unwanted, and I believed—foolishly, incorrectly, with a heartbreaking youthful naiveté—that money meant I never would.

My mother tried to explain to the financial officers that my father had promised to pay my tuition. They were sympathetic but unmoved. Whatever he'd said didn't matter, nor did the bankruptcy case. Both of my parents had signed the documents promising to pay my tuition. Eventually, my mother and I took out loans for thirty thousand dollars to cover my last two years, loans we'd repay at a rate of three hundred dollars per month for, I think, the next twenty years.

For the rest of my time at Princeton, it felt like I was stuck in that same head-down, hands-in-my-pockets hurry, like I was racing through campus, and toward the finish line of my degree, knowing that I could get a call, or a red-bordered letter of my own, in my box in the campus mailroom. *No, we don't want you. Where's your father? Let us talk to him!*

The next summer, I had an internship at the Fund for the Feminist Majority in Washington, DC. The internship was unpaid, but I had a plan—if I worked two weeks of twelve-hour days at Princeton's reunions, I would make enough to support myself during the internship, and have enough left over for books in the fall.

The problem was, my internship started before my check

from Princeton arrived. After three days in Washington, during which I'd gotten myself settled in my dorm at American University and figured out how to take the Metro to work, I was down to my last five dollars. I'd bought a loaf of bread and a jar of peanut butter, but when that ran out I didn't know what I was going to do. I called Fran, and asked if she could loan me a hundred dollars, just until my check arrived.

She turned me down. "You should just ask for an advance on your paycheck," she instructed.

"Fran," I said, trying not to panic. "It's an unpaid internship. There is no paycheck."

"I'm sure if you explain to your boss what's going on, and ask her to lend you some money, you can pay her back when your check gets there."

Of course, I was way too embarrassed to ask my boss, who'd once run the National Organization for Women, to lend me money. Instead, I found a CVS that would accept the credit card I'd gotten, in my own name, used once, then panicked when the $80 bill arrived and vowed never to use again. I bought cold cuts and canned soup and got a second, paying job at a coffee shop in Arlington. I turned down invitations to museums, skipped a trip to the movies, and, with my fellow interns, found a bar that had a spread of dips and vegetables, crackers and cheese, available for free during happy hour. I'd try not to notice the waitress's scowl as I'd load, and then refill, my tiny plate, trying to eat enough to stay full until breakfast.

When I tell that story now, and ask my mother (in a tone I try not to make too accusatory) why she couldn't have just sent me some money—even twenty dollars!—she replies, very calmly, "I probably didn't have it to spare." I think, of course, that if it was one of my girls asking for money, I would have found a way to get her some, even if I can recognize that my mother's refusal gave me the gifts of resilience and self-confidence, of knowing that whatever went wrong, I could count on myself to find a way out.

I knew, from that point forward, that I was on my own, working without a financial safety net. I would have to rely on myself, which made me even more eager to be done with school, to be on my own, saving my own money, weaving my own net so that if I ever fell again, I would be fine.

What I didn't know is that no amount of money would ever be enough to convince me that I would be truly safe. Instability marks you. It leaves you feeling permanently uneasy, as if, at any moment, everything you love could be taken away with a phone call, a conversation, a letter's arrival, the turn of a key in a lock. I didn't know that I'd grow up to write in what would become a very contested genre, that books like mine would be called dumb and worthless, reactionary, and even dangerous, or how I could still feel so worthless, even as the books sold and sold, even when my bank statements told me that I was a success. I could never have guessed the way the compliments and good reviews would evaporate, while the bad reviews and criticism would echo, lingering like slow-to-heal wounds, or that I'd hear them, over and over, in voices that sound like my father, or the creditors on the phone, the summer I was eighteen and worried that I wouldn't be able to go back to college, like the life I'd imagined for myself since I was old enough to imagine any kind of life at all might be impossible, and I'd have to start over again.

I left Princeton with a transcript full of As and *summa cum laude* on my diploma, prestigious internships on my résumé, and folders filled with copies of the stories I'd written and professors' letters of recommendation. Out in the world, I tried, as hard as I could, to believe in my own worth. But sometimes, especially on humid summer days, when I smell cut grass in the air or see heat lightning crackling in the sky or hear the cough and rumble of a lawn mower being yanked to life, the phone will ring and my heart will stop. The phone is still ringing; the phone will always be ringing, and no matter what the voice on the other end asks for, I will never be able to give it what it wants.

Not That Kind of Writer

P rinceton was, by its nature, exclusive. It wasn't easy to get in . . . and, once you were there, you'd continue to encounter little pockets of additional selectivity—the eating clubs you had to bicker to join; the classes you had to apply to take. The university had amazing creative-writing teachers . . . but your tuition dollars guaranteed you nothing more than a chance to study with them. You couldn't just buy a beret, march yourself down to 185 Nassau Street, and announce that you were, henceforth, a poet. You had to submit a short story or an actual poem, and have someone read and evaluate it before you got in.

I applied to every creative-writing class the university offered. My first was with Joyce Carol Oates. There were twelve of us, freshmen and sophomores, either so desperate to impress the professor with our erudition that we wouldn't shut up (one young man, now an award-winning novelist, was so voluble that Professor Oates, normally the most soft-spoken and even-tempered of instructors, snapped, "Mohsin, I'm talking now!") or so cowed by her outsize reputation that we would barely speak. Professor Oates was waif-like and long-limbed, with dark curls and enormous glasses that magnified her big brown eyes. She spoke in a high, thin voice and wore loose-fitting pants and cardigan sweaters in which her spindly limbs seemed to be floating. She didn't walk so much as drift, like she was being pushed around by a delicate breeze, like she existed on some other more ethereal plane than the rest of us.

In her class, I wrote lots of stories about teenage girls from broken homes, which I knew something about, and lots of stories about poor people in Appalachia, about which I knew much less (I'd discovered Dorothy Allison the previous summer). A piece about a boy and his mother visiting colleges was based on the trip that I'd made to look at Princeton and Penn with Fran. "I don't know anything!" was the line I gave the boy in the story. "Not anything!" I don't remember if I said it, but I remember that's how I felt, and I could call up the specifics of the moment, the orange tiled floors and the smell of fried chicken and disinfectant, and how tired my mother looked, and put all of it into what, years and a number of revisions later, became the first short story I ever published, in *Seventeen* magazine.

I loved writing fiction and my two semesters' worth of poetry classes. My first class was with J. D. McClatchy, who'd also taught one of my favorite non-creative classes, Modern British Poets, where we read Auden and Philip Larkin and Stevie Smith ("Not waving, but drowning"). McClatchy was an elegant man, his salt-and-pepper beard carefully trimmed, with perfectly cut tweed sports jackets, and a manner that was wry and refined but never condescending—a line in a poem about the narrator's ability to "make my woman come" earned a lifted eyebrow and an "I doubt we'd say it just like that anymore." In his creative-writing class, we'd spend one week on sonnets, the next on sestinas, and the week after that, villanelles. That was the class where I wrote the poem that won the Academy of American Poets Prize for 1990, which I wish I could find.

The semester after that, I studied with Ann Lauterbach, who was petite and red-haired, with outfits accessorized with green velvet capes and elegant bead and crystal necklaces. I don't remember much of what I wrote for her, but I remember a lot about what I read—particularly, the work of a female classmate who was dating an Israeli guy. Turns out, there are many words that rhyme with "Ofer."

Senior year was my last creative-writing stint. For Toni Morrison's "longer fiction" class, we had to write a hundred-page section of a novel. Somehow, I got the starting time of the class wrong, barging in at ten-thirty for an eight-person seminar that had started thirty minutes earlier. It took me weeks to get over the shame. What I remember from that class was the sound of Morrison's voice. Sometimes she would read our work out loud, in her low, deliberate tone, and occasionally she'd pause, letting a silence swell, then begin again, taking up the story in her thrilling cadences. You'd sit there, transfixed, thinking, *I am truly brilliant.* Then, usually on the walk back through campus, you'd realize that you were, in fact, not brilliant . . . it was just her voice that made your work sound so good.

Out of the hundred and fifty pages that I eventually turned in, there were probably three salvageable paragraphs, and one piece of an idea, which was how easily any young person with a backpack could be mistaken for a student on a college campus. The writing was showy, the point of view shifted unnecessarily, and while I knew enough to use adverbs sparingly, I compensated by piling on the adjectives. If there's a lesson, it's that sometimes you have to write and then discard a mountain of pages before you get to the tiny little bit of usable material. Or maybe it's that everything serves a purpose, even pages that end up in the trash. When I read Malcolm Gladwell's book about how it takes ten thousand hours to master a skill, I added up the months and years that I'd spent writing—as a student, as a journalist, in my spare time—before I sold my first book . . . and, sure enough, the total was just about where Gladwell said it should be. Sometimes the point isn't to end up with something worth showing the world. Sometimes it's just rehearsal.

Writing workshops are notoriously brutal—or at least, that's the impression you get if you read the novels by the people who've survived them—but maybe the brutality doesn't show up until you get to the graduate-level MFA programs. I don't remember any particularly vicious zingers from my workshops, just a male classmate kindly explaining to me that "telekinesis," while a nice rhyme for "senior thesis," did not mean "the ability to magically make things appear out of nowhere," and that some of my sex scenes were anatomically unlikely, if not impossible; and me gently explaining to a male classmate that it was impossible for the narrator to "marinate in the spice of your love" because marination required a liquid.

As much as I learned in my creative-writing classes, the class that taught me the most was John McPhee's seminar, Humanities 404, the Literature of Fact, which I took in the spring of 1990.

Professor McPhee had been a *New Yorker* staff writer for almost thirty years. He'd grown up in Princeton. His father had been a university doctor. Small and slight, soft-spoken and owlish, with thick glasses and a full gray beard, McPhee would sit, or stand, at the head of a long wooden table in East Pyne Hall and speak to us in a quiet, high-pitched voice. You'd have to lean forward to hear him, and none of us wanted to miss a word. I'm sure I'm not the only student who thought that if God had let us pick our own fathers, we would have chosen someone just like John McPhee, if not McPhee himself. He was patient, he was thoughtful and helpful. He made it clear that he expected nothing less than your best . . . and he also made it clear that he'd do what it took to get you there.

Professor McPhee taught his seminar just once every other year. Because it was about how to write nonfiction, it wasn't part of the Creative Writing program, and so it met in the Humanities building, in a beautiful, wood-paneled room with enormous windows and high ceilings. Admission was by application, he accepted only sixteen students, and the only grades were Pass and Fail. You weren't competing for As, but for his approbation. Every week, you would turn in a piece, and you'd meet with Professor McPhee every other week to discuss your work, which would be returned covered in his neat, penciled annotations—a word circled here, a phrase crossed out there, queries and comments written in the margins, a summary of his thoughts at the end.

He believed that any piece of writing could be improved through stringent, concerted, lengthy revision. He did not teach his students to wait for the Muse to whisper in our ear, or to hope for a flight of inspiration to loft our prose to the heights of brilliance. Writers were not people who hung around on misty mountaintops. We were not divine wind chimes waiting for the right breeze to blow. Writers *worked*—like sculptors hacking and chipping away at slabs of marble; like jewelers selecting the proper metals and polishing the best gems; like plumbers or HVAC guys, going into the unlovely guts of a building, unscrewing rusty pipes, cleaning dusty vents, fixing and building from the inside out . . . and revising, revising, revising. Every piece of prose had to be whittled and buffed, fine-tuned and reworked and rubbed down and polished again, until it was as close to perfect as you could get it.

Classes met for three hours on Monday afternoons. We'd sit around the rectangular table in that grand room that seemed to whisper all the boldfaced names who'd studied with Professor McPhee, the prizes he'd won, the books that he'd written, the luminaries he'd profiled, and, most of all, the name of the vaunted *New Yorker*.

We learned to think about the shape of a story, and its component pieces, building each one—the opening paragraph, the final words, the transitions and descriptions and dialogue—as best as we could, fitting them together with care, until the structure was invisible to the reader, and the author, too, disappeared. Writing, at least the way John McPhee taught it, promised the thing I most craved—namely, invisibility. Leading protests and giving speeches were all well and good, but writing could be just as powerful, just as persuasive . . . and it didn't involve a physical self. A writer wasn't a body, just a byline. My words would be sharp and spiky, punchy and pointed; my stories would be swift and lean, sleek and enviable, moving fast and hitting hard. I would not, I vowed, write like a fat girl.

During Week One of the class, Professor McPhee paired us up and had us interview, and profile, one another. It was a punishing task. He got to know us—both from the pieces that had been written about us, and from the way we described someone else. We had to learn to balance accuracy and sensitivity (you didn't want to dwell on the bad skin or bad reputation of the guy, or girl, you'd be seated across from for the rest of the school year). Week Two, you had to go find a piece of abstract art on campus and describe it (I wrestled with a Henry Moore work, affectionately called "the doughnut," an asymmetrical oval of greenish-tinted marble that proved easier to sit inside of than to write about).

In the succeeding weeks, Professor McPhee would bring in a friend or a colleague—a documentary filmmaker, a publisher, a married pair of archaeologists. We'd ask questions (or, in the case of Roger Straus, of Farrar, Straus and Giroux, the subject would deliver a rambling, hilarious, profanity-laced monologue, while Professor McPhee sat, chuckling and occasionally wincing from his seat in the corner). We'd then go off and write a profile of our subjects, one of whom was a documentary director named Tom Spain. I was offended by something he'd said that I'd found sexist, so my piece let him have it. I remember McPhee's notes, penciled in the margins: "If humor is tragedy plus time, this needs more time." It wasn't the first occasion I was forced to think about the line between funny and mean, between punching down, not up, to figure out how to write about the things that made me angry in a way that was powerful, not didactic or unhinged.

As the semester progressed, we were allowed to choose our own topics. I wrote a piece on English bulldogs, the most unnatural of animals, bred to live short, violent lives that would end during fights with bears or bulls; so anatomically implausible that they needed human intervention to mate and give birth. I wrote about the vexing history of the Miss America pageant, which, then and now, is one of my guilty pleasures. Understand that, when I say "wrote," I mean rewrote. Page by page, sentence by sentence, again and again and again. It was hard but exhilarating, the kind of effort that left you wrung-out and hot-eyed and proud because you knew you were doing what the pros did. Even John McPhee, a Pulitzer Prize winner, wouldn't dream of turning in a first draft. Or a second, or even a third. Writing was rewriting. It was the most important thing I learned that semester and, probably, throughout all of college.

My family was always on my mind during those four years. For my last paper for Professor McPhee, I wrote about a spring break trip I took with my sister, Molly. We visited Florida and Molly was in rare form, whether she was angrily filling out an airline evaluation sheet ("Was not provided with beverage of my choice") or going to the movies with me and Nanna and Nanna's gentleman caller, Harold, and messing with the senior citizens who go to the movies to act as interpreters for their hearing-impaired friends and loved ones.

"*Jen*," wrote Professor McPhee. "*This is just first-rate. That is, it is tightly composed and it is funny. It asks questions: Is the dialogue noted or recollected? If noted, when? What percentage of the fact is fact? 100? Where did you go to grade school and high school? Did you have a teacher who liked to teach writing? Has Molly read this? How—if so—did Molly react? Polish it up—one more time—and send it around. Publish it. Molly will sue. But you have insurance. You know how to tell a story.*"

Travels with Molly

Jennifer Weiner
April 20, 1990

My mother's sister, Marlene, and I are at gate C-12 in the Detroit Metro Airport, waiting for Molly. I have flown in from Newark, she is soon to arrive from Boston, and after Aunt Marlene has entertained us for our hour-long wait, we'll be on our way to Florida together. From our vantage point at the big glass window Aunt Marlene and I watch Molly's plane lumber into position. Passengers wearing pale, dazed expressions that spell "In Transit" begin to flood out of the corridor linking plane to airport, and we scan the crowd for my sister. Stomping off the plane, she's not hard to pick out.

Molly stands five foot four in her ratty blue canvas sneakers. Her travel outfit is composed of a pair of white canvas overalls, a faded Run-D.M.C. T-shirt, and a lime-green oversize windbreaker. A green fanny pack is slung loosely around her waist, and dangling from her neck are two gold necklaces, one silver chain, and a leather thong bearing a three-inch plastic replica of a vase. Her dark brown hair is piled haphazardly upon her head, and her tiny round mouth is pursed in its customary grumpy frown. Her small brown eyes monitor our progress. My aunt Marlene reaches her first. She hugs Molly warmly. "I'm so glad to see you!" Molly twists out of the embrace and air-kisses Aunt Marlene's cheek.

"I have a kidney infection," she announces, by way of hello. She hands me her luggage with an imperious gesture. "Take this, oaf," she says.

The three of us walk toward the frequent fliers' lounge. Aunt Marlene has the athletic gait of a longtime runner. Molly's walk is a strange, loopy bounce, somewhere between a runway model's haughty stride and a criminal's defensive shuffle. Loaded with Molly's luggage, I struggle to keep up, but the pair is well ahead of me. Through the stale, anonymous airport air, I can hear Molly discoursing upon her school.

"Yeah," she declares, in her hip, sarcastic tone, "it's pretty much a dump . . ."

The frequent fliers' lounge offers a number of snacks, all of which appeal to Molly. I select a plum. Molly looks at it longingly.

"Can I have your plum?" she wheedles.

Aunt Marlene snorts, "Get your own plum, they're right over there."

"I," Molly declares regally, "have a kidney infection."

"Probably just have cramps," I mutter, but hand her the plum. She accepts it with a brief inclination of her head. She devours the fruit with noisy relish, and turns to me with her hand raised as if she wants to slap me five. When I put my palm out, she bends over and neatly spits the plum pit into my hand.

"This is disgusting," observes Aunt Marlene. Molly laughs cheerfully.

"Kidney infection!" she says. Heads turn, and the businessman in the next seat sniffs audibly, collects his briefcase, and moves to the other side of the room. Molly watches me get up to throw her pit out.

"Bring me some lightly salted peanuts," she says, "I'm sick."

My parents' parents, survivors of the Great Depression, had prudent families, two children maximum. My mother claims today that when she got married she planned on having six kids; and my father, whose only sibling was a sister nine years younger, also felt that he'd missed out on something special. Kids, his philosophy went, need siblings. And so, for whatever reasons, fifteen months after my arrival into the world Molly Beth was born. She would be my roommate for the next seventeen years.

When Molly would pick fights or pull my hair or break my toys, I would complain to my mother, who would sigh in response, "Molly was born angry." As I got older, she would elaborate. "You were a boring baby," she told me. "Slept through the night from two weeks on. Instead of giving you night feedings, we would wake up every two hours to make sure you were still alive. You weren't really into . . . interaction," my mother concluded, "you just liked your mobile a lot."

Molly was into interaction—the more violent, noisy, and energetic, the better. Family myth has it that her first word was not "mommy" or "daddy" but "gimme." Photo albums feature a small girl with a broad smile and dimples, usually in motion and wearing a shirt that read HUG ME. The strained, wearied expressions of those in the pictures with Molly tell the story better.

Molly and I are on the plane that will take us to our grandmother in Florida. Molly is excited about the vacation, and the chance to see our younger brother, twelve-year-old Joe.

"I can't wait to terrorize him," she declares happily. Our seats are near the back of the plane, and behind us is a mother-grandmother-toddler combination. The toddler has a phenomenally deep, wet cough, and within minutes of takeoff Molly has dubbed it the Exorcist Baby. Every time the Exorcist Baby coughs, Molly and I dissolve in laughter. The mother laughs with us. "I bet you're waiting for something to come flying out of her mouth," she says dryly. "No," says Molly, sotto voce, "actually, we're waiting for her head to spin around."

The most important thing about Molly is her temper. From her infancy, her temper has flared up violently, and even now, at the age of eighteen, she throws the temper tantrums of a two-year-old—albeit laced with very adult profanity—when she doesn't get her way. Understandably, that isn't often. All of us—my mother, me, our brothers, Jake and Joe—know enough to tread carefully around Molly. My father's the only one who doesn't have to worry. He left three years ago, so he considers himself immune to Molly's wrath, as he sees her only when he wants to. But the rest of us suffer it frequently. Our fear of her fits, combined with the knowledge that Molly, despite her pretensions otherwise, generally has a good soul, makes us willing to do her bidding. And so—with a blend of good-natured orneriness, a slight touch of nastiness to come, and just a hint of the pitiable—Molly rules our family. Or at least, for the seventeen years we shared a room, she ruled me.

As we begin our descent I point out the lights of Fort Lauderdale. Molly peers haughtily through the window at the cars creeping along the highway. "These people," she remarks grandly, "drive like dump. Also, the stewardesses have not offered me the Beverage of my Choice." She rummages around in the seat compartment until she finds what she's looking for—an evaluation form. She locates the series of questions on "flight attendants," and checks off "poor" after "poor." In the comment section, she scrawls "was not provided with drink." A picture of the founder of Northwest Airlines appears on the form. Molly scribbles horns and a beard on it, and draws a balloon coming out of his mouth with a statement urging the reader to perform an obscene act.

"Molly," I tell her soberly, "I don't think they'll take that seriously." She jabs one pink-nailed finger at the call button.

"Bug off!" she growls.

Nanna greets us at the airport. She nods a distracted hello at me, then turns to Molly with concern etched on her face.

"Mamma told me you have a kidney infection," she says. Molly rolls her eyes and clutches her back dramatically.

"I'm dying," she says sincerely. Nanna glares at me angrily.

"How could you let her come here with a kidney infection? Now take her luggage!" Meekly, I comply. Molly smirks at me until she's distracted by an elderly woman driving something like an electric golf cart.

"Oh, can we get one of those?" she asks.

"We're almost to the car now," my Nanna replies. Molly weighs her options and decides to continue walking.

"I called my doctor, he'll meet us at the apartment," says Nanna. "How's school?"

"It's a dump!" Molly cries, and begins enthusiastically listing her university's shortcomings: bad food, too far away from the college her boyfriend attends, library too far from her dorm, unsympathetic RA, hallmate plays Janet Jackson incessantly, infirmary sucks. Nanna looks at her suspiciously.

"Just what's wrong with the infirmary?"

"Well, for one thing they said there was nothing wrong with

my kidney. They didn't even give me a blood test! They didn't even ask me the right questions!"

Nanna turns to face Molly. "So you don't have a kidney infection," she says. It's a statement, not a question. Molly refuses to give in.

"I *might* have one," she says petulantly. "They forgot to ask me if I was experiencing pain upon urination."

"Well, *are* you?"

"No, but that's not the point."

Nanna throws up her hands in despair. "Molly, Molly, Molly," she says. "What are we going to do with you?" But Molly isn't listening. Kidney pain forgotten, she is dashing toward Nanna's silver four-door, in which, folded uncomfortably in the front seat, is Nanna's boyfriend, Harold.

Molly's most vivid childhood memories are of torturing people. She remembers bathing our infant brother Joe and pouring alternating pitchers of hot and cold water over his back—never hot enough to burn him, just hot enough to make him extremely uncomfortable.

"I liked the noises he made," she explains. She remembers hiding my books, listening in on my phone calls, wearing my clothes to school.

"Kept my life interesting," she said. When she began high school, she found what she solemnly terms her "niche in life"— as a coxswain for the crew team, where her lung power and sadistic impulses were both put to good use.

"Then I could torture people on a professional basis," she comments.

For the three years that Harold has been in Nanna's life, he has been one of Molly's favorite tortur-ees, second only to Joe. Harold, who is eighty-two years old, has experienced what doctors politely term a substantial hearing loss. In other words, Harold, despite hearing aids, is as deaf as a post.

Molly throws open the door of the Buick and flings her arms around Harold's wrinkled neck. Her lips move in a soundless semblance of hello. It's an old trick, but Harold responds admirably. "Hello, Molly," he booms. "Glad to hear it!" Nanna shakes her finger at Molly, who sticks out her tongue in reply. Harold regards this interplay with confusion. As we drive through Fort Lauderdale, he notes the passing attractions in a loud, careful voice. "Heavenly Delights," he reads, "Naked Oil-Wrestling Nightly. Now Hiring."

"I could get a job!" says Molly. Harold, who has only caught the last word, nods with a smile. "Jobs," he intones, "are wonderful things." My Nanna rolls her eyes. "Why I let your mother talk me into this . . ." She glances back at Molly and me. "You'll have to share a bed," she says sourly. "Uh-uh," says Molly, "she could accidentally kick me in my kidney." Nanna screeches onto the freeway. "Too bad," she says.

As long-term roommates, our routine is well established. Without speaking, we arrange ourselves on the sides of the bed that parallel the sides of the room we sleep in at home. I get the bathroom first, she turns off the light, and, after some perfunctory bickering about whether or not this bed is really the most uncomfortable we've ever been in (I say yes, Molly maintains that the bunks at Camp Tanuga were worse), we fall asleep.

At three a.m., Molly wakes me up. "Can you die from a kidney infection?"

No.

"If I needed a new kidney, would you donate one of yours?"

Sure, whatever.

"Do you think there are alligators in that pond out there?"

Molly, we're on the third floor.

"Oh."

There is silence for about ten minutes. Then, just as I am

drifting back to sleep, Molly mutters, so softly that I almost miss it, "If there's something really wrong, will you tell Nanna that I need to see the doctor again?"

Sure.

"Bring me some orange juice." Seventeen years of training conditions you well. I get up, search out carton and glass, but by the time I return Molly is sound asleep again.

Our wake-up routine is as well established as the one for going to sleep. Molly sneaks over to my bed and begins to jump on it, singing "Get up, you sleepyhead, haul that heinie out of bed," until I smack her or my mother makes her stop. Today she's made accommodations for the fragility of the hideaway bed, and contents herself with yanking the covers off me and making fun of my nightgown until I grab my bathing suit and slink into the bathroom.

"How's your kidney?" I ask sarcastically.

"Much better, thanks," she answers. "In fact, I think I am well enough to go to the beach."

Nanna drops us off at the beach at eleven-thirty, and promises to pick us up by four. Molly stalks along the burning sand, looking for the perfect spot. "How about here?" I ask. As usual, I am carrying everything. "We have to find interesting people we can be near," she says.

"And why is that?"

Molly looks at me as though I'm crazy. "So we can eavesdrop, of course." Finally she finds three who suit her: a very skinny blond girl in a white string bikini sharing a blanket with two short, swarthy, heavyset men whose necks and wrists are liberally festooned with gold chains. One of the men is extremely tan; the other is deathly pale. Both have flabby bellies and hairy backs.

"Yuck," I say, but Molly motions me to be quiet.

"I wonder if they're brothers or what."

I try to get interested. "Yeah, and I wonder which one of them the girl's with."

Molly gives me her you-must-be-crazy look again. "She's sitting on one of their *laps*." Embarrassed, I run into the water. When I come back, Molly is full of news. Her words tumble over one another as she rushes to tell the story.

"The girl—her name's Deedee. Well, she went up to their hotel room to get some Cool Ranch Doritos, and as soon as she was gone they both started talking about all the action they were getting."

I look at the men with new interest. One of them is sleeping, his mouth lolling open, his hands loosely cradling his belly. The other is lazily perusing a copy of *Penthouse Forum*. Deedee's chest is powdered with Dorito debris, and she's smearing her bony arms with suntan lotion.

"Gross," I say.

"You should hear how she pronounces Bain de Soleil!" Molly whispers. "Now go buy me a hot dog."

"Don't you want to come with me?" I offer hopefully.

Molly waves me away, her brown eyes intent upon the trio. "I wish I had binoculars," is the last thing I hear her say as I head down the boardwalk in search of a hot dog. When I come back with the hot dog, a large Coke, and little plastic packets full of mustard and relish and ketchup, Molly is composing a note on a postcard that features a grinning alligator and bears the legend WELCOME TO FLORIDA!

"Dear Deedee," it reads so far. "Your boyfriend is seeing other women. Bain de Soleil is not pronounced exactly the way it is written. You can do better than Rich."

"How do you know his name is Rich?" I ask.

Molly sips her Coke and hiccups. "I am a champion spy."

"But of course," I say, and run back into the water. When I

return I notice that Molly's legs have ugly pink streaks running down the back.

"I think you need to rub your sunblock in better," I tell her. I toss her the tube.

"Bug off," she says sleepily. She's shifted her attention away from the Deedee/Rich saga, and is engrossed in V. C. Andrews's latest.

"Well, at least put some on my back," I tell her.

Molly grimaces. "No unnecessary touch!" she commands.

"Molly," I tell her, "it's not unnecessary. I'm your sister."

She flings the tube back at me. "Why don't you just put your shirt back on," she grumbles.

By four o'clock, the streaks on Molly's legs are more pronounced, and my back is roughly the color of a stop sign. Nanna is displeased. "I told you not to get too much sun!"

I explain that Molly has refused to put lotion on my back.

"What's your problem?" Nanna demands.

Molly defends herself: "You know I don't like touching people."

Nanna is bewildered. "But she's your *sister*."

"Doesn't matter," Molly says.

"Meshuggenah!" Nanna snorts.

"Oy vey!" Molly replies.

We go out for early bird specials at my Nanna and Harold's favorite Italian restaurant. Nanna and Harold are both having eggplant parmigiana. I'm eating chicken. Molly is poking half-heartedly at a meatball.

"Eat!" says Nanna.

"*Ess!*" says Harold.

"*Mangia!*" enthuses the waiter.

"Uh, can I have a doggie bag?" asks Molly. Molly's status as a family legend was made by her temper, but is perpetually ensured by her distaste for things corporeal—touching people is one, and eating is another. We are used to this sort of performance, and aren't overly afraid that she'll starve. The meatball is stowed in a doggie bag with a minimum of fuss, and we proceed to a movie.

We have arrived early enough to get good seats—Harold on the outside, long legs stretched into the aisle, my Nanna next to him, with me next to her, and then Molly. As the previews begin, an older couple attempt to take two seats next to Molly.

"Excuse me!" the man says.

"Shhhh," says my Nanna again.

Molly, outraged by this gravest of unnecessary touches, whacks his Bermuda-clad bottom with her meatball bag. "You pervert!" she cries. Half of the theater turns to look. The man sinks into the empty chair next to Molly with an air of abject humiliation.

The first ten minutes of the movie are uneventful, but slowly Molly and I begin to notice something strange. As the actors on the screen say their lines, about half of the people in the theater repeat them in loud stage whispers to their hard-of-hearing companions. The result is a kind of three-part harmony.

"I'll be going now," says the actor.

"Huh?" say half the people in the theater.

"*He said he'll be going now,*" choruses the rest of the audience. Even my Nanna is busily translating for Harold, with occasional pauses to ask me for lines that she herself has missed. Molly invents a new game. Unceremoniously dropping her meatball bag on the floor, she leans over in her seat and begins feeding Nanna misinformation.

"I have good news," says the actress.

"Huh?" says Harold.

"She says she has blue shoes," whispers Molly. Harold's brow furrows in puzzlement as Molly's whispers get wilder.

"I love you," the actress murmurs softly.

"Huh?" says Harold.

"I'm having Elvis's love child," Molly says. Nanna purses her lips and reaches over to pinch Molly's arm. She gets mine instead.

"Ouch!" I yell.

The two rows in front of us all go "Shh!" at once. Molly picks up her meatball bag and whacks me smartly. "Stop disrupting the entertainment," she says.

Nanna has promised to take us all to the flea market in the morning, so she wakes us up early, and by eight-thirty we're down in the parking lot. She opens the driver's door and gasps. Molly, it seems, has accidentally left her meatball in the car, and the humid Florida night has saturated the new upholstery with the smell of oregano and decaying meat.

"MOLLY!" she roars.

"What did I do?" Molly demands. Nanna reaches into the backseat and removes the offending meatball.

"Oops," says Molly in a small voice. She throws the meatball out by herself and makes profuse apologies, trying to work herself back into Nanna's favor.

The flea market is uneventful. Molly is on her best behavior, offering suggestions on watches or T-shirts, promising that if we go to the beach again she'll put lotion on my back, even offering to drive to the airport in the afternoon to pick up our mother and brothers.

"Not a chance," says Nanna, gathering her purchases. "I'm taking you out to breakfast, I'm dropping you off at the beach, and I'm turning you over to your mother as soon as she gets here. You're too much for me!"

Molly is aghast. "You'd trade me in for one of the boys?"

"I'd trade you in for both of them," says Nanna grimly.

Molly sulks all the way to the restaurant, where, to our

amazement, she orders the lumberjack special and proceeds to finish everything—eggs, bacon, home fries—except the stack of six pancakes. She drops her fork queasily, silent for once.

"Uhhgh," she says weakly.

The waitress looks sympathetic, my Nanna unmoved. "Would you like to take those home?" asks the waitress, pointing at the pancakes.

Nanna snaps the clasp of her wallet with a final-sounding click. "Absolutely not," she says.

Molly and I are lying on the beach. Or rather, I am lying on the beach, while Molly is huddled miserably under the sparse shade of a palm tree. The sun, she claims, makes her feel too full.

"I wasn't that bad, was I?" she frets.

"You were pretty awful," I tell her honestly. "Mocking Harold was a bad idea, and Nanna's car reeks of meatball."

Molly giggles. "At least she'll remember me when I'm gone." Cheered, she spreads her towel and steps gingerly into the sun, clutching the sunblock. "I'll do your back," she offers. "Want a hot dog?"

Soon things are back to normal. I'm trying to read while Molly is regaling me with stories of her soap opera, which she never fails to identify as "the Emmy Award–winning *Santa Barbara*." "Okay, so Gina's house burned down, but Abigail owned it and won't give her any of the insurance money 'cause she knows that Gina once had an affair with Chris—Abigail's ex-husband, really her brother, but she didn't know—"

Suddenly Molly breaks off. "Uh-oh," she says.

"What?" I ask, but then I see what she has seen. Through the glare rolling off the sand, through the humid haze of a Florida afternoon, coming toward us as inexorably as soldiers are Nanna and our mom.

"Mom had to ride all the way back from the airport in that meatball car," I whisper.

Molly clutches V. C. Andrews to her like a shield. Her eyes dart nervously to the left, making sure that the lifeguard is still in his chair should witnesses prove necessary. "I'm doomed," she whispers. The two women draw closer. Their feet raise sandy dust, their eyes unforgiving.

"She hasn't looked this mad since the dog threw up on the Persian rug," I observe. "Shouldn't have invented that kidney infection."

"She probably heard about the Harold thing," mutters Molly.

"She probably heard about my *back*," I offer. Nanna waits on the sidewalk while my mother plows on toward Molly, who is seized by a new fear.

"Oh, God," she murmurs, "what if she got my grades?"

"I'm out of here," I say, and I dart away, but not before I hear the sound of my mother's fingers closing firmly around the burnt flesh of Molly's shoulder. The words "meatball," "kidney," and "utter ingratitude" follow me out to sea.

Girl Reporter

I graduated from college with grandiose ambitions, big plans, and thirty thousand dollars of student loans. I knew that I wanted to write. My dream was to write novels. Unfortunately, we were no longer living in a time when I could present myself to a wealthy czar or nobleman or nobleman's wife and ask if he or she was interested in being a patron, or patroness, of the arts, and supporting me while I perfected my craft, and dashed off the occasional sonnet about his or her brave character and good looks. Nor were my parents interested in funding a year in a garret in Paris, or in Brooklyn, so that I could write a thinly veiled account of their divorce and how it had hurt me.

I needed to find a J-O-B, one where I'd be paid to write, where I was, per Professor McPhee's advice, writing every day. The two fields that came to mind were advertising and journalism. I rejected advertising immediately. No way was I going to be a shill in corporate America, using my talent to sell debt-ridden citizens useless crap! Besides, I was convinced, for absolutely no reason rooted in reality, that I'd end up working on the tampon campaign, and that my professional life would be spent finding synonyms for the word "absorbent."

(True story—years later, my agent called me up. "I think I know what you're going to say to this, but I need to run it by you anyhow," she began. I could hear the reluctance as I asked what was up. Turns out, a "feminine protection brand" had asked if I wanted to be their campus ambassador.

I was instantly enthralled. "Would I have to dress up as a giant tampon?" I demanded.

"I don't know," Joanna answered.

"Could I dress up as a giant tampon?" I continued.

"I'm going to take this as a no," said Joanna.

"No! No, it's not a no! I need you to find out if there are any strings attached!"

"I'm hanging up now," Joanna said.

"Just give me some time," I said. "You have to admit, it's a lot to absorb.")

So journalism it was. I was lucky enough to be selected as one of the first class of "fellows" at a new summer program run by the Poynter Institute, a journalism think tank in St. Petersburg, Florida. The institute picked a dozen liberal-arts graduates who hadn't been journalism majors but wanted to work for newspapers. They paid us a stipend, helped us find housing, and spent six weeks teaching us the fundamentals of reporting.

If John McPhee's class had been about structure and language, the rhythm of good prose, and the beauty of the perfect word, then the Poynter fellowship was all about the mechanics of reporting. There was less emphasis on beautiful sentences or seamless structure and more of a focus on accuracy, on making sure the pertinent facts were in the story, that sources were quoted correctly and that their names were spelled right. Our job as journalists was to give readers news they could use, information that would help them make decisions about everything from politics to how to spend their weekend. We covered a city council meeting. I profiled a nurse at a local abortion clinic, and tried to endure the muggy heat of a Florida summer as I drove my rental car to my assignments. It was grueling and exhilarating and humbling, because, as it turns out, being a good writer and being a good reporter are far from the same thing. A writer can be invisible, but a reporter has to be both present and persistent, showing up with a notebook or asking questions over the phone. I was shy. Talking to strangers wasn't easy. But I wanted to write, and as far as I could figure, this was the best way to learn, to get paid to write every day in a way that I hoped would help me get better.

During the final week of our fellowship, the institute had a job fair. My résumé made it into the hands of Knight-Ridder's corporate recruiters and, in short order, I was offered a job as the education reporter for the *Centre Daily Times*, a small paper in State College, Pennsylvania. My job started in September, just before the deadline my mother had given to be out of her house and supporting myself.

It was 1991. I rented, for three hundred dollars a month, a two-room apartment on the third floor of a brick Victorian house on East Linn Street in Bellefonte, Pennsylvania. My place had wall-to-wall shag carpeting in an unlovely and stain-disguising shade of brown, a rattling radiator in a boxy metal cage that jutted into the center of the living room, and a harvest-gold kitchen with peel-on wood veneer on the cabinets and linoleum on the floor. The floors tilted, in a way that made me feel constantly, slightly tipsy, and there were two deep, narrow dormer windows—one in the bedroom and one in the living room/dining room/kitchen.

I did my best to decorate, with family cast-offs and tag-sale finds. A third of an old sectional from our living room became my couch, and an old dresser housed my TV. I bought a wobbly wooden table and two metal-frame chairs at a secondhand shop, and put my king-size futon on a donated queen-size box spring on the bedroom floor. (The way the futon hung over the box spring always reminded me of the lunch-meat-and-miniature-bread sandwich in *This Is Spinal Tap*.) The dormer cutout in the bedroom was just wide enough for a twin-size bed—I called it my guest suite—and the one in the living room was the perfect size for the folding metal card table that I'd be using to write on for the next ten years.

Bellefonte was a small town about ten miles from State College, and the *CDT*'s office, and about five miles away from the State Correctional Institution at Rockview.

Bellefonte was grittier than Simsbury. Few of the houses had swimming pools or well-tended lawns. There were no country clubs, no fancy boutiques, no art galleries or bookstores or cute little cafés . . . but there was a library, and a video rental store, and a pretty park full of friendly ducks that would eat bread crusts right out of your hand. Fran and I went to the BI-LO supermarket and stocked up on basics—chicken broth and rice, chuck steak and onions, garlic and carrots, apples and bananas and salad stuff. Then Fran drove away, and I got into the minivan that my mother had sold to me for the last of my bat mitzvah money to go exploring. I turned the key and, instead of the car starting, I heard an ominous *thunk*. I got out and found what appeared to be the entire engine lying on the pavement. I'd gotten a AAA membership as a graduation gift, so the tow to the repair shop was free, but the van needed hundreds of dollars' worth of new parts, and I had to rent a car so that I could get to work (Fran: "Ask if there's a company car they can lend you!"). Not an auspicious start to my employment.

Shopping options in State College were limited. My work wardrobe boasted pieces from Lane Bryant and T.J. Maxx and Marshalls back at home—lots of long cotton tops and stirrup pants, boxy jackets with shoulder pads, floral skirts worn with white hose and pumps from Payless. At home, I'd wear my favorite casual top, a extra-large blue cotton hooded pullover with a pouch in front for my hands. Chris Isaak and Enya were on "repeat" on my Discman, I took step class at the gym, and I went to Sears and bought a TV—my first major, adult purchase—because, not so far out of high school myself, I was obsessed with *Beverly Hills, 90210.*

My job was to cover the five local school districts in the paper's circulation area—their board meetings, their outstanding students, their teachers' strikes. I was also responsible for typing in five districts' worth of school lunch menus once a week—and if there's anything that slaps the taste of F. Scott Fitzgerald out of your mouth faster than having to sit there typing "Hot dog with bun, tater tots, fruit cup, your choice of skim or chocolate milk," I don't want to know what it is.

Even though my beat was education, reporters at small papers end up covering everything. Breaking news about the bagel shop on College Avenue closing? That's you. House fire? Car crash? Sewage board hearing that nobody else can attend? All you. The fires were actually pretty big deals. State College had some hot firemen . . . or at least it had strapping guys who looked appealing in their turnout gear, with hoses coiled around their shoulders and axes in their hands. When news of a fire came over the scanner, I'd fight the other young female reporters over whose turn it was to cover the blaze and who'd gotten to go to the last one.

In my two and a half years at the *CDT*, I wrote about everything—usually, at least at first, badly. I'd profile artists and writers, and get their names wrong, or the names of their books or their spouses wrong. I'd write about proposed tax increases, and get the decimal points wrong, and show up at work the next morning to find thirty-two furious voice-mail messages on my phone, most of which would be from the senior citizens who seemed to comprise much of the *CDT*'s subscription base, and who had nothing to do but linger over the day's paper, hunting for errors.

To this day, I'm not sure why I was so awful. Maybe it was a lack of supervision: the paper was understaffed, the editors were overwhelmed, and the reporters were mostly twentysomethings, most of us at our very first job. Maybe it was the difference between the desultory pace of writing opinion pieces whenever I felt opinionated versus the grind of churning out two or three or four pieces a day about a variety of topics, some of which interested me intensely, some of which you couldn't have paid me to care about. It was a learn-as-you-go situation, and I tried to get better and enjoy myself. After a year, I moved from Bellefonte to the second floor of a carriage house in Boalsburg, on the expansive grounds of Boal Mansion. I had a roommate and a boyfriend, a tall, handsome guy who'd started at the paper a year after I had, and along with my fellow reporters, we'd all find ways to have fun after hours for as little money as possible. We'd go hear local bands or out for ten-cent wings and five-dollar pitchers of beer at local bars. I'd cook, or we'd go hiking in Bear Meadow, or swimming at Whipple Dam, or for grilled sticky buns at Ye Olde College Diner on College Avenue. Life felt like it was moving in the right direction—even if, sometimes, I'd come across a profile of a former classmate who'd sold a novel or of a twenty-three-year-old who'd been hired to write for *Saturday Night Live*, and I would feel sick with jealousy, plunged into despair, positive that I would be stuck in State College forever; that I'd die broke and unfamous, with my student loans still outstanding.

Still, most days, I couldn't believe that I was being paid to write, even if it was the princely sum of $16,000 a year, a few thousand dollars less than annual tuition at Princeton had cost. But I didn't care . . . and I wasn't proud. Whatever needed to be done, I'd do it.

Which is how, a year or so into my tenure, I found myself dressed in a skirt and cute suede pumps, rolling a tranquilized bear across a cornfield.

Happy Valley, where State College is located, has at its heart Penn State University, and the sophisticated town that had grown up around it. There were ethnic restaurants and movie theaters, fancy clothing stores and a new, modern library. As you got farther away from the campus, there were golf courses and new construction, gated communities of condominiums and McMansions where nostalgic PSU alumni could purchase second homes and be within walking distance of Beaver Stadium and Nittany Lions football games.

But if you drove five miles in any direction, it was *Deliverance*. Maybe not *Deliverance*, exactly, but it was distinctly agrarian, which was a whole new world for a suburban girl like me.

The first summer I worked at the paper, in 1992, a bear had been ravaging area cornfields. The bear would amble through the rows, pulling off ears of corn at random, eating its fill before basically passing out in a food coma in the middle of the field. It would roll around, crushing the cornstalks, before arising, decimating a few more plants, and strolling off along the ridges of Mount Nittany, on its way to the next farmer's fields.

We'd been getting calls about the bear—first from farmers, then from game wardens who were trying to catch it. I'd written a few little squibs, my own humorous takes about the hungry bear and where it would head next. So it was that on a Monday morning, the city desk phone rang, and an excited warden announced, "We caught the bear!"

"Good for you!" I said.

"Do you want to come see it?" he asked.

Initially, I did not. It was a bear. I was a young woman who'd taken pains with her appearance that morning, because I had a school board meeting that night. I was not interested in schlepping twenty miles into the hinterlands to get a look at the local wildlife.

The game warden wore me down. "Oh, c'mon, aren't you curious? You've been writing all these stories about the bear! You should come see!"

Reluctantly I went to the newspaper parking lot, climbed in my minivan, and drove. And drove and drove and drove. Out of State College, into Bellefonte, through Centre Hall, up and over Mount Nittany, all the way to a farm on the very edge of where the *CDT* could claim penetration. There was the warden, all crisp khaki and gold badge, wide-brimmed hat and wider smile. And there, maybe ten feet away, standing on its hind legs with one of its feet stuck in a trap, was the bear.

I'd never been that close to a bear before. The first thing that struck me was the smell. The bear reeked. Think elderly, unwell, rotting-from-the-inside black lab, with top notes of halitosis and spoiled meat. The bear was enclosed in a seething fog of fleas, a grayish nimbus that clung to its greasy-looking fur, lifting briefly whenever the bear moved, then settling down around it again. It was clacking its teeth, which, I learned, is what bears do when they're angry, and regarding me and the game warden with unmistakable resentment. I wasn't scared, exactly—the bear was trapped, and I figured if it started moving toward us, I could run and it would get to the game warden first—but my trembling knees and the sweat at the back of my neck were all signs that this wasn't the same as looking at an animal in a zoo.

"Now watch this," said the warden. He pulled out what looked like a rifle, took careful aim, and fired a dart full of animal tranquilizer high into the bear's hip. The bear clacked and glared. Then it started to wobble. Forward and backward, forward and backward, in steeper and steeper arcs, until finally it pitched forward onto its face. The flea-fog buzzed, lifted, then resettled. The game warden approached. He peeled back the bear's black, dog-like lip and used pliers to pull out one of its milk teeth—this, he explained, was so his bosses would know the bear's age. He pierced the bear's ear, punching a red plastic tag through a hole in the cartilage, so that the bear could be identified if it was ever captured again.

"Okay," he then instructed. "We've got to get the bear in my truck."

I blinked at him. "We?"

"Oh, come on!" he urged. "When are you going to get a chance to touch a bear?"

"When had I ever wanted to touch a bear?" I replied.

"Don't worry," said the warden, explaining that the bear would be out for hours, maybe even all night . . . and wasn't I curious?

Of course, I was. It was how I'd ended up being a reporter; it was how I then ended up, in my pumps and skirt, knuckle deep in coarse, oily fur, rolling a passed-out, reeking bear across a field, then heaving him up a ramp and into the back of a game warden's pickup truck. We drove the bear ten miles down the road, found a ledge, and rolled the bear, still unconscious, onto the ground. On the way back to the office, as I tried to wipe the grease off my hands, a few things occurred to me. First: I would not be wearing this outfit to the school board meeting. In addition, at some point, the bear was going to wake up, have no idea where it was or how it had gotten there, minus a tooth, plus a brand-new piercing. It was like the worst fraternity initiation ever!

I went back to the office and wrote up my story, which ran with a picture I'd taken. (The paper couldn't spare another body, so one of the staff photographers gave me a camera, preset and loaded, with the instruction "Just point and push the button and DO NOT touch anything else.")

The story joined my fattening pile of clips—my profile of the special ed teacher whose students seemed to win a collect-the-box-top contest every month, my coverage of a lengthy teachers' strike, a piece about a four-room schoolhouse that was closing after eighty years, and a story about high school students' reaction to Magic Johnson's announcement of his HIV-positive status. For one of the stories I was proudest of, I figured out the longest bus route in the most rural school district, and for a week got up at the crack of predawn and rode the bus with kids who, for their entire educational careers, had spent the hours from six a.m. to seven-thirty on their way to school.

I'd also started to write op-ed pieces about the inscrutable demographic pie-slice that people were just starting to call Generation X, and some of those columns—one about my wish for two sets of winter holidays, so that children of divorced families wouldn't have to split their time; another considering the efficacy of Take Back the Night marches—had been picked up by bigger papers in Pittsburgh and Philadelphia.

By 1994, all of this was good enough to get me a job as a feature writer at the *Lexington Herald-Leader*. I came to Lexington in February 1994 and stayed long enough to join a synagogue, date both of the Jewish guys my age, and cover the Kentucky Derby—and, more important, the Derby parties, where I shook Ivana Trump's hand.

That fall, there was a rare job opening at the *Philadelphia Inquirer*, one of the flagship papers in the Knight-Ridder chain. (I loved working for Knight-Ridder, primarily because my Nanna pronounced it *Knight Rider*, and I'd have to explain to her, over and over, that I was not, in fact, employed by a sentient car.)

The *Inquirer* had been running my Generation X columns, and I'd talked to the editors there, who'd wanted to hire me, but had to wait until someone else left. When I came on board, it was with the condition that I give up my perch on the op-ed page and settle into writing features for at least a few years. That was a bargain I was happy to make. I'd learn everything I could about how to write a great feature, a Nora Ephron–esque feature, and then either I'd resume my column and become the next Anna Quindlen, mining the specifics of my own life for generational truths, or I would write a novel or a screenplay or a novel that turned into a screenplay, and I'd finally have enough money to have kids and not freak out about being penniless.

The *Inquirer* was my dream job. No more news. No more numbers. No more school lunches. Back then, the paper had a budget to let a reporter spend a week or even longer reporting a single story, or travel to do it. So off I went, on trains and planes and company cars, in search of stories.

I wrote about a group of factory workers in Michigan who were on the verge of losing their jobs when a lottery ticket they'd bought as a group won them millions apiece. I covered the Democratic National Convention in Chicago, hanging out with Philadelphia's delegates, and I traveled to the presidential inauguration in Washington, where I saw Bill and Hillary Clinton slow-dance in Union Station's grand rotunda. I went to Atlantic City for the Miss America pageant, and to Deerfield Beach, Florida, for a report on my Nanna's gefilte fish, and I did my best to add whatever celebrity coverage I could muster.

I saw Kathie Lee Gifford having her eyelashes combed out on the steps of the Philadelphia Art Museum, where she and Reege had come to tape. I interviewed Wendy the Snapple Lady on a promotional swing through town. In general, though, not many stars came to Philadelphia. When it was announced that the *12 Monkeys* director had picked Philadelphia to stand in for its dystopian city in ruin, Philadelphians whipped themselves into such a frenzy that features reporters were dispatched across the city to cover Monkey Madness and hunt for Bruce Willis and Brad Pitt. The assignment I pulled was gay bars. "Do you know something we don't know?" one of the patrons at Woody's, a venerable watering hole for men who prefer men, responded when I asked if there'd been any Pitt sightings.

Sometimes the movie studios or television production companies would come to New York and make their stars available to the media—even reporters from Philadelphia. The publicists would stick their celebrities and director in hotel suites, where the talent would endure what were officially called roundtables and were less politely known as "gang bangs," fielding questions from reporters from all over the country who'd made the trip, sometimes on the production company's dime (the paper always paid my way).

Getting one-on-one time was the goal . . . and, if I couldn't get that, I would try my hardest to get an actor to say something original, something that a dozen of my competitors weren't also going to report. I once followed Shannen Doherty, in New York to promote the Kevin Smith opus *Mallrats*, into a ladies' room, where she unburdened herself to a publicist. "Why do they all keep asking me the same things?" she demanded. Locked behind a stall's door, I think I pretended to pull out the world's smallest violin to play for her.

Sometimes the stars were lovely. Sometimes they were depressed. Adam Sandler, promoting *Happy Gilmore*, seemed so unhappy that I offered to bring him home to Philadelphia and make him chicken soup, even though I knew that his corporate minder in the next room could very well have chosen to have me removed. Sometimes they were boring, so programmed that they seemed less like people than like creatures that had been built in a lab, for the express purpose of entertainment. Brandy, who was then best known for starring in *Moesha* (as opposed to being a singer and eventually the big sister of the guy who'd costarred in Kim Kardashian's sex tape), was especially robotic. And sometimes I never got to meet them at all. I had a scheduled interview with Minnie Driver yanked out from under me after I'd made the trek to New York, because I refused to take a blood oath and promise not to ask her about being dumped by Matt Damon on *Oprah*, an incident I'd eventually deploy in fiction, where Minnie Driver became Maxi Ryder (#geniusatwork).

I also covered the larger world of entertainment. I wrote about the phenomena of *South Park* and *Iron Chef*, and the brand-new genre of reality TV, ushered in by Mark Burnett's *Survivor*. When the Oxygen network debuted, I watched Lifetime, which had previously been the only existing network for women, for twenty-four hours straight and wrote about what I saw. When a publisher dropped a book called *Cooking with Friends*, I cooked a week's worth of recipes and wrote about whether eating "misery meatloaf" or "stay-at-home pasta" made me any more sleek and hip and amusing, like the stars on the NBC sitcom.

I was happy. I was making enough money to live comfortably. I loved my job. I loved my apartment. I had a best friend and a nice Jewish boyfriend I'd been dating for two years. Aside from my ongoing, mostly fruitless efforts to lose weight, I was content. I thought I had nearly everything . . . but of course that's not how that story went.

Nanna's Gefilte Fish

This Special-Occasions Dish Is an Acquired Taste. And Making It at Home Is a Tall Order. An 81-Year-Old Expert Describes the Process—Which Includes Airing Out the House Afterward.

By Jennifer Weiner, INQUIRER STAFF WRITER
December 8, 1996

DEERFIELD BEACH, Fla.—There are Jews who serve gefilte fish maybe once a year, decanted from glass Manischewitz containers, garnished with a carrot or two, served, picked at, and whisked away so they can get on to things they like better.

There are Jews who recook the canned stuff in their own broth; or who make their own from pre-ground fish.

Then there is my Nanna.

And if you are my Nanna you do neither of those things. You buy your own fish, fresh. You have Mike the fish guy save the heads, bones, and skin, so you can make your own broth. You grind the fish yourself. You cook it all day, with your fan running and your AC turned up. Afterward, you dot your surroundings with little bowls of vinegar "to get rid of the stink."

And when you fly to one of your daughters' houses for one of the Jewish holidays, you and whichever grandchild comes to pick you up wait by the baggage carousel for a Playmate cooler—the plastic kind that college guys keep their beer in—triple-wrapped in newspaper and garbage bags, enrobed in masking tape and labeled, simply, FISH.

Gefilte fish, which means, literally, filled fish, is a special-occasions dish mostly because it's incredibly time-consuming to make, requiring pots, pans, fresh fish, a fish grinder, and an especially high tolerance for the smell of simmering fish heads.

The dish often is a combination of whitefish, pike, pickerel, and carp (if you like carp, which my Nanna does not), ground and mixed with eggs, onions, and matzo meal, formed into patties and boiled for hours in a vat of fish broth.

The finished product looks like hamburger in black and white, if you're feeling charitable; like brains if you aren't. It's an acquired taste, considered a delicacy by adults who grew up eating it, and a fate worse than death by children who grew up eating Happy Meals.

My Nanna's is out of this world, and it's much in demand, so she'll make it for special dinners as well as big Jewish holidays, turning out enough to donate to friends, coconspirators, and her down-the-hall neighbor, who can't help but smell the boiling fish.

Recently, I wandered into the gefilte-fish-making process by accident. I'm in Florida on business, a concept which my Nanna doesn't quite get. "So if they're paying you to be here . . . does that mean you still get paid for a week's work?"

"Yes," I say.

My Nanna—Faye Frumin—is 81, but she looks just the way she's looked all my life, a small, trim woman with her face set in the same determined lines that you can see in her wedding photographs. She lives in a South Florida compound called Century Village East, home to about 15,000 senior citizens, spending their golden years sitting in the sunshine, sustained by the occasional, all-too-rare visit from a child or grandchild. Or great-grandchild, of which my Nanna has none. This lack will be a major topic of conversation in the hours ahead.

When I arrive, she's sitting by the window and looks startled when I tap, which is typical, because a long time ago my family decided that I was a complete incompetent in terms of real-world dealings, which means that everyone's delighted whenever I manage to turn up anywhere at all.

"You're here!" she says, and hugs me.

Today is Wednesday. On Sunday, she's giving a dinner party for a few friends, plus "that nice young couple that used to live next door." (Careful questioning reveals that the members of this nice young couple are both in their 60s.) Tomorrow, she's making fish.

Shopping is our major activity: mostly, I think, because my mother, her daughter Fran, hated it so much, and Nanna feels the need to compensate.

When my mother's four children were young and defenseless, she was known to dash up and down the aisles of the local Marshalls, a shopping cart in front of her and a determined look on her face, grabbing indiscriminate fistfuls of children's clothing off the clearance rack and muttering, "This'll fit someone."

Nanna, on the other hand, likes to shop. And she's much more careful. She considers fit and style. She follows trends.

In the dressing room she clucks her tongue at my sunburn, pokes my stomach. "Stop eating so much!" she says. Then she redeems herself by ferreting out a terrific pair of black suede loafers from the size 10 rack, and paying for everything.

Back at the Village, Nanna is wiped. We call my mother. I

report on my activities in Miami. I got a sunburn, I tell her. And a blister from Rollerblading.

We have dinner at a big, noisy steak house. "You can order the chicken without skin here," Nanna says helpfully. So I do.

She is delighted when I pick up the check: "I like going out with you!" she says.

Back home, we get ready to sleep. Tomorrow is a busy day, and Nanna's got the menu and schedule, on the phone pad, to prove it:

(1) Soups: Borscht or Bean?
(2) Gefilte fish, kugel, pickles, beets, olives, red peppers, bread, and rolls.
(3) Coffee and Cake.

* Thursday: Pick up fish; pick up bread.
* Thursday: Make fish.
* Saturday: Make kugel and soup.
* Sunday: Finish kugel, set table, make iced tea and coffee.

On Thursday at 7:30 a.m., I wake to the smell of chopped onions.

"Get up," says Nanna. "It's time to get the fish."

But first we have breakfast with Nanna's friend Helen from the thrift shop. Helen is beautifully attired, perfectly accessorized, carefully made up, and completely deaf. She communicates with my Nanna by talking directly into her face.

Me, she communicates with by grabbing both of my hands and getting psychic emanations. "I see success!" she proclaims. "Do you see any babies?" asks Nanna.

Then it's off to Pops', where Nanna buys her fish. Rows and rows of recently deceased bluefish and monkfish and catfish stare up at us in regimented, iced lines.

Nanna asks after the whitefish, debates the merits of buying a frozen pike, which is brought out from the freezer for her inspection. Eventually, she decides on just the fresh whitefish.

"No carp?" I ask.

"I don't like carp," says Nanna, tapping the glass case disparagingly, right above where a big red blank-eyed carp reposes. "Such an ugly fish, I couldn't stand to look at it."

What happens next?

If you are my Nanna, you go to Dora's and grind the fish in her Mixmaster. You add the onions and matzo meal. You also add eggs and whip it all into a frenzy. This will bind the fish.

Then go home to make your broth. Combine your fish heads, bones, and skin with water, onions, and carrots, sliced horizontally, so that when you serve, each piece of fish gets a pretty carrot on the plate.

How much water? How many onions? Nanna shrugs. "Enough," she says.

Simmer the broth until everything's soft. Add water until the pot's full. Bring everything to a boil. Form your ground fish/egg/onion/meal mixture into little balls ("or big ones, if that's what you like"). Boil the fish balls for "two, two and a half hours." Fish them out. Then strain your broth, retaining the carrots, and put everything in the refrigerator and chill, and "it turns out delicious."

Air the house out for three days.

Renaissance Fran

This is how I found out that my mom had, at age fifty-four, decided to, as her kids now say, park on the alternate side of the sex street. I was twenty-six, sitting at my desk at the *Inquirer*, writing a story and minding my business, when my phone rang. It was my brother Joe, who'd come home from college to do his laundry, as one does. Searching in my mom's bathroom for toenail clippers, he'd come across a cache of love letters. Actually, they were love Hallmark cards . . . and they were all signed with a woman's name. There were female belongings in the guest room, weird new foods in the fridge.

"There's a woman living here," Joe reported.

Huh? I called Fran and said, "What's going on?"

"Oh, nothing," she said, cheerful as ever.

"Joe says there's a woman living in the house."

There was the briefest pause. "Oh," said Fran. "That's my swim coach."

I consulted my calendar. "Fran," I said. "It's not an Olympic year."

There was another pause, this one longer. "Actually," said

Fran, her words tumbling together, "I met a woman and we're in love and she moved in."

Then I was holding the phone, a dial tone buzzing in my ears, my jaw probably somewhere around my chest, stunned and numb and thinking the same thing I'd thought eleven years previously, when my mother pulled off the New Jersey Turnpike to tell me that my father wasn't going to live with us anymore. *I don't know anything. Not anything.*

Looking back, there'd been signs, signs that had been there even when she was still married, if we'd known enough to look. The short hair. The lack of makeup and high heels and interest in fashion. (Then again, there are a great many straight women in New England who go around barefaced in their L.L.Bean parkas, so many of them that my ex-husband and I used to play a game called "Lesbian or Just from Vermont?") The Holly Near concerts. The vacations in Provincetown.

I was in my twenties, no longer living at home, technically too old to be too freaked out by anything my parents did—at least, according to the guidebook that, oh, wait, does not actually exist for adult children whose parents come out!

The idea that my mother had been lying about who she was—unable, perhaps, even to be honest with herself—was deeply disconcerting. What must her life have been like? How had she felt all of those years? And what did it mean for all of us, going forward?

The truth is that I *was* freaked out. And confused. And—if I'm being honest—upset. It wasn't entirely, or even largely, the same-sex thing, although it did put an interesting spin on the situation: no child, not even an adult one, wants to spend any length of time thinking about a parent's having sex, and that's especially true if the parent is having more interesting, edgier sex than you are.

It felt like everything was suddenly backward, reversed, the street signs written in some foreign language, the road maps torn in half. My brothers and sister and I, we were the ones who were supposed to be out there sampling different romantic partners and trying to get our futures figured out. My mom was supposed to have answered all of her questions . . . or at least, presumably, the big one, the one about which gender she preferred. Certainly divorced women dated, but they didn't just all of a sudden start dating women, did they? And what did it mean about our history? Did it mean that, for all the years of her marriage, through the birth of four kids, my mother had been living a lie?

What was the deal with Dad? we'd ask. And, *Why did you marry a man if that wasn't where your interests were?* And, *Did you even want kids in the first place? Would you have just been gay if it had been more of an option? And was the sex awful? Like, was every thrust a stab of shame?*

The four of us had questions. (Those last two were Molly's.) Unfortunately, Fran did not have answers. She was like a swoony teenager, whispering and holding hands and giggling and sneaking off with her girlfriend, who was unpleasantly gruff and triangle-shaped, with a tiny head topped with tight blond curls and a body that widened as it descended. We did not see the appeal of this woman, who, in lesbian-joke fashion, had moved in somewhere between their second and third date. Fran was behaving in the tremendously irritating way I'd probably behaved with the first boys who'd reciprocated my interest; doing the things I will likely find tremendously irritating when my own daughters have their first loves. When the four of us came home for that first post-revelation Thanksgiving, we found my mother's new ladyfriend permanently affixed to her side, except for the few minutes every hour when she'd go stand on the deck to smoke Marlboro Lights and hate men. Suddenly there were motivational posters on the walls—an artistically lit shot of dolphins leaping out of the water with the phrase TEAMWORK: EVERYONE PULLING TOGETHER—and the house smelled like sandalwood incense and Opium and cigarette smoke. My mom had never liked cats—we'd always had dogs—but now there was a cat in the house, a six-toed, mostly feral creature that shredded the furniture and hissed at my brothers. Self-help books lined the bookshelves, with titles like *Healing Your Inner Child* and *The Art of Transformational Suffering* and *It's Not What You're Eating, It's What's Eating You* alongside Fran's fiction and the medical textbooks my father had left behind.

That Thanksgiving, Molly and I were dispatched to the guest room or the pullout couch. There was a new lock on the door of the bedroom that my sister and I had once shared, a room that had been repurposed as the new ladyfriend's "safe space." ("Are you kidding me?" I remember demanding. "Is the laundry room dangerous?")

Nor was my mom willing to ease into her new identity. The only thing I can compare it to is when a girl joins the Girl Scouts, and she's so thrilled about her new affiliation that she's going to wear her sash and uniform to school the next day, whether the troop's having a meeting or not.

That was Fran and lesbianism.

My mother was out to everyone—her old book-club friends, her boss and her fellow teachers at the alternative high school where she worked. She was out to the neighbors, to waitresses and pharmacists and bank tellers, possibly even the joggers trotting past our house during the weekly Monday-night fun runs. She was thrilled with her new girlfriend, her new identity, and all of the new aesthetic and cultural options that it gave her, because being gay didn't just mean a new partner, it meant an entirely new life, with new icons and entertainment options, new fashions and music and reading material. Suddenly Fran had new sets of friends—her partner's circle of female companions, and "the boys," as they called the gay men with whom they'd play bridge. She was frequenting different restaurants, listening to the

Indigo Girls ("Yes, Fran," I would say, rolling my eyes world-wearily. "I've heard of them"), slapping rainbow triangle stickers on her car's back bumper. It left the four of us feeling like our childhood had somehow been invalidated; as if one of the certainties undergirding our lives—that our parents had loved each other, at least for a while—had vanished.

I wish I could report that my siblings and I were kind and patient, or at least accepting and tolerant, about my mother's new life and about her partner, a woman whom Fran seemed to have as much adopted as fallen in love with. The truth is that, feeling ill at ease and discomfited and displaced, we retreated to the familiar ground of mockery. In our imaginations and in the impressions that we'd do for one another and for our friends, Fran's new girlfriend became the distillation of every cliché and stereotype about lesbians, gay gym teachers, smokers, cat owners, and readers of self-help books. The fact that she was a cliché whose company Fran preferred to ours only made things worse.

It would have been confusing and strange, even if there'd been another functional adult with whom we could make sense of this sea change. By then, however, our father was long gone. He'd resurfaced, briefly, in 1996, to announce that he was getting remarried and to invite us to the wedding, a horribly tense affair. Molly boycotted. Jake went to be polite, I attended because I was curious, and Joe went with the mission of destroying the open bar. The nuptials were held at an inn in Lakeville, Connecticut—ceremony by the water, reception in the inn's restaurant. The three of us got there early and waited on the lake's slippery, muddy shore. When the justice of the peace arrived, we looked at one another and wondered if she was our father's new bride.

In fact, his second wife was in her thirties and looked like a version of my mother at the same age—tall, with short hair, a round face, and a body I couldn't see much of beneath her loose lace gown. As it turned out, she was pregnant when they got married, and she was still pregnant, six months later, when my father left her. Over Christmas, during the first and only trip I'd ever make to the house they'd bought a few towns over from Simsbury, she led me down to the basement rec room and poured out a not-surprising tale of woe. My father was awful. Abusive. Strange. He yelled at her, locked her out of the house, made stuff up, pretended to be sick, lied about going to the hospital and suffering a heart attack. I sat and listened and nodded sympathetically as she cried, her maternity sweater pulled tight over her belly. Inside, I was not sympathetic. *You married a man who has no relationship with his four existing children,* I thought. *A man who's never paid his child support consistently. Why did you think you'd be any different?*

In the ten years since he'd left us, my father had only gotten stranger and scarier. In Lexington, months before, he'd called my apartment, late one night, his voice slurred, and delivered a rambling monologue about how my mother hadn't wanted to sleep with him. He'd called her a "dyke" and said he'd been tricked into a sham marriage. I remember my entire body cringing, toes curling and fists clenching in the universal posture of Do Not Want. I didn't want to hear it, didn't want to think about it, did not want to know one single thing about their sex life or lack of same.

Except now I didn't have a choice. Fran was out and proud, and frequently clueless, because being gay doesn't equip you with gaydar, or undo thirty-plus years spent as a straight lady in the suburbs. Arriving at a new identity so late in life made for some embarrassing missteps. "Jenny," Fran would say, dropping her voice to a whisper after she'd called me at work, "do you know who's one of us?"

"Who's that?" I asked, lowering my own voice.

Fran would pause and take a breath before triumphantly whispering the words "Rosie O'Donnell!"

"No way," I said, deadpan.

Fran either didn't hear my sarcasm, or chose to ignore it. "Oh yes! Yes, she is! I met someone who knows someone who met her girlfriend!"

(True story—years later, I was on a talk show and Rosie was one of the guests. After twenty minutes of my brilliant publicist Marcy Engelman wrangling with Rosie's people to broker an introduction, a hallway meeting was arranged. It took about twenty seconds of gushing admiration before Fran announced, "And I'm gay, too, I just came out a few years ago . . ."

Rosie looked my mother up and down—the short hair, the loose-fitting, all-cotton clothing, the clogs. "You were with men? All those years?" she asked, in her Long Island honk. "What were ya thinking?"

I decided to go to the ladies' room before Fran answered.)

That first year, as part of her new lifestyle initiative, my mother announced that she needed to go to Florida and come out of the closet to her then eightysomething-year-old mom.

"You don't think you could just tell Nanna you've got a new roommate?" I asked. I was, again, on my phone, at my desk at the paper.

"I'm not hiding," Fran replied indignantly.

As soon as I realized that she was serious, I asked the only question that any writer worth her salt would ask: "Can I come?"

Fran was outraged. "Jenny. My life does not exist for your amusement!"

"Yeah," I said. "It kind of does. Remember how you told me that everything was material?"

Fran knew she was beaten. I bought myself a ticket. Then I called my sister, who was living with a boyfriend in Indiana.

"She's doing what?" Molly asked. "Oh my God. What is wrong with her?" Then, "You'll get me a ticket, right?"

I did . . . and Molly and I flew down to Fort Lauderdale for what the four of us were already calling the Spillage in Century Village.

A word about the Village—it's in Deerfield Beach, a gated community of ten thousand retirees, most of them Jewish, waiting for death or their grandkids. Whichever comes first. Ambulances drive in a constant loop, their sirens quiet, their lights off, just waiting for someone to need them.

At the Village, there's security—you have to drive past a gatehouse and give your name to a guard before you're admitted. Because the guard is typically a Village resident in a polyester uniform, we've learned over the years that any Jewish-sounding last name will get you in.

My sister and I were coming from Indianapolis and Philadelphia respectively, while my mom was flying from Hartford. I'd tried to coordinate our flights so that we'd arrive at the same time, and I'd begged Fran not to say anything until we were there . . . but by the time Molly and I collected our luggage, my mom was already in Nanna's car, sitting behind the wheel, looking peaceful and content. Nanna, in the passenger's seat, was looking like she'd been hit by a Trailways bus.

"So, Nanna," said Molly, tossing her suitcase into the trunk and hopping into the backseat. "What's new?"

Shoulders slumped, lips pursed, Nanna shook her head. "I'm not ready to talk about this," she said.

As the oldest of four, I know my role. I'm the peacemaker, the one who smooths over the cracks, calms things down, and directs everyone's gaze to the bright side. "I know it's a big change," I said. "But she's found someone to be with! Someone to love! And love is a wonderful thing!"

Nanna sighed . . . and then, glaring at our mother, she unscrewed her lips long enough to deliver a line that would live forever in Weiner family infamy. "Frances was always difficult!" she spat.

Molly and I looked at each other. *Difficult?* What the hell did "difficult" mean? Was it some kind of generational code word for gay? (Maybe not, but it quickly became sibling-code for the love that once never spoke its name. "Did you see what Kanye West just tweeted?" Molly would ask. "He sounds so difficult." "I know!" I said. "And I don't get a difficult vibe from Kim Kardashian at all, so go figure.")

We pulled up to the Century Village gatehouse. My mom was too pleased with herself, too cheery, to remember to give the guard Nanna's last name. Nanna, in the passenger's seat, was too distraught to remind her, and I was on the wrong side of the car. Thus, it was Molly who cranked down her window, leaned into the sticky Florida sunshine, and yelled, "Rosenpenis!"

The gate went up.

This, by the way, happened over Passover. Yes, my mom chose the feast of the Exodus to come out to her mother, thus ensuring that, indeed, that night would be different from all other nights.* Molly and my mom and I walked into Nanna's living room, where my aunt Marlene and several cousins were already waiting. A few of them were flipping through old photo albums, looking over pictures of my mom and her sister as girls. Quickly, Molly pulled the other albums off the shelf. She handed one to me and took one for herself, and we sat together on the couch. Standing in the doorway, even in the midst of her shock and confusion, Nanna seemed to be touched by the tender family moment . . . until Molly yelled, "Everyone! Look for signs!"

The funny thing was that we found them. Picture after picture showed little Frances in pants, beside Marlene in a dress, or Fran in her beloved cowgirl outfit, with a hat and a vest and a badge, and two toy guns strapped around her waist. *Difficult.*

---

* It's a Jewish joke. Ask a Jew if you don't understand.

The years went by. Fran and her first girlfriend broke up, and my mother moved on to a much more suitable, age-appropriate partner, Clair, who was a mom, who did not hate men and did not seem any more overtly damaged than the rest of us. Best of all, as far as Nanna was concerned, Clair was a nurse practitioner, who sometimes traveled with her own blood-pressure cuff. Even though Clair's specialty is all things gynecologic, she's always been happy to discuss Nanna's various ailments and medications.

That helped. So, honestly, did *Will & Grace*, and other shows that depicted gay people as regular folk, just like you and me, only usually more fashionable and with better senses of humor. Once Nanna started to admit that the women accompanying her daughter on visits to the village were more than just Fran's friends, other village people began to confide in her . . . and it turned out that many of them had a son or a daughter, a niece or a nephew, a grandchild or a great-grandchild or even a former spouse who was That Way. In ten years, same-sex relationships moved from the margins to the mainstream, and my grandmother, to her credit, was flexible enough to make peace with her daughter's new identity.

Thirteen years later, Clair is still my mom's partner. She has a good sense of humor and the ability to laugh at herself, at the way she lugs around a nylon tote bag full of files and notebooks (the bag o' work) when a normal woman might carry a purse, even when she's just going to dinner or the movies; and how she'll take along a wheeled crate full of even more files and notebooks (the box o' work) for longer trips. Clair can't walk past a golden retriever without petting it and remarking on its beauty; can't drive by a garage sale without stopping and buying something; and has subtly inculcated my daughters with her politics, to the extent that my eight-year-old completed her Persuasive Writing assignment by telling Donald Trump, "You say you want to make America great again? How? You have not convinced me." Clair is a good egg, and Lucy and Phoebe adore her. She spent her childhood summers on Cape Cod, and knows how to find every hidden freshwater pond and protected ocean beach (and where to park for them). She loves swimming and biking and canoeing, and, for years, has led our annual shellfishing expedition to the tidal flats in Eastham, laughing cheerfully when her kayak gets stuck in the mud, gamely ignoring Molly's running, Marlin Perkins–style commentary. "Today, we are hunting the elusive bearded clam . . . oh, wait! I think I see one now!"

Back in the 1980s, Clair and her then partner, Deb, along with a turkey baster, a Dixie cup, and a donation from a willing gay male friend, became the parents of a boy named David who is, without exaggeration, the nicest person in the world. David is the kind of young man who volunteers to spend his vacations with his elderly grandparents, passing the days helping them out around the house and the nights watching the political documentaries that they favor. For three months after college, he worked as my "manny," tending to newborn Phoebe, who had to spend twenty-four hours a day in a canvas-and-Velcro harness to keep her hips in place. Most twenty-three-year-old guys would not be topping the list of "people I want caring for a tiny baby with a medical condition," but David is different. To this day, Phoebe's face will go practically radioactive with joy if she hears she's going to spend time with "big David."

So now Lucy and Phoebe have Flair—Fran and Clair. They have my mom, and their dad's mom, and what they call a "bonus grandmother," who shows them how to pick beach plums and find clams with their feet, who takes Phoebe out for doughnuts on Sunday mornings on the Cape and found Lucy a horseshoe-crab charm necklace, and we have David as part of our lives. My mother is happy, even though there are still some interesting moments. When Massachusetts legalized gay marriage, it was front-page news in the *New York Times*. I was at the table in Cape Cod, reading the story, when then six-year-old Lucy came in for break-fast and asked what the fuss was about.

"You know how some girls like boys, and some boys like girls," I began. Lucy nodded her curly head.

"Well, there are also girls who like girls, and boys who like boys."

Lucy's forehead wrinkled. "You mean, like, to kiss them?"

"That's right."

Lucy's eyes widened. "EW!"

"What do you mean, 'ew'? Lucy, you know people like that!"

"I do NOT," Lucy insisted. From behind the breakfast bar, Fran and Clair raised their hands. Lucy stared at them, eyes wide. "EWWWW!"*

As good as things have gotten, the four of us still want to know my mother's story. Every family holiday—Thanksgiving or Passover or bar and bat mitzvahs—is the same. We eat the meal or attend the party, we do the dishes, and then everyone gathers in the living room to interrogate Fran about her love life. "When did you know?" "Did you date women in your twenties?" and "Is this going to happen to me?" are the most common questions. (Molly is fond of demanding, "When did the urges start?" But that's Molly.)

"You couldn't have kids back then if you weren't married," Fran will tell us calmly. She used to get flustered, to shift in her seat or narrow her eyes when we'd question her, but now she just sits there, unruffled and serene. "I wanted to be a mother. I always wanted that."

I believe that she wanted children . . . but I think that most

---

* Lucy would like me to tell you that her "ew" was about kissing in general and not same-sex smooching.

people want love, too. I wonder what my mother's life might have looked like if she'd been born ten, twenty, thirty years later. Would she have settled down with a lady and had babies via DIY artificial insemination? Would she have ever been with men at all, or would it have just been women, or would it have been both? And what was her marriage like?

I'll never know the answers, especially to the last question. "You can never know what's going on inside someone else's marriage," Fran always told me . . . and this, of course, is true.

My Girls

Looking back from almost twenty years' distance, I think that the breakup that precipitated *Good in Bed* was the kind of thing you go through only once . . . because you couldn't survive any more than that.

My story began with a setup. After I'd started working in Philadelphia I'd met a guy. A friend of mine from Lexington who'd gone to graduate school with him gave him my number. He called me one day at work, and then that night, and we talked for hours, a conversation that began with stilted getting-to-know-you exchanges and ended with whispered declarations of what I'd do to him if he were there with me, not hours away in New Jersey. At which point, he said, "I'm coming down."

"Now?" I asked. It was already after midnight, and it was a work night.

"Now," he said . . . and I was enchanted, impressed by his impulsivity, the strength of his desire. I was also terrified. On the phone, I could play the seductress, could murmur promises about which body part I'd put where, but in person, it was different. What if he didn't think I was attractive? What if I opened the door and he gave me a sheepish smile or a shrug, and turned around and went back to New Jersey?

I got so busy worrying about whether he'd like me that it never occurred to me to wonder whether I'd like him. When he arrived, it was a shock. There were things that I liked right away—his height, his sweet smile, his inquisitive gaze—but there was also something distressingly simian about him. He had long hair and long arms and a round, hard lump of a belly, hunched shoulders, and bad posture. It all added up to a first impression of *chimpanzee*. Also, there was his smell. It wasn't that he smelled bad, exactly—his scent combined a little bit of old library book, a little Head & Shoulders, a little marijuana—it was that he didn't smell good to me. I am a great believer in the importance of scent, and in the notion that a couple can get through a lot together if they enjoy each other's conversation and appreciate each other's smell.

But there he was, brown eyes crinkling in the corners, looking at me in a way that let me know he liked what he was seeing, or, at least, that he wasn't appalled. I opened the door, smiling back, ready to make good on my promises. Inside, however, things did not start well. His hands were cold and clammy, and he was a terrible kisser, whose perfectly normal-looking lips seemed to instantly flatten on contact, leaving me with the sense that I was kissing teeth. He did not, it emerged, believe in putting chemicals on his body, which, alas, included factory-made deodorant, and it turned out that he hadn't had a lot of experience with women. He was raw material, happy to let me mold him, at least hygiene and kiss-wise. And, if I hadn't fallen instantly in love with him, I was immediately besotted with his family. His long-married parents, who were very much in love, lived in a beautiful house in the Jersey suburbs, its sides and trim unpeeling, and a swimming pool in the back—a house that reminded me of my own house before everything went south. His folks invited me to celebrate Passover and break the Yom Kippur fast and go on vacations with them. His mom clipped my stories out of the paper and took me shopping for a new comforter after I bought my first actual bed. At meals, his father sat at the head of the table, asking his children thoughtful questions about their jobs and their friends, listening to their answers. I wanted them to adopt me . . . but, barring that, I wanted their son to marry me so that I'd keep them in my life forever.

At some point, after a few years together, between perusing friends' wedding registries and baby-name books and idly wondering what wedding-dress silhouette was the most slimming, I realized I should ask Mr. Right whether I should go ahead and book the hall. We had a long, tortured conversation full of twenty-eight-year-old angst—Who are we? Where are we going? What do we want out of life?

Our answers to the last question should have alerted me that all was not well. I wanted fame and fortune . . . or, at least, I wanted to publish a book and earn enough money that my kids would never be pulled out of a college class-registration line. He wanted to enjoy life, to have as many good times as he could, an endeavor that was possibly going to include following the band Phish for a year. I hated Phish. I disliked all jam bands, with their endless, noodling guitar solos, their twelve-minute drum breaks, the wordless interludes where the male fans would time their head-bobs to their knee-bobs and the girls would twirl in endless, dizzying circles. Where are the lyrics? (Not that the lyrics ever improved things much.) What's the point?

By the end of our talk, we'd agreed to split. In my mind, this was a "let's take some time apart and talk about things" break, because I couldn't imagine us not being together.

He must have thought it meant something different, more permanent. Which I learned, a few weeks later, when I called him on a Friday night and heard a reluctant "Hang on," followed by a long, muffled pause and the sound of faint conversation and giggling. Female giggling. He lived, as I well knew, in a studio apartment, with only one telephone, which he kept on the windowsill, right next to the king-size bed that his parents had bought him (along with the sheets, and the comforter, and the pillows, and the apartment).

I was devastated. This was heartache like a physical illness, an incurable case of the flu. I couldn't sleep, couldn't sit still, couldn't exist in my own skin. I couldn't eat and, for the first time in my adult life, briefly approached something resembling thinness. I didn't even care, which was a sign of just how badly I was doing. The truth was that I'd had doubts of my own about the relationship and whether he was The One. Where I was driven, he had a more laissez-faire view of life. Where I'd been not exactly neglected but certainly not spoiled, and was accustomed to taking care of myself, he'd been cosseted by those loving parents, who gave him everything—a car, spending money, and vacations. He didn't like my dog. I didn't like his friends, a motley collection of good-natured stoners. I loved great food and dreamed of the restaurants I hoped to someday be able to visit; he was a vegetarian whose favorite meal was cheese pizza. In retrospect, we were obviously ill suited for each other, and we probably would have made each other spectacularly unhappy . . . but I couldn't see it then. Once we'd parted, and he'd found someone else—a giggler! If he'd wanted a giggler, why had he been with me at all?—the situation instantly clarified itself in my mind. This man, whom I had callously discarded, was the only one who would ever love me or understand me or want to see me naked. If I didn't get him back I'd die alone . . . and it would be one of those horrible, single-girl-in-the-city deaths where nobody even knows you're gone until the neighbors notice the horrible smell seeping into the hallway, and when the cops break down the door, you're nothing but a decomposing corpse, and the dog has eaten your face (I found this possibility especially terrifying because my rat terrier, Wendell, was a very small guy, and the face-eating would have taken him a very long time).

I called my ex. I went to see him. I wrote. I tried to make a case for getting back together. He wasn't having it. "Goodbye," he told me, kindly but firmly, over and over. I should have salvaged the shreds of my dignity and let him go . . . but I couldn't. I hung on, calling and writing, trying to explain myself, to say the magic words that would convince him to take me back, until there were no longer dignity-shreds to save. I was, you'll remember, twenty-eight. This was the third serious relationship of my life. I hadn't been single since I was sixteen. I didn't know how to be alone, and I didn't want to learn. I wanted to be married. To him. I wanted to buy the dress that would magically make me look like Stephanie Seymour in the "November Rain" video. I wanted to choose the invitations, register for china, get an announcement in the *Times*, to live out the Disney-princess-for-a-day fantasy. I wanted my relatives to make the trip east, where they'd be forced to admit, *I guess we were wrong. Turns out, someone does love her.*

If you've ever been twenty-eight and heartbroken, you might know the steps to this dance. I would begin each day by reading his horoscope in the morning and getting depressed if it said he'd be having a good day for love. At work, I'd scour the nascent Internet for his stories, trying to divine his mood and romantic status by reading between the lines of newspaper pieces he'd written about insurance fraud and freeholder elections. I mooned over pictures and old letters. I did drive-bys, which would have been pathetic under any circumstances, but were especially sad, given that he lived two hours away. I signed up for a clinical trial of a new weight-loss drug, convinced that if I was thin he'd want me back (even though my weight, unlike friends and taste in music and general attitude toward life, had never been a point of contention). Nights, when I'd lie awake, or early mornings, when I couldn't sleep, I would drive around aimlessly in my little Honda Civic, and I'd listen to the radio. This was 1998, the Year of *Titanic*, and I would cruise the streets of Philadelphia with Wendell on my lap and tears streaming down my face, singing "My Heart Will Go On." I wasn't sure it was true. I couldn't see my way out of the sadness, couldn't imagine a time when I wouldn't be dragging myself through my days, weighed down with thoughts of what he was doing and thinking and fantasies about what might have been, and what his new girlfriend looked like, and what she was, or had, that I wasn't, or didn't. Every house I drove past was a place we'd never live; every weekend that went by was another forty-eight hours that we'd missed out on spending together.

The worst part was how much I'd wanted to get married—not necessarily because I wanted to spend my life with him, but because I wanted to be done with being single. I was ready for the next part—being a wife instead of a girlfriend; being a mother, and giving my kids all the things I'd never had. Now I was faced with having to go back out into the world of single people, blind dates and first dates and nights at clubs and bars, where I knew that what I had to offer—wit, smarts—didn't matter as much as being attractive, where inevitably, I'd wind up alone at a table, minding my more attractive friends' purses. When JDate launched, I put up a profile with an actual picture and an actual description of my actual physique. I met a whopping total of two guys—the only two who'd been interested. (One of them, I later learned, was responding to every single profile posted by any woman between the ages of twenty-one and thirty-five.) The first one told me, upon minutes of our meeting, with what was probably meant to be a kind smile, that he "didn't feel any chemistry." Fair enough. The second guy was tall and gangly, with thick glasses, so skinny that he looked breakable. He'd come to Center City to meet me at the Pink Rose Pastry Shop, one of my favorite bakeries (I had several). After coffee and pie, I was walking him back to his car, trying to figure out what to say if he asked for my

number, when he picked up the pace until he was racewalking . . .
then jogging . . . then running. Literally running away from me.
Maybe eating the dessert I'd ordered had been a mistake?

I didn't want a new guy. I wanted my old guy back. I talked
about him endlessly, obsessively, for months, until finally my best
friend, Susan, sat me down. Susan is tall and striking, a few years
older than I am, with dark hair and dark eyes and no shortage of
men in her life, and what she said, in her own inimitable, cut-to-
the-chase fashion, let me know that there was no future. "Jen,"
she said. "None of us liked him that much."

Once your best friend says that, it's over. You can't get back
together with the guy your friends don't like, unless you're willing to find an entire new group of friends . . . and I wasn't. I
would have to endure single life again, with all of its humiliation
and rejection. I'd have to find a way to get along without him.

It wasn't long afterward when something inside of me rose
up, insisting that enough was enough. I remember thinking,
What do I know how to do? And the answer came back . . . *I know
how to tell a story.*

I would, I decided, tell myself a story. I would be my own
Scheherazade, spinning a tale to keep myself alive, night after
night, entertained and away from the dark snares of my imagination, my fantasies about what he was doing with his new girl, and
what new humiliations might await me out there in the clubs
and bars, a world where smiling guys would approach me, holding business cards emblazoned not with their phone numbers
but with information about how to join their pyramid weight-
loss schemes, or the Internet, which, thus far, had proved every
bit as brutal. I would write my way out of my heartbreak, write
my way to a happy ending . . . and, if, by the end of it, I had a
story that other people might like, that happy ending might be
the publication of an actual book. Not marriage, not a reunion
with Mr. Right, not the kids and the house and the white picket
fence, but not nothing, either. A happy ending of a different kind.

I took stock of the positives. I loved living in Philadelphia, which seemed to be constructed on a more human scale than either New York or Washington, where I'd spent summers during college. Center City, where I lived, was completely walkable. Everything I needed—the supermarket, the movie theater, my gym, my vet, my dentist, my doctor, the bank and the bookstore and the library, museums and galleries and dozens of great restaurants—were all an easy stroll along tree-lined cobblestone streets, past stately brick row houses with engraved plaques on the front, explaining which historic personage had once lived there. There were all kinds of hidden spots, secret gardens and pocket parks and stamp-size green lawns with fountains and sculptures, if you knew where to look. Every spring, the dogwood and cherry and magnolia trees on my street would blossom, perfuming the air, raining petals down on cars and pedestrians. Every September, the trees' leaves would change to orange and crimson and gold, turning the city into a watercolor of fall.

The *Inquirer*'s offices were two and a half miles away from my apartment. Most days I'd walk to work, zigzagging my way northwest, crossing South and Lombard and Pine Streets, then walking up my favorite block of Delancey Street, where all the houses had flags hanging over their front doors. I'd walk past the fountain in Washington Square Park, then up Walnut Street, across Chestnut and Market. Through Chinatown, which smelled like the fish the vendors would display on crushed ice outside of their shops, and through the Reading Terminal, where mornings smelled like the cinnamon buns the Amish bakers were preparing. My office was in a white skyscraper on Broad Street, nicknamed the Ivory Tower of Truth. In the basement locker room, I'd get cleaned up from my walk, put on my working-girl skirts and tops, fill my water bottle, and be at my desk by ten. At night, I'd walk back as far as the Reading Terminal, then take the Phlash, a big purple bus designed to ferry tourists around town. It stopped at Fourth and South Streets, two blocks from my apartment. I'd hit the gym for a step class or a Stairmaster session, walk Wendell, eat dinner, and write.

In every place I'd lived, from my first apartment in Belle-fonte to the shared carriage house to my garden apartment in Lexington to, now, my first apartment in Philadelphia, I'd made a place for writing. From Pennsylvania to Kentucky and back again, I'd set up my folding bridge table—under the eaves, in spare corners and second bedrooms—and put a corkboard above it, filled with inspiration (a thumbtacked copy of a story about surviving rejection, with tales of woe from Joyce Carol Oates and John Updike), and, eventually, rejection letters from literary quarterlies and big-deal magazines ("Dear Writer, Thank you for your contribution. Unfortunately, we find it does not meet our current needs. Best of luck in placing it elsewhere").

My apartment on Monroe Street was the nicest place I'd lived since Campbell Hall at Princeton. It had hardwood floors and a galley kitchen with a dishwasher and a garbage disposal. There were closets in all of the bedrooms, plus a coat closet and a pantry, and big windows that looked down at the row houses across the street and the cars parked along the curb. There was central air and a washer and dryer in the basement, where I had a storage cubby for my college papers and my bike. All of this cost six hundred dollars a month, and the landlord was deeply apologetic when she had to raise my rent to six hundred and fifty.

The apartment had two bedrooms. The smaller bedroom, all the way at the back, looked out over a shared yard. That was where I slept. I painted the walls pink, installed my new queen-size bed, and hung my framed Humane Society poster, a simple line drawing of a woman embracing a puppy, on the wall. The second bedroom was my office. On the far wall was the folding bridge table, draped in a blue-and-white Indian-print cloth I'd found back in State College. There was a foldout pink-and-green jungle-print love seat from Pier 1, and a dresser that I'd trash-picked and stripped and repainted in shades of cream and brown. I put a printer on top, and my nine-by-twelve envelopes and reams of blank paper inside. On the other side of the desk was a flip-out wooden bookcase from Target that I'd filled with my favorite books: Erica Jong and Adrienne Rich, *Rubyfruit Jungle* and *Almost Paradise*, *Disappearing Acts* and *Mr. Bridge* and *Mrs. Bridge*, Tama Janowitz and Jay McInerney, and, eventually, all the first-person-*Sex-and-the-City*-single-girl books that would be classified as "chick lit," along with *A Writer's Guide to Literary Agents*. I hung a poster of a sleeping child against a midnight-blue background with the alphabet over my desk—A is for Apple, B is for Ball. I'd bought it at an art fair, when I was twenty-two and couldn't afford much art, because I'd loved it so much, and I'd dreamed of hanging it in a baby's bedroom someday.

I wrote on the Mac Classic that my father had bought me the summer before my senior year, one of the handful of times he saw me during college, after I'd told him that I'd do better on my senior thesis—and on graduate-school and job applications—if I didn't have to fight my classmates for time in the computer lab. My father must have been flush if he'd spent almost a thousand dollars on me. I remember feeling guilty, wondering which of my siblings he'd be stiffing as a result.

So I began. On nights, after work; on the weekends, between brunches and bike rides; and, most of all, on my walks, with Wendell and to the office, I imagined a girl who was a lot like me and a guy who was a lot like my ex. I gave the girl a version of my family (absent dad, funny/bleak siblings, mom who'd come out of the closet in her fifties and hooked up with a much younger woman). I gave her my problematic body and a variation on my job, and I gave her my dog, only in the book his name was Nifkin. (Years earlier, I'd overheard my brother Jake, who'd been in a fraternity, use the word in a sentence that I'm pretty sure was "I'm going to powder my nifkin." I badgered him until he told me that "nifkin" was the same as "taint," the space between a guy's balls and his asshole.)

I knew that Cannie Shapiro's story was going to share its broad outlines with mine. I also knew that heartbreak, while exquisitely painful, is fairly common. In order to make her story compelling, I knew I'd need to raise the stakes, to make her agony more vivid and palpable than that of the average dumped girl. Luckily, my life provided plenty of raw material. A few years before I'd met the guy who'd broken my heart, I'd gone out on a few dates with a writer in Philadelphia. There weren't any fireworks—I remember his kisses as being distressingly wet—and we'd had a perfectly typical parting (I thought he'd call, he didn't; I was sad for a few days, then I moved on). Then, a few years later, I came home from work, opened up one of the lady magazines to which I subscribed, and found his byline on top of a story about sex. Specifically, about good sex, and how to have it. The title was something like "Ten Tongue Tricks That Will Make Him Beg for More" . . . and I remember thinking, *This guy? This guy is passing himself off as an expert? This guy is giving good-in-bed advice?*

The memory lodged somewhere in my mind . . . and years later, when I started to think about Cannie, my subconscious obligingly kicked it to my forebrain, and I had my first big what-if. What if you're dating a journalist and you break up and he gets a gig writing sex advice for one of the big women's magazines? What if his columns are all about you and your body? What if he basically outs you as the fat girl to the entire reading universe and uses your insecurities as fodder for his columns, so you're not only alone and heartbroken, but ashamed and exposed?

I imagined a girl who works at a newspaper, a girl who has broken up with a guy, but thinks she's going to be all right—there are, as they say, other fish in the sea, a lid for every pot, and somewhere out there is her fish, her lid. Then her phone rings and it's her best friend saying, "You need to go look at this magazine right this very minute," and she goes bouncing down to the newsstand and opens it and sees her devastation.

I've always loved the place writing can take you, when you're so deep in the narrative that it feels almost like the pages are writing themselves . . . like there's a story out there, somewhere, already in existence from beginning to end, and all you're doing is transcribing it, or carving away the obscuring rock to reveal the art underneath. Writing *Good in Bed* felt like that. Every weekday I would go to my job and report my little heart out, writing about movies and books and politics and celebrities. Every night, after a home-cooked dinner that was always ten Weight Watchers points or less, I'd return to my bedroom, sit in the folding chair, and fall back into the story: where I was invisible, where happy endings were possible, where my heroine always had the perfect zingy comeback at the moment it was required, instead of thinking of it three days later when no one cared. In the world of the story, I could forget about the loneliness of my real life, the fear that I'd never find my fish, my lid.

I'm not sure any writer who's lucky enough to publish more than one book ever gets to write with the fearlessness and the freedom that you feel when you're working on the first draft of your first novel, when you don't have an agent or a publisher, when you haven't told a soul. My spare bedroom, in my Philadelphia neighborhood, was only an hour and twenty minutes away from Manhattan, but as far as the publishing world was concerned, I might as well have been in Nebraska or North Dakota or on the moon. I didn't have an agent or an editor. I didn't have connections or names to drop. I wasn't living in Brooklyn, where every third person on the subway platform in Park Slope seemed to be toting a manuscript. I think I told maybe three people what I was doing, and one of them was my mother, who didn't believe me. "Oh, yes, the novel," she'd say when I brought it up, draping her hand across her forehead in an affected fashion.

I remember getting stuck on a plot point, where Cannie's been to see Bruce at his father's funeral and he's made it clear he has no interest in getting back together. What happens next?

I wondered. Does she meet a new guy? Have a breakdown and move back in with her mom and her mother's new girlfriend? Quit her job and go live in a vegetarian ashram so she can attain spiritual enlightenment and finally wear a single-digit size?

I fell asleep with possibilities arrayed in my mind and woke up with my answer, as clear as if someone had written it down on a legal pad while I was sleeping. They have sex. She gets pregnant. ("Oh, Cannie," I heard Susan asking in my head, in a line I'd eventually give to the fictitious BFF in *Good in Bed*, "what did I tell you about sex with the bereaved?") Cannie tells Bruce, who wants nothing to do with her and nothing to do with the baby. What does she do then?

All day the story would churn in the back of my mind, so that by the time I returned to my desk at night, I'd have the next few pages right there waiting. It felt sometimes like a Möbius strip, because I knew that Cannie's salvation—like mine, I hoped—was going to come through writing. She would realize that her parents had done the best they could, had given her what they had to give her, and that her job was to take it and grieve what she'd lost and then move on. I wanted her to find love . . . because it was a story I was telling myself, and because, even as a staunch feminist, that was what I wanted; a guy who'd promise to love me forever, who'd give me a ring, who'd stand up in front of his family and mine and the whole entire world and say, *I choose Jennifer.*

But I also wanted my girl to find peace within herself, to find her own resilience, to know that she was strong enough to save herself and save her baby and fight her way toward her hard-earned happily-ever-after. I wanted her to know that, even if her happy ending did not include a man, she would be fine.

Some of the scenes were ripped straight from the headlines of my own life. My mother's romance with her much-younger girlfriend became Cannie's mom's affair with the gruff, raspy-voiced, self-help-book-loving Tanya. The awful colleague who

torments Cannie was a composite of a few of my less supportive coworkers. The too-cool-for-school New York City publicist who denies Cannie an audience with the movie star Maxi
Ryder was a not-even-thinly-veiled version of the publicist
who wouldn't let me chat with Minnie Driver; Bruce became
a version of my lost love, albeit an obnoxious, cartoonish, self-
righteous, and frequently stoned version. It was not the most
charitable portrait. But I was twenty-eight, and I'd just wasted
three years of prime fertility and six months of tears on this guy,
who had then ghosted me so thoroughly that it felt like he was
trying to pretend that the relationship had never even happened.
I was not in the most charitable mood.

I remember the moment when I decided to name Cannie's ex
Bruce Guberman. A plastic surgeon with the last name Guberman had billboards lining I-95, advertising his skill as a liposuc-
tionist. I took his last name, added Bruce (for the rhyme and for
Springsteen), and felt my mouth moving into an unfamiliar shape
that it took me a little while to recognize was a smile. Then I followed *Salon* columnist and *Bird by Bird* author Anne Lamott's
advice to women writers using their exes in fiction, and I gave him
a tiny little penis—because, as Lamott wrote, no man will ever cop
to being the inspiration for a character who is hung like a grape.*

As natural and joyful as most of the writing felt, there were
times when it was harrowing. When I had to write the scene that
I was dreading—Cannie's reckoning with her father, her memory
of him throwing silver dollars in the water, telling her to jump,
reassuring her that she could do it, that she could swim, that she
already knew how, that she'd always known—I dipped into my
savings and rented a cabin advertised as a "writer's shack" called
Lis Sur Mer on the Outer Cape for a week in September. My

---

* You can imagine my dismay when, many years later, I found myself panned in that very same
publication for mocking Bruce's tiny penis. I felt like the kid in those long-ago don't-do-drugs
PSAs, shouting, "I learned it from you, Dad!" or "*Salon!*" You know, whichever.

plan was to go home for Yom Kippur, break the fast with Fran and her book-club buddies, then go to Cape Cod and write for a week. The little cottage was perched on top of a bluff in Truro, overlooking Cape Cod Bay, and it was everything the website had promised. The single room held a spool bed and a little desk in front of a window, which had panes made of wavy old glass. There was an outdoor shower enclosed in a cedar fence, with a mermaid painted on the wall. The beach was down a long flight of splintery wood stairs. When the tide went out, the water left loops of drying seaweed, like layered necklaces on the sand, and when I slept I kept the windows open and I could hear the waves all night long.

Each morning of my makeshift writer's retreat, I'd go for a long walk along the water. Then I'd write. I ran an extension cord from the inside of the cottage out to the picnic table, where I'd set up my Mac. (This was 1999, and not everyone had laptops.) I'd work for a few hours, then have lunch, then write some more and go for a swim. It was September, but summer was still holding on; the temperature was in the seventies every day and the water was almost as warm. I'd always loved swimming, the sensation of weightlessness, the way my boyfriends could carry me in the water the way they never could on land, how my body wasn't an embarrassment or a shame, but was purely functional, even graceful, with my arms stroking smoothly, my hair fanning out behind me. I'd think of Kurt Vonnegut, describing his ungainly body in the introduction to *Welcome to the Monkey House*, writing, "I am six foot two and weigh nearly two hundred pounds and am badly coordinated, except when I swim. All that borrowed meat does the writing. In the water I am beautiful."* The bay was

---

* Years later, toward the end of his life, I did an event with Kurt Vonnegut, and he was awful to me—cruel and cutting, and basically calling me out as a hack in front of an audience that, sadly, included my mother. I was so shocked and so brokenhearted that a man who'd been my junior high favorite, a guy who could write a line like "in the water I am beautiful," was being so awful that I promised myself that if I ever had another chance to appear with—or even meet—one of my writing heroes, I'd skip it.

so clear I could sometimes catch glimpses of fish, and feel their silvery scales brush against me, and see crabs scuttling sideways, balanced on their legs, pincers held pugilistically aloft, hurrying out of my way. Wendell would act as my lifeguard, pacing along the shore, watching me, occasionally doing a desperate, tooth-clenched dog paddle, swimming out to make sure I was okay before he'd turn and let the waves carry him back to the sand.

My rental ran from Sunday to Sunday. On my last Saturday night I sat inside the cottage and yanked the window closed. The wind was whipping up the waves and Wendell was napping un-easily on the bed, opening his eyes whenever a gust shook the cabin. Before the weather had turned, I'd been outside, in the sun, and I'd gotten through the hard scene about the father, how he'd loved his daughter in spite of what he'd said and done to her. I was inside, warm and safe, when I wrote the very last paragraphs and typed the words THE END. By Sunday morning, the temperature had dropped twenty degrees and the wind was screaming, churn-ing the water into froth, bending the pine trees toward the ground. I inched home on Route 6, creeping along the two-lane highway, through what had become one of the worst storms of the year, with my lights on and my wipers flailing at the rain. Wendell was trembling in his carrying case on the passenger's seat. My Mac was in the backseat, seat-belted in place, and I remember thinking that the most important things I had on Harvest Hill Road were right there with me in the car.

I stopped in Connecticut, halfway between Truro and Phil-adelphia. "I finished my novel," I told my mom. "Oh, yes, the novel," she said, and rolled her eyes. She was getting ready to sell the house by then, and all of my stuff—my books and bookcase, my bed and my clothes—was either gone, boxed up in the base-ment, or in my apartment in Philadelphia. *I guess I don't live here anymore*, I thought. But that was okay. In that moment, I felt entirely adult, certain that I could take care of myself and be fine.

Back in Philadelphia, I printed out what I'd written, put it in a box, and set it aside, on top of the little table in my office. A few weeks later, I took it out, imagining it was something I'd picked up at the bookstore or from the "New Fiction" shelf in the library, trying to figure out whether what I'd written would appeal to anyone besides me. At that point, I'd read enough fiction to have some objective sense of whether what I'd done was any good . . . and I wasn't sure, but I thought I had something.

Thus I began the next stage in my march toward publication—finding an agent. My goal was to sell the book before I turned thirty. I had six months and a number of obstacles. The Internet was still a brand-new thing. If you wanted to learn about literary agents, you went through the back door, reading the dedications and the acknowledgments of the books you loved, trying to see if an agent was named and thanked (99 percent of the time, one was). Then, instead of zipping over to an agency's website to see if they were accepting submissions, you went to a reference book that listed literary agencies. You prayed the book was up-to-date and that you weren't writing to an agent who was retired or, God forbid, dead. You looked up the address and their submission guidelines, and you sent a query letter, a chunk of your work, if they were amenable, and a self-addressed stamped envelope so that if they rejected it—*it*, not *you*, I reminded myself—they could send it back for free.

I came up with a list of twenty-five agents, including one dream agent, a woman who'd represented half a dozen of my favorite books, including one of the hottest among the young-woman-in-the-big-city books that *New York* magazine had recently praised. I knew that we'd be a perfect fit; that as soon as she read my proposal she'd be delighted to take me on as a client; and that we'd work together over many books, for many happy years. In fact, I was pretty confident that most, if not all, of the agents I was asking would want to work with me. Princeton degree? Studied with

Toni Morrison? Fiction in *Seventeen* and *Redbook*? Worked at the *Philadelphia Inquirer*? What agent wouldn't be interested?

The answer came, with swift brutality: almost all of them. Out of the twenty-five letters I sent, I got twenty-four rejections.*

My Dream Agent wrote me a lovely letter, saying that while I was "obviously a writer," she was "failing to connect with my characters at this point in my life." "What does 'at this point in my life' mean? Menopause?" I wailed to the new boyfriend I'd acquired during the six weeks when the novel was sitting in its box, aging like fine wine. At twenty-nine, I couldn't imagine being menopausal . . . and, of course, I thought that anyone should have been able to connect with my lovingly crafted and brilliantly realized characters.

Sadly, that was one of the more helpful rejections I got. A few more agents' letters actually gave me a few words of encouragement or a reason for their decision—*this is good, someone will want it, but it's not right for me*—but most didn't bother. They sent form letters or, in some cases, form postcards, the better to pack in maximum pain for minimal expense. *Sorry, not taking new clients. Not interested in new fiction. Not interested in new women's fiction. Not interested in new young women's fiction. Not interested in you.*

Three weeks after sending my first batch of twenty-five query letters, I'd gotten only a single request to see the manuscript. I sent it along and was preparing another round of queries as 1999 was turning into 2000. "Take a break," Adam, my new beau, urged, and we planned a trip to Las Vegas, where I'd never been. On our last day away, I called my answering machine, which I was doing, by that point, three or four times a day, hoping that I'd gotten a phone call saying "yes" instead of another letter or postcard saying "no."

---

* Note to aspiring writers: This is actually not that many rejections in the grand scheme of things. I know published writers whose rejection count is in the triple digits. Never give up. Never, never, never give up.

"Hi, my name is Famous Agent," the message began. "I've read your manuscript, and I'd like to offer you representation."

Adam and I booked a table at Picasso, one of the celebrity-chef-run spots I'd dreamed of patronizing, where even without wines, a meal could cost more than a hundred dollars. I spent my last night in Las Vegas too excited to sleep, thinking that this could actually be happening, that my story could become a book. I changed my plane ticket, called my boss to arrange for a few more days' worth of vacation, and flew to California to meet Famous Agent in person.

She was a tiny, energetic older woman with a no-nonsense manner, whose airy, light-filled, white-walled office was lined with framed covers from the books written by the authors—over a hundred in all—that she represented. I was so excited that I was practically levitating. *Remember this*, I told myself as she showed me around and introduced me to her staff—her assistants and interns and editors, almost all of them young and female—and I thanked her, over and over again, while I tried to remember names, remember book titles, remember everything.

When she said, "I loved your book, but we need to think about some changes," I agreed immediately. After years as a reporter, and everything I'd learned from John McPhee, I was perfectly willing to make changes, and believed that even a good manuscript can always be made better. The truth is, at that point, she could have told me that the change required was a sex change, and I would have flown immediately to Sweden to collect my new penis. I was that thrilled with the idea that this woman, with her star-studded roster and decades in the business, was going to be my agent, and that with any luck, my book was going to be a book.

I flew home in a state of joyous disbelief and floated around Philadelphia, working the phrase "my agent" into every conversation, thinking about how I'd pose for my author photo, and how I'd tell the story of finding my agent to the inevitable re- porters who'd be writing profiles of me when the book came out.

A few days after I got home, Famous Agent called. It was seven o'clock my time, four in the afternoon for her. I'd gotten home from work, changed into my uniform of leggings and a loose T-shirt and was walking around barefoot, awaiting in- struction. She did her business via speakerphone, and I paced my apartment with the phone tucked under my chin and a reporter's notebook in my hand, scribbling notes during her static-spiked pronouncements. "The heroine of this book is fat," she began, her voice rising in disgust on the word "fat." "I talked to a film agent I work with, and we both think that no one wants to see a movie about a lonely, pathetic fat girl."

It was the first pinprick in my bliss balloon. *Lonely, pathetic fat girl?* Sure, Cannie was lonely, but I didn't think she was pa- thetic. I thought she was resilient! A survivor! And size sixteen wasn't that fat . . . was it? And who was talking about a movie, anyhow? Of course I'd love it if the book became a movie, but, for starters, I just wanted the book to become a book.

"Maybe she could be, you know, like, fifteen pounds over- weight," the agent suggested. "Like, normal fat."

If she's fifteen pounds overweight, I thought, *then she's Bridget Jones with a bat mitzvah.* And as much as I'd loved Bridget, I'd found her obsessing over a relatively minor weight issue grating. A hundred and thirty-five pounds? Feh. Call me when the first number's a two—or even a three—then we can talk. And what's all this about *normal fat?* What does that make me, and my mom, and my editor at the paper, and my favorite college professor, and a bunch of my friends? Freakish fat? Stop-and-stare-at-the-fat-lady-fat? When half the women in America wear a size fourteen or larger, how can a size sixteen be that unacceptable? And if she was so disgusted by my fictional doppelgänger, what had she thought about me?

"Next issue," the agent continued, her brisk manner suggesting that she had many more important matters to attend to. "There are all of these sex scenes, where it's the fat girl having sex. And I just . . . it's all just kind of . . ." She did not speak the words "grossing me out," but I heard them anyhow.

"You know," I said, in a tone just short of tart, "fat people have sex, too." By then, I was bewildered. This woman had seen me. In person. She knew she wasn't on the phone with Twiggy. Did she realize that I was a size sixteen? Didn't she think that I'd be insulted at the dismissive, even derisive way she was talking about the impossibility of a fat girl having sex or a happy ending?

There was more. "I'm not sure about the title," the agent continued. "I'm not sure we should call it *Good in Bed*. What do you think about *Big Girl*?"

I'd been prowling up and down my hallway as we spoke. That comment—even more than the one about fat, even more than the one about fat sex—froze me in place. I had many thoughts about *Big Girl*. Most of them were some variation on the phrase "Hell, no." I thought it was a terrible title, for many reasons. *Good in Bed* was fun and inviting, a little naughty, a little mysterious. *Big Girl*—its two syllables sounding, to my ears, like the twin thuds of heavy stones plummeting into a scummy pond—was not fun or inviting or naughty or mysterious. It was judgmental, unkind, even didactic—Big Girls Don't Cry. Big Girls Do Go to Weight Watchers.

In addition, this was the age before e-readers. There was no hiding your shame, no telling the world you were reading *Anna Karenina* when it was actually *Fifty Shades of Grey*. Would women pick up a book called *Big Girl*? I wasn't even sure that I, an actual big girl, would want to be seen carrying a book entitled *Big Girl*. Anyone who saw me would know! A book called *Good in Bed* would be a different story. That book I'd be proud to carry . . . because it made me sound sexy. And maybe there'd be pictures.

In the space of a single phone call, I had gone from exhilarated joy to agonal misery and serious self-doubt. This was, after all, the only agent who'd shown any interest in representing me, and she had a client list packed with name-brand bestsellers and prizewinning literary luminaries. She was a very big deal; she clearly knew her business. But, still, the changes she'd suggested didn't feel right to me. They felt like they'd make the book more generic, less specific, less authentic, less true to itself and to me. But what if she was right? What if I didn't do what she'd told me to do and then nobody published my book?

I spent a cocktail-punctuated weekend ruminating, changing my mind every twenty minutes. I'd think, *Of course she's right, I need to fix this, there's a reason there's never been a hit novel that had a genuinely plus-size woman as the heroine, unless she started out that way and lost weight. Judith Krantz never had a fat heroine.* Then I'd think, *I can't change it. There need to be books out there where the big girl's happy ending doesn't depend on magical weight loss that she achieves by following a diet that exists only in fiction.*

After I'd finished *Good in Bed*, I'd read about another British book, a bestseller about an overweight newspaper reporter (hey!) who meets a guy online, seduces him with a fake picture, and then drops a hundred pounds in about ten minutes before they meet. *As if.* The book concluded with the journalist snagging a different hot guy, along with some tacked-on-sounding nonsense about how she had gained *some* of her weight back (but not all of it, because ew), and how she was living happily as a size eight (because happiness as a size eighteen would have been not just fiction, but science fiction). Those were the narratives available to me—the slightly overweight girl who believes she's enormous, the genuinely plus-size woman who has to suffer, and change, before she can be the heroine of her own life story. Neither tale appealed. I could not, would not, put a book like that into the world, a book that told girls like me that only our fretting-over-fifteen-pounds sisters could play the heroine, that we were unacceptable, unlovable, unworthy unless we shed half of our body weight. I knew so many women who were not skinny and who had wonderful, happy, fulfilling lives, with great jobs and friends and family and partners. Why couldn't I tell a story about one of those girls?

I'd drift into dire fantasies about making the changes and having my protagonist being called a copycat. Then I'd sink into even more dire imaginings about not making the changes and having readers repeat what the agent had said—that they found Cannie repellent, unseemly, gross, that they didn't care about her story, that she wasn't the kind of character they wanted to spend a few hours with, and her happy ending was clearly a fantasy, because no girl who looked like that could hope to get a handsome man to love her.

Back and forth and back and forth I went. I asked myself the central question, the one that had always helped steer me successfully through life: *What would Billy Hunnenwell Winthrop Ikehorn Orsini Elliot do?* But even that wasn't much help. When Billy launched Scruples, her Beverly Hills boutique and passion project, it was an exact replica of Chanel in Paris, and nobody came, and it took Spider Elliot convincing her that California shoppers craved a different kind of experience—less reverential, more fun—before she redid the place and made it a success. Was the agent my Spider? Was the first draft of my book Billy's first try at Scruples? Did I need to swallow my pride, take a seat, and listen to the experts? Was I dooming myself to humiliation and financial ruin—or at least relative obscurity—if I didn't?

I was getting confused, even as I impressed myself with my almost total recall of Judith Krantz's oeuvre, so I asked a different question: *Who did I write this book for?* That one, I knew how to answer. I'd written it for me, and girls and young women like me. My girls: the ones who wouldn't lose fifteen pounds and fit into a bikini, the ones who were always hearing *You've got a great personality* or *You have such a pretty face.* The purse-minders, the wallflowers; the ones the wingman who'd agreed to "take one for the team" took home from the bar. The ones who nod in sympathy when their friends talked about street harassment, but whose lived experience involved more shouts of "lose some weight" than cat calls and leers. The ones who hardly ever saw themselves—their physical selves—reflected in stories where the heroine got the guy, the job, the money, the power, the happy ending. Maybe there'd never been a bestseller with a girl like that as its star . . . but what if there had been? What difference could that have made in my life, the way I saw the world, and what I let myself hope for from it? If nobody had attempted to write the happy ending for girls like me, then why couldn't I be the one to try?

I had my answer, even if it wasn't the answer I wanted, even if it meant I'd need to start my agent-hunt again. I wanted to publish the book I'd written, with the heroine I'd imagined, and the happiest of endings. I wanted to toss the book like a life buoy to those girls and women, and to the girl I'd been, and tell them, *Hold on to this, and I promise you, it'll be all right.*

If I made the changes the agent had asked for, the book wouldn't feel like my book anymore. It would feel like a compromise, like a soup that too many cooks had tried to season. Maybe I'd never find an agent. Maybe my agent would never find a publisher. Maybe the book would be published and only twelve people would buy it and I'd be related to eight of them and I'd know the other four from Weight Watchers . . . but I was going to try my hardest to get it into the world the way I'd written it, for myself, and for all those girls like me.

On Monday morning I wrote Famous Agent a letter. I thanked her for her time and her thoughtful comments, but I said that I believed we had different visions of the book. I went back to my guidebook, drawing up a list of another twenty-five agents to query. Then I called one of the young editors I'd met on that trip to California, a woman who did freelance work for Famous Agent, and with whom I'd chatted a few times on the phone. I told her that I didn't think it was going to work out with her boss, and that I didn't want to get her in trouble, but did she know any other agents? Preferably one with free time and low standards.

As it turned out, that editor, whose name was Liza Nelligan, did know someone. She'd worked with a young agent named Joanna Pulcini, who worked for Linda Chester, a big-deal agent in New York with her own lengthy list of bestsellers. "Joanna hasn't sold a lot of fiction," Liza cautioned me. "But I think she'd really respond to this book."

I sent the manuscript on a Thursday, with a letter explaining who I was and how I'd come to hear about her. On Monday morning I was sitting at my desk at the *Inquirer* when the phone rang.

"I loved your book!" enthused a high-pitched voice that sounded like it belonged to an eight-year-old girl, or a dog's squeaky toy. "It spoke to me!"

I remember sitting there, the telephone pressed to my ear, as the newsroom buzzed and simmered around me, thinking, *How?*

"That's great!" I stammered . . . and we made plans to talk. I took the train in to the city and met Joanna, who was a year older than I was and who looked like a miniature version of Courteney Cox, shiny brown hair and enormous blue eyes, in an agent-y uniform of a chic navy-blue sheath dress and pointy-toed high-heeled shoes. Joanna took me to lunch at Marcus Samuelsson's restaurant, Aquavit, and over herring sashimi and deconstructed Swedish meatballs, we talked. We talked about my book, about our lives, about her work as an agent and mine as a reporter. I remember she tried to tell me that one of the reasons Cannie spoke to her so specifically was that she'd had bad skin in high school, and how I smiled and said, "Not the same, but thanks for playing." Years later, I learned that Joanna had heard all about what happened with me and the first agent, and had been worried that I wouldn't want to work with her because she's so tiny. Which is funny, insofar as some of my best friends are thin. I love small people! I don't discriminate . . . but I do love to think about Joanna, the night before I came up to the city, pounding down high-calorie shakes and chanting, "Must . . . get . . . bigger!"

Joanna and I had a lot in common. We'd both grown up in small towns, then moved to big cities, working our way up in our respective fields, currently trying to figure out if our new guys were the right guys, eager to get on with it, to be wives and mothers in addition to working girls. We hit it off immediately, even though she's all sweet sincerity and I am more prone to sarcasm and dark moods; even though she's a good Catholic girl and I'm Jewish; even though her vocabulary is pristine and mine is studded with vulgarities. As we started working together, I quickly discovered that Joanna was taken aback by anything more than the most vanilla sex scenes, and that she never curses, and so I made it my secret mission to shock her as much as I could.

"Joanna," I'd urge her, just for fun. "Say 'blow job.'"

"I won't!" she'd say, giggling, covering her blushing face with her hands.

"Just say it," I'd wheedle.

"I can't!" she'd say, ducking.

"Just once!"

"Nooooo!"

"Do it for me?"

She'd part her fingers, open her mouth, and say, "blow job," in a tiny, apologetic whisper.

"Now say 'cocksucker'!"*

---

* Note to aspiring writers: Sometimes I'd put special treats into my books, knowing that Joanna would find them and be horrified. In the short story "The Guy Not Taken," an unhappy mother of a newborn discovers that her ex-boyfriend is getting married. I had her realize that she could access her former beloved's wedding registry (she remembered his password) and had her sign him and his new bride up for a food scale, and then a Hitachi Magic Wand.

I sent Joanna the story. A week later, I got it back with the note that I'd expected: *What is this*, with "Hitachi Magic Wand" circled. No worries! I thought. My editor will know what it means! A week later, it came back with the same passage circled and the same question inked in the margin—*What is this?* At which point I realized that I am a pervert.

• • •

Joanna and I worked on the manuscript for months. We cut. We tightened. We shifted sections around, amplifying some scenes, trimming others back. Finally, Joanna decided that the book was ready to go out to publishers. By then she'd been laying the foundation, taking editors out for breakfast or lunch or drinks and saying, "I have three words for you! Good in Bed!" Then she'd refuse to tell them anything else, including whether the book was fiction or nonfiction or a memoir or what. By May, publishers were buzzing, eager to discover what Good in Bed was all about.

Joanna sent the book out on a Thursday. By Tuesday, we had our first indication that a house wanted to buy the book. On Thursday night, I took the train up to New York, splurging on Amtrak instead of the more affordable New Jersey Transit and somehow losing one of my fancy new shoes on the trip. The next morning, my brother Jake ran to Nine West to buy me a pair of black slides with chunky heels while Joanna and I met to strategize over coffee. Joanna had set up a day's worth of meetings with interested editors. We began making our rounds and, by ten that morning, the first editor we'd met with had made an official offer, which Joanna fielded in the backseat of the Town Car she'd hired for the day. "That's not the number we had in mind," she said crisply, before hanging up. When she told me what the number was, I lunged across the backseat, grabbing for her phone, saying, "Call them back! Call them back and tell them that's plenty!"

We ended up meeting with three different editors at three different imprints, and while I liked them all, it was clear that Greer Hendricks was the right fit. Age-wise and life-experience-wise, she was right where Joanna and I were. She got Cannie on a visceral level—her yearnings, her insecurities, her ambitions, her desire to build a happy life with the right person. She'd also, over a weekend's time, convinced her entire team to read a four-hundred-page manuscript . . . so not only did we meet Greer, we met her marketing director, her publicity chief, and other members of the team who'd be instrumental in bringing the book into the world.

The whole day was a blissed-out, sunny blur that I remember in bits and pieces. Someone told me she'd missed her subway stop because she'd been so wrapped up in Cannie's story. Someone else asked if I was okay basically signing up as the public face of my plus-size heroine. ("Sure." I shrugged. "It's not like people who see me are going to think the only reason I've been to Lane Bryant was for research.") I remember asking editors questions not just about this book but about the next one, and being instructed, "If anyone asks if you consider yourself a literary or a commercial writer, say commercial," and not really understanding where, exactly, the division was, or why it was such a big deal. (FORESHADOWING!)

Joanna gave the editors a "best bids" deadline, which meant they had until the end of the next day to make their best offers. All of them were very close, money-wise, so I got to pick the team with which I felt the most affinity, and I signed on with Greer and Atria for a two-book deal, of which *Good in Bed* would be the first book, for the staggering sum of $550,000.* Publication was set for twelve months hence, in May 2001. I'd wanted to sell a book by the time I turned thirty. I missed it by six weeks.

People say that the happiest day of a writer's life is when she gets to tell her parents—or, in my case, my mom—that someone is publishing her book. I drove to Connecticut to make my big announcement. "Hey, Fran," I said. "Remember that novel you didn't believe I was writing?"

"Oh, yes," my mother said, rolling her eyes. "Your novel."

"Well!" I said. "Simon and Schuster has acquired it as part of a two-book deal for more than half a million dollars, and foreign rights have already been sold in sixteen countries!"

---

* Note to aspiring writers: Back in the day, a first-time novelist could actually command a staggering sum like that. TIMES HAVE CHANGED.

My mother stared at me, her eyes filling with tears. She hugged me, enfolding me in her arms and her signature scent of baby powder, chlorine, and the JCC's complimentary shampoo. Then she started to cry. "I'm so proud!" she whispered. It was a beautiful moment.

Then Fran pulled away and looked at me, beaming. "So what's it called?" she asked.

Shit.

"*Good in Bed*," I mumbled.

"What was that?"

"*Good in Bed*," I said, a little louder.

Fran's brow furrowed. "*Good and Bad*?" she asked.

"No," I said miserably. "No, it's *Good in Bed*."

Fran pulled back, looking horrified. "Jenny," she demanded, "how much research did you do!"

The road to publication was not entirely without bumps. That weekend in Connecticut, I gave Fran the manuscript and explained that there was a character loosely based on her. I gave her the deal I'd extend to friends and family over the next fifteen years, telling her that of course, I didn't want to cause her any pain or embarrassment, and that she should flag anything that gave her pause, and that I would cut or change it. I then had to listen to her read what I'd written, sitting in the family room with a book of my own, hearing the sound of flipped pages punctuated by laughter, then cries of "Jenny, goddamnit!"

Back in Philadelphia, I did not quit my day job, which meant that I stayed at the *Inquirer* for the year between the day the sale was announced and the day I left for my book tour. While most of my colleagues were supportive and kind, a handful seemed to decide it was their personal mission to make my work life as miserable as possible.* One editor seemed to take a special

---

* Note to aspiring writers: Having your colleagues find out about your six-figure advance is not always a recipe for goodwill.

delight in tormenting me. She'd send me on the absolute worst assignments—the more mundane and less glamorous, the better, and if she could send me somewhere mundane and unglamorous in the middle of the night, well, that was best of all! When the paper eventually did publish a profile of me, she edited the piece and made sure it included ugly gossip about my family[*] and criticism ("self-absorbed and ambitious") from former colleagues who were allowed to take shots anonymously (and who considered "ambitious" an insult). It was not quite what I'd imagined, back when being the subject, instead of the author, was just a pleasant daydream.

In spite of the work woes, the entire run-up to being an official, capital-*A* Author felt charmed, like someone had looked at the previous twenty-nine years of my life and said, *Okay, now here comes your reward.* With zero connections in the publishing world, I had to ask/beg writers I admired, but did not know, to give me those quotable endorsements called blurbs that appear on the book cover. I wasn't optimistic, and hoped, at best, for two or three nice quotes. I ended up with six beautiful blurbs, one of them from Susan Isaacs, my role model and hero. *Good in Bed* got a starred review in *Kirkus.* ("It's been so long since I've seen one of these that I almost forgot what they looked like!" my publicist said.) Then it got a starred review in *Publishers Weekly.* My publisher agreed to a sixteen-city tour (Greer now jokes that it was supposed to be only twelve cities, but Joanna accidentally-on-purpose misread a "2" as a "6"), and, as the cherry on top of the fantasy sundae, HBO optioned the film rights.

My new boyfriend, Adam, a lawyer, was smart and funny and delighted to be at my side during those months when it felt like every phone call brought some new piece of unbelievable good news. He'd celebrate every great blurb and review, he'd listen,

---

[*] Stay tuned. It's coming.

patiently, when I bitched about the inevitable bad ones, and he was supportive when, as a prepublication treat, I decided to take my mom and Molly on a weeklong vacation.

"Jenny, I couldn't," Fran demurred.

"Come on," I said. "There must be someplace you've always wanted to go."

"I can't."

"Yes, you can!"

"It's too much!"

"I can afford it!"

"Fine! Rancho la Puerta! William F. Buckley and his wife spend a month there every year!" I wasn't sure why Fran considered their patronage a persuasive endorsement, but we went. And it was lovely.

Best of all, the guy who'd broken my heart, who'd declined to take my calls, who'd gone off with a giggler? I saw him again, after I'd sold the book, after I'd met Adam, after everything was wonderful (except my weight: I lost twelve pounds, kept six and a half of them off, and had finally decided, for the time being, that I would try to love, or at least tolerate, my body just as it was).

Adam and I were in New York City for a Bruce Springsteen concert. That July, Springsteen was playing at Madison Square Garden for ten nights. Madison Square Garden holds twenty thousand people. I'm not sure, mathematically speaking, what the chances were that my ex and I would end up in the exact same row, on the exact same night . . . but there he was. When I saw him sauntering down the staircase, all ponytail and patchouli stink, with his (tiny) new girlfriend in tow, I freaked out. I told Adam who he was, grabbed my cell phone, and fled.

Locked in the handicapped stall of the ladies' room, sweaty and hyperventilating, I called Susan and gave a whispered account of the night's events, ending with the line "I don't think

I can spend three hours sitting next to him, and it's going to be three hours. Four if there's encores."

"Stop whining," Susan instructed. "This is the great wheel of karma spinning around. You have a boyfriend, and you have a book deal, and you need to go back out there and face him."

I had a single tube of lipstick in my purse. In the Madison Square Garden ladies' room, with excited New Jerseyites all around me, I did everything I could possibly do to myself with that one cosmetic. The lipstick was lipstick. It was rouge. It was contouring cream and it was eye shadow. I would have waxed my legs with the lipstick, had I believed it to be possible. Finally, after I'd gotten myself looking as good as I could, I pulled back my shoulders, lifted my chin, marched back into the arena, and took my seat.

My ex-boyfriend looked at me. "Hi," he said.

"Hi," I said back. (Sparkling dialogue!)

I asked how he was doing and feigned sympathy when he told me that his paper had gone through a round of layoffs and that he'd been among the casualties. When he asked me how I was doing, I told him that, actually, I was doing quite well. I had written a book, and Simon & Schuster had acquired it, and foreign rights had been sold all over the world.

My ex looked surprised, then stung. Playing what was clearly the final card in his hand, he indicated his girlfriend and said, "This is my girlfriend, Bitchface."*

I smiled. "And this," I said, indicating my boyfriend, "is my fiancé!" Except—oops!—Adam and I were not yet engaged.

Adam smiled manfully. My ex looked gratifyingly dismayed. The lights dimmed and Springsteen took the stage, and I sat down. On top of my left hand, in case either my ex or Bitchface thought to look for a ring, which I did not have, on account of not being engaged yet.

---

* Not her actual name.

Although it was several days before I regained full sensation in my fingers, my run of good fortune continued. A few months later, Adam proposed, and *Good in Bed* was published. It sold solidly in hardcover and took off in paperback, turning into a word-of-mouth success story, a book that's buoyed not by an expensive ad campaign or critical consensus, but by a much more rare and gratifying force—readers, specifically female readers. Mothers were telling daughters, sisters were telling sisters, women were telling their best friends and yoga buddies and neighbors and coworkers—*you need to read this book*. Best of all were the letters I got. *Thank you for telling this story. Thank you for not having Cannie get thin. I found this book right after a breakup, and it saved my life. My whole life, my father told me I was fat and ugly, and this book made me think that maybe I'm okay.*

Good in Bed sold and sold—and not just to my family or my Weight Watchers friends. It went on to spend almost a year on the bestseller list. It was, as they say, a dream come true . . . and I was on my way.

Two in a Million

Good Housekeeping, August 2009

There are friends who are loyal, steadfast, and supportive; friends you can call in the middle of the night or the middle of a breakup, who stay by your side no matter what.

My friend Susan, in addition to being all these things, is also the friend who does not hesitate to send me e-mails marked "urgent" that include images of a celebrity with a lamentable amount of plastic surgery (memo line: "must discuss") or to share her insights about why that famous author should have known her much younger husband was gay. ("His eyebrows looked better than hers did. Hello!") The friend, in other words, who, come death or disappointment, can always make you smile.

We met the way single girls meet in the city. I'd just moved to Philadelphia to work at the city paper and didn't know a soul except for the editor who'd hired me. I was walking my dog, Wendell. Susan was walking her dog, Daisy. The doggies sniffed each other. Susan and I eyed each other. Finally, one of us (I'm guessing it was her) said something (I'm guessing it was sarcastic). That's how it started. Like true love, or finding the perfect black cashmere cardigan with a three-quarter sleeve: we just clicked.

Susan was sophisticated and glamorous, with a mane of inky black hair and a string of brokenhearted ex-boyfriends. When we first met, she lived in a tiny jewel box of a row house, with an ornate wrought-iron headboard and a sleek little couch covered in buttercup-yellow leather. I had a sensible brown bob, a practical denim couch, and a collection of not-terribly-disappointed exes whom I could count on one hand and have fingers left over. Based on appearances alone, we shouldn't have worked. But we bonded over our mutual love for roast chicken, the same sense of the absurdities of life, and, these days, by Susan's refusal to take me, or anything else, too seriously. (While everyone else oohs and aahs if one of my books gets optioned for the big screen, Susan's impressed only because my dealings with Hollywood may bring her one step closer to meeting longtime crush Peter Strauss.)

Over the years, we've seen each other through major life transitions: weddings and kids' birthdays, C-sections and biopsies, the deaths of dogs and of parents. We've talked each other off the ledge. When Susan wanted to drag a heavy planter in front of her ex-boyfriend's garage so he'd run over it with his Lexus, I persuaded her that it was a bad idea and that, if she went through with it, I'd be unavailable to pay her bail. When I wanted to drive all night to convince a boy that we were meant to be together, Susan sat me down and gently but firmly explained that no, we actually weren't. Other friends will reassure you that oh, no, that dress your cousin wore to your wedding wasn't *so* bad. Susan will devise a scorecard for guests' fashion infractions (thigh-high slit, no bra, flaming red dress) and, at the end of the reception, hand it to you as a memento.

There are friends who tell you, "Someday you'll laugh about this." Susan's my best friend because, with her, "someday" is always now.

With Child

Adam and I spent a year planning our wedding and got married in October 2001, at the Mutter Museum, which houses Philadelphia's collection of medical oddities, including rows of syphilitic skulls and, that fall, an exhibit about food-borne illnesses. "Most of our brides choose to keep the exhibits closed during cocktail hour," the museum director said. Adam and I agreed that my family was such a freak show that the museum's offerings would struggle to compete. "Open those doors!" I said.

Our wedding was six weeks after 9/11, which meant that some of the guests with small children were naturally reluctant to get on planes, while all of our ninety-and-over relations—the people we'd invited to be polite, without actually expecting their attendance—decided to make the life-affirming gesture of appearing in person at our nuptials, in some cases with hired attendants or the daughter they wanted there to help them to get to the bathroom and cut their food. Both of us were oldest children, the first in our families to get married, and we—I—wanted a big celebration, dinner and dancing, the rabbi and the chuppah and the big white dress.

At thirty-one, I was six years older than the average first-time bride in America. But in the East Coast city where I lived, thirty-one seemed just right, and certainly not out of line with my friends and my peers.

I had lured Adam out of his apartment on Rittenhouse Square and into my neighborhood, east of Broad Street, and we'd used my advance for a down payment on a three-story row house around the corner from my Monroe Street apartment. It was long and tall and narrow, with a twisty staircase, and rooms stacked up vertically instead of stretched sideways, but it had a little L-shaped bricked garden and four bedrooms, including a tiny one down the hall from our bedroom on the second floor that would be perfect for a baby. I'd had the walls painted a buttery yellow and I'd put dozens of Ikea postcards in colorful frames, tying each with a bit of ribbon, and hung them in neat rows beside the window. There was, just barely, room for a crib, and a glider, and a changing table. The one big window looked out over the garden that I'd filled with bright annuals in the springtime, round barrels full of impatiens and posies and phlox. I had a little patch set aside for zucchini and tomatoes, and I was coaxing roses to climb up the walls.

Our plan was to wait a year, maybe two, before starting a family, enjoying each other and our lives as newlyweds. Then one day, six months after our wedding, I took a break from my writing and went downstairs to collect the mail. A new *Newsweek* was on top. YOUR DECLINING FERTILITY, blared the cover. SELFISH SINGLE LADIES THINK THEY CAN POSTPONE CHILDBIRTH FOR-EVER WHILE THEY SELFISHLY FOCUS ON THEIR CAREERS, BUT THEY ARE WRONG AND THEY ARE GOING TO DIE ALONE EXCEPT FOR THEIR WINE AND THEIR NINE CATS, the subhead added. (I might be paraphrasing, but not by much.) Worst of all, the cover was illustrated with—I kid you not—a photograph of one of my college roommates. She was a year older than me. She, too, had spent her twenties establishing her professional life, earning a PhD, building her career. She, too, had recently gotten married . . . only, unlike me, she was already trying to conceive, and was having trouble, BECAUSE FEMINISM AND MADONNA HAD SOLD HER A LIE AND TOLD HER SHE COULD WAIT AS LONG AS SHE WANTED TO WAIT EXCEPT BIOLOGY HAS OTHER IDEAS AND NOW YOU'LL DIE ALONE.

I stood by my front door, feeling faint. Oh, God. I *had* been selfish. I'd been blind. I'd been ignoring the biological realities, blithely living my self-centered, single-lady life, taking it on faith that I'd get married in my late twenties or early thirties and pop out a few kids at some point in the ensuing decade and that everything would be fine. I'd been worrying about the wrong things—terrorism, or a repeat of September 11's horror, or a president whose response was to put in place menacing and barely constitutional measures designed to protect "homeland security." Clearly, the real threat was much closer, and had nothing to do with bombs or planes or racial profiling . . . and no, things would *not* be fine. I was probably already too late, and if I didn't start trying to conceive at that exact moment I was going to spend my declining years dressing up my cat in baby booties after my husband had left me for a nubile nineteen-year-old who'd be able to give him an heir.

I called Adam at the office. "Can you come home for lunch?" I asked. He came home. There was no lunch. ("Not even a sandwich?" he asked sadly, trudging back down the second-story hall with Wendell, who'd never quite made peace with his presence, barking smartly at his heels.) Approximately fifteen minutes later, I was pregnant. Thanks, *Newsweek*!

The timing was not great. The magazine came out in the summertime. I was supposed to go on a book tour for *In Her Shoes*, my second book, that fall. In August, a few days after a home pregnancy test revealed why my breasts were swollen and achy and AT&T commercials were making me cry, I drove myself to Connecticut, where the book tour was beginning. My mother, who'd been swimming, wrapped herself in an ancient beach towel and came to greet me. She looked me up and down as I rolled my suitcase into the hallway.

"Jenny, are you pregnant?" she demanded.

Standing in the laundry room, feeling the heat of the house pressing down on me (my mother did not believe in using air conditioners, preferring to cool the house with fans), I started to cry. Or maybe I'd been crying already. I cried a lot over those nine months. "I thought it would take longer than it did! I thought I had declining fertility!"

Fran just stared. "I had four kids," she said slowly. "My sister had four kids. Why would you think you'd have any problems getting pregnant?"

"It's *Newsweek*'s fault!" I blubbered. "They said it would take at least six months and that I needed to start trying right away!"

Fran shook her head. I went to the bathroom to barf. For the next two weeks, I was queasy and achy and permanently exhausted as I made my way across the country, from Boston to Atlanta to Minneapolis to Nashville to Denver to Los Angeles, and points in between, reading every how-to-be-pregnant book that I could find along the way. (Alas, I bought *What to Expect When You're Expecting* at the same time that I purchased a copy of *Best Fetish Erotica* from Amazon. *BFE* had the same cover image as *In Her Shoes*—two pairs of sexy stilettos, pretty feet side by side—and I wanted to check out the competition, which made sense to me but was undoubtedly perplexing to the Amazon algorithms. "Based on your previous purchases, we have recommendations for you!" the banner on my home page would read. Half of the recommended books would be erotica of the S&M variety. Half would be pregnancy books. I wondered whether anyone from Amazon's headquarters thought it was weird.)

Back home after the tour, I planned for my pregnancy and delivery the way I'd readied myself for every other major event in my life—by overpreparing, committing reams of facts to memory, and reading everything I could find.

In 2002, there was a lot to read. Pregnancy and childbirth, especially as experienced by a privileged white lady such as myself, had become a kind of blank screen, where shifting attitudes and neuroses and double standards and conflicts and attitudes about gender and knowledge and power were projected . . . and many contemporary feminist thinkers who were having their own children were writing about the experience, making me reevaluate my own expectations.

There were articles about the rise in the C-section rate, and whether doctors were doing them unnecessarily, to avoid the risks, and attendant lawsuits, of vaginal births going bad. There were stories about whether the medication doctors gave laboring women affected babies, or kept mothers from being sufficiently in touch with their bodies to give birth naturally. The message I got was that a good mother threw off the shackles of Western medicine, and the chemical bondage of epidurals and Pitocin, and labored the way God and Nature intended, without medical intervention or a ticking clock or chemicals that would speed up the process for a doctor's convenience or an insurance company's bottom line.

Of course, all the writers agreed that breast-feeding was best, an assumption that wouldn't be reexamined for another decade. Back then, if you weren't committed to breast-feeding exclusively for a period of at least six months, well, you might as well be giving your baby Dr Pepper in a phthalate-filled plastic bottle, so of course I was determined to nurse.

There was also the debate about hiring help. Babies, we were instructed, needed their mothers, not day care or nannies or paid caregivers, so if you were a good mother and you had the financial resources, then you would stay home for as long as you could, no matter how high-powered your position or how much you'd invested in your work. The *New York Times Magazine* ran a story about the "opt-out" generation—bright women with Ivy League degrees leaving their jobs to stay home making baby food and crafting with their kids—and once again, my college classmates were pictured in the piece, their photographs Exhibit A of the opt-outers. Ambivalence about staying home, or boredom or dissatisfaction with life with a newborn, were never mentioned, and pregnancy and new motherhood were depicted as candy-coated, peachy-toned bliss. "I don't want to be famous; I don't want to conquer the world; I don't want that kind of life," read a quote from one of my Princeton sisters. Her words—and the story itself—told me that, as soon as I'd conceived, I was supposed to have stopped wanting these things, too, and made me feel uneasy—and guilty—because I hadn't.

Not only that, but pregnancy was now also supposed to be sexy. I remember my own mom, pregnant with my younger brother, in billowy, peasant-style maternity tops (I remember them mostly because she continued to wear them for decades). I recalled Lady Diana, swathed in yards and yards of disguising white cotton. Pregnancy had been when ladies got to take a break from being toned and firm and cute and sexy all the time. It was when you could relax a little, when you could (however temporarily) retire your status as Object of Desire and be a glowing, loosely clad Madonna.

By the early 2000s, all that had changed . . . thanks, in part, to our Madonna, who along with other celebrities was flaunting her toned body and her baby bump, wearing sexy, revealing, body-con clothing for the duration of what the Victorians used to call her confinement. Not only that, but the stars would give birth, then emerge from the hospital precisely the size they'd been nine months previously, toting their babies as if they were the most desirable luxury-brand accessories, in a manner that made it clear that motherhood wasn't slowing their social calendar, widening their waistlines, or dulling their sexual appetites at all.

Designers rolled out cutting-edge maternity fashion in the tiniest sizes. Shelter magazines and catalogues featured nursery porn—decked-out babies' rooms with hand-carved cribs and cradles, beautifully upholstered gliders, color-coordinated curtains and comforters and crib bumpers and sheets. Every new issue of *People* or *Us* would have photographs of some famous new mom, babe in arms, with a husband or partner beaming in the background and no paid help in sight.

I read and watched everything I could find, every book, every TV show, every magazine. I studied blogs and birth plans, and devoted myself, like the A student I had once been, to having the best pregnancy, followed by the best possible labor and delivery, that I could, treating my journey into motherhood like another test that I'd ace if I studied hard enough.

Adam and I took classes in the Bradley Method of "husband-coached childbirth," which instructed, "*Natural childbirth is an important goal since most people want to give their babies every possible advantage, without the side effects of drugs given during labor and birth . . . Couples are taught how they can work with their bodies to reduce pain and make their labors more efficient. Of over 1,000,000 couples trained in The Bradley Method nationwide, over 86% of them have had spontaneous, unmedicated vaginal births. This is a method that works!*"

Together we interviewed obstetricians and midwives, going in with a page-long checklist of questions. *How many of the births you've attended in the last six months ended with C-sections? How do you feel about medications? Will you let Jen labor for as long as her body requires, or do you expect delivery to occur within a certain time frame?* We hired a doula, because, of course, that's what you did, what our friends and birth-class buddies were doing, to ensure that the delivery would proceed as optimally as possible. In between the relaxation exercises and the high-protein diet and the pain endurance techniques, where we'd have to hold ice cubes in our hands,* we worked on our birth plan, which spelled out, specifically and at great length, exactly what we wanted and did not want. We wanted a calm, peaceful, dimly lit environment, with a diffuser scenting the air with lavender and a CD of whale songs playing softly in the background. We did not want fluorescent lights, unnecessary interruptions, loud noises, or Pitocin, a drug commonly administered to kick-start labor. We did not want an epidural, or any pain medication. We wanted me to be able to move around the room, untethered to monitors, free to crouch or rock or squat or get on all fours as my body—my body, which knew how to do this and was, in fact, made to do this—dictated. We did not want frequent internal examinations, continuous fetal monitoring, or any extraneous medical interventions. By the end, the birth plan ran upward of ten pages, and I was still worrying that we'd left out something important. Should we spell out, explicitly, that we didn't want our daughter wrapped in a pink blanket if something gender-neutral was available? And that one of us wanted to give her the first bath?

By the time Lucy's due date arrived, I was as ready as I'd been for any exam. My bags were packed, with clothes for me and two cute but non-pink outfits for her, both washed in non-allergenic, not-tested-on-animals organic detergent. I had a Boppy pillow and a Bugaboo stroller and a Baby Björn, which I prayed would fit over my newly extra-enormous chest. The wardrobe of onesies and cute little hats and socks had been washed and dried and lovingly folded in the brand-new dresser with the changing table on top. All was in readiness. We had everything but the baby.

Lu was due on April 28, and I made the rookie mistake of

---

* Holding an ice cube in no way resembles the pain of delivering a baby.

telling people the exact date—not "sometime this week," or "the doctor says late April or early May." When the day came, my phone rang from seven a.m. until ten at night. Unfortunately, that was the only thing that was happening. There was nothing to report. No contractions, not even a twinge. Nothing. Then it was the end of April. Then it was May. Then the baby was a week late. Nothing. Eight days late. Nine days past my due date. Nothing, nothing, nothing. At ten days—and at this point I was going in for daily checks of the baby's heart rate, with the technicians assuring me that she was fine, just not showing any inclination toward leaving—my extremely understanding obstetrician sat me down. He knew, he said gently, that I'd been set on natural childbirth, but nature was not cooperating, and that at this point, the risks of continuing the pregnancy were starting to outweigh the benefits of letting nature take its course. "The uterine environment is decompensating," he said, his face uncharacteristically serious, his voice grave. "What does that mean?" I asked through my tears. "Does it mean the schools in there are getting bad?"

I was sick with sorrow. I felt like I'd failed, like I'd flunked the test that I'd studied so hard for, the biggest, most important test I'd ever take, the one whose results would not only affect me but would also affect an innocent child.

I cried all afternoon as Adam tried to reassure me that things would be fine. I sobbed through dinner. I wept myself to sleep. My daughter hadn't even been born, and I already felt like I'd let her down by being unable to give her the optimal birth that would have left her in the best possible position for the best possible health and future.

Already, I could see the dominoes fall—she'd be sickly from the drugs they'd give me. She'd have trouble forming loving attachments, having been unceremoniously ripped from my body instead of making her own leisurely way out. Of course she'd have trust issues. She wouldn't get into the right preschool, which would keep her out of the best private school, which would prevent her from getting into the top high school, which would end her chances for the Ivy League, which would doom her to a life as a scullery maid. Possibly one in my employ, because she'd probably also be one of those kids who never left the house.

I knew what my own unhappy childhood had done to me, how it had colored my view of the world, how I tended to see the majority of people as harmful and malevolent, enemies who'd hurt me and everyone else as much as they could. I wanted to do better by my own children. Now I had—already—failed.

About six hours before my scheduled C-section, I woke up with a stomachache. *Oh, great,* I thought. *I'm a bad mother, I'm having major abdominal surgery in the morning, and now I've got indigestion.*

Then the pain went away. Then it started up again. After three or four rounds of this, I realized that I was—praise God—having contractions. I woke up Adam, called my doctor, canceled the operation, and settled in triumphantly to wait.

After about twelve hours of on-and-off contractions, we walked six blocks to Pennsylvania Hospital, with me towing my suitcase behind me, like a brave pioneer woman preparing for a new frontier. Unfortunately, it turned out that I was barely dilated at all. "Go home," said the nurse. "You'll know when it's time to come back."

I went back home, and I did everything the books recommended. I walked. I took a bath in the tiny third-floor tub we'd installed for the baby. I drank teas made of raspberry leaf and nettle, applied evening primrose oil and extra-virgin olive oil to all the recommended places, and ordered spicy eggplant for dinner, except after I'd ordered it I remembered that I wasn't supposed to be eating, in case I ended up needing a C-section, which

I wouldn't, I was sure, because now my body was kicking into gear, just the way God and Nature intended. I bounced on my giant inflatable birth-ball. I breathed through the contractions. I watched the timer on my BlackBerry. Twelve hours later, back at the hospital, I checked in again, underneath a banner that read AMERICA'S BUSIEST MATERNITY WARD. Was that a good thing? I wondered. Wouldn't it have been more of a comfort if the sign had said BEST and not BUSIEST? And shouldn't I have worried about this sooner?

In spite of all the home remedies and the contractions (painful but endurable), I was still barely dilated, but the nurses agreed to let us stay and put us in a small, rectangular room with the walls painted beige, a private bathroom with a shower, and a single bed. After twenty-four sleepless hours, Adam immediately claimed the bed, lay down, and conked out, leaving me to squat, bounce, shower, pace, moan, and endure, as the hours dragged by.

The contractions would grip me, leaving me groaning and breathless, fists clenched and brow furrowed. They were like nothing I'd imagined, nothing I'd read about, less like a "really bad menstrual cramp" or squeezing of a melting cube of ice and more like a previously unexplored force of nature, like being seized and tossed by my own private hurricane, something so powerful and enormous that I couldn't even comprehend it. I had never felt so scared or so small. I'd have one contraction, then another, then another one after that, the time between them shortening, and I would think, *This is it* . . . then they'd taper off and stutter to a halt again. Finally, after twelve hours of laboring in the hospital (during which I'd had no sleep, nothing to eat, and nothing but ice chips to suck), the baby's heartbeat was starting to dip.

So it was a C-section after all. All that pain, all that struggle, all that planning, all that hope, all for nothing. I hunched forward on the edge of the bed, shivering, trying not to think too much about how big that needle had looked before the anesthesiologist plunged it into the space between my vertebrae and my doctor eased me down onto my back. I couldn't feel anything below my waist but pressure, and tugging, and I knew better than to look—even what I could make out from the distorted reflection in the lamp above my belly was distressingly bloody. I shut my eyes. Adam squeezed my hand. And then I heard a faint, indignant cry. I held out my arms . . . and there was my baby.

So motherhood did not get off to a propitious start. I was sick with guilt about the C-section, sick with the certainty that I could have toughed it out, talked to the doctors and convinced them to let my labor continue, convinced that the drugs and C-section had affected my body and hers. Back in my room after the surgery, I was so exhausted and dehydrated that I couldn't stop shivering. My teeth chattered and my body trembled in spite of the heated blankets the nurses piled on top of me. Worst of all, my milk didn't come in. Lucy wasn't terrifically interested in nursing—as happy as I was to have her in the world, that's how unhappy she was to be there—but even when I held her, skin to skin, and maneuvered her mouth where it was supposed to be, there was nothing doing.

So Lucy went to the nursery, where they fed her formula, which I'd learned to think of as the devil's own rancid spittle, a few steps removed from poison. I was lying in bed, with IVs in both arms, shivering so hard that the bed was shaking, hating myself for being so weak, hating my body for betraying me and failing her.

At home, things did not improve. I'd imagined an easy recovery, easy nursing—I had breasts, didn't I?—and a cheerful, easy-to-understand baby. I thought, after all of the studying I'd done, that I'd do as well at motherhood as I had on all of my tests.

Of course, that's not the way it worked. I had a beautiful, perfect pink pearl of a baby—a perfect pink pearl who could morph, in the space of ten seconds, into a furious, red-faced shrieking dervish. I was using nipple shields, which would sometimes stay on my breast in the proper position but would usually fall off and need to be reaffixed. Even when they stayed in place, Lucy wouldn't nurse—she'd turn her head away from my breast, sometimes slapping at it with her little starfish hands, like a bald man trying to shake a piece of candy out of a recalcitrant vending machine. She would only take bottles, she was crying all the time, and I couldn't figure out how to soothe her—because, it quickly emerged, I'd spent so much time on the pregnancy and childbirth-preparation end that I hadn't spent enough time on the actual raising-the-baby aspect of things.

I wasn't sleeping. I was skipping meals, spending hours trying to feed and comfort my baby, then stuffing fistfuls of whatever food I could find into my face when I realized that I was starving. Not only did I fail to lose the baby weight, I actually gained weight in my first months as a new mother, which left me even more thoroughly demoralized. My breasts hurt. My stitches hurt and tore and got infected and took forever to heal. Lucy cried every time I put her down. She screamed when I picked her up. She shrieked when she was hungry, and when it was time to change her diaper, and when I settled her in her stroller for a walk or her crib for the night, and for no reason whatsoever.

I tried to do everything perfectly, but things kept going wrong. My attempt at round-the-clock baby-wearing ended when a combination of an imperfectly knotted Moby Wrap and the dishwasher that I'd been trying to load ended with Lucy narrowly escaping impalement on the knives in the silverware basket. Co-sleeping kept me up all night, terrified that I'd roll on top of the baby. Sleep-training didn't work—it turned out that Lucy was perfectly capable of "crying it out" for a solid hour, and I usually cracked after ten minutes, going in to soothe her, which I was not supposed to do. And scheduling was impossible. The perfectly sensible-sounding routine of E.A.S.Y.—that's *eat*, then *activity*, then *sleep*, then (ha!) *you time*—would fall apart, because Lucy would fall asleep immediately after eating . . . or she would eat, then do her activity, then want to eat again, without any sleep at all, or any of the promised respite that I was supposed to get.

"Babies cry," my mother told me, holding her arms out for my squalling, red-faced child. Fran's bemusement at my plans and my books—*so this is how people do it these days?*—was giving way to real anxiety. By then I was crying almost as much as the baby. I was going days without finding time for a shower; the piles of unwashed laundry were reaching mountainous proportions, there were dishes stacked in the sink, half-emptied grocery bags on the counters, beside heaps of unsorted mail and unpaid bills, and I was angry all the time, angry at my husband for not being psychic and not knowing exactly what I wanted exactly when I wanted it; angry at the baby for being so hard to soothe and please; and most of all, angry at myself.

The situation was far from ideal. Adam had lost his job while I was pregnant and was taking some time to find a new one. Instead of asking for his help with the baby or with the housework, I was trying to give him the time and space he needed to conduct a proper job search. Of course, I ended up resenting him horribly—for every shower he took that lasted longer than thirty seconds and was uninterrupted by a baby's shrieks, for every outfit that wasn't lacquered in spit-up and applesauce, for being able to leave the house for hours at a time without the encumbrances of car seat or diaper bag or stroller or baby, even though I was the one insisting that he shower, dress, and leave. I was jealous of his freedom, angry that he seemed to have no problem dumping all of the child-care and financial obligations on my shoulders, and furious—red-faced, fist-clenched, head-spinningly furious—every time I came home from playgroup or a pediatrician's appointment to find him on the couch, in the air conditioning.

He saw that I was frantic. He would offer to help with the baby, but I was determined to stick to the plan, where he worked and I took care of Lucy. *Oh, no,* I'd say. *You need to spend your time on your job search. I've got this.* Or, if I was exhausted enough, I'd let him try . . . but, of course, I couldn't ever just let him change a diaper or feed her a bottle. With the words of whatever book I'd read most recently chorusing through my brain, I'd explain to him—sometimes patiently, sometimes not so patiently—that he was doing it wrong, wiping her wrong, holding her wrong, burping her wrong, wrong, wrong, wrong, wrong, wrong.

Adam must have felt like he'd lost both his job and his wife, along with any semblance of a calm and happy home life. I felt abandoned and lonely and permanently infuriated. Then, as if full-time newborn care wasn't enough, I decided—for no reason that was even remotely rooted in reality—that I needed to write another book that very minute, and that if I didn't get back to work, if I couldn't secure the next chunk of my advance, if we didn't have some money coming in, then we'd go broke and lose the house and be out on the street.

It was sheer, delusional panic, and if I could go back in time I would sit myself down and tell myself sternly, *Relax, you've got enough money saved up that you don't have to worry for years.* But I couldn't see that through the fog of my self-loathing and terror, and so I added "write five pages a day" to my to-do list.

Initially I'd imagined that writing would come as easily as it always had; that I'd start working in the cheerful little nursery, with its yellow walls and tiny pink crystal chandelier, and the window covered with a sheer curtain panel embroidered with pastel butterflies—it had, after all, once been my office. I would sit in the glider with my laptop on my lap and Lucy asleep in her Moses basket at my feet, or tucked into the crook of my arm. She'd nap and I'd write, and then we'd go for a walk to the grocery store and have a home-cooked meal on the table by the time Daddy got home.

This, of course, did not happen. Lucy's naps ranged from fifteen minutes all the way up to a sumptuous half hour. Most days, by the time I'd located my laptop, realized the battery had died, dug the charger out from underneath a pile of magazines and newspapers, and plugged it in, she was awake again . . . and Lucy was not the kind of baby who would happily stare at her fingers or suck on her thumb from the comfort of her state-of-the-art bouncy seat while Mommy wrote novels. She was, instead, the kind of baby who, at six months, determined that she was done forever with her pacifier, and signaled this new development on I-676 by flinging it from her car seat at my head.

One afternoon in August, when Lucy was three months old, I'd taken her out to run errands. It had been an awful night, where she'd been up and down, never giving us more than a ninety-minute respite, and I was exhausted and on edge, but determined to stick to our schedule of eating and activities. We'd gone to the grocery store and the hardware store, and came home with half a dozen plastic shopping bags, plus the diaper bag and my purse, shoved into the stroller's inadequate undercarriage or dangling from its handlebars. It was ninety degrees and humid. I was soaking with sweat. Lucy woke up and started to cry as I tried to heave the stroller up the front step and maneuver it through the front door . . . and once I got there, I saw my husband on the couch, in his boxer shorts, fast asleep. He didn't get up to help me with the stroller into the house—or at least he didn't do it fast enough. I was so angry that I could feel my fingers curling into hooks in preparation for ripping his face off . . . and I was certain that if a jury of my peers was assembled, the twelve mothers of newborns would not only acquit me but would build a statue in my honor.

That was the moment that broke me. Something had to

change. If things didn't get better, I'd end up hurting someone or losing my mind. I needed some help. So, even though I'd planned on staying at home for a year, I was forced to acknowledge, with sorrow and regret and a metric ton of guilt, that so far, stay-at-home motherhood was killing me. I couldn't just roll with it; couldn't accept that chaos and sleeplessness were my new normal. I'd get frustrated at the way Lucy seemed secretly intent on screwing up anything I'd have the temerity to try to organize. A friend and I would plan to meet for lunch and Lucy would stay up all night, finally falling asleep at eight in the morning and staying passed out in her crib until two in the afternoon. Or I'd feed her, then load the diaper bag, then strap her into the stroller, then walk six blocks and smell something awful and realize she'd had one of those clothes-wrecking blowout poops—the kind where the shit sprays all the way up the baby's backside and leaks out of the diaper to soak the stroller underneath—and have to turn around and go back home. We'd go on a plane trip, and she'd screech for three hours straight, earning me endless stink-eye from fellow travelers, until five minutes before the plane landed, at which point she'd conk out. Everything was a struggle. Everything left me feeling frayed and miserable and incompetent.

By September, I'd found a sitter, a calm and serene and lovely young woman named Jamie, and I started to work first ten, then fifteen, then twenty hours a week. It helped. Getting dressed, combing my hair, putting on grown-up clothes and going to write in a coffee shop down the street, leaving my baby with someone who was warm and loving and patient (and who could be all of those things because she got to give the baby back to me and go home at the end of the day) did wonders for my mental health. Almost immediately, I started feeling better. Then, of course, came the guilt *about* feeling better. *A good mother would not have left her baby this early*, I would think, remembering those content-looking moms in the *Times*. *A good mother would not have hired a sitter. A good mother would have found a way to make it work.*

Every day gave me the opportunity for new screw-ups, new occasions to feel like crap. When Lucy was six months old, I booked a speaking engagement at a synagogue outside of Baltimore and I brought the baby along. I felt comfortable doing this, because I'd taken her out to dinner a few months before and she'd slept through the entire thing like a potted plant in a pink onesie, and I knew that if she didn't sleep, Adam, who was coming with me, would quickly whisk her away.

You can probably write the ending to this sad chapter. Somehow we drove all the way to Baltimore and were in the synagogue before realizing that the diaper bag was lacking the crucial component of "diapers." Adam went to find a place to buy them, leaving me with a fussy baby and an increasingly disgruntled event coordinator. I was on a panel with a beloved bestselling local mystery writer and a woman who'd self-published a memoir about surviving the Holocaust. Adam and Lucy were seated right up front. The mystery writer brought down the house. The Holocaust survivor moved the crowd to tears. I quickly decided that I could not follow a story about Auschwitz with my planned raunchy passage about blow jobs, and was rifling through my manuscript to find something that felt more appropriate when Lucy started to cry. There I was, on the stage, sweating and stumbling through my speech, trying to shoot psychic messages out of my eyeballs and into my husband's brain: *take the baby out of here!* Alas, he didn't hear.

I apologized my face off. It didn't help.

The next day, the event organizers sent me a chilly e-mail saying they hoped I'd "learned my lesson" about where it was and was not appropriate to bring a baby. Then they cc'd me on an email to my booking agent, asking for their money back.

I was mortified. For years, I'd prided myself on doing well at work, on never missing a deadline or letting a boss down, on always doing my best. I was never going to be the prettiest girl or the thinnest or the most popular. By then, it was also clear that I wouldn't be getting any Best New Mom prizes. But I could damn well be the hardest worker, the best prepared . . . and now I'd screwed up so badly that the people who thought I'd be a fun, engaging speaker wanted a refund.

I was damned if I did, damned if I didn't, damned if I tried to split the difference, damned no matter what. In the winter of 2004, the *Atlantic* published a piece by Caitlin Flanagan, a scathing indictment of nanny culture and the selfish, self-centered upper-middle-class white women who pay other women to care for their babies. It felt like it had been written specifically for me, a poison-tipped arrow aimed right at my heart, as punishment for my wicked working ways.

Flanagan's essay, "How Serfdom Saved the Women's Movement," pointed out (correctly) that our modern world has become absurdly child-centric. "In the past month," she wrote, "I have chaperoned my children to eight birthday parties, yet not attended a single cocktail party (do they even exist anymore?)." She observed (again, correctly) that "almost any decision a woman makes about child care is liable to get her blasted by one faction or the other." Then, with barely a paragraph to pivot, Flanagan unloaded on the privileged, educated white ladies who hired—and underpaid—their black and brown nannies.

Never mind that my sitter—I could not bring myself to call her a nanny—was white, with a college degree, or that I was paying her more per hour than I'd made at my first two newspaper jobs. Never mind that none of my working-mom friends were exploiting their help. Never mind that I doubted that the black and brown women Flanagan was caping for had subscriptions to—or time to read—the *Atlantic*. The target of her story was guilty white moms, and her words kicked me right in the guts. A mother who chooses to leave home to work was a mother who had forfeited her children's love.

"The professional-class working mother—grateful inheritor of Betty Friedan's realizations about domestic imprisonment and the happiness and autonomy offered by work—is oppressed by guilt about her decision to keep working, by a society that often questions her commitment to and even her love for her children, by the labor-intensive type of parenting currently in vogue, by children's stalwart habit of falling deeply and unwaveringly in love with the person who provides their physical care, and by her uneasy knowledge that at-home mothers are giving their children much more time and personal attention than she is giving hers."

There it was, in black and white, in the pages of a magazine I respected. Children love the woman who takes care of them. "At-home mothers are giving their children much more time and personal attention." And women "who have chosen to separate themselves from their children for long hours of the day . . . feel a clawing, ceaseless anxiety about this." I felt guilty, for sure, but I wasn't sure I felt the "clawing, ceaseless anxiety" that Flanagan had identified. I wasn't anxious about leaving Lucy with Jamie, because Jamie was lovely and competent and kind, and wasn't undone by Lucy's crying the way that I was, and because giving myself permission to leave made me a better mother when I came home.

Leaving, clearly, was best for me . . . but it was not, per Flanagan, the best for my baby. After I read the *Atlantic*, it was as if every previous instance of self-doubt and self-loathing—hating my body, doubting that I was qualified to be at Princeton, worrying that I'd never find a man to love me—were only warm-up rounds that had existed to prepare me for this, the Mother of All Shame. Failing yourself is one thing. After all, who are you really hurting if you fake your way into a school you never deserved to attend, if you never get thin, if you never find love, if you die alone with your nine cats and the paramedics have to saw a hole through the wall to remove your gigantic, bloated corpse? Just yourself. Possibly the paramedics who'd have to haul you to the morgue. Maybe the person who should have been admitted to

Princeton in your stead. But if you screw up a baby? The implications were endless and awful.

Maybe if I'd been leaving my daughter with a nanny so I could slave away at a law firm or a big bank, trading the misery of motherhood for work that I hated in order to earn a desperately needed paycheck, it would have been different. But I loved my job—so much so that it hardly ever felt like work. I loved the balance that working gave me. I loved how writing let me lead a kind of double life, attending to the realities of the quotidian world while simultaneously living in the world that existed only in my head. So I wrote when Lucy was a baby, in spite of the guilt. When Lucy started preschool, I adjusted my hours, and the sitter's, with the school year, fitting my work life around her schedule. I learned to grab time whenever I could, keeping my laptop with me so I could write if she fell asleep in the car, or while she skipped and somersaulted in Little Gym, where I became an expert at figuring out how to look up at the precise instant she'd scamper past the glass windows between the parents and the gym, then quickly go back to my screen, then look up again during her next cartwheel or flip. Work was giving me happiness and autonomy, even if it did make me an object of suspicion in a culture that preached attachment parenting and baby-wearing and co-sleeping; one that encouraged nursing on demand for as long as a kid was willing and told moms that by putting their babies in front-facing strollers instead of wearing them strapped to our backs or our chests, we were implicitly rejecting them, literally pushing them away.

By then, I also knew what to do with pain and guilt and shame and sorrow—spin them into fiction! With *Good in Bed*, I'd wanted to write honestly about weight, and screwed-up, funny families, and finding happiness in spite of it all. With *In Her Shoes*, I'd wanted to write honestly about weight and sisters; about being stuck with the label your family gave you as a girl and growing out of it, or into it, and finding happiness in spite of it all. My third book was going to dip into the realm of magical realism. It was going to be about an orphaned girl, horribly scarred, who found out that she's the descendent of Diana the huntress. I was a hundred pages in when I had Lucy, and, in short order, a new story to tell. I wanted to write honestly about motherhood. I wanted to tell the truth that the glossy magazines hadn't hinted at, the story that the advice and how-to and call-to-arms opinion pieces never mentioned. I wanted to talk about how undone I was by my baby, how unprepared, how giving birth made me a different person, how it was like a bomb erupting in the middle of my marriage, leaving carnage and resentment and distrust and guilt in its wake.

I thought about one of my favorite poems, Elizabeth Bishop's "One Art"—a villanelle, one of the first I'd learned in Professor McClatchy's class—the lines that go,

> *It's evident*
> *the art of losing's not too hard to master*
> *though it may look like (Write it!) like disaster.*

I would write it, like disaster . . . and that story, and the ones my fellow yoga moms and playgroup moms shared, became *Little Earthquakes*.

I'd always wanted at least two children, but I'd been so thoroughly shamed and undone by my initiation into motherhood that it took me years to believe that I hadn't caused Lucy irreparable harm, that I was ready to try again. Eventually, I did, and once again, I got pregnant pretty much immediately. Phoebe Pearl was born on the last day of November in 2007.

Things were different the second time. When my obstetrician, who remembered how desperately I'd wanted natural childbirth and how heartbroken I'd been about my C-section, asked if I was interested in trying for a VBAC (vaginal birth after C-section), I gave him a smile and told him that I thought I'd spent enough time in labor to last for my entire life. We pulled out our phones, loaded our calendars, and agreed on a date, and when it came I arrived at the hospital well rested and well hydrated, pedicured and waxed, and, most important, with an armada of help lined up and waiting for me at home. When Phoebe's lungs failed to clear because she hadn't been squeezed on a trip down the birth canal, and she ended up spending eighteen hours in the NICU, I refused to feel bad about not attempting a vaginal delivery. When she was diagnosed with hip dysplasia that required her to wear a wee little harness that pulled her legs up and out into a froggy sort of split, around the clock for the first three months of her life, I did not pore over the early weeks and months of my pregnancy and try to figure out whether something I'd done or eaten or neglected to do or eat had caused it. Nor did I feel guilty for refusing a "push prize" and asking instead for a doula who'd spend every night from ten p.m. to six in the morning at our house. When Phoebe woke up, Tia would bring her to me. I'd nurse her, burp her, cuddle her, then hand her off and go back to sleep.

Phoebe was a different kind of baby than her big sister, easygoing and cheerful, a good eater and a good sleeper who fell easily into the promised routine of eating, activity, then sleeping for a while, then waking up to do it again. Some of that was just her nature, the personality she was born with . . . but some of it, I have to believe, was because she had different parents than her sister: a father who was working and had his confidence and self-esteem back, and a mother who was much more forgiving and much more relaxed, a mother who wasn't a neurotic, self-loathing, guilt-ridden wreck.

Breast-feeding went much more smoothly, in part because I knew that Lucy, who'd been mostly formula-fed, was perfectly healthy and was, so far, exhibiting none of the dire effects that nursing advocates (or, as I'd come to think of them, the Nipple Nazis) promised were awaiting every child whose mother hadn't loved him or her enough to nurse exclusively; in part because I was better rested and better hydrated before my delivery, so it didn't take a week for my milk to arrive, and in part because I had lowered the bar. I knew that it wouldn't be easy or natural, and that I would need help. I had a lactation consultant work with me in the hospital and at home. I nursed Phoebe, as best I could and as frequently as I could, and when I gave her bottles of pumped breast milk or even formula, I didn't let myself feel like a failure.

As my girls have gotten older, I've been able to realize my strengths as a mother, and I've tried to forgive myself for my weaknesses. I've learned that I'm just not great with newborns . . . but give me a toddler or a preschooler, a kid who can talk, and I can spend all day chatting with them, reading them books, swimming with them, making cookies with them, whatever they require. I've learned that I don't have the patience for board games . . . but I can, when presented with an armada of stuffed animals, give them all names and personalities and individual voices, and make up adventures for them. Craft projects and beading make me want to shoot myself . . . but I love popping my girls into a kayak or a canoe and spending a day on the water.

These days, I try, in my own small way, to be a corrective to the culture that makes women feel like they're disgraces if they can't do it all by themselves, to the magazines stuffed with shots of celebrities where the kids and mom are all clean and perfectly clothed and coiffed and there's never a nanny or paid caregiver in sight. Whenever people ask about the work-life balance, or how to manage a writing career with motherhood—and, unlike male authors with young children, I get asked about it all the time—I don't lie. "I have a ton of help," I tell them. I say that I'm very lucky to be paid well for what I do, and that the money allows me to pay people well to do the things I don't want to do—the housework, the laundry, the grocery shopping—so that I can spend my time either working or being with my girls.

When Lucy was six weeks old, I was sitting cross-legged in my bed, with the baby arranged on a pillow on my left thigh, my instruction sheet on my right thigh, and my glasses slipping down my nose. As my mother regarded me dubiously, I stuck the silicone nipple shield on my breast, lifted Lucy's head, then tried to line up breast and baby and nipple shield. The trick was getting Lucy to latch on before the shield fell off, a feat I couldn't manage without either a doula or extra arms. The baby was crying. I was crying. My mother left the room, went to the kitchen, and poured me a glass of Manischewitz, a sweet kosher wine that is, along with fruity mixed drinks, the only kind of alcohol I can tolerate. "Drink this," she instructed. I drank. She looked at me and said the words I will never forget, the ones I tell to any new mother who asks me, the ones I'll repeat to my own daughters, if they have kids. "It doesn't have to be perfect," she told me. "It just needs to be good enough."

My mother did her best, and I am, for the most part, okay. I did my best, and it seems to be working . . . and if my brilliant, intense older daughter or my sweet, sunny younger one become mothers, whatever they do will be good enough, too. I only hope they won't beat themselves up the way I did, won't read a dozen different parenting books and try to adhere to the advice of each one. I hope they'll know, whether they nurse or don't nurse, work or don't work, co-sleep or baby-wear or not, that their children will grow up and walk and talk and love them. I hope they'll listen (but do any daughters listen to their mothers?) when I tell them that loving your baby is the most important thing and that, as the Talmud says, all the rest is commentary.

Never Breastfeed in a Sweater Dress, and Other Parenting Tips I Learned the Hard Way

DO NOT hate yourself if you need an epidural, if your baby needs formula, if you need a break. The object is survival and the two of you getting out alive and intact. Whatever it takes to make that happen is fine.

DO always check the diaper bag before you leave the house, and bring more diapers and clothes than you think you'll need.

DO NOT wear a sweater dress while breastfeeding. Seriously. Do not.

DO keep baby nail clippers in the car, so that when your baby falls asleep in her car seat (thus totally blowing her nap), you can at least get a few nails clipped.

DO bring earplugs when flying with a baby, as well as a small gift for the flight attendant and drink coupons for anyone stuck in the blast zone if a meltdown occurs. Remember—it's nice to appease fellow passengers, but the flight attendants are the ones you really need on your side.

DO NOT judge the mom with the screaming baby on the plane. Chances are she's already mortified and miserable, and unless she somehow snuck aboard your private jet, you agreed to take your chances when you got your ticket. Buy yourself a drink—and maybe offer her one, too. Put in your headphones. Deal.

DO understand that near-sightedness can be a gift. If you can't hire a full-time housekeeper, you can forgo the Lasik surgery and regularly wearing your glasses and/or contacts so that your entire life looks like a soft-focus Monet blur and you don't really see the dust. Or you can decide that no woman on her deathbed ever looked up at her loved ones and croaked out, "I wish I'd wiped down the floorboards."

DO NOT try to do it all yourself. Don't be a martyr. Don't stand when you can sit, don't sit when you can lie down, take a nap whenever possible, and take whatever help you're offered.

DO know that any bra can be a nursing bra, any top can be a nursing top, any stroller can be a jogging stroller, and any kid's party can be a drop-off party, if you have the courage of your convictions.

DO NOT be picky. One of my relatives was great about offering to help with my daughters, but I worried that she was too rough with them and that she wasn't following my explicit instructions about naps. One of the playgroup facilitators told me, "Your daughter is going to meet all kinds of people in her life, and they're going to treat her all kinds of ways. By letting this relative spend time with Lucy, you're teaching your daughter to learn to get along with people who aren't just like you, and to be her own advocate . . . and that's a gift." Obviously, don't entrust your kids to caregivers who are abusive or cruel, but different? Different is okay.

DO keep it in perspective. At the end of the day, these are #firstworldproblems. You and your baby are not wanting for clean water, electricity, or medication.

DO be prepared for the inevitable moment when your child sounds like a spoiled monster. When Lucy was three, I signed us up for swimming lessons at the gym in Philadelphia's gay neighborhood, and was mortified when Lu refused to get in the water. "I don't *like* this pool! I only want to swim in Provincetown!" she wailed. The handsome man swimming laps in the next lane popped his head out of the water and looked at Lucy sympathetically. "Oh, I hear that, Mary," he said.

DO NOT be surprised when the instant your kid pulls off her socks on a thirty-degree day, or you give her a sip of your iced coffee, or you hand her your iPhone to play with, someone will appear out of nowhere to judge you.

DO NOT give a new mom cute baby clothes or baby toys. She probably has enough of both. Hire someone to clean her house, or go over and tell her you're doing her laundry and do not take no for an answer. She will thank you in her prayers.

DO NOT be fooled. All of those celebrity moms who won't shut up about how "hands-on" they are, or how they'd never hire a nanny? Well, maybe they don't have nannies, but they do have an armada of assistants . . . or a live-in grandmother . . . or a sister, or a spouse who is picking up the slack. At the very least, they had people who helped them look good in those pictures.

DO tell the truth. There's still a lot of stigma around needing help and not doing it all yourself. I know it can feel shameful to talk about your nanny or sitter or how your own mother moved in with you for three months after your baby was born. Say it anyhow. Own it. You'll make it that much less painful for the next mom who ends up putting her kid in day care, or leaving the baby with Grandma for the night, or the weekend, or the week.

DO let your husband or partner help. Even if they're doing it all wrong. Even if they put the diaper on backward. Good enough is fine.

DO NOT attempt to use your kids to heal your own childhood wounds. As someone whose mother was indifferent to fashion, I was dying to give Lucy a beautiful wardrobe of brand-new clothes . . . but as soon as she was old enough to express an opinion, she made it clear that all she wanted to wear was navy-blue elastic-waist Lands' End yoga pants and T-shirts with "no words." That was it. That was all. Those sparkly, miniature lavender fleece-lined UGGs, tulle tutus, and sweet little pearl-buttoned cardigans? That was my dream. Not hers. I made peace with a child who wanted to dress like an eighties aerobics instructor and let it go.

DO take every chance you get to tell stories about your kids when they were babies, especially ones involving nudity or excretion. Thus the tale of the day I brought eighteen-month-old Phoebe to Starbucks for story time. I was waiting for my coffee when Phoebe stood in front of the window, bracing her hands on the glass. As her face reddened and an unmistakable smell filled the air, an older lady approached. "Oh, look at you! Aren't you pretty?" she crooned. "What's your name?" "POOPING!" Phoebe grunted.

DO understand that, when all is said and done, your kids are going to find something to blame you for, no matter how hard you try, and that they will grow up to be who they were destined to be, no matter what you do. A large part of this is out of your hands. Try your best, treat yourself well, and forgive yourself as frequently as possible.

Nanna on the Silver Screen

Different writers have, I imagine, different reactions the day the phone rings and it's someone—a publisher, an agent, a manager, or in my case, my brother-slash-manager—saying, "They're going to turn your book into a movie." Some writers probably think of the money or the acclaim, or how a film will secure their place in the canon or on the bestseller list. Some might dream of themselves in the audience at the Oscars, or walking the red carpet at the Hollywood premiere, or becoming BFFs with the stars. I had a different dream. What I wanted—all I wanted—was to be, for once in my life, the number one grandchild, at the top of the eight-grandkid heap, secure in my Nanna's affection

My second book, *In Her Shoes*, had been optioned shortly after its publication. I cashed the check and tried to forget about the possibility of an actual film because I knew, from my stint as a reporter covering the world of entertainment, and also from my brother, who was starting his own career as a movie producer, that the odds weren't in my favor. Most books that get published never get optioned; most books that are optioned never get turned into movies. Smart writers, I'd been instructed, take the money and get on with it.

I permitted myself maybe a single afternoon of Hollywood daydreams, banked the check, got pregnant, settled more deeply into my life in Philadelphia, and started writing something new.

Every once in a while, my brother Jake, who'd brokered the film deal, would call with an encouraging update. They want to get Susannah Grant to write the screenplay, he told me one afternoon when I was writing in my bedroom, with Wendell perched on the arm of the big chair where I worked.

"That's great," I said. Susannah Grant had written the screenplay for *Ever After*, a Cinderella update that I'd loved, and was one of the credited writers on *Erin Brockovich*, which had won Julia Roberts her Oscar. But even after Susannah Grant's services had been secured and she turned in her first draft, I was dubious. The script was brilliant—so good that there were choices that Grant made or details she'd added that I wished I'd thought to put in the novel. Still, I knew that a great screenplay could be a great beginning or the end of the road; that the executives who fell in love with the project can get fired, the director who was so hot to do the film can get busy or distracted; that the two potential leads don't have the same two months free. For a book to actually become a movie, the stars must align in a rare and perfect way . . . but, in my case, they kept lining up.

"They're asking Curtis Hanson to direct," Jake said.

"Fantastic." I had loved *L.A. Confidential*, and loved *Wonder Boys* even more, but I was six months pregnant by then, unwilling to get distracted by big-screen chatter as I tried to find the best doula in town and figure out whether she was available on my due date.

It wasn't until Jake told me that Cameron Diaz was interested in playing Maggie, the flighty party girl whose beauty hasn't kept her from feeling like she grew up, stunted, in her smart big sister's shadow, that I let myself think that it might be real. By the time I got The Call—the one announcing the first day of principal photography, which triggers the payment of the second part of the option fee, and which, more important, means that a movie is actually going to happen—I was six weeks postpartum, bloated and sleep-deprived and too tired to think of anything except how, finally, I was going to achieve one of my major life goals. Finally, I was going to get to be the number one grandchild.

The first thing I did was make one of the rare mentally healthy decisions of my life. *I told the story I wanted to tell in the book*, I told myself. *It's there, and no one can change a word of it. I had my chance to tell Rose and Maggie's story. The movie is going to be the filmmakers' chance, their chance to tell the story their way.*

I decided that if they asked for my input, I'd give it . . . but I wouldn't try to force it on them. If there were changes in the script that gave me pause, casting that I found problematic, bad wardrobe, bad music, bad whatever that led up to a bad movie, I'd just tell myself that the book was still the book, and that even a terrible movie might make more people want to read it.

The second thing I did was to call Nanna.

"Nanna!" I said. "You know how they're turning *In Her Shoes* into a movie?"

Nanna allowed as to how, indeed, she'd heard the news.

"Well! They're going to be shooting parts of it in Florida! And I'm wondering if you'd like to be an extra!"

Nanna, who was almost ninety at the time, paused. "Jenny," she began, "I'm not much of an actress."

"Oh, no. You don't have to say anything. You just have to be there."

Another pause. I held my breath. "I'll think about it," she finally said.

I'll think about it?

I was surprised, to put it mildly. If someone asked me to be in a movie, I would do it. If it was Rachel, Ronnie, Michael, or Stevie, I figured, Nanna would be in the movie, no questions asked. "Damn lesbian mother ruining everything," I told Molly, who had joined our brothers in L.A. by then and was mostly concerned about making her own on-camera appearance.

The next morning, Nanna called with the good news. "I'll do it!" she said.

At which point I got to learn an inconvenient truth about Hollywood: unless you've made special contractual arrangements, or are Philip Roth, or a writer who's a much bigger deal than I am, you do not get to dictate any aspect of the casting. Which meant that I got to enjoy some next-level begging, calling everyone I knew associated with the film and trying to make my case. *Please, it's my Nanna, and she's almost ninety years old, and if she could just appear on-screen for a minute I'd be so grateful and so happy, because I really just want to be the number one grandchild, except it's never going to happen because my mom came out of the closet and she had this awful girlfriend who sounded like Marge Simpson's sisters, and . . .*

Okay, okay, someone finally told me. Nanna's in.

Molly shot her scene first, on a soundstage in L.A., where she played a secretary in Rose Feller's law firm. When the film-makers asked if I wanted to be an extra, Molly told me to go for it. "It's really fun!" she promised. "And it's your book! You should be a part of it!" The night before I was set to report to the street in Philadelphia where they were shooting, Molly called with her expert counsel. "Okay, do NOT do your hair and makeup. They'll have people who do that, and if you go in all made up they'll just have people who do that, and if you go in all made up they'll just have to wash it off your face."

Excellent, I thought. To this day, I am famously inept with makeup. I never got the hang of eyeliner, either crayon or liquid or liquid-to-powder or gel; never mastered the application of fake lashes to augment my own stubby ones; I never knew, until I was an embarrassing way into my twenties, that you were sup-posed to do something with your eyebrows other than lament their failure to resemble the tidy arches you saw in magazines. I can do lip stuff—lip balm, lip gloss, even, if I'm very careful, lipstick. Other than that, I'm lost . . . so, I was glad and relieved that the movie would offer professional help.

Early the next morning, I found myself standing in an empty Mexican restaurant, hair uncombed, face bare, in a throng of perhaps two hundred Philadelphians, looking around in vain for hair and makeup assistance. Of which there appeared to be none. Even though it was three in the morning, her time, I called my sister. "Molly!" I hissed. "There's no hair and makeup here!"

"Oh," she yawned. "Well, maybe that's because I was a featured extra and you're just background."

Thus, in what will probably be the only book-to-film adaptation of my work, you can see me for a span of ten seconds, walking alongside my agent, looking like a naked mole rat who's just wandered in from a windstorm. Joanna and I are strolling behind Toni Collette and Brooke Smith in the Italian Market scene. We're carrying shopping bags. Between takes, we discussed our motivation. I decided that we were shopping for broccoli and we were going to make broccoli soup for a crowd of our vegan friends, then concentrated on making Joanna, who was, at the time, between homes, break character. "Joanna!" I said as the cameras rolled, "when we met all those years ago, did you ever imagine that you'd be living in a van down by the river?"

Then it was time to fly to Florida for Nanna's feature film debut.

It started like the coming-out-of-the-closet trip. I got off the plane and into the humidity, this time without my sister but with baby Lucy in tow. Fran and Nanna were in Nanna's Camry at the curb. By six o'clock, the baby and I were stowed in the backseat, and the complaining commenced. "Do you know what time my call is?" Nanna demanded. "They want me on set at six a.m.!"

Part of me was bemused to hear my grandmother, who'd lived her entire life in Detroit and its suburbs and then in a retirement community outside of Fort Lauderdale, dropping the Hollywood lingo like she was the reincarnation of Army Archerd. I was also amused by her objection to the early-morning obligation, given that Nanna does not sleep. I know this because years ago my sister and I went on a Carnival Cruise with Nanna. In a berth that felt about as large as an airplane lavatory, Molly and I would lie on our bunk beds and listen as, at four-thirty in the morning (sometimes five), Nanna began the day's activities: moving her belongings from one crinkly plastic bag to another while conversing with her late husband, Herman, in Yiddish.

My mother and I assured her that we'd wake her up in time. We had dinner late—six-thirty. We went back to Nanna's place in Century Village and watched a little *Raymond*. (Even though I know it can't be true, I am convinced that there's a channel in Florida that plays nothing but *Everybody Loves Raymond* reruns.) At nine, Nanna bid us goodnight, then tried to slip into her bedroom and close the door behind her.

"Where are you going?" I asked.

"It's none of your business," she said, with the cordless phone in her hand.

"Who are you calling?"

"None of your business, stinker!" she said. "You'll put it on the computer!" I had a blog, at the time, which Nanna referred to as "the computer." She lived in fear of me putting her words "on the computer" while remaining strangely untroubled about showing up in my books. "If you must know, I am calling the sheriff's office."

"Why," I asked, "are you calling the sheriff's office?"

"Oh, they call me every morning."

"Why do they do that?" As soon as the words were out of my mouth, it dawned on me. "Nanna," I asked, caught somewhere between horror and hysterics, "are they calling to see if you're still alive?"

She drew herself up to her full five feet two inches and gave me a frosty glare. "It's called the Call of Life," she said.

I bit the inside of my lip, took a steadying breath, and asked, "What happens if you don't answer? Like, if you're in the shower or something?"

No worries, Nanna said. "They call back!"

And what if you still don't answer?

"Jenny," said Nanna. "You know those ambulances that just drive around and around and around?" She turned toward her mirror, giving a single, satisfied nod. "Well, one of them stops."

We woke up early the next morning, got Nanna installed in the Camry, and hit the highway, heading a few exits north on I-95 until we reached the community where they were filming. As we rolled slowly down a lane lined with tents and groups of people, lights and cables and cameramen, canvas tents and paparazzi and port-o-potties, I saw Nanna's eyes get big.

"Is this all for you?" she breathed.

No, I explained. Oh, no. This is all for Cameron Diaz (whose name I was, at that point, saying as often as I could, because Nanna kept calling her Carmen Diaz).

We met a smiling, cheerful PA, who whisked Nanna off to hair and makeup. She emerged, her short white curls beautifully coiffed, her makeup tasteful and flattering. I felt my stock rise. Then came wardrobe. Nanna came out dressed in a beautiful blue-green gown. Designer label. I felt my stock rise higher.

The scene she'd been cast in was the "senior prom," where Ella, played by Shirley MacLaine, danced with her suitor, with both of her granddaughters, Cameron Diaz and Toni Collette, looking on. The room they were using was filled to capacity with the actors and the extras, the camera and light and microphone operators, the director and his assistant and the hair and makeup people, taking up every available inch of space. I waited outside, holding baby Lucy and watching on a monitor. Nanna sat at a table for ten, in profile, her folded arm resting on the tablecloth, a heavy bracelet of gold links at her wrist. Outside, watching take after take on the monitors, I saw, with relief, that she was in every one. Uncuttable. Which was good news, because how awkward would it have made the holidays to have to try to explain to Nanna that she'd been left on the cutting-room floor?

After an hour, the director called, "That's a wrap! Moving on!" I slipped into the building, stepping carefully over the cables and behind the cameras until I reached Nanna's table. She got to her feet and she hugged me hard, whispering, "I am so proud of you!" in my ear. Then she turned to the roomful of people—the director, the stars, the cameramen and the boom mic operator, the hair and makeup ladies, with their leather holsters full of hairspray and brushes, and announced, "Everyone! This is my granddaughter, the author!"

It was one of the best days of my life. Not only that, but I knew, for that one brief and shining moment in time, that I was, unquestionably, the number one grandchild.

Of course, six weeks later Cousin Rachel had a baby, sending me right back down to the number five slot. But the buzz and excitement for the movie continued to build. Each week, it seemed, *People* and *Us Weekly* would publish pictures from the set, while the more serious publications put MacLaine on their short list of potential Best Supporting Actress Oscar nominees.

Best of all, I got to escort Nanna to Los Angeles as one of my dates for the Hollywood premiere, along with my mom, my siblings, and Nanna's baby brother Freddy (then a youthful eighty-seven) and his wife, Ruth, who drove down from San Francisco for the weekend.

The studio flew me out to Los Angeles and hired someone to tend to my hair and makeup—which, let me assure you, is something you really want if you are planning on being in photos with Cameron Diaz. Or, you know, in the same room or zip code or country as Cameron Diaz. The makeup artist was friendly and sweet, and we got to talking, and I asked if I could hire her for the rest of the afternoon to do my mom and my sister and my Nanna. "Sure," she said. "No problem!"

She finished Molly first, coaxing my sister's long, dark brown hair into beachy waves and doing a dramatic smoky eye. Nanna took her all of ten minutes (Nanna has a very definite sense of how she wants her makeup to look). Then the makeup lady turned her gaze toward my mother, who smiled back, bare of face, unplucked of eyebrow, short and gray of hair.

"Ooh, blank canvas!" she said. "Can I play?"

"Sure," said my easygoing mom.

The makeup artist unlatched an aluminum suitcase full of tools, brushes, pots of powder, palettes of eye shadows. She mixed, then airbrushed foundation onto my mom's face. She lined her eyes and applied false eyelashes, painted her lips and contoured her cheeks and teased her half inch of hair into a stylishly tousled cap. With her face painted, her hair styled, in a black dress and sheer black hose and, for once, shoes that were neither orthopedic nor sneakers, my mother looked objectively amazing.

As it turned out, we weren't the only ones who thought so.

We rode in the studio-provided limousine to Grauman's Chinese Theatre. We walked the red carpet as flashbulbs flared, exploding in a blinding fusillade, and reporters shouted questions. We watched *In Her Shoes*. ("It was excellent" was Uncle Freddy's review. "I didn't fall asleep once!") Then it was time for the afterparty, which was held at Spago.

It was a scene—there's no other way to say it—straight out of a movie. Waiters circulated with hors d'oeuvres, bits of sushi and miniature cheesesteaks that had been flown in from Philadelphia. Shirley MacLaine held court in a booth in the middle of the restaurant, posing for photographs and talking at length with Nanna. There was music and toasts and excited chatter . . . and then the unbelievable happened: a man asked for my mother's phone number.

I don't remember who he was—only that he was connected to the film in some professional capacity, that he and my mother had been enjoying a pleasant conversation, and that, at some point, he asked if he could get the digits. Startled, my mother looked at him and blurted something to the effect of *I am a gay lesbian American woman in a committed relationship!* (In my retelling, the guy just shrugged—this being L.A.—and said, "Can I watch?")

My mom told my sister-in-law. My sister-in-law told my brother Jake. Jake told Joe. Joe told Molly. Molly told me. By the end of the night, we were all outside, waiting for the Town Car to arrive and laughing at this surprising turn of events. *Oh my God. Can you even believe it!?*

All of us were laughing except Nanna. Nanna was not laughing. Nanna was regarding her difficult daughter with a gimlet eye and poking one perfectly manicured index finger into the flesh of my mother's upper arm. "You see that, Frances? You see? If you'd just wear a little lipstick, you could get right back in the game!"

A few years ago, I did a fund-raising event for a women's shelter on Cape Cod. There were four authors there, all of whom had had their books turned into movies—me, Claire Cook, Jacquelyn Mitchard, and Alice Hoffman. At the beginning of the afternoon, once we'd all arrived, the organizer announced her plan to show a brief snippet of each film, then have us comment on the experience of seeing our book make its way to the big screen.

First came a scene from *The Deep End of the Ocean.* Jackie Mitchard spoke graciously about the unbelievable good fortune of not only having her book chosen as Oprah Winfrey's inaugural pick, but having it turned into a film with Michelle Pfeiffer. Next, a bit from *Must Love Dogs.* Claire Cook told a story about writing her first book in her minivan during her daughter's swim practices, and how included in the process the filmmakers had

made her feel, inviting her onto the set, even giving her a director's chair monogrammed with her name. The scene from *In Her
Shoes* was one with Nanna, so I got to talk about her stint as an
extra. Finally, the organizers played the clip from *Practical Magic*,
a scene in which a drunk and rowdy Nicole Kidman and Sandra
Bullock traipse around the kitchen in their nightgowns, dancing
and singing "Put de lime in de coconut." The lights came up. The
audience looked expectantly toward the stage. Alice Hoffman
leaned into the microphone. Eyes narrowed, she bit off each syllable as she said, "I FUCKIN' HATED that movie!"

If more writers were really honest, Alice Hoffman–level
honest, there would be, I imagine, a lot less carefully temporized
"I wanted it to be the filmmaker's story to tell" and a lot more "I
fucking hated that movie." I think of some of my favorite books
(*Shining Through*, *A Prayer for Owen Meany*), and the botches
that Hollywood has made of them. I knew—how could I not?—
that by signing the rights to *In Her Shoes* away, there was risk
involved, risk that the movie wouldn't look anything like what
I imagined, that it wouldn't reflect the heart or the soul of the
story I'd set out to tell.

The experience of translating *In Her Shoes* from book to film,
up to the week of its release, had been as close to perfect as any
novelist had a right to hope for. Were there quibbles? Of course. I
wish Toni Collette had found a way to gain more weight and look
more like Rose as I'd imagined her. When Collette was cast I was
thrilled, because I knew she had no problem, physically or mor-
ally, with playing the big girl. She'd gained weight for her star-
making turn in *Muriel's Wedding*, which made her the next best
thing to a genuinely right-size woman—at least she was willing
to be the right size temporarily.

Unfortunately, she'd just finished making a movie where she
was playing a grief-stricken mother. The part had required her
to be practically emaciated and, unlike those of us whose natural

gifts include the ability to gain weight just by thinking about dessert, she struggled mightily to put on even a handful of pounds for *In Her Shoes*. For a while, I was getting updates from the West Coast. "She's gained five pounds!" they'd tell me. Whoopee, I'd think. "She's gained ten pounds!" they'd say. So have I, I'd quip. Just since this phone call started. Seriously, guys, does she need me to go out there and give her lessons? Somebody tell her about doughnuts! She made it to fifteen pounds. Then things got quiet. Finally I got the call I'd been expecting but dreading: "She's hit the wall."

"What wall?" I asked Susan. "There's a wall? I've never found a wall!"

But these were minor issues, especially given what could have gone wrong. The filmmakers could have cut out the explicitly Jewish aspects of the story. They didn't. They could have eliminated the senior-citizen characters, reasoning that the over-seventy set isn't buying as many tickets as young men. They didn't do that, either. They didn't turn Maggie's dyslexia into something showier, or have her growth emblemized by something more visual than reading. There are men in *In Her Shoes*, but it's a story about sisterly love, and also the love of books, of stories, the redemptive power of words. That's not an easy thing to show in a movie, and the filmmakers pulled it off.

In Her Shoes, the book, came out in the fall of 2002. The film rights sold fast, the stars aligned, the actors and director and screenwriter signed on, and the movie was ready to go by the fall of 2005 . . . which, in film-land, where projects can advance and retreat toward completion for years, is an almost unheard-of pace. The speed, the ease, the excellence of the director and the screenplay and the cast, not to mention how much fun I'd had with my family, had all conspired to make me believe that this would be, from start to finish, completely positive, an unmitigated joy.

The first hint I got that the experience might be something other than complete and total bliss was when my brother called to say that the "tracking" indicated that the movie would likely finish in third place at the box office its opening weekend, behind *Flightplan* and a new *Wallace and Gromit* cartoon.

"What's tracking?"

Jake patiently explained that tracking involved polling people to ask about their potential interest in seeing a film.

"What can I do?"

See if you can rally your readers, Jake advised . . . and I did.

Then came the reviews. Many were positive. A few were puzzled, or even outright hostile, that a respected director like Curtis Hanson would lower himself to truck with a chick flick. Some of the critics took aim at my book, in ways I still find incomprehensible—I know what "glib" and "masochistic" mean on their own, but was bewildered when the *New York Times'* Manohla Dargis described my characters that way. *Girlie trash* seemed to be the minority opinion . . . and for the most part, despite my get-out-the-viewer campaign on my blog, the filmgoers stayed home.

I felt guilty and sick to my stomach for the three weeks that the movie was in theaters, weeks during which the producer, with whom I'd become, if not friends, then at least friendly, apparently lost my number. More than anything, though, I was unprepared. I'd readied a suit of armor to wear if the movie turned out to be a disappointment; if it betrayed the spirit of my story; if, instead of a plump dog walker and her stunning sister in search of a connection to their long-lost mom, the film was about a pair of hot stripper-sisters on a road trip to Vegas in search of another hot stripper. I was ready for that. I wasn't ready for a really good movie that flopped in spite of its excellence.

Writers get asked the same questions a lot. *Where do you get your ideas?* is number one with a bullet, *What time of day do you write?* and *What kind of laptop do you use?* and *Could you introduce me to your agent?* are also top ten. "Do you think they'll make another one of your books into a movie?" is one I hear a lot. My go-to response is a shrug and a smile and a few practiced phrases about how a bunch of them have been optioned and, hey, anything could happen, and with Hollywood, you just never know. A slightly more honest answer is to explain that the filmmakers did such an amazing job with *In Her Shoes* that I'd be worried that subsequent experiences could only disappoint. More honest than that is explaining that, because the film didn't make money, nobody in Hollywood is breaking down doors to bring anything else of mine to the big screen. The part I don't talk about, because I think the very definition of ungracious is to complain about the movie that got made of your book, is how hard it was to live through; how I felt like I personally was disappointing people, that my work was damaging their reputations, that I was tainting their profiles or their legacies with my girlie tales about mothers and daughters and sisters. I am in no rush to live through that specific hell again. Let someone else climb aboard the Tilt-A-Whirl, I think sometimes, let someone else take that ride.

These days, a movie's life doesn't end when it leaves the theater. There are many different ways for viewers to find a film, and the business of criticism has become livelier and more fluid. At the end of 2005, *Entertainment Weekly*'s Owen Gleiberman put *In Her Shoes* on his list of the ten best movies of the year, and viewers kept finding the film—on airplane screens, on cable, on DVD.

Whenever it's on TV—and it seems to happen a few times a year—I'll get tweets and Facebook posts from people telling me how they loved the movie, how they watch it with their sister, how they used the e. e. cummings poem from the book at their own wedding. It was fun and heartbreaking, and there were moments of triumph and joy and moments of disappointment and sorrow. Kind of like life. And, of course, the book is still the book, and the book is still in print, and available for downloading. The movie, and the experience of it, didn't change a word.

Appetites

Years ago, an interviewer asked the writer Grace Paley whether she considered her novels political. Paley, I imagined, gave her interlocutor a long and level stare before answering, "I write about women. So, yes."

Nobody's ever once asked me whether I consider my novels political. And I can see why: they come with pink covers, adorned with shoes and women's body parts; their tone tends toward the breezy, and they always have happy endings, because I think that real life gives real people enough sad ones. But if someone ever were to ask the question, I would point out that, in my books, it's fat women getting the guy, getting the great job, getting the big success, getting all of it, sometimes, at once. Are my books political? I give plus-size women happy endings. And, in today's America, that is a political, even a radical, act.

Disclaimer: I am not a doctor. I am not a therapist. I am not even a talk-show host qualified to dispense healthy living and body-image advice. What I am is a size-sixteen-and-mostly-okay-with-it woman who's read many women's magazines, studied a number of dress-for-your-shape tutorials, digested several—okay, more than several—self-help books, and also spent her entire adult life living in a larger body. During which time I have dated, gotten married (TWICE!), had babies, participated in sprint-distance triathlons, hundred-mile bike rides and ten-mile runs, wrote a bunch of books, and enjoyed myself . . . a lot.

Getting here was, as they say on *The Bachelor*, a journey. I spent most of my twenties on a diet—an entire decade spent measuring out my life, not in coffee spoons but in four-ounce portions of chicken breast and half-cup servings of pasta. I did Weight Watchers, Atkins, and South Beach; low-carb and no-carb. I worked with a private nutritionist for six months, paying a very nice young woman to encourage me to eat frozen grapes instead of cookies and to weigh me once a week. I was part of a clinical trial of one of the drugs that was eventually marketed as part of fen-phen, the successful weight-loss medication eventually yanked off the market after the women who took it started having heart attacks.

Like a great many women in America, I can look at any food—an apple, a hard-boiled egg, a scoop of ice cream—and tell you how many calories it has, how many of them are from carbs, how many are from fat, and probably how many Weight Watchers points it is worth. I tell people that I'm bad with numbers and hopeless at science, but I can talk for hours about engineered foods and the evils of white carbs and high-fructose corn syrup and can instantly calculate how many miles on the treadmill correspond to any given dessert.

None of that knowledge helped. None of my diets worked—at least, not in the long term. I'd lose fifteen or twenty pounds, keep it off for a little while, and then those pounds would come back, and sometimes they'd bring their friends. And, of course, with weight comes shame. In spite of my professional accomplishments, in spite of how full and rich and interesting my life was, I felt like a failure. *Why can't I get this under control?* I would think . . . and, inevitably, *if I could just lose ten, twenty, thirty, forty pounds, then I'd have everything I wanted. Then I'd be happy. Then I'd deserve to be happy. The size I am now, I don't deserve to be happy, I don't deserve to be loved, I don't deserve good things . . . but when I'm thin, then I will.*

I can't blame myself for feeling that way. The books I'd grown up on, the shows and movies I'd absorbed as if through osmosis, the advertisements and images that wallpapered my life, all told me the same thing: *fat women deserve nothing*. Fat women are hideous, punch lines, grotesqueries, jokes, and they qualify for nothing good that the world has to offer.

Of course, that isn't true. There is no magic weight, no magic size, no magic number on the scale where, as soon as you hit it, confetti rains down and a band starts to play and hidden doors slide open and Daniel Craig walks through them to lift you in his arms (because, thin as you are, he totally can) and carry you into the life of uninterrupted bliss that you just know could be yours, if you only wore a size two dress.

Life is what happens when you're busy making other plans, the saying goes. For too many women, I think that life is what happens when you're planning on, or trying to, lose weight. *As soon as I lose ten/twenty/forty/eighty pounds, then I'll buy that dress/take that trip/wear a bathing suit/go dancing. But not until. I don't deserve fun, or pretty, nice things. I don't belong in the world at my size.*

So you don't buy the pretty dress to fit your current body— because why spend money on something that won't fit your new, theoretical thin self? You choke down chalky SnackWell's cookies (remember those?) or frozen Atkins meals or green juice or cabbage soup, and deny yourself the foods you really want to eat. You don't swim or wear shorts or sleeveless shirts because you don't want people looking at the body you've been taught to think of as an offense, an affront. You get used to never seeing anyone who resembles you, anywhere—not on Broadway, in the movies, in the magazines, on TV, not unless she's a punch line, or a sidekick, or maybe the "before" on one of those radical weight-loss shows. You make love with the lights off, which has, if you're like me, probably resulted in more than one elbow-to-eye-socket injury and maybe even the words no woman ever wants to say— "um, you need to move that up a few inches." When you read the celebrity tabloids, you skip over the shots of starlets in their evening gowns, but linger over reports of what they eat in a day and wonder if you, too, committed to a regimen of hot lemon juice and vinegar and dinners of sashimi and spiraled zucchini then you could look that good. You deprive yourself until you're weak, faint, embarrassing yourself by drooling every time an Applebee's commercial comes on. Then you cram whatever's handy down your throat, and you don't even taste it, and you eat more of it than you'd intended, and you hate yourself even more. Rinse, repeat. Forever. No matter how old you get, no matter how successful you are, how much you earn, or what kind of good you do in the world, you're not allowed to stop. If you're fat, you've lost the game. If you're thin, you win—only thin is a moving target, always receding into the distance, growing ever smaller, and you are never allowed to stop trying to hit it.

Except—as it turns out—you can make peace with a larger body. I did. And I am here to tell you that life on the other side is pretty solid.

For me, it was a gradual change.

Maybe it started when I went to see Margaret Cho. She was doing her stand-up act at Rutgers—talking about her mother, talking about her childhood, talking about her failed ABC sitcom where executives told her she was too fat to play the part of herself. "You know what?" she asked. "Being thin is like trying to hold a basketball underwater." You can do it, she implied, but at what cost? And what else could you be doing with all that strength, all that time, all that effort, that you were focusing on the ultimately pointless task of keeping the basketball submerged?

By the 1990s, there was an increasing body of research that showed, conclusively, what Cho suggested and what almost anyone who's been on the Weight Watchers merry-go-round can tell you: diets don't work. Losing weight, it turns out, is the easy part. It's just like every online commentator is ever so happy to explain—you take in fewer calories than you burn. But keeping it off is harder—is, in fact, almost impossible—because when you lose weight your body decides you're living through something cataclysmic, like a famine or a war, and that it needs to hang on to every calorie you can give it. So your metabolic rate drops, which means you've got to eat less—in some cases, a *lot* less—to maintain your loss than a person who'd spent her whole life at that weight. In the stories I read, people who'd dieted off significant amounts of weight and kept it off described that feat as a full-time job. They logged every mouthful in a journal, they measured their portions precisely, they exercised, up to two hours every day, and they could never relax their vigilance, not even for a weekend.

Did I want to live like that? Did I want "thin" to be my job? Wasn't there more important work that I could do? By my late twenties, I had spent a solid ten years obsessing about my weight. I worked out regularly, because I liked being strong and fit and flexible, and because a session at the gym always left me feeling better than I'd felt when I walked in . . . but I decided that I was done with diets. If that meant I'd narrowed my fashion options or the size of the pool of men who'd want to date me, so be it. I didn't need every man in the world to love me . . . I needed only one.

I dated as a larger woman, fell in love, got engaged, and loosened my grip on the reins a little bit. I'd found a good man who loved me, just as I was . . . so maybe it wasn't unthinkable that he'd love me even if there were a few pounds more to love? We both enjoyed good food, and we had the money to spend on great restaurants, or on cooking great meals . . . and both of those things, it turned out, were much more fun than those Weight Watchers meetings, where members tried to convince each other that a sliced apple was an acceptable, even delicious, substitute for cake.

I got married in a plus-size wedding gown (note to bridal-gown designers—if ever there was a garment for which "vanity sizing" would be appropriate, yours would be it). I went on book tours and felt fine—after all, I was famous, or at least book-famous, for creating plus-size heroines who got happy endings in spite of their bodies. It wouldn't do for me to show up skinny, right?

Then, when I was thirty-three, I got pregnant. This was the moment I'd been waiting for ever since I'd learned where babies came from, because A) I wanted a baby, and B) I'd finally have an explanation for my appetite and a permission slip to eat, at last, to my heart's content. For the first time in my adult life, I could just focus on what my body was doing, not on how it looked.

Big mistake. Huge.

And so, at last, here were brownies, deliciously dense; crisp-skinned roast chickens and meltingly tender sugar-roasted pork; voluptuous sea-salt caramels and dark-chocolate-covered pretzels. There were hoagies and banh mi and baked brie; there was cornbread and fritters and fried dough.

I gained a lot of weight when I was pregnant—to this day, I don't know how much, because I refused to look at the scale when they weighed me at my checkups. Then, after I had Lucy, I gained even more.

I'd always been bigger (and, more to the point, hungrier) than most of the women I knew. I'd grown up watching people leave plates half full, declining snacks, even skipping meals, and I'd never been able to understand it. *How can you just leave that there? Aren't you going to finish it? Aren't you still hungry?* I was always hungry. It was like I'd been born without an "off" switch.

I'd never known what it was to feel that I'd eaten enough. I'd been unable to follow that long-ago nutritionist's advice about just getting used to being "a little bit hungry all the time." I hated being hungry. Nor could I imagine a circumstance that couldn't be improved by the addition of something delicious.

These were different circumstances, though. This was a different hunger. I was eating not to feel, piling food on top of emotions I couldn't handle, using ice cream and cookie dough to tamp down the misery of failing as a mother, and my fears about whether my husband would find another job, what it meant for our financial situation and our marriage if he couldn't and if all of the financial and child-rearing responsibilities ended up being mine. Food was my answer to everything. Bad day? Have a cannoli. Irrational terror about going broke and ending up homeless? Have two. Sleepless night, cranky baby, not even thirty seconds of privacy in which to change my tampon? That's why God made foie gras.

By the time Lucy was two, the first number on the scale was a 3 . . . and I was scared. I couldn't lose the weight that I'd gained, because I'd never been able to lose weight and keep it off, so why would this time be different? My blood pressure and cholesterol were both edging into the danger zone, and I was sure that diabetes, which runs on both sides of my family, was just around the corner . . . except, like many fat women, I was skipping checkups, too afraid of going to the doctor and getting the inevitable what-are-you-doing-about-your-weight talk to find out.

I was stuck. On the one hand, I did not believe that my worth resided in my appearance; I knew that there had to be a way to live happily in the body that I had. But I didn't feel good. I longed for the days when I'd been "just" a size sixteen. I didn't want to be thin, I just wanted my old, Jen-size body back . . . only now there was a way to get it, a way that worked.

I'd been initially repelled by the idea of weight-loss surgery; grossed out, specifically, by the former girl-band member who'd once been my size, then had her stomach stapled, and was suddenly showing up in *Playboy*, and on the cover of *People*, with her entire body slipped into the leg of her size-twenty-eight jeans, and talking about how, for the first time in her life, she felt pretty and sexy and desirable. I felt personally betrayed. Wasn't she supposed to have felt pretty and sexy at her former size? Wasn't she carrying the banner for the rest of us big girls? Who would carry our banner now?

I was deeply conflicted . . . but, surreptitiously, I bought her book and began studying the surgery. I went online, browsing before-and-after pictures, reading stories about people who said that, for the first time in their lives, they knew what it was to feel full. And they were able to keep the weight off that they lost. It sounded like a dream come true.

I researched for months and found the best surgeon in the state, who told me that I could expect to lose about a hundred pounds, a figure that would put me back in the neighborhood where I'd spent most of my twenties. I attended the practice's here's-how-you'll-be-eating-now classes, memorized the binder they gave me, resigned myself to always having protein first, turning bread into a special treat, and knowing I'd get sick if I had too much sugar. I tried not to feel like a hypocrite, telling myself that I was doing this for my health—so I'd be able to get down on the floor comfortably when I was playing with Lucy, so I wouldn't leave her motherless too soon.

It's true that some of my decision was motivated by health and comfort . . . but some of it was caving in to external pressure, to everything the world said about larger bodies. Maybe, if I'd been stronger or happier, I could have figured out how to be in the world at a size twenty-eight instead of a sixteen; how to deal with not fitting into airplane seats or not being able to buy clothes at even the plus-size shops at the mall; how to let it roll off my back when snarky local bloggers posted pictures of me at my heaviest to illustrate posts about what a wonderful guy my husband was and how could he stand being married to *her*?

I could have tried harder . . . but I was so beaten down, so tired of fighting, so sick of my weight and my size being one of the preoccupying issues of my life. I didn't want to be skinny, or pose in a men's magazine, or worm my way into a cast-off plus-size pant leg. I wanted to have a normal appetite and my old body back. I wanted to take the issue of weight off the table. I wanted to know, for once in my life, how it felt to have enough, and for reasons science didn't entirely understand, people who had weight-loss surgery had much better luck at reducing their risks of diabetes, and at keeping the pounds off, than the dieters. I wanted something that worked, instead of the screw-you yo-yo of losing weight and then gaining it back, and losing it and gaining it. Again.

I had the operation in January 2006, and woke up in the recovery room feeling like I'd done ten thousand sit-ups, then had my midsection run over by a bus. I was lucky that I didn't have any complications and that I was still, in my heart, the A student who'd do what it took to get a gold star. I followed the rules, subsisting, first, on protein shakes, gradually reintroducing bites of soft-boiled eggs and lean protein into my diet. I walked laps around the hospital floor as soon as they let me out of bed, and went back to the gym as soon as I was home. There was trial and error, and so much throwing up those first few months after I ate the wrong foods, or even too much of the right ones, that it barely even bothered me when it happened. Eventually, I got to the point where I could eat almost everything, in moderate portions—a piece of bread here; a few forkfuls of dessert there. Best of all, for the first time ever, I had an off switch. I knew what it felt like to be full, to say, *No thanks, I've had enough*, and mean it, to leave food behind and not make plans to run back when nobody was looking and gobble it down.

At the end of the first year, the period during which most weight-loss surgery patients lose the majority of their weight, I'd shed almost exactly the amount my surgeon told me I could expect. I was back to my pre-wedding, pre-baby body, back to being a size sixteen, sometimes able to fit into the so-called "straight" sizes, sometimes shopping in the plus section. I could eat normally for the most part. I wasn't thin . . . but it didn't matter. Taking things further would have involved preoccupation and effort—keeping the basketball down. Where I'd ended up, I decided, was fine, and probably where my body was meant to be all along . . . and in the decade since the operation, that's where my weight has stayed.

I committed to the new rules of eating. I exercised for an hour a day most days of the week. I ate my protein first. For the first time in years, I studied my body in the mirror, letting myself look at what the weight gain and loss and pregnancy and surgeries had left me with—my belly, jiggly and soft, cross-stitched with silvery stretch marks and scars, my thighs, muscular underneath a solid and seemingly immobile layer of cellulite, breasts and upper arms that both appeared to be subject to a more stringent gravity than the rest of me. It was nothing you'd pay to see in *Playboy* . . . but it was mine, and I knew that I'd have to make peace with it.

I committed to turning off the voice in my head, or at least turning down its volume, when it told me that I was too fat to deserve happiness. I was a mother now, the mother of a daughter. I wasn't just responsible for myself and my own body issues—I was at least partially responsible for the way Lucy would grow up seeing the world and her own place within it.

I thought about how the symbolism and rhetoric of dieting did or did not fit into a feminist framework. If feminism's goal is for women to be more present in the world, to step up and be counted as equals and (politely and firmly but never ever shrilly or stridently) ask for what is ours, what kind of sense would it make for me to spend time and money trying, literally, to diminish myself, to take up less space, to make myself ever smaller? How would working out feel if I shifted the focus from *I wish I were thinner* to *I want to be stronger*? What would it be like to just set that burden down and never pick it up again and just live, as best I could, in the body that I had?

I worked on it. I practiced following every negative, self-critical thought with a positive one. *My legs look strong*, I'd think, after noticing that I was, once again, the biggest person in barre class. Or *I'm getting a lot more comfortable in these poses*, I would say, after noticing that I was also the biggest person at Bikram yoga. I would try to reframe my body in terms of what it could do, not whether it was aesthetically pleasing to strangers I'd pass on the street, even in the face of skepticism and intractable societal norms (after I had completed a four-day, two-hundred-mile bike ride, the first thing one of my coworkers asked was "How much weight did you lose doing that?"). I would remind myself that it's not my job to give erections to random men on the Internet, and that if strangers don't like the way I look, they can exercise their option of not looking.

Baby steps. I wore a sleeveless dress. On TV. People tweeted about what a pretty color it was, not about my upper arms looking like pans of dough on their first rising. At a friend's urging, I trained for a sprint-distance triathlon, and not only lived to tell the tale but was one of the first women in my age group out of the water (best part—looking over at a fellow swimmer and thinking that she was topless, with extremely hairy nipples, before realizing that I'd swum all the way up to the men's group). I made a point of looking at larger bodies on the Internet—models, athletes, fashion bloggers, other writers—until I'd shifted the needle of *normal* in my own head. (Science shows that this works. The more larger bodies, older bodies, real-people-in-the-real-world bodies you see, the more you move your own needle of what constitutes "normal.")

Day by day, inch by inch, it's gotten to the point where I can mostly live my life in the body I have, and, for the most part, enjoy it.

Not that it's perfect. I have days where I catch a glimpse of my face reflected in an iPad's black screen and shudder. I still spend too much time and money trying to look, if not like a model in a magazine, then at least my best. I've tried Botox. I color my hair and wax my legs and pay for someone to paint my toenails and glue fake lashes to my real ones (my argument is that they make it look like I'm wearing makeup when I'm not, thus saving time, money, and effort). I resent the time I spend on my hair and makeup and the shapewear I squeeze myself into before television appearances and public events—men, I suspect, don't require much more than powder and a comb—but I do it anyhow. I can't walk into a Sephora without dropping at least fifty dollars on whatever miracle serum or lotion or anti-aging crème they're promoting, and when the Cape Air representatives ask me how much I weigh so they can balance the passengers on the nine-seat plane, I rapidly run through the benefits of absolute honesty versus the potential of the plane going down if I shave fifteen (twenty) pounds off the number.

But most days I'm, if not happy, then reasonably content. What I've learned will be familiar to any woman who's ever worried about her weight—which is to say, all women. There's nothing revolutionary here . . . but my daughters' pediatrician once told me that, sometimes, to get a kid to eat a vegetable, you have to put it on her plate ten times. Ten times, before she'll consider taking a bite. Maybe it's the same with self-acceptance—you have to see the same chestnuts and platitudes repeated over and over before they land.

Maybe this, right here, will be someone's tenth time. Maybe there's some eighteen-year-old who will read this and not have to waste the next decade of her life hating herself . . . or a new mother who will decide to focus on her new baby and her growing family instead of her stretch marks and her belly . . . or a woman somewhere who will decide to go for that bike ride, take that new job, smile at that cute guy, because maybe, just maybe, she's fine, right now, just as she is.

A Few Words About Bodies

Weight and Diet

You are never as fat as you think you are.

Seriously, you're not.

Ten years from now you will look at pictures of yourself and think, "God, I was so thin." (You will also wonder what you were doing with your hair and clothing, but that's neither here nor there.)

Nobody is judging you as harshly as you're judging your own body. Wartime tribunals do not judge murderers and spies as harshly as you're judging your own body.

The phrase "horror show" can properly be applied to a late-night airing of *Saw*. Not to your thighs or anyone else's.

When you feel insecure, follow the money. Which people and industries profit when women hate themselves?

Every time you judge another woman's appearance, an angel gets a gallstone.

Every time you think evil things about yourself, your daughters can hear.

Yes, even if you just think it.

Yes, even if you don't have daughters.

Unless you are an actual supermodel, it is not your job to look like a supermodel. Similarly, unless you are a porn star, you need not devote hours of your time and thousands of your dollars to looking like one.

Thinness is not a job requirement. Nor are perfect beachy waves, poreless skin, or a jiggle-free midriff. Can you do your work? Are you hurting anyone? Are you as present as possible for the people who need you? If the answers are yes and no and yes again, then you're just fine, as is, right now.

Understand that being out in the world, with billboards, magazines, and the Internet bombarding you with hundreds of images of artificially perfected women, is like exposing yourself to an ongoing low dose of radiation. It will eventually make you sick. Take preventative steps: look at real women, either in real life or online. Follow athletes and activists on Instagram, not just models and actresses. Teach yourself to see beauty in the unconventional . . . and in the women you love.

Give other women compliments. Learn to accept compliments with grace, not self-deprecation.

When you start in with the I'm-a-disaster-oh-God-look-at-my-ass, ask yourself: Would you talk to a friend that way? To your daughter? What would you say if you heard a friend talk to herself like that?

Remember Naomi Wolf's lesson: "*A culture fixated on female thinness is not an obsession about female beauty, but an obsession about female obedience. Dieting is the most potent political sedative in women's history; a quietly mad population is a tractable one.*"

Hungry women are easy to lead and easy to fool and extremely easy to sell stuff to. Diets are the tool of the patriarchy. Also the devil. And they don't work.

Remember the way you lived in your body before you learned to see only the wrong in it. Remember being a girl and how it felt to float in the bathtub, jump in mud puddles, race around the block, climb trees, lie in bed on a hot night with a crisp cotton sheet on top of you. Think of your body as a mansion that houses your spirit, not as an unruly hedge you're constantly pruning and tending and trimming, or a bonsai tree you're trying to keep small.

Consider the money you've spent on concealer and hot rollers and SlimFast and Spanx, on paid diet programs and hair extensions and diet frozen dinners that tasted like thawed cardboard. Consider the time you've spent in step class and nutrition seminars, watching your Fitbit and cooking steamed vegetables. Imagine how you'd feel if you'd donated that money to some worthy group or cause and spent that time taking a painting class or writing poetry or adopting a dog or going for walks in the woods.

Think of exercise as a vitamin you take to ward off unhappiness. Find a sport or activity that you enjoy that gets your heart rate up, and try to do it most days of the week. Bonus points if it's something that lets you be with your friends, train toward a goal, be out in nature, or practice patience and kindness toward yourself. Try yoga, or a mud run, or open-water swimming, or riding your bike—and if none of those are for you, try something else.

Dig out all of your favorite pictures—of yourself, of your mother, your grandmother, your best friend, your bridesmaids, your sorority sisters. Please note that "favorite" does not mean "the ones where you look the thinnest." Find the shots where you look happy, put them in the prettiest frames you can find, and put them where you can see them, every single day.

Do not postpone life until ten pounds from now. Go on the trip. Wear the strapless dress. Go ziplining, or water-skiing, or swimming with the dolphins. None of us are guaranteed a future. Even a supermodel who's finally hit her goal weight could step outside and be hit by a bus. Putting off joy until you're the right size could mean you'll never experience it at all.

And remember—no woman ever said, on her deathbed, *I wish I'd eaten less cake.*

Food

There are many things that taste as good as thin feels. A partial list includes cannoli, canelés, fresh doughnuts, homemade Toll House

cookies, Korean fried chicken, samosas, saag paneer, Korean bar-
becue, o-toro sashimi, that brisket with the onion-soup mix that
my mom makes for Passover, chocolate birthday cake, English
muffins with apricot preserves, mashed potatoes, pommes frites,
and the apple dumplings with condensed-milk ice cream that
they serve at the restaurant down the street.

Learn to tell the difference between hungry and sad and angry
and bored. Honor each feeling with what it requires. Eat when
you're hungry, cry when you're sad, deal with your anger and
boredom, but don't stuff them down with food, or booze, or men,
or pills, or whatever else might be available.

Look at what you're eating for breakfast, for lunch, for dinner. Is
that what you'd feed someone you love?

Every time you choke down a protein bar in the car or eat
freezer-burned ice cream over the sink, an angel picks a fight
with her neighbor.

Use food to take care of yourself. Treat yourself like your own
guest. Boil an egg. Toast some bread. Use an actual plate. Sit in a
chair. Slow down. Taste what you're eating. Enjoy it.

If you want to eat ice cream, eat ice cream. Buy your favorite flavor.
Let it thaw to the proper creamy consistency. Scoop it into a bowl.
Sit down. Eat it with a spoon. Yes, the calories still count if you
eat supermarket-brand rocky road straight out of the cardboard
container standing in front of the freezer, so why not get the good
stuff—your favorite stuff—and really enjoy it?

Spices, like mascara, should be replaced every six months.

Always buy the best-quality chocolate that you can find.

In fact, always buy the best-quality everything that you can find.

Learning to cook is not hard, and you don't need a ton of fancy tools or exotic ingredients to feed yourself well. A few pots and pans, good knives and a cutting board, and you can put a meal on the table.

Eat as much real food as possible. If you're craving a treat and you have time, make it yourself. Want cookies? Bake your favorite variety. Enjoy the smell of the chocolate chips, the tap of the eggshells on the rim of the bowl, the slippery slide of the egg separating from the yolk, the sensation of pushing a wooden spoon through butter and sugar, the smell as the cookies bake. Put the cookies on a rack to cool, then put them on a plate, and serve with milk and a napkin. Sit, and enjoy.

Fashion

In order to look her best, every woman needs two things: good bras and a good tailor. Bras first: go to either a specialty lingerie shop, if your town or city has a good one, or a good department store (Oprah and I recommend Nordstrom). Get yourself measured. Yes, there is a bra that will fit you . . . and your clothes will look better when you've got the right bra.

A good tailor can turn your T-shirts into bodysuits so they stay tucked in; can rip out seams and sew in lace panels so the floaty white lace shirtdress that looked beautiful on the flat-as-a-board model will fit your chest, too; can shorten your jeans so you're not stepping on the hems and add snaps to wrap dresses so they're alluring without being indecent. When your clothes fit you right, they look 100 percent better.

Don't wear anything that pinches or itches or makes it hard to move or breathe—at least, not on a regular, non-special-occasion basis.

Wear what makes you happy and what feels good against your skin. If that includes busy patterns or horizontal stripes or bright colors or any of the hundreds of things that you've been told not to wear, wear them anyhow if they suit you and make you feel good.

Anything that doesn't—donate it, sell it at a consignment shop, or give it away.

No, I don't care how much you paid for it. If you haven't worn it in over a year, it needs to go.

If you don't know what makes you look beautiful, take pictures. Ask a friend. Consult the Internet and find fashion bloggers and Instagrammers with your body type. Check out their outfits of the day, how they incorporate trends, how they accessorize, what their hints are for looking your best. Look at their pictures every day, as an antidote against self-loathing, to inoculate yourself against the images you'll see all day of women who don't look like you, and the hundreds of messages you'll hear saying that your body is wrong and flawed and shameful.

Take care of yourself. Wear sunscreen, every day, on your face and your hands (one reality star whose Twitter feed I follow recommends keeping a bottle in the car so you won't forget and subject your skin to the sun that comes through the windows). Always take off your makeup before you go to bed; get your hair trimmed and colored as often as it takes for it to feel good.

Find a scent you love and wear it every day. Even if you're hanging around the house in leggings and your favorite old T-shirt (your flattering, well-made, non-holey, non-stretched-out leggings and your cute, well-cut tee), smelling delicious can make you feel well dressed.

Tell yourself you're beautiful. Even if you feel stupid saying it. Even if you can't say it out loud. Act like you believe it, even if you don't. Keep your chin up and your shoulders back, as if you are the ruler of all you survey. Carry yourself with confidence, and that's what the world will see.

The F Word

Allure, October 2012

Okay," I said to my daughter as she bent over her afternoon bowl of Cinnamon Life. "What's going on with you and J.?" J. is the ringleader of a group of third-graders at her camp—a position Lucy herself occupied the previous summer. Now she's the one on the outs, and every day at snack time, she tells me all about it, while I offer up the unhelpful advice I've been doling out all summer long. Find other girls to sit with. Ignore them. Be yourself. Be patient. It does get better.

"She's bossy," Lucy complained.

"Mmm-hmm," I said as I returned the milk to the refrigerator, thinking that my daughter can be a little on the bossy side herself.

"She's turning everyone against me," Lucy muttered, a tear rolling down her cheek. "She's mean, she's bad at math, she's terrible at kickball. And . . . she's fat."

"Excuse me," I said, struggling for calm, knowing I was nowhere in calm's ZIP code. "What did you just say?"

From the way her eyes widened, I knew that she knew she'd done what her sister, four-year-old Phoebe, called a Big Bad. "She is fat," Lucy mumbled into her bowl.

"We are going upstairs," I said, my voice cold, my throat tight. "We are going to discuss this." And up we went, my blithe, honey-blond daughter, leggy as a colt in cotton shorts and a gray T-shirt with Snoopy on the front, and her size-sixteen-on-a-good-day mom.

I'd spent the nine years since her birth getting ready for this day, the day we'd have to have the conversation about this dreaded stinging word. I had a well-honed, consoling speech at the ready. I knew exactly what to say to the girl on the receiving end of the taunts and the teasing, but in all of my imaginings, it never once occurred to me that my daughter would be the one who used the F word. Fat.

I am six years old, in first grade, and my father is hoisting—that's really the only word for it—me up into the backseat of the family's Chevy Suburban. "She's solid. She weighs sixty-five pounds," he's telling a friend. I have no idea why he brings it up, what it means, if sixty-five is a little or a lot. It is a number, two digits, out of context. It means nothing. My father's arms around me, the bristle of his beard against my cheek, the smell of his soap, the starch of his shirt—that means everything.

I am eight years old, sturdy bare legs dangling at the end of the padded plastic examination table while my pediatrician, a woman with short, dark hair, a soothing voice, and disconcertingly cool hands, tells my mom to stop packing me two sandwiches for lunch. "One should be fine," she says. And my mother, overweight herself, nods and says nothing. I know—and probably my mom does, too—that one would not be fine. The hunger pangs would start around ten a.m., and by lunchtime I'd be bolting my sandwich, gobbling the cut-up carrots my mother dutifully packs and eyeing Roseanne Webster's Hostess cupcake, offering to trade my apple for someone's squished half peanut butter sandwich. Hungry, always hungry.

I am ten, watching my sister poke at her peas and nibble a forkful of meatloaf before pushing her plate away. "I'm all done."

It's like watching a magic trick, and I don't get it. How do people do that, I wonder, cleaning my plate, wheedling for seconds, accepting, instead, a bowl of the dietetic Jell-O the well-meaning pediatrician had prescribed, a red goop that tastes like chemicals and shame. How can anyone say no to food? I'm beginning to recognize that there are people born with an off switch, people to whom food, even the most delicious, is simply fuel.

Then there are people like me, who eat every bite and still want more, who sneak into the kitchen when the house is dark for slices of white bread slathered with margarine, sprinkled with cinnamon and sugar. I have no off switch. Happy, sad, lonely, content—the one constant in my life is hunger. I will never be able to take food or leave it; instead, I'll take it, and then take more.

I'm fifteen, five foot six, 145 pounds, most of it breasts and muscle thanks to three-hour varsity crew-team workouts every day after school. My parents, in the process of separating, have shipped me off on a teen tour to Israel. The group is filled with a full complement of mean girls from my own high school and from a neighboring town, a wealthy Jewish suburb where Fiorucci jeans and Benetton tops are the order of the day, neither of which my parents would have bought me even if they had fit. There are five girls named Jennifer making their way across the Promised Land with my group that summer. "Oh, not the fat Jennifer," I hear one of my tour mates saying matter-of-factly to another as we hang out by our kibbutz swimming pool, holding his hands out away from his hips to indicate my girth, "the other one." So that is me: not the Jennifer who loves to read, or who listens to the Smiths and is the most sought-after babysitter in town. Not the Jennifer on the honor roll, the one who can swim a mile without stopping: the fat one.

I am incandescent with shame, knowing that fat is by far the worst thing you can be. Fat is lazy, fat is gross, fat is sloppy . . .

and, worst of all, fat is forever. Michelle has a full-on Frida Kahlo mustache. Kim has terrible skin. But Michelle could wax and Kim could go on Accutane; I am going to be fat—and, hence, undesirable, unlovable, a walking joke—for the rest of my life.

I walk back to the dorm, eyes brimming with unshed tears, swearing that I'll stop eating bread, sweets, desserts, anything, to lose ten, no, twenty, no, twenty-five pounds before school starts again. I'll wake up every morning and run five miles. I'll find a pair of Fiorucci jeans and an Esprit sweater-vest, and the mean girls like Michelle and Kim who hadn't invited me to their bat mitzvahs even though we'd been going to Hebrew school together twice a week for five years would be forced to acknowledge, due to the boys' appreciative glances, that I was one of them.

My resolve lasts until dinner that night: discs of fresh-baked pita, still warm from the oven; bowls of hummus topped with a slick of olive oil; chicken schnitzel, pounded thin and deep-fried. I gain twenty more pounds before I finish high school as one of four graduation speakers: the fat one.

Then I'm eighteen, sitting in the dining hall across from the crew coach. It's winter break, and everyone else has gone home except the rowers stuck here doing two-a-days, working out in the tanks that smell of chlorine and ancient sweat every morning, lifting and running every afternoon. I'd been a good rower in high school, good enough for Princeton to recruit me, but now I've gained the freshman fifteen, plus the fifteen pounds one of my many bulimic classmates should have gained but didn't. (In the innocent days of 1987, I thought it was perfectly normal for brilliant girls with perfect SAT scores to have blue fingertips and a fine coat of downy blond fur.) "If you want to stay on the team," the coach tells me gently, "you're going to have to lose a lot of weight."

I bow my head in wordless—and now familiar—devastation.

No matter that I am strong or that I work hard. I have no off switch. I am bigger than the other girls, and that is what matters; that is all that matters. The coach relegates me to the worst boat and never makes eye contact with me again. The next year, I quit the team and join the school newspaper. I find my place, my calling. On the page, at least back in the glorious pre-Internet era, you're nothing but words and a byline. On the page, nobody can tell that you're fat.

I am thirty-three, and after two days of unmedicated labor followed by an emergency C-section, the doctor places my newborn daughter in my arms. I am shaking with exhaustion, weepy with hormones. My midsection feels like it's been ripped open and scooped out, stitched together with burlap thread and knitting needles. I tuck the tiny bundle against my chest, unwrapping the blanket with trembling hands to sniff the intoxicating scent behind her ears, curled like the buds of flowers, and brush my lips against her cheek. First, I make the traditional new-mother inventory: ten perfect fingers, ten toes like pearls. Then I make a less typical assessment, examining the shape of her body, the width of her baby hips, the creases of her adorably pudgy thighs. At eight pounds, eleven ounces, almost two weeks overdue, she's one of the biggest babies in the nursery. As I look at her roommates, some plump and adorable as the infants in diaper ads, others scrawny and jaundiced, I'm far too embarrassed to ask my doctor the only thing I want to know: Will she be normal, or will she be like me?

Now, at forty-two, I've made as much peace as a plus-size woman can make with her body. I might be big, but I'm plenty strong. I've run 5Ks and 10Ks, completed hundred-mile bike rides and triathlons. In my career, my weight has never held me back. I've worked for national newspapers, written bestselling novels, had a book turned into a movie, cowritten a TV show that made it on the air. I have a job I love, two smart, funny daughters, a rich, full life with wonderful friends, and a man who loves me . . . but I know that, when the world sees me, they don't see any of this. They see fat.

My daughter sat on her bed, and I sat beside her. "How would you feel if someone made fun of you for something that wasn't your fault?" I began.

"She *could* stop eating so much," Lucy mumbled, unwittingly mouthing the it's-just-that-simple advice a thousand doctors and well-meaning friends and relatives and weight-loss profiteers have given overweight women for years.

"It's not always that easy," I said. "Everyone's different in terms of how they treat food. You know how Phoebe is with ice cream? How sometimes she'll gobble it right up, and sometimes she'll let it sit there and melt?" Lucy managed a quavery smile, then looked at me, blue eyes wide, waiting for me to go on.

I opened my mouth, then closed it. How do I walk the line between the cold truth and helpful fiction, between the way the world is and the way I wish it was? Should I tell her that, in insulting a woman's weight, she's joined the long, proud tradition of critics who go after any woman with whom they disagree by starting with "you're ugly" and ending with "no man would want you and there must be something wrong with any man who does"? Do I tell her I didn't cry when Gawker posted my picture and someone commented underneath it, "I'm sorry, but aren't chick-lit authors supposed to be pretty"?

Does she need to know now that life isn't fair, or can she have a few more years of thinking that it might be that way? I feel her eyes on me, waiting for an answer I don't have. Words are my tools. Stories are my job. It's possible she'll remember what I say forever, and I have no idea what to say.

So I tell her the only thing I can come up with that is unequivocally true. I say to my daughter, "I love you, and there is nothing you could ever do to make me not love you. But I'm disappointed in you right now. There are plenty of reasons for not liking someone. What she looks like isn't one of them."

Lucy nods solemnly, tears on her cheeks, the look of the Big Bad still on her face. "I won't say that again," she tells me, her voice shaky, and I pull her close, pressing my nose against the part in her hair, inhaling the scent that is hers alone.

We're both quiet, and I don't know if I said the right thing; I may never know. So as we sit there together, shoulder to shoulder, thigh to thigh, I pray for her to be smart. I pray for her to be strong. I pray for her to find friends, work she loves, a partner who adores her, and for the world not to beat out of her the things that make her who she is, for her life to be easy, and for her to have the strength to handle it when it's not. And still, always, I pray that she will never struggle as I've struggled, that weight will never be her cross to bear. She may not be able to use the word in our home, but I can use it in my head. I pray that she will never get fat.

"Some Say a Parent Should Teach a Child to Swim"

Imagine the happiest person you know—the one who's never down, never sad, never irritated, the one who's just preternaturally pleased all the time.

Then give that person brain surgery so that he or she is physically incapable of experiencing unhappiness.

Voilà. You've got my mother.

I always knew that Fran was good-natured to the point of being oblivious, but that truth was hammered home one summer afternoon a few years ago on Cape Cod. Fran, who is now retired, spends the summers with me and my husband and daughters in our house in Truro that overlooks Cape Cod Bay. She and Molly and I were on the beach. I was flipping through *O* magazine and it had one of those quizzes that magazines in general and *O* in particular seem to feature every month: "What's Your Happiness IQ?" "How Happy Are You?" "Could You Be Happier?" "Probably, You Could Be Happier: Let's Find Out, Shall We?"

"Hey, Fran," I called to my mom, who was as usual planted in a folding camp chair with a pink terry cloth visor propped cock-eyed on top of her head, wearing a skirted floral-print swimsuit at least thirty years old ("Vintage!" she's been known to protest when Molly and I point out that her swimsuits are older than her kids, or that her toaster dates back to the days when she was still into men). "Want to take a quiz?"

"Sure," said my ever-obliging mother.

So we began.

"When you think about people in your life, do you focus on the ones who've disappointed or hurt you?"

Fran waved her hand dismissively. "I don't even remember people like that."

"In most ways, my life is close to ideal. Agree or disagree?"

Fran beamed, indicating the sand, the water, her grandkids. "Sure!"

"Are you ever irritated when people cut you off in traffic?"

A shrug. "Who notices?"

"Do you get angry when, for example, the shopper in front of you in line at the supermarket pulls out a pile of coupons?"

Another shrug. "I'm not in a hurry. I'd just read my book!"

At some point, I started making up questions. "If you checked into a hotel and thieves broke into your room and sedated you and removed one of your kidneys and left you in a bathtub filled with ice cubes, what would you do?"

My mom considered. "You can get along fine with one kidney, right?"

"If someone carjacked you and took your clothes and money and left you stranded naked on the street, on a scale of one to ten, how angry would you be?"

Fran thought it over. "Things happen."

Finally, we were finished. Fran went back to her *New Yorker* and I tallied up her score. People who scored lower than forty were instructed to seek professional help. Forty to fifty meant that you were getting there, but that your "pleasure center" could use a reboot. Fifty or above meant that you were reasonably content. Sixty or higher was a solid happy. Seventy or above meant you had achieved a state of Buddha-like self-actualization and bliss. Above eighty meant you might have taken the quiz while intoxicated.

Fran's score was ninety-eight, which more or less corresponded to "lobotomy."

I'm exaggerating—but not by much. Of course my mother worries—about money, about her children and her grandchildren and her partner and the possibility of a Donald Trump presidency. Occasionally she will get angry or frustrated or fed up. But, for the most part, my mother is cheerful. Even in the throes of the divorce, even in the ten years after, when she devoted what little free time and money she had to taking my father to court and trying to get him to pay the tens of thousands of dollars in child support that he owed her, Fran was happy.

These days, she and her partner of thirteen years will bicker, sometimes in a manner that hints that Fran sees Clair as her fifth child, just as in need of her guidance and expertise as the rest of us . . . but, for the most part, my mother goes where she wants, does what she wants, lives the way she wants, riding her bike or playing bridge, and is supremely content.

Sometimes I wonder whether growing up with my Nanna's expectations, with a stern mother who just wanted her to behave and be a good girl, with equal emphasis on "good" and "girl," somehow froze my mom, emotionally, at ten years old, where your settings are *Happy* and *Not My Problem*; where emotions like sorrow or frustration or anger are far off on the horizon, where bad moods blow over, where it's always easier to avoid a conflict, to smile and pretend—or in her case, believe—that everything's fine. Sometimes I wish she could get over her distaste for confrontation long enough to stand up for us—for me. If, to use a random example, a wedding guest who was explicitly, repeatedly informed that a wedding was adults-only shows up with a squalling toddler, there are mothers who will march right up, say, "Absolutely not," and make arrangements for the toddler and, probably, the guest to be whisked away before the bride even notices. Then there are mothers who will, literally, throw their hands in the air and say, "I can't do anything about it," and "I don't want to upset Nanna" (even though the toddler's presence ended up upsetting my new in-laws and their relatives, who had considerately obeyed our requests and left their children at home).

But I also believe that, just as there are people inclined toward melancholy and depression, there are those more outfitted for pleasure and joy—people who look at most conflicts or arguments or differences of opinion and decide *not worth it*. My mom is one of those people. If the self-help section has it right and happiness is a choice, my mother chooses it, every day, over and over again. She is so chill that she's practically frozen; unsinkably optimistic, astonishingly serene. She's kind of a miracle.

No matter what's happened with the four of us, how far we've come or how much we've achieved, Fran keeps it real. She remains unimpressed with our accomplishments, unfazed by our achievements, barely willing to make any kind of concession that suggests that we're no longer twelve. Whenever I visit the new house she shares with Clair, I sleep on the pullout couch, unless one of my siblings has claimed it first. I spent my fortieth birthday on an air mattress on the floor of her bonus room while my daughters slept in the bed. My sister took me out to see *Hot Tub Time Machine*. Fran brought me a Carvel ice cream cake. It was awesome.

One of the greatest joys of my career is going on book tours.

I know that most writers hate it—the city-a-day pace, the grind of the early-morning flights and nighttime readings and hours spent in between in airports or in cars, en route to bookstores to sign stock. They hate the shifting time zones, the home-sickness, not to mention the public speaking.

Lucky me—my anxieties do not include talking to crowds. I like to travel, even in our post-9/11 atmosphere, where it's gotten less and less thrilling and increasingly degrading.

For me, the best part of a book tour—in fact, the best part of being a published author in the first place—has been taking my family along for the ride. Which meant that, on my first tour, I got to answer the question: What happens when you take the cheapest woman in the world and bring her on an all-expense-paid ten-day book tour with cars and drivers and four-star hotels?

"Look at her," Molly whispered as Fran wandered, wide-eyed and bewildered, through the lobby of the Regent Beverly Wilshire—the *Pretty Woman* hotel, where I still couldn't believe my publisher was putting me up. "She looks like she's been clubbed."

We observed as Fran inspected the elaborate floral arrangements, taking a tentative sniff, then as she turned to stare at a trio of well-dressed women swanning by, heels clicking briskly on the marble floor.

"She's saying something," Molly whispered.

We edged in close enough to hear my mother murmuring, "It's too much."

Molly and I decided we would make a *Wild Kingdom*–style documentary entitled *Fran in the Wild* . . . except, of course, her "wild" was luxury. From Atlanta to Dallas to San Francisco to L.A., Molly and I followed Fran around hotels and in and out of Town Cars, delivering a Marlin Perkins–esque voice-over, just loud enough for Fran to hear. "At first, the animal is wary of its new surroundings," I said as Fran wheeled her suitcase into a hotel suite, having waved off the offer of assistance with her luggage. "Let's watch as it attempts to acclimate to a strange environment."

Fran touched the bedspread, flicked on a lamp, flipped open the room service menu, and hissed as if she'd been scalded.

"Twelve dollars for a cup of chicken-noodle soup?!?"

I drifted after her, in the direction of the bathroom, as Fran squirted L'Occitane lemon verbena lotion into her hand, sniffed it, rubbed some on her arms, pocketed the little bottle, then examined the selection of soaps and shampoos.

"My assistant will now attempt to provoke the wild Fran," I announced as Molly sidled up to the minibar. Fran's head snapped around.

"DON'T YOU TOUCH THAT!" she shouted.

Molly paused, her hand halfway to a Diet Coke. "What?"

"DO. NOT. TOUCH THAT. Do you have any idea how much that costs? I can get you a six-pack of soda at the Rite Aid down the block for the cost of one Diet Coke!"

"The animal is angry," I murmured as Molly flipped the tab of her soda. "Watch as the predator continues to taunt it."

"Jenny, I can hear you! Put those Oreos down. CUT THAT OUT! Oh, you two are going to drive me crazy!"

Eventually we'd leave the fancy hotel and go to a bookstore for a reading. Fran, being Fran, would prowl the stacks, occasionally chatting with other customers before the reading began . . . and if my mother is insecure amid the chandeliered ceilings and elaborate floral displays of a Ritz-Carlton lobby, she is completely confident about her take on modern fiction.

"I just read the most amazing novel!" I once heard her say. It was my first book tour, and I was busy signing a stack of *Good in Bed. Here it comes*, I thought, swelling with satisfaction.

"It had everything," Fran continued. "Great characters, drama, heartbreak, humor . . ."

I preened expectantly. "What is it?" the shopper asked.

"*Empire Falls*!" said Fran. "By Richard Russo! Do you know his books?"

At which point, I pulled her aside and explained that, unless I received confirmed reports that Mrs. Russo was somewhere in the wilds of Maine, pimping my books to unsuspecting shoppers, she was not to promote his work on my tour.

It's no accident that my siblings and I all ended up somewhere in the entertainment industry, with jobs that revolve around some version of storytelling. I write; Molly works as an actress and body double. ("Watch *CSI* tonight," she'll sometimes text. "When they find the waitress's body in the dumpster, those are my legs!") Jake produces movies, and Joe Weiner, Fran's baby, is an entertainment attorney, whose job involves hunting down possible reality-TV fodder. (Recent assignment—a trip to Texas to meet with a man who runs a tire repair shop along with his five beautiful daughters. "Did you meet the daughters?" I asked. Joe shook his head, looking dejected. "Their dad says they're only around when the cameras come out.")

As enthusiastic and constant a reader as she's been all her life, my mom is an even more devoted swimmer. It's her exercise and her mental health; self-care translated into an hour of laps in the Olympic-size swimming pool at the West Hartford JCC, where a tiled quotation from the Talmud over the deep end reads, "Some say a parent should teach a child to swim."

My whole life, I've watched my mom do her laps, either at the indoor pool or at the pool in the backyard of our house on Harvest Hill Road. Her stroke is the crawl, her pace is slow and deliberate. She'll lift one curving arm out of the water, hand extended, scoop-like, and she'll bring the arm down, her feet churning steadily behind her and the skirt of her swimsuit trailing in her wake.

"Swim," I think, is allegorical, a stand-in for all the other stuff parents need to teach their children to keep their kids afloat in the world, but my parents took the swim part literally. It was my dad who actually taught all of us how. We used inflatable armbands back then, yellow plastic doughnut-shaped things with a hole in the middle, called Swimmies. First, Dad would have you swim with just your left Swimmie in place. Then you'd paddle around with just your right Swimmie. Then you'd leave the Swimmies on the shore. Dad would toss a silver dollar into the deep end, and down you'd go. My mom has taken over duties for the next generation. Both of my daughters learned to swim in Gull Pond, in Wellfleet on the Cape. Fran would carry them into the water, put them down, show them how to put their faces in the water and blow bubbles. "Kick! Kick! Scoop! Scoop!" she'd call, and hold out her arms to catch them when they jumped off the dock.

When I think of my mother, I see her in the water, in the pool or in the bay on the Cape, holding baby Lucy or baby Phoebe under her armpits, keeping her afloat. My mother taught both of my daughters to swim, and taught them both, along with my half brother David, how to ride bikes. She doesn't believe in training wheels or inflatable vests or rings or any of the modern inventions designed to keep kids safe (she has, I am happy to note, made a concession for helmets). When it comes to bikes, her method is ingenious: she takes the pedals off and lowers the seat so that the kid can reach the pavement with his or her feet. "Glide!" she'll call as the kid pushes off and glides for an instant, then wobbles, then slams his or her feet back down.

"Don't worry!" I will yell, slightly out of breath from running alongside. "Just try again! It's okay! I'm right here! I'll catch you!"

"Jenny, get back here," my mother will tell me, exasperation and affection mingling. "You will NOT catch that kid. You'll hurt your back. Just let them go."

"But . . ."

"Just. Let. Them. Go." She'll wait until I've walked back to stand beside her, then call to the kid on the bike. "Try again! Push! Push! Push! Now glide!"

Eventually it always works. I back off. Fran reads her book, keeping one eye on the kid as they glide up and down the parking lot, sometimes wobbling, sometimes falling, sometimes crying. There are scrapes, there are wails of pain, there are exclamations of "I hate this!" and "I'll never learn!" But eventually everyone gets back on the bike and tries again. When the kid can glide the length of the Corn Hill Beach parking lot, the pedals go back on the bike. As it turns out, balancing is the hard part, and once a kid can do that successfully, pedaling and steering are no big deal. With Lucy, then Phoebe, then David, I've watched as each kid yells, "I've got it!" and then, with decreasing wobbles and increasing confidence, goes pedaling away.

It's a metaphor, of course. Teaching a child to swim means learning to let go. If you hold on too tight, the child won't figure it out, or be able to trust in her own ability to keep herself afloat. If you're always there to catch and comfort and soothe and smooth the way, the child never learns how to catch herself, how to comfort herself, how to get back on the bike or in the water and try, once more, to do the thing that scares her. There have been times I wished my mother had stepped forward to defend me or fight for me or move mountains to make sure that I got what I needed. Now that I am a mother myself, though, I can see the benefits of parenting with an open hand. *Some say you should teach a child to swim* . . . but the Talmud doesn't say anything about testing the waters for them, or clearing obstacles out of the way, or making sure the other swimmers won't be unkind. You teach them how, as best you can, and then you let them go.

Fifteen years after my first book was published, my mother, like many animals whose environments have changed, has adapted. She can enjoy a Four Seasons with the best of them, but the frugality that underpins her behavior and informs her life view has not budged. She will insist on carrying her own luggage (currently a donated duffel with a Teamsters' logo on the pocket). She'll tell people that my books are "page-turners" and extol the virtues of whatever she's currently loving, from Eloisa James's memoir of Paris to Geraldine Brooks's newest novel.

People talk about never losing their childlike sense of wonder; of wanting always to see the world with a kid's innocence and delight. For me, it's different: I always want to see the world the way my mother does, where it's one adventure, one wonderful new experience, one delicious meal after another; where there are no strangers, just people you haven't recommended Richard Russo's book to yet, and where it's never embarrassing if you're having a good time.

Years ago, we were traveling between Philadelphia and Florida. The night before, to kick off our vacation, we'd gone to the best Mexican restaurant in town and ordered, basically, everything—the spicy street corn, the ceviche sampler, the guacamole with pistachios and chili flakes, empanadas filled with this and burritos full of that. It was way too much food, and I thought it was only a reflex when my mom asked them to pack up the leftovers, even though no one would be home to eat them.

The next morning we boarded a plane. I'd gotten my daughters settled, with my mom and my sister a few rows behind us. The plane took off, we reached our cruising altitude, the captain turned off the FASTEN SEAT BELT sign, and all was well. Until I started smelling garlic. Lots of garlic. Plus chilis and black beans.

"What is that?" I whispered. Lucy unbuckled her seat belt, clambered onto her knees, and turned around, peering through the crack between the seats.

"Fran is eating nachos!" she reported.

"The nachos from last night?"

"Yes!"

I stood up, squinting. Fran, with a Styrofoam clamshell open in her lap, gave me a cheerful wave. I spent the rest of the trip reviving a skill I'd perfected as a child, when she'd pull the jar of peanut butter out of her tote bag during, for example, the changing of the guard at Arlington National Cemetery. "Is that your mom?" the woman sitting beside me asked. I smiled and shrugged and said, "I've never seen her before in my life."

Mean Girls in the Retirement Home

New York Times, January 2015

About eighteen months ago, my ninety-seven-year-old grandmother went out to dinner with some friends. As Nanna got out of the car, she tripped over her friend Shirley's cane, fell to the pavement, and came down hard on her elbow. Back at home, she headed to the kitchen to get some dessert—"and my left leg just crumpled."

At the hospital, the doctors ordered X-rays but couldn't see anything wrong. After two weeks of therapy, Nanna was sent home, but she'd made up her mind. After thirty years of living in Florida, twenty-eight of them as a widow, and most of those spent insisting that the only way she'd go back to her native Michigan was "in a box," Nanna asked her older daughter, my aunt Marlene, to find her a sunny place near Detroit.

Last summer she moved into an independent living facility with access to a range of services and activities. She has her own apartment with a kitchen, but can eat her meals in a dining hall.

After giving her a few days to unpack and settle in, I got her on the phone. How was it going?

"Well," Nanna began. Her apartment was lovely. The food was just fine, and there were all kinds of classes and courses to while away the hours. "Have you made any friends?" I asked, in the same chipper tone I used when my younger child returned from her first day at kindergarten.

There was a pause. Then: "They won't let me sit at their table!" Nanna cried.

"Wait, what? Who won't let you sit at their table?"

"You try to sit and they say, 'That seat is taken!'"

"Oh my God," I said, instantly thrust into a painful flashback of junior high, when I walked into the cafeteria and was greeted with the sight of leather purses looped across the chair backs and the sound of one girl with dramatically plucked eyebrows announcing, "Those seats are taken!" I hadn't known enough to carry a purse. I had a lunchbox. (And it would take me another decade to figure out the eyebrow thing.)

"And just try to get into a bridge game," Nanna continued. "They'll talk about bridge, and you'll say, 'Oh, I play,' and they'll tell you, 'Sorry, we're not looking for anyone.'"

"Mean girls!" I said. "There are mean girls in your home!"

"It's not a home," Nanna said sharply.

I considered. "Here's my advice," I said. "Find a bridge four-some. Figure out which one of them looks weak. Then hover."

When I was young and innocent—say, last summer—the idea of ninety-year-olds in pecking orders, picking on those at the bottom, was a joke. Everyone knew that the real danger to the elderly came from unscrupulous relatives, con artists, or abusive caregivers. We've all heard sad tales of senior citizens being beaten, starved, or neglected by the people paid—usually underpaid—to care for them.

The notion that a threat to seniors is their peers is somewhat new, and usually played for laughs. It goes against a truism handed down from mothers to daughters for generations: this, too, shall pass. Mean girls are not girls, or mean, forever. High school doesn't last forever; everyone grows up. But Nanna's experience suggests otherwise. It says that the cruel, like the poor, are always with us, that mean girls stay mean—they just start wearing support hose and dentures.

A recent Cornell University study by Karl Pillemer proves the point, showing that aggression among residents in nursing homes is widespread and "extremely high rates of conflict and violence" are common. According to the study's news release, one in five residents was involved in at least one "negative and aggressive encounter" with another resident during a four-week period. Sixteen percent were cursed or yelled at; 6 percent were hit, kicked, or bitten; 1 percent were victims of "sexual incidents, such as exposing one's genitals, touching other residents, or attempting to gain sexual favors"; and 10.5 percent dealt with other residents' entering their rooms uninvited or rummaging through their belongings.

Whether you're brawling on the playground or battling over the best seats in chair-cercize, bad behavior is constant, and the rituals for trying to get in with the in-crowd don't change much. Nanna's quest for "the Cadillac of walkers," a four-hundred-dollar number not covered by Medicare, mirrored my search a decade ago for the nearly thousand-dollar Bugaboo that would signal to my urban-mommy cohort that I belonged.

What transforms with age are the criteria for judgment: not looks, not wealth, not the once-coveted ability to drive at night. When you get to be Nanna's age, you're reduced to a number—the younger the better. Even in a residence for the elderly, the eightysomethings will still be cold to the ninety-five-year-olds. Now ninety-nine, my Nanna is completely cognizant of what's going on. Her memory, both short- and long-term, is excellent.

But once her new neighbors heard her age, they knew they didn't want her at their table.

"My question is, are they rude? Are they nasty? Or is it that she's not hearing, or is interpreting something that's not really something? I can't tell," says Aunt Marlene. "I think there's definitely cliques. I don't know if there's a way to alleviate the feeling of being left out. At ninety-nine, do you end up with a group? Does that happen? I don't know. At first I thought it just takes time. Now I wonder—maybe this is the way it is. Maybe you can't expect anything else."

Bad behavior doesn't change. Nor does the response from the ones on the sidelines, watching and hoping for the best. Even with lowered expectations, it's hard. I fret about my first-grader getting shut out of the Four Square game or my sixth-grader sitting alone at lunch. My mom and her sister wonder if their mother is suffering the same kind of isolation, exclusion, and loneliness; the pain of having outlived every single one of your contemporaries, of having lots to say and no one to listen.

Nanna tries. Every day, she takes a class: Yiddish, current events, even iPad 101. She gets dressed up for dinner, with a pretty scarf, a new sweater. She's gotten to know her neighbors, table-mates, even the one who forgets her name between one dinner and the next, and she's joined a mah-jongg game—"even though I haven't played in years." The ledge outside her front door is home to a little stuffed bear, dressed in University of Michigan regalia, a hopeful sentry, and maybe a conversation starter.

I try, too. Over Thanksgiving, we celebrated Nanna's ninety-ninth birthday, with all twelve of her great-grandchildren on hand to tour the new apartment. Down in the lobby, my six-year-old, Phoebe, and I met a beautifully dressed, immaculately made-up woman sitting on a bench with a cane, waiting for her niece to take her to Thanksgiving dinner at five. It was two. "Do you want to see my kitty?" she asked, and my daughter happily agreed. I learned that, like Nanna, the woman had moved in over the summer, was a Michigan native, and seemed sharp and aware. Feeling like a guy at a bar—another echo of another acceptance-and-rejection ritual—I asked for her number.

Then Phoebe and I took the elevator back up to Nanna's apartment, where the refrigerator door is covered with pictures of her children, grandchildren, and great-grandchildren, and I announced, "Nanna, I think I made you a friend."

Judging Women

A young woman stands on a stage in an emerald-green bikini. The legs of the bottom are cut high enough to put any hint of upper-thigh jiggle or pucker on display. The wired cups of the top hoist her breasts toward her chin. Her high heels turn her posture into an S-curve—hips thrown backward, chest thrust up. She shakes her glossy ringlets down the tanned skin of her back, and as up-tempo pop plays, she struts across a makeshift stage in a hotel ballroom in Boston. Hitting her first mark, a masking-taped X on the wooden boards, she stands, hands on her hips, legs apart, eyes on the crowd, trying to project poise and command and looking, instead, slightly angry and maybe even the tiniest bit deranged. "What's wrong with being . . . what's wrong with being . . . what's wrong with being con-fi-dent," Demi Lovato asks rhetorically as the woman spins in a slow, graceful turn. The crowd—two hundred people, almost all of them female—squeals its approval. A young man with a hoarse voice shouts her name.

I bend over my scoring sheet and write down "10." In the Miss America scoring system, "physical fitness in swimsuit" counts for only 15 percent of a girl's final score (the pageant people are trying mightily to refer to the contestants here as "women," with mixed results, and, at the end of close to nine hours in Pageantland, despite forty-five years as a feminist, I'm having trouble not thinking of them as girls myself). "This isn't about judging the girl's body," we've been told by our shepherds for the night, two middle-aged men named Rocky and Dana, both longtime Miss A. volunteers, both warm and enthusiastic and gay. "You're looking for confidence. Poise. Does she command the room? Does her personality come through? Is she a standout? Is she our Miss Massachusetts?" Rocky and Dana have also told us, repeatedly and insistently, that they don't want us to merely pick their Miss Cambridge and Miss Boston, the titles the two winners of tonight's pageant will eventually hold. They want their winner to ultimately be crowned Miss Massachusetts, to be the girl who will win the title this July in Worcester. The one who will head to Atlantic City in September. The one who will do what no Miss Massachusetts in the ninety-five-year history of the Miss America competition has ever done—bring home the crown.

Going into my inaugural judging experience, I've decided to give all the girls a ten in swimsuit, with the belief that A) you can't judge physical fitness just by looking at someone ("Have them run a mile!" I've joked. "Make them do a barre class!") and B) the idea of handing out scholarship dollars based, at least in part, on how good a girl looks in a bikini is absolute bullshit and in complete contradiction of my deeply held belief, communicated at least once a day to my daughters, that It's What's Inside That Matters.

But now that I'm sitting here, with the girls on the stage and my pen in my hand, I don't want to give all of them tens anymore. The twenty-year-old with the tiny, tight body, strutting like she grew up with a catwalk in her living room? Easy ten. But what about the high school senior whose orthopedic condition was misdiagnosed, who spent four years in a wheelchair and is onstage, in a blue bikini, with twelve-inch surgical scars visible on both of her hips? What about the MIT graduate who lost fifty pounds and is still much curvier in her swimsuit than her competitors . . . but is up on the stage anyhow, with her eyes bright and her shoulders thrown back and a big I'm-the-one-that-you-want smile on her face?

And what about the redheaded teenager, so scared she's practically trembling, who is in recovery from anorexia, whose platform is about eating-disorder awareness and whose performance was a dance set to music, and her own voice speaking over the beat, telling the story of the director who told her "you're too fat to wear that costume" and set her on a road of obsessive calorie and carb counting that ended with her hospitalization? What courage does it take for her to be on this stage, in scraps of nylon and Lycra, letting us look at her body and rate it?

I give the redhead a ten. I give the curvy girl a ten. I give the girl with the scars a ten. I give the girl with the perfect body and composure an eight. I tell myself that I'm doing what second-wave feminists called "unworking," where you'd get hired at a sexist corporation and then screw up your job so badly you'd cause the place to rot from the inside out, but the truth is, I'm not sure what I'm doing anymore, if I'm taking the Miss America pageant seriously or if I am seriously trying to undo it; if I want to burn it all down, or get someone to give me a crown of my own.

For as long as I can remember, I've had a love-hate relationship with Miss America. I love the spectacle of the pageant—the women in rows, beaming as they announce the names of their states, and how at home in the peanut gallery (and in later years on Twitter), I'd say things like "she doesn't have a chance," and "top ten, for sure," and "are you kidding me with this?" I loved the talent competition, especially when the contestants strayed from the old reliables—belting Broadway standards or trilling operatic arias or playing the piano or dancing—and dipped into pageant-specific skills, such as baton twirling, Irish step dancing, rhythmic gymnastics, dramatic monologues, or—please, God—ventriloquism, as Miss Ohio did in 2015 ("Performing ventriloquism, while singing 'Supercalafragalisticexpialadocious,'" is a phrase that I could hear *The Bachelor* and *Miss America* host Chris Harrison say forever). I loved snarking on the gowns during Evening Wear, I loved going all righteously feminist during Swimsuit, I loved doling out tidbits of Miss A. lore that I'd picked up during years of viewing and research ("Did you know that Debra Maffett, Miss America 1983, competed three times for Miss Texas before she allegedly had a ton of plastic surgery, moved to California, and won her state title there? Do you know that it wasn't until 1999 that the Miss America Organization lifted its ban on competitors who've had abortions?"). I loved the suspense of the slow final reveal, from fourth runner-up, to third, to second, until there were just two women left, gripping each other's hands as they stood in the spotlight. I loved the inevitable crying, and the way that, after all these years of pageantry and progress, nobody's figured out a reliable way for the outgoing Miss America to affix the crown to the new winner's head, which means that each year's show ends with tears, roses, and endless, result-free fumbling with bobby pins.

When I was hired at the *Philadelphia Inquirer*, I was thrilled for many reasons, and Miss America was one of them. Philadelphia is less than an hour away from Atlantic City. It's pageant-adjacent. In 1998, after some patient waiting and some hard lobbying, I was sent to Atlantic City as the *Inquirer*'s on-the-ground reporter. It turned out to be a big year. Kate Shindle, who'd grown up in New Jersey but won her regional crown in Illinois (she'd gone to Northwestern for college), was the controversial winner. Her platform was AIDS awareness—a big deal for an organization whose representatives usually embraced less hot-button causes. Not only that, but Shindle's father had been a Miss America board member. Although he'd resigned well before his daughter's win, this news led to charges that, somehow, the fix was in. If the pageant itself hadn't been enthralling enough, the behind-the-scenes drama made it unforgettable.

So that was the love of the love-hate dyad—the pageant, the drama, the way its arrival was a signpost of my year, signaling the end of summer, the beginning of fall, sweaters and colorful leaves, fresh notebooks and new teachers, the chance, every September, that this year would be better than the year before.

The hate, of course, came from knowing that I could never, ever be that girl. No matter how hard I worked out or how long I dieted, no matter what I did to my face, no one would ever be struggling to stick a rhinestone crown on my head. Miss America doesn't need to be a beauty—actually, cute, girl-next-door/ local-newscaster looks seem to serve contestants better than the kind of ethereal, drop-dead gorgeousness that sells perfume and haute couture. Regardless, Miss America rewarded something I would never have and could never get. It was a yearly reminder that the woman who was what boys wanted, who was what everyone wanted, who represented our country—"there she is," as Bert Parks used to sing, "your ideal"—was a woman who was pleasant and pretty, admired and beloved; a woman who looked, who was, nothing like me.

There are five judges for tonight's Miss Boston competition. There's me: novelist, newspaper columnist, pageant skeptic. There's our veteran judge, Patty Haggerty, whose short hair, big glasses, and impeccable posture all suggest the principal whose office you don't want to get sent to. Dr. Danica Tisdale Fisher, who runs admissions for the summer program at Phillips Academy in Andover, is another Miss A. vet. In crisp pants and low heels and glasses, you wouldn't immediately peg her as a former beauty queen, but that's what she is—the first-ever African-American woman to hold the Miss Georgia title and a top-ten Miss A. finalist in 2004. With degrees from Spelman, Temple, and Emory, she's a prime example of what the Miss America Organization likes to say that it's about: education and accomplishment and giving back, not just looking hot in a bikini. A Miss America crown can lead to big things—Kate Shindle had a solid career on Broadway; Vanessa Williams, who lost her crown after *Penthouse* published nude photos in 1985, is a singer and an actress. Gretchen Carlson, 1989, was a Fox News anchor and is currently suing the network's head for sexual harassment. However, the title is no guarantee of future fame and fortune. Google the Miss Americas of the 1980s and 1990s and you'll find a number of stay-at-home mothers–slash–"Christian recording artists" who live in places like Branson or Nashville and host public-access cable shows, or give speeches in favor of abstinence and against abortion. Dr. Tisdale, with her job at an elite boarding school and her doctorate degree, is undoubtedly one of the stars in the pageant's crown.

To balance the panel are two middle-aged white men. James McCabe is an executive in the hospitality industry ("he is now back in New York City helping to run the tallest hotel building in the Western Hemisphere," says his bio), and Paul Shipman heads media relations and brand development for the Connecticut Food Bank.

Our first job is the private interview competition, which the audience won't see. For ten minutes, we'll grill each of the women about her platform, her talent, her pageant experience, the results of the previous night's presidential primaries, whatever we like. Per our instructions, this gives us the "opportunity to learn as much as possible about the contestant's Qualities and Attributes to fulfill the titleholder position."

The sessions turn out to be a lot like press conferences—not hostile, exactly, but we're not just pitching softballs. From the high school senior whose platform is accessibility for the handicapped, Danica wants to know, "Why did you write that you were 'forced to use a wheelchair'? Isn't that language problematic?" We ask about their politics, their academic ambitions, their travel plans. "I'd love to visit Dubai," one contender has written on her bio. "Why Dubai?" asks a judge. "With all the places in the Middle East that are so rich in history and art . . ."

"Oh, I just love shopping," the girl—the young woman—burbles. "And every time I see those amazing malls they've got on TV . . ."

The five of us have been strictly forbidden from discussing the contenders, or even exchanging glances once they've left the room. I suspect that if we could, though, we'd all be rolling our eyes.

And so it goes. For every piece of Pollyanna-ish nonsense or garbled bit of Scripture ("I am a firm believer that positive energy generates positive outcomes"; "My parents say I was born with the heart of a servant"), for each serving of incomprehensible word salad ("Due to my parents' divorce, I immensely value cohesive family units, which I have not always had"), for every glaring typo in the paperwork (one young woman's platform involves "Drub Awareness"), for every platform that sounds like a *Saturday Night Live* skit first draft ("Dancers for Cancer"), there's a girl who's sharp or funny; a girl who's lived through something difficult and come through it with a story to tell.

The MIT graduate has, for example, a half dozen different volunteer commitments—endeavors that sound serious, as opposed to mere résumé padding—that she manages along with the pursuit of her PhD. "I'm a foodie," she says, explaining that one of her life goals is to visit every Michelin-starred restaurant in the United States. She's got an easy laugh and a figure suggesting that she's no stranger to bread and butter.

Another contender, with an anchorwoman's poise and a politician's cool, is currently attending Harvard. One does stand-up as a hobby. ("What travels around the world but never leaves the corner?" she offers when we ask for a joke. "A stamp!") Two girls are still in high school; three are in graduate school.

There's the girl whose sister is an addict (a quick under-the-table Google shows that the sister has been arrested a bunch of times for crimes including prostitution). There's the redhead whose eating disorder took her down to eighty pounds, with doctors telling her parents that they weren't sure she'd survive. The girl advocating for wheelchair accessibility spent years using a chair after doctors misdiagnosed her hip condition as "growing pains."

All of this serves as a reminder that it's hard to be young and female—even in America, even if you're exceptionally talented, smart, dedicated, pretty. And all of these young women are intelligent, articulate, accomplished, and driven . . . but to my surprise, not all of them are pretty. While there are a few who could probably drop jaws in a crowd and stop traffic on the street, the majority are just regular, healthy, well-tended American girls, and a few have probably occasioned whispers—*she does pageants? She thinks she could be Miss America?*

With almost every girl, I ask some version of the same thing: How does it feel to compete for scholarship dollars based, in part, on how you look in a swimsuit? "We're going to be judging your bodies," I say, sweeping my arm in a gesture that includes all five of us. "Isn't that creepy?"

Nobody's got a perfect answer. Responses range from versions of *It's a necessary evil* to *It is what it is.* I get excited when one girl—woman—mentions the male gaze, and I wait for her to elaborate on her discomfort with pandering to it, but her response trails off into a mishmash of politically correct words and phrases—*confidence* and *poise* and *you have to get used to people looking at you.* At first that last part sounds meaningless . . . except it's not meaningless, it's true. Whether you're a beauty-queen contender or a would-be news anchor or just a college freshman walking across the quad, simply existing as female means that people will be looking and judging and making determinations about you based on how you appear to them. Given all that, it probably makes perfect sense for these young women to spend hours, weeks, years of their lives trying to conform to that gaze, to be the thing it wants to see, its perfect object of desire, its ideal.

Getting through all fourteen girls' interviews takes up most of the afternoon. By five o'clock, I'd kill for a nap. Instead, we grab a quick meal in the hotel restaurant, with the judges from the Miss Outstanding Teen contest. Then we head up to the ballroom for the big show (Patty Haggerty has traveled from New Hampshire with a garment bag that turns out to contain a black satin sleeveless sheath that displays her slim figure and toned arms. Once a pageant girl, always a pageant girl).

The show, I am delighted to learn, is more or less the Miss America pageant in miniature, complete with opening dance routine, set to the Black Eyed Peas' song "I've Got a Feeling," where it's easy to tell which competitors had dance training versus the ones who don't dance between pageants. The girls wear black dresses and high heels. They form lines and parade across the stage, moving their arms in time to the music, smiling politely at the emcee's banter.

The first onstage component we judge is the "onstage question." Each contender has submitted a question, which one of her competitors will answer. Donald Trump and gay marriage are covered, with varying degrees of success. The Harvard undergraduate gives a thoughtful reply about whether lowering the drinking age might cut down on drunk driving. "And after I've spent all day in classes, then at work, why are my elected officials allowed to tell me I can't have a glass of wine?" she asks. I'm confused, until I remember that, even though she's got the poise and presence of a forty-year-old, she is, in fact, just twenty.

She also has something weird going on with her makeup. Maybe it's the lights, or some odd reflection from her giant, Pageant-with-a-capital-*P* earrings, but her skin looks . . . gray. In Swimsuit, in Evening Wear, as she plays the piano during Talent, I keep staring . . . and, yep, she's gray. Like, corpse-colored gray. Weird.

Some of the girls—women—are truly gifted; some have more personality than they do native ability. The MIT girl doesn't have the best voice, but she sings a song about believing in oneself from *La Cage aux Folles* that brings down the house. "I am what I am. I don't want praise, I don't want pity," she sings, with such nuance and conviction that it's her performance we remember, not the belter who tears through a Céline Dion song, not the conservatory student who dances and sings "The Laughing Song" from *Die Fledermaus* in a halter top and harem pants decorated with dangling gold coins.

The five of us—and the rest of the audience—quickly learn the difference between a national-champion-level step dancer and a girl whose parents probably dragged her to step-dancing lessons one summer during elementary school. One of the modern dancers is so strong and flexible that her performance resembles a gymnastics floor routine, a dizzying series of backbends and bouncy round-offs. Another's dance relies so heavily on sultry looks and a lick-your-lips-stick-out-your-chest pose that I wonder whether her preparation consisted of repeated viewings of Aerosmith videos.

There are a few standouts—a "comedic monologue," a performance of a scene from *Waiting for Guffman*, which could have gone horribly wrong, but was so funny that it's all I can do not to clap (judges are forbidden from applauding). The Harvard girl plays a tricky Bach Solfeggietto, delivered with a precision that's dazzling and also, somehow, grim, like Liberace, if Liberace had no sense of humor and would maybe rather be doing your taxes than playing the piano. It's technically impressive, but joyless; showy but no fun, which is sort of how I'm feeling about this Miss herself, only maybe, I tell myself, it's the odd clay-y makeup.

In the end the women stand onstage, hands linked, in their evening gowns. Some are purchased-for-the-pageant confections, encrusted with sequins, in TV-friendly jewel tones. Others look like repurposed prom gowns. While they wait, we're totaling our scores. Take your private interview score, multiply it by 2.5, add it to Lifestyle & Fitness in Swimsuit, which is multiplied by 1.5, plus Talent times 3.5, plus Evening Wear times 2, then the onstage question times 0.5. ("You can just add up your scores," a sympathetic emcee whispers as he hears me muttering under my breath about how I hadn't been told there'd be math.) My top two are the curvy MIT grad and the *Waiting for Guffman* girl, a college freshman in musical theater who attended a performing-arts high school in Georgia. As it turns out, she's the only one of my two who's made the composite Top Five, and she ends up as our Miss Boston, with the Drub Awareness girl—pretty and poised and also, it should be noted, from a southern pageant state—as Miss Cambridge.

The MIT girl is the fourth runner-up. She also wins Miss Congeniality, the prize her fellow contestants vote on, and seems genuinely touched to get it. The eating-disorder survivor wins a prize for her talent and accepts it with a tremulous smile, seeming to want nothing more than to get off the stage and go home.

At the end of the night, back in the judging room, the five of us debrief with Dana and Rocky. "What happened with Alissa?" Rocky asks, sounding crestfallen. Alissa is the Harvard girl. "She won Talent. She won Swimsuit. I'm going to have a difficult conversation with her."

We talk about her assurance—how it teeters on the line between impressive and arrogant. We praise her smarts, her talent, her poise. Then there's silence. Then finally someone—me—blurts, "I think maybe her makeup could have been a little bit better."

The floodgates open. What was that? asks another judge. Contouring powder? Contouring gone horribly, horribly wrong? "She looked gray!" "She WAS gray!" "What happened?" "It was awful!"

"She doesn't have any homosexual men in her life," Rocky reassures us. "We can work on that. We can fix it." This we know—at the beginning of the day, Rocky explained that he and his team of coaches and trainers and voice instructors can fix just about anything, except a young woman who gives a bad interview ("Just don't give me stupid," he pleads).

And what about the MIT grad? he asks, sounding still a little scold-y. Turns out, we all loved her. Some of us—me, I think—more than others. I hold my breath, waiting for someone to say something about how she was, clearly, at least twenty pounds heavier than the next-biggest girl, that her hair, fine and a little limp and clearly unenhanced by extensions, didn't look like pageant hair, how she needs a diet and a trainer and a makeover, but no one says it. The closest to body-shaming we get is Danica's mild suggestion that her two-piece did her no favors. "She should wear a one-piece, if that's where she feels comfortable."

Rocky nods. "I tell them all the time, you can win Swimsuit—you can win the whole thing!—as a three," on the one-to-ten scale. "It's all about confidence." He seems—he is, I'm pretty sure—unhappy that the curvy, funny girl wasn't one of the winners, and his sorrow is shocking, in a wonderful way. If this is who the expert, the pageant guy, wants as his Miss, maybe there's hope. Maybe there could have been hope for me. (And, as it turns out, there's even a second chance for Alissa Musto, the Harvard girl who steps up to replace Miss Cambridge after Miss Cambridge decides to focus on her studies and, in July, goes on to make Rocky and Dana the happiest men in the Commonwealth when she becomes Miss Massachusetts. By the time you're reading this, there's a chance that she could be the first Miss Mass to go all the way and that someone will have jabbed, unsuccessfully, at her head with bobby pins—that she could be, in the end, our ideal.)

At the end of the night, there's time for the local title-holders from all over New England—who, it seems, comprise half the audience—to take the stage and greet the crowd. Again, I'm pleasantly surprised. There are traditional Misses—big hair, little bodies, crowns and sashes and big, shiny grins—but there's a young woman in a sweater-vest and gray pants and flats who looks like she came from a part-time job at a library, and another in a vintage-style skirt and sweater set who's a dead ringer for a young Adele. Up close, you can see that these could be any girls, at any high school or gymnastics meet: there's bad skin underneath the makeup; padding in at least a few of the bras; imperfect bodies teetering on high heels. And, even in New England, there's a black winner, a Miss from Rhode Island with a wild Afro, who walks up to the microphone holding her six-year-old cousin's hand. "I wanted her to see how wonderful pageants are!" she says, and lifts her hand in a practiced gesture. Her cousin smiles and gives her own shy, tentative wave. I smile back at her, trying to make eye contact. I wish I could give her a crown. I wish, a little ruefully, that someone had given me one.

It's not until the very end of the night, when the judges are posing with the winners, that I realize how blinding the lights are, and that, from the stage, it's impossible to see anything of the audience at all. Up there, the potential Miss Americas aren't seeing friendly faces or loved ones' smiles, approval or disdain or anything at all—just darkness. While we are judging, they are looking into the abyss.

Twitter, Reconsidered

I love social media. Like Oprah loves bread, like millennials love selfies, like Romeo and Juliet loved each other before their untimely deaths, that's how much I love it. I love what it gives me—attention, a voice, a community, a chance to do my own publicity and marketing in a low-key, authentic way, a bunch of smart, snarky friends, authors and activists, experts in publishing and politics and even porn, who are constantly gathered 'round the virtual watercooler, ready to talk to me (or talk among themselves and let me eavesdrop). It's everything I never had as a lonely, nerdy girl, and everything I'll never get as a female genre writer in a world that still privileges literary men's voices.

My initial foray into the World Wide Web came via snail mail. Before *Good in Bed* was published, I had hundreds of postcards made, with the book cover and laudatory quotes on the front, my tour dates and a picture of my dog on the back. I used the baby Internet to build a list of every group or shop or book club or organization that might even be remotely interested in a story about a plus-size reporter who finds her happily-ever-after. I dug up their addresses and wrote them each a note, with the date I'd be in their city highlighted, signed with my name and a little doodle of my face.

My mother's then girlfriend had built me a website with a funny bio and a link to Amazon and many pictures of my dog. In 2002, my husband had launched his own blog and encouraged me to add one to my website. "That's fantastic!" my publisher cheered, before asking, "What is a blog, exactly?"

I'd just found out about weblogs myself, but I knew I wanted one. An online diary would be a way to stay in touch with my roots as a journalist, a way to talk about news and pop culture and gossip of the day, a way to talk directly to readers, and remind them of my existence between books—a crucial hustle when you can't count on the *New York Times* to do that job. I blogged for years, about my life, my writing, my writing life, my adventures as a new wife and mother. I talked about the time I was signing books at a Borders and a woman shyly approached my table, and how I thought she was going to ask for a signed book but what she really wanted was a token to unlock the bathroom door (I gave it to her). I described the bookstore in Dallas where the manager thought I was asking for copies of *When Bad Things Happen to Good People* instead of *Good in Bed*. (I signed them.) When *In Her Shoes* was made into a movie, I blogged about that process, from my day as an extra to the night of the premiere to the day it became clear it was going to be a flop. All through that awful release week, I posted excerpts from the best reviews I could find and basically promised readers a pint of my blood if they'd buy tickets. It didn't work, but at least there'd been a place for me to try.

When Twitter came along, I embraced it, too, feeling like it had been tailored for my hand. Tweeting was like blogging in miniature, blogging in real time, from the line at the coffee shop or the carpool pickup lane or the parents' holding pen at Little Gym. I was thrilled when the medium turned into what it is today: a worldwide soapbox, a democratizing force giving voice to the voiceless, a place where everyday people can find an audience and where their ideas can gain traction. It's where movements coalesce, where evildoers are exposed, where wrongs are righted and justice prevails.

Twitter, of course, is also a cesspit of crude, hateful misogyny, insults and name-calling and poorly considered tirades, rapid-fire escalations played out in impulsive and regrettable hundred-and-forty-character bursts. It's a place where, I hope, I've done some good, and a place where, for sure, I've had some fun, and a place where I've been horribly humiliated and made mistakes and said things I wish I hadn't said.

The problem with Twitter is that there are no take-backs. There's no way to edit a tweet once it's been tweeted, and while you can delete something you've thought better of, the Internet is forever . . . as many celebrities have learned to their sorrow. I learned the hard way to check the trending topics before tweeting anything, to make sure that there's no school shooting, no horrible violence, no civil war outbreak or celebrity death before I start gossiping about which author's been using the same headshot for a decade, or which literary critic's similarly long-lived cartoon avatar looks absolutely nothing like her. I try my hardest to deprive myself of that little frisson of self-righteousness that comes with joining a group as it points out someone else's misstep or stupidity. I try not to pile on myself, to jump on the victim of the day just because everyone else is jumping, and to take a deep breath before clapping back at the haters, remembering that even though I might feel like a picked-on nobody, it ain't necessarily so.

I joined Twitter in 2009 and, according to its helpful counter, I've sent just over twenty-seven thousand tweets, which sounds like a lot until you notice the nonstop word-sprayers who've topped six figures in less time. Through the years there have been plenty of tweets and posts and updates that I was proud of—ones that were pithy or funny or pointed, or ones that even, in their tiny way, moved the march of progress forward. There are also plenty that I wish I could reconsider, and a few times when I found myself in pitched Twitter battle, being body-slammed across the World Wide Web. Here are some of the tweets that I remember.

"Jason Mesnick is a tool."
Tweeted March 2009

With these five simple words, a calling—nay, an obsession—was born.

I had been a *Bachelor* devotee for the first few seasons, and fell away after I had a baby and the silliness of Lorenzo Borghese's season (remember him? the Italian prince?) became too much. As the years went on, I'd watch sporadically, and I just happened to be channel-surfing when bachelor Jason Mesnick, torn between Melissa Rycroft and Molly Malaney, stood on a balcony and cried. And then, as producers captured each delicious teardrop, he cried and cried and cried and cried and then he cried some more, and it was glorious and hideous and wonderful and awful and exactly what you want in your reality TV. And then, when you thought things couldn't get any weirder or worse or more embarrassing, Mesnick ditched Rycroft, the woman he'd chosen, on live TV, during the "After the Final Rose" special, and asked for Molly's hand instead.*

I had my Facebook fan page open at the time and I couldn't believe what I was seeing, so I posted an update, sharing my feelings about Jason with my Facebook friends. Five minutes later I had three hundred comments. Clearly there were people out there watching, people who wanted to discuss what they were seeing . . . and I was more than happy to talk about it with them. I moved over to Twitter, where I could follow *The Bachelor*'s many hashtags, tracking the conversation in real time and live-tweeting the show,

---

* The show—nay, television!—will never top that.

providing my own running commentary on its foibles, its excesses, its double standards and sexism, its drunken participants (the guy who slurred "Why am I not raping you right now?" at a fellow contestant), its demeaning challenges (a slow-speed race down a Beverly Hills street where women sat on tractors, in bikinis), and the money shots of jilted suitors sobbing in the backseat of a limousine. Live-tweeting was a way to love and hate the show at the same time, to be entertained by its boy-meets-crowd-of-girls, boy-culls-crowd-of-girls, girls-get-dumped-and-cry, while also recognizing and shining a disinfecting light on its narrow beauty standards, its relentless heteronormativity, its frustrating lack of diversity, what it says about desire versus the performance of desire; about true love and, with ever-recurring declarations about "journeys" and "fairy tales," the propagation of old, punitive myths about how happy endings work and who deserves to get them.

It has also been a way to make friends, to connect with a like-minded community of viewers and mockers, people who watch it lovingly and people who watch it ironically and people like me, who find a way to do both. As much as I love *The Bachelor*, I love watching it with Twitter even more.

"Dear Y.A., don't let the bastards get you down! Your friend,
Chick Lit"
Tweeted January 2013

This remains one of my most-retweeted tweets (almost a thousand retweets, which in my world is basically the equivalent of a National Book Award) . . . and I think I know why.

For years, chick lit—breezy books about young women in big cities—was reviled as the infected boil on the body of literature, the books where intelligence and insight went to die on their way to the shoe store. People *hated* chick lit. Even—especially—feminists, some of whom seem determined to prove that they weren't hairy-legged man-haters by finding something made by women that they, too, could mock. Female bloggers published posts entitled "Nine Reasons Why Chick-Lit Authors Should Be Kicked in the Head Until They Are Dead." Literary writers published a collection called *This Is Not Chick Lit*, billed as *Original Stories by America's Best Women Writers* (I joked that my ballot must've gotten lost in the mail). Chimamanda Ngozi Adichie, who'd go on to write the famous, Beyoncé-sampled "We should all be feminists," contributed a story, and Gloria Steinem's approving blurb appeared on the cover.

My problem, back in 2000, was that I didn't realize that I was writing chick lit. When *Good in Bed* was published, the term was only beginning to be used widely . . . and the first round of stateside single-in-the-city books hadn't been despised at all. In fact, they'd been celebrated on the cover of *New York* magazine, praised as smart and poignant takes on how modern women were living. I thought I was writing that kind of novel, a book with humor and heart and something to say, a story about a single girl in search of a happy ending that was not entirely dependent on a guy and that might amuse and comfort the girls and women like me. I did not realize that my book, with its fanciful script title, with its tempting slice of cheesecake, and its curvy naked legs on the cover, was the print equivalent of a flesh-eating virus with the potential to rot the very foundations of literature.

I didn't know . . . but the world was happy to instruct me. As much as women loved it, and as much as *Good in Bed* connected, there were critics and bloggers who disdained chick lit, with its pink covers and images of engagement rings, purses, and martinis, as everything that was wrong in publishing, and possibly the world. Female writers of literary fiction tried to lock in their spot as Authors of Quality and high-minded cool girls by insisting that, oh no, *their* books weren't chick lit, and by being as critical as they could about books that were. Chick lit, thundered an (anonymous, of course) editor, was "hurting America." It was driving real literature off the shelf, forcing high-end writers to turn their framed MFA toward the wall and insert gratuitous scenes of giggly brunches and drunken sexcapades into their serious works of fiction. A National Book Award–winning female writer told young female writers to "shoot high" and eschew imitations of "the derivative, banal stuff"—like chick lit. The novelist who wrote so movingly about women's place on "the second shelf" bemoaned the prevalence of "slumber-party fiction," easy-reading books where the heroines were crafted to feel like your best friends. Things reached a head when Lena Dunham—millennial feminist icon Lena Dunham!—told the *New York Times Book Review* that she detested "airport chick lit," books with sparkly engagement rings and baby carriages on the cover, or, really, any story that was "motored by the search for a husband."*

It was not a lot of fun, living through that era as one of the genre's more popular and outspoken writers whose first book did, indeed, end with a proposal. It was hard to be the one on the front lines insisting, over and over, that not only were these books not so bad, but they weren't always just about shoes and bags and husband-hunting, and they were surely no worse than thrillers and mysteries, genre books that got respectful mentions in the *Times* and whose authors were hardly ever accused of harming an entire nation.

Want to make the world holler? Be female . . . then stand up and say, *This thing that I created, this thing I made as a woman, for other women, is worth something.* Oh, the fun you will have! From the online literary critic whose "close reading" will not only pan your books but also you as a human being to the publisher, renowned for his gentlemanly ways, who will tell a reporter that your books don't deserve any attention and also are not as good as Jonathan Franzen's—whom he happens to publish—your life will be a carousel

---

* To be fair, Dunham lives in Brooklyn, a borough where, I am fairly certain, they send cultural critics to appraise the contents of residents' shelves, and if you're found with an unironic copy of anything by Danielle Steele, you're run out of town and forced to live on Staten Island.

of delights. Especially if your last name is Weiner. Turns out, not even the snootiest, most MFA'd critic can resist making the same "WHIN-er" jokes you've been hearing since the second grade.

The good news? Nothing lasts forever. By 2012 or 2013, the anti-chick-lit tsunami started to recede as the critics locked in on a new target—young adult books. Suddenly, lighthearted tales of bad dates and happy endings weren't the problem. Grown-ups reading *Twilight* in the subway were.

The day I sent the tweet, *Slate* had published a piece called "Against YA." Its author, Ruth Graham, had gleefully tweeted the day before that she knew her article would raise hackles, and indeed, it read like a provocation, as it told adults that they "should be embarrassed if what [they're] reading was written for children." Put down your *Hunger Games* and for God's sake pick up something worthwhile!

Young adult authors were predictably peeved. Plenty of librarians and booksellers and writers joined the chorus of "who are you to judge" and "at least people are reading something." I think my tweet caught on because it pointed at the cyclical nature of whose turn it is to sit in lit-land's dunking booth—how it's always someone, how it's usually books that are written by women, for the pleasure of other girls and women (the "Against YA" movement was preceded by a brief but violent sortie against *Fifty Shades of Grey*–style erotica), and how the hatred has as much to do with times and with trends as it does with intrinsic value.

I dream of a day when there's not a separate category for women's fiction, when the *Times* gives chick lit its due and covers it like male-genre books . . . and wouldn't it be nice if something lowbrow and male ended up in the crosshairs for once? It might never happen, but a girl can dream of the day when the critics decide that YA is A-OK—or that at least they can give it a break—and turn on science fiction or Westerns. Look out, estate of Louis L'Amour! #yourenext

If supporting Planned Parenthood is radical, then I am radical.
And so is my mom. And my Nanna. #IStandWithPP
Tweeted July 2015

My support for Planned Parenthood should not have come as a surprise to anyone who knows me. I've been a feminist my entire life, and I think that my fiction reflects that—not that my books whomp people over the head with a KEEP ABORTION LEGAL poster, but because I hope that I write about the issue around reproduction with sensitivity and also in a way that makes it clear that if women can't control their reproductive lives, they can't control their lives at all.

Of course, if you're someone with a following and a platform but you didn't get that following or that platform from politics, stepping into that contested land can get tricky. Basketball star Michael Jordan famously refused to endorse Harvey Gantt in his Senate race against famed racist Jesse Helms, quipping that Republicans also buy sneakers. Not only do they buy sneakers, but they buy books. Before I tweeted, I wondered: Was it worth wading into the fray and potentially alienating readers?

Most novelists don't. At least, not many of the ones I'd consider my cohort group. They use social media to post recipes for tarte tatins and pictures of their kids; they run jewelry giveaways and offer free movie tickets; they support other writers and talk up the books they're reading. I do most of that, too (except not the pictures of my kids, because their father and I believe that they deserve their privacy, and should not be used to boost my brand, and also because there are stalkers, and if the two of them want to blast selfies and bikini shots all over the Internet, they can do it when they're old enough to understand the consequences, and also the concept of permanence).

But I digress.

In 2015, Planned Parenthood was once again under attack. A right-wing group had cobbled together film footage purporting to show Planned Parenthood doctors selling baby parts for fun and profit. Politicians and presidential candidates and right-wing pundits joined in, demonizing Planned Parenthood, lying about what it did and whom it served, holding chest-thumping contests about how awful Planned Parenthood was and which one of them would defund the organization fastest and most completely. Christian extremists took the rhetoric as marching orders: in Colorado, a man stormed into an abortion clinic and killed three people while shouting "No more baby parts." Because pro-life.

I have never had an abortion. This is the result of being careful 90 percent of the time and being lucky the other 10. When I was working in State College and my health insurance didn't cover birth control, I went to the local Planned Parenthood affiliate for my checkups and my birth-control pills. I knew, from personal experience, that Planned Parenthood offered more than abortions . . . and I also knew that sometimes abortion is the absolutely correct choice, and that women—especially the ones who've used Planned Parenthood—need to stand up and protect it, to say, "Here's what Planned Parenthood is all about, and here's what it's done for me." Last but not least, my mom's partner, Clair, is a Planned Parenthood employee. I see how hard she works and I know whom she's working for, and it's not privileged white ladies like me. Her clientele is young, poor, diverse, less likely to have access to the kind of care that money guarantees.

I wasn't surprised at the blowback, the disappointed Facebook fans and Twitter followers who said, either with snark or with sorrow, that they came to me for entertainment, not politics, and that they'd been faithful readers but that they'd never buy my books again. I tried to accept it with equanimity, only occasionally tweeting a snarky "BUT HOW WILL I PAY FOR MY ABORTIONS NOW?" I spoke the truth as I'd lived it, and with the knowledge that simply sending a tweet was a relatively risk-free way to take a stand. Planned Parenthood had been there for me, and for women I loved, and I wanted it to be there for my daughters and their friends and all the girls and women who need birth control, need breast exams, need cervical cancer screenings and free condoms and yes, sometimes, abortions . . . and if that costs me readers, so be it.

> Left my yoga mat at Whole Foods and now I can't go back and get it because clichés.
> Tweeted April 2015

This actually happened! It was a nice yoga mat, too.

> @jenniferweiner sensing pattern. Little Freud in me thinks you would have liked at least to have had opportunity to sleep way to top
> Tweeted by Andrew Goldman, October 2012

The history: Goldman was the *New York Times* writer who conducted the Sunday magazine's cheeky Q and A with the famous and sort-of famous. His shtick was to ask provocative, in-your-face questions, and let readers watch his subject squirm on the hook. When he interviewed Whitney Cummings, he inquired, "On those Comedy Central roasts, your fellow comedians liked to joke about how you slept your way to fame. How accurate is that criticism?"

I was offended! I think that Cummings was, too, judging from her answer: "Do you know any example of anyone who's ever slept with a producer or whatever that has gotten them anywhere?" she retorted. I tweeted something about "Holy shit, in this day and age, are we really implying that successful ladies only got to the top on their backs?" Goldman responded on Twitter that, hey, Comedy Central had made jokes about it and thus it's fair game. I tweeted back that the *Times* should have different standards than Comedy Central, insofar as the *Times* is a respected purveyor of facts and Comedy Central has "Comedy" right in its name. Cummings joined in to theorize that Goldman hadn't been breast-fed long enough; Goldman tweeted that his mom had died, so there, and everyone went back to their respective corners.

Months later, Goldman did a Q and A with Tippi Hedren, who had just released a memoir describing how Alfred Hitchcock had hit on her, but that she'd found him repulsive. Then Goldman asked her whether there were any directors she would have slept with to further her career. Ugh. Here we go again. I tweeted, "Saturday am. Iced coffee. NYT mag. See which actress Andrew Goldman has accused of sleeping her way to the top. #traditionsicoulddowithout." Goldman tweeted back about his little Freud, implying that I was sensitive to illusory charges of sleeping-to-the-top because I'd never had the chance to do so myself.

I was, as it happened, once again a single lady at the time. I can tell you exactly where I was when I read that tweet (walking down the hall from the elevator to my boyfriend's apartment, prepared for a quiet day of writing, with my laptop in my purse). I can tell you exactly what I was wearing (my gray velour overalls and a long-sleeved purple T-shirt). I can tell you how I got dizzy for a minute, how my knees quivered and my hands shook, how I felt like someone had hit me in the gut with a battering ram. I staggered through Bill's door, skin icy, heart racing, shoved my phone in his hand, and said, *The* New York Times *just told the world that I'm too ugly to fuck.* Of course it wasn't the *Times* saying this, but it was the *Times'* guy, and it did, indeed, feel like the entire institution had risen up to pass judgment on my attractiveness, or lack of same. And how does Andrew Goldman even know what I look like! I railed. My Twitter avatar is a headshot—and it's a cute one! And his avatar is a rodent in a fedora! And is he so stupid that he doesn't realize that publishing's run by women? Does he understand that, in my line of work, I couldn't sleep my way to the top even if I was interested? And I've got two kids! Clearly, someone thought I was fuckable, at least twice!

Bill tried to calm me down. My friends assured me that I

looked fine and that Goldman was the one with the problem. None of it helped. I felt deeply ashamed and furious and sick—sick that there were men who thought that way; that there was so much vileness and bile maybe an eighth of an inch beneath a normal-seeming man's surface; sick that this guy was married with children, kids—maybe even daughters—he was influencing with his noxious views; sick that this was still the way the world operates, where the fastest way to silence a woman is telling her that she's ugly and thus not worth hearing from . . . and most of all, sick that it had worked.

Goldman spent the day on Twitter digging in his heels, first saying he'd meant his tweet as satire, then taking predictable shots at chick lit and insisting that his question to Hedren hadn't been sexist. I spent the day writing boldly about how despicable Goldman's remarks were, and how physical beauty should not be a litmus test about who is and is not allowed to have opinions, and how I would tell my daughters, every day, that it's who they are, not how they look, that counts. Meanwhile, I was inside, with the door locked and the shades drawn, huddled in a three-sizes-too-big brown cardigan with the hood pulled up. I didn't want anyone to see me. I didn't want to see myself.

Things got worse. The editor in chief of Gawker—who, as it turned out, was Goldman's good friend—published a screed entitled "Andrew Goldman Is Not a Misogynist and Neither Am I," tweeting about my "bonkers assertion" that Goldman's questions to Cummings and to Hedren had been sexist in the first place (because, I tweeted back, if a lady isn't ugly, she must be crazy!), and then asking if, since he couldn't call me ugly or crazy, he could at least call me stupid, citing my online biography, which referenced my love of reality TV, as proof that I was a big dum-dum.

Good times.

Goldman eventually apologized, saying that his wife told him he was behaving badly. I accepted his apology, figuring that a guy who had a wife, who knew what he'd done was awful and whom he was willing to heed, deserved a second chance.

Initially, it didn't seem like he'd get in any trouble at all. Goldman's editor, Hugo Lindgren, slapped his wrist, saying, "My feeling is that he had an unfortunate outburst and that he will learn from it." The *Times'* public editor, Margaret Sullivan, wasn't as inclined toward leniency. She called Goldman a "highly replaceable freelancer" and faulted his "level of obscenity and hideous misjudgment." When Goldman e-mailed me to say that, unsurprisingly, in the wake of Sullivan's column his job was in peril, I wrote to Jill Abramson, who was then the *Times'* editor in chief, to say that he'd made a mistake but did not deserve to be fired. I was still deeply rattled by what he'd written, but I wanted to shake it off . . . or at least act as if I could.

Eventually, Goldman was suspended for a month. He did his time and stayed at the paper until the summer of 2013. Interviewing Diane von Furstenberg, he'd asked her about her marriage in a way she found over-the-line offensive. Von Furstenberg complained to Jill Abramson, and Goldman—who, per Gawker, was already on a short leash because of "the Weiner debacle,"* was finally fired. Which just goes to show that maybe there's nothing you can't say to, or about, a woman, you just have to be careful to say it to, or about, a woman with less power and fewer connections than you.

I thought then, and think now, that Goldman's bad behavior was a symptom, that it was connected to institutional sexism in the world in general and at the *Times* specifically. It was no surprise to watch him go from mocking my looks to mocking my books. Goldman worked at a place where the culture supported different treatment of male and female writers—the former as deserving of respect and attention, the latter not necessarily worth more than mockery. Goldman was only echoing, in much

---

*   Which was, by the way, the alternate title for this book.

cruder terms, what editors at the paper felt about me, specifically, and writers like me in general—that we were beneath their notice, that our books were jokes, and if our work isn't serious, then our bodies and faces are probably laughable, too.

I still have mixed feelings about the Goldman mess—about what he said, about how the tweet led, at least in part, to his losing his job, about how I handled the whole thing. I knew that having my appearance put on blast that way was the equivalent of someone sticking a splinter into the root of an infected tooth. That was my sore spot; it was going to hurt.

I know that people say stupid, hurtful, cruel things in the heat of the moment, and lash out, sometimes inappropriately, when under attack . . . I know that I have, and I've regretted it . . . but it bothers me that this was the first place that Goldman's mind went, that it was, maybe, the first place any man's mind would go. *She's got a problem with what I wrote? She must be ugly. Or maybe I'll just say she is and that'll shut her up.* It made me sad and suspicious. It made me wonder, with every guy I'd speak with or meet, whether it was what all men were thinking, deep down, or maybe not so deep down—that any woman with a voice or an opinion or a criticism of their work must be ugly, must be sexually frustrated, must be unattractive and undesirable, and thus unimportant.

Worst of all, it made me quiet. Goldman wanted to shut me up, and for a while, he did. For weeks, I was gun-shy about social media, not to mention the men I'd interact with in real life. I walked around with my head down and brushed my teeth with my eyes closed, which is A) dangerous, and B) no way to live and nothing I want to show my daughters.

In the end, the *Times* found other writers to fill in for the column, eventually hiring Ana Marie Cox. It turned out that the highly replaceable freelancer was . . . highly replaceable.

In 2014, Goldman wrote an essay for *Slate* about losing his job, pinning the blame on the "little Freud" tweet and on Sullivan's column, which, he said, "pretty much did me in at the *Times*." He didn't say that I tried to defend him. He never even mentioned the von Furstenberg mess, or acknowledged that maybe his inability to understand his company's guidelines about social media, was the real problem—that it's one thing to perform insult comedy on your interview subjects, but another to do it with your readers. Goldman also wrote that "what made [his] column great" was his "mouthiness," his willingness to ask those in-your-face questions, to, at his editor's urging, "draw some blood." Maybe that's the saddest part of the story—that Goldman believed that he was a great writer, that asking *Glee* star Matthew Morrison, "Imagine you had the ability to see the number of a woman's sexual partners on her forehead. What's the highest number you could see and still take her seriously?" was speaking truth to power, or that asking Condoleezza Rice what it felt like to be booed at a Broadway show made him a force of righteousness, that he was a tremendous talent muzzled by the Big Bad Feminists, instead of a guy with the same bag of tricks as half the drive-time shock jocks in America who should have read his employee handbook more carefully.

PS: God, give me the self-confidence of a mediocre white man.

If your three-year-old says she "just wants to hold" the bottle of sparkly red nail polish, she is full of shit.
Tweeted April 2011

Still true.

Imagining Saint Peter, greeting new arrivals, gently suggesting that Scalia might be more comfortable at a "slower-track" kind of heaven.
Tweeted an hour after the news of Justice Antonin Scalia's death, February 2016

De mortuis nil nisi bonum, says the Latin—speak nothing but good of the dead.

Except what if the dead said rape victims can't sue their alleged attackers, thought minorities weren't smart enough to keep up at top colleges, and claimed that until fifteen years ago, everyone in history "understood" marriage was between a man and a woman?

On the one hand, yes, I get it—even the most terrible people are somebody's father, somebody's husband, somebody's brother or son. Antonin Scalia was survived by nine children, his wife, and Justice Ruth Bader Ginsburg, who somehow became his dear friend.

But his policies hurt people. Comparing gays to child molesters, calling their "lifestyle" "immoral and destructive," likening the "moral disapproval of homosexual conduct" to distaste for "murder or polygamy or cruelty to animals" is the kind of language that gives people permission to hate gay men and women, to kick their queer kids out of their houses so that they end up living on the street, to taunt them into suicide, to beat them or kill them.

I thought about it. Then I tweeted it. I got a lot of approval, a lot of "damn, that's cold," and a handful of "you have no class" and "show some respect," and, inevitably, variations on the theme of "too soon."

On Twitter, it's always the delicate balance of risk and reward—do I make the funny, provocative, in-your-face quip, then deal with the pearl-clutchers who feel compelled to tell me how awful I am and how they'll never buy my books again? Or keep quiet and hope someone else says what I'm thinking?

In this case, there were a lot of fans, and a few "you are unbelievably rude." Of course, the way I'm wired, the "you're an awful, classless monster" were the comments that stuck, so in retrospect, I think I should have kept my mouth shut.

If I'm Joan Didion's dog, I'm not liking my chances.
Tweeted November 2011

This one was right on the edge of funny versus awful. Joan Didion is, of course, a magnificent writer and a national treasure who has suffered unimaginable losses and written about them in a way that has brought comfort to thousands of grieving readers.

She's also someone who, to be completely crass and reductive, is profiting from her loved ones' deaths. Her husband dies—she writes a book. Her daughter dies—she writes a book. And we all know that, in a post–*Marley & Me* environment, books about dogs and about the beloved canine's inevitable demise, are huge bestsellers.

It made me laugh, the image of Didion sitting at her desk, a blank piece of paper before her, bereft of ideas, clad in black, with her Céline shades covering her eyes. The dog wanders into view, wagging its tail hopefully. Didion stares at the dog. Stares at the blank page. Looks at the dog again. The dog whimpers unhappily. Didion looks down at the page again. When she looks up, the dog is cringing by the door.

How about #Franzenfreude?
Tweeted August 2010

When my first book was published, in 2001, I had a modest set of aspirations. I wanted to go on a book tour, even if nobody showed up at my readings. I wanted to see the book for sale in stores, even if the only people who bought it were my friends. And I hoped for a review in the paper I'd read for my entire life, the *New York Times*.

The *Times* is the holy grail for most writers.* Being reviewed

---

* And by "most writers," I mean "in my head."

in the paper means you've really, truly made it—or at least, that's how it felt to me. But even before I was a writer, back when I was just a reader, I knew that a book like mine wasn't the paper's normal fare. Music critics at the paper wrote about opera and Top 40; TV critics covered sitcoms as well as PBS's twelve-part series on slavery; restaurant critics reviewed Per Se and the under-twenty-five-dollar-a-head ethnic eateries in the boroughs. Every day, in every section, the paper made an effort to be broad and inclusive, to recognize that its readers weren't all rich or male or even New Yorkers. Then I'd open up the Sunday paper and a version of the *Paris Review* would land in my lap. The book critics mostly ignored popular fiction and stuck to capital-*L* Literature . . . unless they were reviewing the popular fiction that men read.

Just as galling as what looked, to me, like straight-up sexism was the paper's church-and-state separation of its daily and Sunday critics. The daily people weren't allowed to talk about what they were reviewing with their *Book Review* counterparts, which meant that you could read a mixed-to-positive review of a literary novel on Thursday, then a mixed-to-positive review of the same book, by a different critic, in the Sunday section.

In previous decades, a writer who disapproved of the Gray Lady's policies would have had to content herself with muttering imprecations to her spouse, her mom, her friends, her dog. But in the brave new world of social media, that same writer could hit Twitter and broadcast her displeasure to the world.

I'd noticed the gender/genre divide for a while, and for years had blogged about what I'd seen in the *Times*—how many male writers were getting the hat trick of two reviews and a profile, how many women were seeing their books relegated to the Style section, how dismissive the paper was when it deigned to even mention chick lit, how lucky I felt when *Good in Bed* earned a few positive words in a Janet Maslin beach-book round-up, and that I was allowed to sneak my book into my wedding announcement. When Twitter came along, it became even easier to give assessments, almost in real time, of what the paper was doing or not doing—how there were three pieces on the new Nicholson Baker book, which would go on to sell fewer than ten thousand copies, but the only mention of the new Terry McMillan, which was in beach bags across the land, came in a snide reference in the Inside the List column, to her divorce; how the paper quoted or mentioned Gary Shteyngart more than eighty times in five years, and no female writer came close.

When the paper joined in the coronation of Jonathan Franzen in 2010, I shouldn't have been surprised.

Franzen had emerged onto the cultural landscape in 1996, when he wrote an essay in *Harper's* bemoaning the lowly position of the literary novelist in the world of ideas. Interspersed with his insistence that writers like him deserved to be more relevant were attacks on the long, long list of things he disliked. Franzen called bestsellers "vapid, predictable and badly written." He attacked his peers, literary writers who put their e-mail addresses on their book flaps, as embarrassments. He complained that "our presidents, if they read fiction at all, read Louis L'Amour and Walter Mosley," and even went after his own brother for failing to understand that Franzen's work was "simply better" than Michael Crichton's.

Then came Oprah. In 2001, she made Franzen's dreams of relevance come true by choosing his third novel, *The Corrections*, for her popular TV book club. Franzen accepted her invitation, then spent the next two weeks trashing Oprah's taste, denigrating her viewers, fretting that her sticker on his masterpiece would keep serious, male readers away, and generally acting like such a pretentious, elitist ingrate that even Harold Bloom came forward to condemn him. Oprah rescinded her invitation, with the frosty declaration that "it was never [her] intention to make anyone uncomfortable." Franzen issued a few limp sorry-not-sorries, and the world moved on.

In 2010, Franzen was back with a new novel. *Time* magazine put him on its cover beneath the headline "Great American
Novelist" (never mind that *Time* was among the long list of institutions Franzen had sneered at in his *Harper's* essay). The *New
York Times* wrote half a dozen stories in the run-up to *Freedom*'s
publication, posting the first of two glowing reviews online days
before the book's release, profiling the author, then writing about
the public's feelings about Franzen, behaving as if its job was to
sell the book, not cover it. Some female writers were less than
amused. Jodi Picoult tweeted that she wasn't surprised to see the
Times lavish ink on "another white male literary darling," and
I wrote about how, even in a world where the *Times* typically
gave the lion's share of its attention to men, this seemed exces-
sive. When Lizzie Skurnick, who wrote the Sunday *Magazine*'s
"That Should Be a Word" column, tweeted to ask what to call
the Franzenfrenzy, I was working on my own book at the Truro
Public Library. I dashed off, "#Franzenfreude," without first consulting the German-to-English dictionary that I don't have, because I never studied German (it isn't a language that Jewish
families tend to urge their children to acquire).

It turned out, of course, that the "freude" part of "schaden-
freude" means "joy." It also turned out that, in spite of my very
compelling hashtag, the *Times* was in no hurry to relinquish its
unofficial duties as Franzen's personal publicist. Instead of pulling back, the paper doubled down, running more stories about
Freedom and Franzen, even dispatching a reporter to cover
Franzen's book-release party. Her breathless account of the evening—a list of the members of "literary Elysium" who attended,
descriptions of the cut of the *New Yorker* book editor's dress and
the "high-ceilinged rooms awash in the romantic luster of the
Colonial era"—concluded with the citizens of Elysium, including Franzen's editor, Jonathan Galassi, and *Salon* book critic
Laura Miller, lining up to take shots at the "detractors who've

groused at his good fortune." The whole thing ran beneath the completely objective, not at all biased headline "In This Galaxy, One Star Shines Brightest."

It was gross. It was bad journalism. It was completely disingenuous of the *Times* to report on the "good fortune" of the bright star that it had been instrumental in creating. It was also not Franzen's fault. He'd been a jerk about popular fiction, he'd been a dick to Oprah and her readers, he'd turned up his nose at the kind of attention and praise that most writers would have killed their own mothers, or at least hobbled their pets, for. But he was just the right kind of writer (white, male) in the right place (New York City) at the right time, with the right publisher (Farrar, Straus and Giroux) to enjoy the *Times'* largesse. And the great good fortune didn't end with the newspaper. Oprah, after years of preaching that women shouldn't go back to men who'd hurt them, made *Freedom* a book-club pick and invited Franzen back to her show. Franzen managed to stop insulting her long enough to collect her endorsement, and the attendant hundreds of thousands of sales that her imprimatur guaranteed, before going back to his regularly scheduled Oprah-bashing. It looked like Status Quo 1, Jealous Grousing Detractors 0.

But, in the days and weeks after the Franzenfrenzy subsided, the social-media conversation continued to simmer—about whose books were getting reviewed, and where, and by whom, and with what language; about who were the "right" writers to drive the conversation, about whether change was necessary, about whether change was possible. People kept talking. Back then, their number included Franzen himself, who acknowledged that, yes indeed, women's books were packaged differently, and treated differently, than books by men . . . and then people started counting.

At the very end of what felt like a very, very long summer, I was having dinner at the Wicked Oyster in Wellfleet when my phone pinged. About ten people, from my agent to my editor to my sister to my mom, were e-mailing the same link, asking "Did you see this?"

"This" turned out to be a story in *Slate*, where a reporter had actually gone through and counted up how many men and how many women the *Times* had reviewed in a just-shy-of-two-years period. The news for *Times* defenders was not good.

Of the 545 fiction books reviewed in the *Times* between June 29, 2008, and August 27, 2010, 338 were written by men (or 62 percent of the total) and 207 were written by women (or 38 percent of the total). Of the 101 fiction books that received two reviews in that period (one in the newspaper during the week and one in the weekend's *Book Review*), 72 were written by men and 29 were written by women.

I remember sitting in the dining room and saying, loudly enough for the sunburned, red-pants-wearing diners at neighboring tables to turn and stare, "I told you so!"

The *Slate* count was only the first of the damning tallies. That year, an organization of women in the arts called VIDA started counting, not just at the *Times*, but at a range of high-end newspapers and magazines. Its first Count, which would become an annual event, appeared in 2011. The organization used pie charts to illustrate the problem. What they found was shocking, even to me.

In 2010, the *Atlantic* reviewed books by 10 women and 33 men. *Harper's* reviewed 21 women and 46 men. The *New Yorker* published articles and short stories by 163 women, 449 men. At the *New York Review of Books*, a whopping 88 percent—or 133 of 152 articles—were written by men. And in 2010 the *New York Times Book Review* reviewed 283 books by women, 584 books by men.

The numbers prompted stories and pointed headlines. "Few Female Bylines in Major Magazines," from the *Columbia Journalism Review*. "Where Are the Women Writers?" in *Mother Jones*. "Voices Unheard: Female Bylines Still Lacking in

Male-Dominated Literary Magazines" on Yahoo.com. Editors were called on to justify their pies. Some were defensive. Others were contrite. "It's certainly been a concern for a long time among the editors here, but we've got to do better—it's as simple and as stark as that," said David Remnick of the *New Yorker*.

In the five years since *Freedom* was published, there's been some improvement. In 2011, the *Atlantic*'s bylines were 28 percent female. In 2014, they were 40. The *New Republic* inched up from 23 to 27 percent. The *New Yorker*'s percentage rose from 30 to 33 percent, while *Harper's* went from a dismal 23 percent to 32 percent. Best of all, from my perspective, the *Times* hired a (female) editor of the *Book Review* who seems to have effortlessly corrected its gender imbalance, and who launched a column called "The Shortlist," which makes room, sometimes, for romance and popular fiction. Which would be great . . . if you didn't know that the paper devotes regular columns to crime fiction and science fiction and horror, to YA and children's books and even self-help, but still has no regular, dedicated space for romance or commercial women's fiction.

So—baby steps. But also an example of how Twitter can at times be a force for good, a way to raise awareness, to point out a problem, to chart progress, and to cheer when things get better.

Once again, my milkshake has failed to bring even a single boy to the yard.
Tweeted February 2013

Again—still true.

In a court document, Bill Cosby says he gave drugs to women before sex.
Tweeted by the *Washington Post*, November 2015

I think you spelled "before he raped them" wrong.
Tweeted by me, November 2015

The "here, I fixed that for you" or "I think you spelled that wrong" trope has become a popular one on Twitter, with readers crossing out and rewriting, offering real-time corrections of what they see as bad hot takes on everything from rape to race to whether Jerry Jones is "running" or "ruining" the Dallas Cowboys. The Cosby scandal generated dozens of the "fixed that for you" tweets and posts. Even in these enlightened times, it seems like writers and editors still struggle with the distinction between sex and sex crimes, between a man who takes a woman to bed—which is sex—and a man who takes a woman to bed after he's laced her tea with Rohypnol—which is rape.

The Cosby case itself is an example of Twitter working right. In the Philadelphia area, we'd all heard rumors and allegations about Bill Cosby for years. *Philadelphia Magazine* had reported extensively on the story that Cosby had drugged and raped Andrea Constand, an assistant basketball coach at Temple . . . but the story hadn't gained national traction. Twitter was what nailed Cosby's coffin shut, with people retweeting jokes that comedian Hannibal Buress made about him, and people tweeting their own hilarious captions under images of Cosby grinning and mugging, after his social media team made the epic mistake of asking Twitter to "meme me!"

The Cosby story illustrates that if you're going to be out and about and online, you'd better understand the way the wired world works. Twitter is ultimately a tool, and as is true with all tools, you can use it for good and for evil. It's a hammer that you can use to build or tear down; a knife that can cut oppressors or turn in your hand if you're holding it wrong. For many of my cohorts, social media isn't optional—these days, publishers are, if not requiring, at least strongly urging their authors to engage with their reading public, and only a handful of high-end writers can decide to just skip it.

But Twitter doesn't come with a handbook. Publishers don't offer tutorials to their writers about what to tweet and when and how and to whom (although maybe they should). It's trial and error—in my case, a whole lot of error, coupled with instances where I've tweeted first, regretted later.

When I think about my life online, I remember the scene in *The Breakfast Club* where Ally Sheedy's rich, weird-girl character is asked what her parents do that's so bad. With her eyes welling and her voice trembling, she whispers, "They ignore me." I know how that feels.

I know what it's like to be ignored, dismissed, written off as beneath notice, or even contempt. Maybe that's why, whether it's an institution or an individual, a *New York Times* freelancer suggesting that women sleep their way to the top, or a country-western DJ who was dismissive and rude to me, and a bunch of other accomplished women, while he fawned over a former NFL star, there's some deep and deeply wounded part of me that cries out for justice, or at least some acknowledgment that what happened was neither fair nor kind. And so I dive into the tweet-storm, fingers flying, heart pounding, elbows up, and if I don't end up saying something I regret, it's a guarantee that I'll get to hear something regrettable said about me.

Being a woman with opinions on the Internet guarantees that you're going to be criticized, sometimes politely and thought-fully, sometimes in ways that make you contemplate calling the cops. Speaking up gets you eye-rolls and sighs and anonymous criticism; it gets you called an attention whore and "a notorious baiter," "strident" and "subliterary," an "imperfect vessel" and an "unfortunate spokeswoman." Over and over, you hear you're just a mouthy bitch, that you're just jealous, and that you're no Cynthia Ozick, which is not a thing you were aware you were going for.

It's easier to be quiet.

But here's the thing, the one I frequently tell myself when my feelings are smarting and I can't sleep at night. Activists aren't here to make friends. We are here to say the things you don't want to hear, to smack you in the face with inconvenient truths, to comfort the afflicted and afflict the comfortable, to force the world to improve. As Elie Wiesel said, "Neutrality helps the oppressor, never the victim. Silence encourages the tormentor, never the tormented."

In other words, if nobody says anything, nothing gets better.

Sometimes I wish I could, per Aaron Burr, tweet less, smile more. As the years have gone by, I've done a better job of picking and choosing, stepping back and weighing the risks versus benefits.

But sometimes, someone has to say something . . . and sometimes, if that someone has to be me, then so be it. With any luck, when I die (many, many years from now, next to my husband, in bed, with my dog curled up beside me and a large half-eaten piece of chocolate cake nearby), I hope that my obituary won't just say "bestselling author." I hope it will say "bestselling author and activist," or "bestselling author who tried to do some good and leave things better."

TLA: *The Bachelor* and Me

Life Lessons with *The Bachelor*

@jenniferweiner

"Will he look cute in wedding pictures" is a very important
question to ask before making a lifelong commitment. #notreally
#bachelorette

@jenniferweiner

Internet went down. I may have possibly used the word
"emergency" with my provider. #bachelor

@jenniferweiner

Oh, Ben. Pretty sure you can't say, "I have traditional values" when
you're wooing four women on a reality show. #bachelor

@jenniferweiner

"I feel like I'm in a fairy tale," says Court. Yeah, I remember when
Cinderella went hot tubbing, in a bikini. On national TV. #bachelor

@jenniferweiner

We're off! Whenever I say, "I need something from you" in
the bathroom, it's usually toilet paper, not declarations of love.
#thebachelor

@jenniferweiner

"Nick and I talked a couple of times over text." In 2015, that's third
base, right? #thebachelorette

@jenniferweiner

She wouldn't let her guard go down/She joked and was the cute
class clown/True love she sought, but did not get/Will she be a
bachelorette?

@jenniferweiner

In other news, I keep getting older and these women just stay the
same. #bachelor

Bachelor Time Can Be Family Time

@jenniferweiner

Sean's mom's biggest concern is that her son isn't "absolutely

sure." Also, herpes. But she's not talking about that.
#bachelornation

@jenniferweiner

I actually want Courtney to get a hometown. I need to see
what kind of parents produce that. And then not be them.
#bachelor

@jenniferweiner

My parents probably prayed for my husband, but in a totally
different way from the Seans. More like, "God help that guy."
#bachelornation

@jenniferweiner

And the seven-year-old is now watching the #bachelor with me. I
give up. Somewhere, the Tiger Mother is laughing.

@jenniferweiner

Four-year-old pulled my highest heels out of the closet,
announced, "When I am on the #Bachelor program, I will wear
these!" #uhoh

@jenniferweiner

Emily tells Brad being a parent's not all fun and games. Word.
Sometimes the kids need you when you're trying to watch the
#bachelor.

@jenniferweiner
"This lady is a crybaby!"—my eight-year-old. Hard to refute.
#bachelorette

@jenniferweiner
Just accused the four-year-old of "not being here for the right
reasons." #bachelor

On Fashion and Grooming

@jenniferweiner
Jade's face says "I am so, so sad." Jade's chest says, "Hello,
world!" #thebachelor

@jenniferweiner
Sean wonders if Catherine can settle down and start a family.
Her mouth say yes. Her nose piercing says, "I'm outta here."
#bachelornation

@jenniferweiner
And Lindsay has TAKEN OFF HER SHOES. Because Sean NO
LONGER DESERVES HER in heels. #bachelornation

@jenniferweiner
Brad and his Stubble of Difficult Decisions has arrived. Here we go!
#bachelor

@jenniferweiner

Serious q: do the #bachelor ladies do their own makeup? I imagine Emily in the bathroom with a spraygun set to Disney Princess. #bachelor

@jenniferweiner

Anyone else having a hard time taking seriously the declarations of a woman who appears to have forgotten to put on pants? #bachelorette

@jenniferweiner

Weatherman in a banana hammock: cloudy with a chance of shame. #bachelorette

The Bachelor Only Gets Better with Cocktails

@jenniferweiner

So the shocking outtake is that Em spilled wine and cursed. Scandal! Or as it's known in my house, Tuesday. #bachelorette

@jenniferweiner

Anyone else wonder how he can keep all their names straight? I get my kids mixed up after half a beer. #bachelor

@jenniferweiner

Drink every time someone says "journey," "chemistry" or "fairy tale." Or Jake shows his abs! #bachelor

@jenniferweiner

Ben and Lindzi slide deep into a gorge. Yeah, that means sex. I'm drinking. #bachelor

Spelling and Grammar, *Bachelor*-Style

@jenniferweiner

"There is no doubt that it will be him and I at the end of this." Ben and his ladies are trying to kill me with their grammar. #TheBachelor

@jenniferweiner

Eesh. Two vocabulary and emotionally-challenged people trying to have a conversation about feelings. It burns. #TheBachelor

@jenniferweiner

We're at Jef's ranch. Where, in my imagination, the cattle are all branded with Jef's missing F. #bachelorette

@jenniferweiner

"We're always kissing, because I feel that that's how he can really express himself to me." Also, he doesn't know many words. #bachelornation

@jenniferweiner

We're off! "Although I see Catherine as my wife, I equally see Lindsay as my wife as well." And the English language wept. #bachelornation

And Don't Forget the Supporting Cast

@jenniferweiner

An elephant lumbers onscreen. It's enormous and wrinkly and eating while it walks. It's now my second-favorite character. #bachelornation

@jenniferweiner

"Emily didn't pick you," taunts Sean's nephew. Who has now become my all-time favorite person on this show, ever. #bachelornation

@jenniferweiner

The crew member checking his Blackberry as Tierra weeps is officially my favorite #bachelor shot, ever. EVER.

Miss

Over the course of her reproductive life, one out of two women will lose a pregnancy—through either miscarriage or abortion. American women are only just beginning to talk about abortion out loud, to have a conversation about the choices we make and how it feels—if we're sorry or relieved, or if we don't feel much of anything at all.

There's still very little talk about miscarriages, in spite of how many women have had them. So here, with regret, is my contribution to the literature.

This is what happened to me.

Adam and I have been separated since 2010, peacefully divorced since 2013. We get along, for the sake of our daughters, and also because, in spite of the demise of our marriage, we still genuinely like each other. Adam's career has taken off. He's one of the country's go-to guys for campaign finance and election law. He lives in an apartment right around the corner from the house where I still live and does an excellent job of parenting our girls. The girls are with me every day after school, and they get to see their dad almost every day, too. Bill's been living with me for the last year, and he's a calm, gentle partner, another male presence in Lucy and Phoebe's life, another man who loves them. No girl can ever have enough of those.

It's Friday right before Christmas, a normal, busy day. I ride my bike fifteen miles to my therapist's office (the bike ride's almost as helpful as the actual therapy). Then I take the train back home, drop off my bike, meet Phoebe at the bus stop, and take her to the little bookstore around the corner to buy a gift for the birthday party she's attending.

The plan is, get Phoebe in the car, take her to her friend's house in Center City, then get on the highway and drive an hour to Berwyn to pick up Lucy, who's hanging out with a friend, and drop her off at the movie theater near our house, where she's seeing *Star Wars* with her dad. A typical, if slightly harried, early evening with children . . . except at some point around five, I start losing my mind. Maybe I'm tired from the bike ride, or chilled, because I didn't have time for a shower, but, after we've bought our goodies, I hear myself snapping at Phoebe to hurry and get in the car. When we're halfway to the party, she notices that she's forgotten the present, and I sigh and whip the car into an illegal U-turn.

"Mommy, are you mad?" Phoebe asks in a tiny voice.

"I'm not thrilled," I tell her. "I wish you'd remembered to bring it. I wish I'd remembered to check." I look at the clock and realize that I'm not going to make it to Berwyn to get Lucy back in time for the movie, so I call Adam to ask if he's home from work. I get lucky, he picks up, and as soon as he agrees to take Phoebe to the party, I drop her off and start the hour-long ride to pick up my eldest daughter.

On the ride home, things do not improve. When Lucy starts giving me her usual twelve-year-old sass, I'm snarky instead of jokey or patient or even just quiet, and after a five-minute recitation of her preteen woes, I tell her, "I think we're done on this topic," and I turn up the *Hamilton* soundtrack.

I know that I'm not behaving like myself. I need to calm down, put things in perspective, realize that being late to a party or a movie, or even showing up gift-free is no big deal. The next day I resolve to do better, and when the girls go to Adam's, I go to the gym. After ninety minutes of Restorative Yoga with my favorite instructor, holding poses for long intervals, ending flat on my back with my legs up against the wall, I go to my favorite bakery, reasoning that sfogliatelle will make everything better, and that, after ninety minutes of sun salutations and listening to a long talk about intention, I deserve something sweet. I'm standing in line when a horde—there is no other word—of drunken Mummers shove their way into the store and start bellowing off-key Christmas carols, to the delight of the other patrons and the ladies behind the counters. Mummers are a unique-to-Philadelphia phenomenon, one of the few things about my city that I genuinely cannot stand. Mummers are men who, on New Year's Day, get gussied up in elaborate, sequined costumes, some of which are basically women's dresses, and twirl parasols and parade down Broad Street in troupes or string bands. Some Mummers are accomplished musicians with dazzling choreography. Others are drunken thugs. They march in brigades trailed by slow-moving vans packed floor to ceiling with cans of Coors Light. These princes among men start drinking first thing in the morning, then stagger up to, and back from, the parade route in their polyester frocks, peeing into convenient gutters and against the walls of row houses (including—every year—mine), and snarling, "What's your problem, bitch? You've never seen one of these before?" when you ask them to do their business elsewhere.

Today's Mummers are from Category Two, and they appear to have been warming up for the New Year's festivities. Once they've shouldered their way into the bakery, they bellow off-key versions of "Rudolph the Red-Nosed Reindeer" and "Frosty the Snowman" and "Silent Night." "And none of this 'Happy Holidays' crap!" hollers their ringleader, a gentleman in a top hat and a stained Eagles sweatshirt, who jingles a cluster of bells to emphasize his point. "It's 'Merry Christmas,' not 'Happy Holidays,' am I right?"

I roll my eyes at the woman in line behind me, who's wearing a hijab and holding a little boy's hand. Then I notice that she doesn't look annoyed or amused. She looks scared.

Her instincts aren't off. It's been less than a month since a radicalized American and his bride from Tehran shot up an office holiday party in San Bernardino, less than two since the terrorist bombings in Paris. Donald Trump is giving daily speeches telling voters that we need to keep Muslim immigrants out of America—"until we know what's going on"—chewing over the phrase "radical Islamic terror," which he says whenever he can, and repeating claims that he saw Muslims cheering on 9/11 after the Twin Towers went down. It is not a good time to be in a hijab and out in public; not a good time, really, to be any kind of American, except a God-fearing Christian one. And a man, of course. Always better to be one of them. Because it's Merry Christmas, not Happy Holidays, am I right?

I stand in front of the woman, my body angled so the drunken Christmas-insisters can't see her. I listen as she quietly interrupts the cashiers, who are clapping and singing along, and asks if there's another way out of the bakery besides the front door. I leave without buying anything, pushing my way through the fog of beer and rum surrounding the Mummers, knowing that I'll never be back; that this place is done for me. When I get home, I am crying. What's going on in the world? I ask Bill, trying to catch my breath. Why are people so awful? What if the Mummers spotted this woman and tried to do something to her? How did she explain to her little boy why they had to sneak out the back?

By the end of this recitation, I am crying so hard I can barely breathe, and Bill is looking at me with considerable alarm. I go upstairs, run a bath, take deep breaths. I realize that my reaction isn't in proportion to what I've seen, which was sad and scary, but which did not end in violence. In my head, I run through a checklist: Am I taking my medication? Getting enough exercise, enough sleep? Did I eat breakfast? Is there anything else going on?

At some point, I realize that I should have gotten my period the week before. Well, that's it, I think. Menopause. I'm forty-five, so this is probably about when I hop on the hormonal roller coaster for the next five years or so. At some point, just to rule out the obvious, I rummage through my bathroom cabinets and locate an ancient pregnancy test. I pee on the stick. Less than ten seconds later, there are two emphatically blue, make-no-mistake lines.

Positive.

After I get over being freaked out, I'm excited. I'm actually pretty thrilled. Yes, my kids are older, but at eight and twelve it's not as if they're so old that a sibling would seem ridiculous. Except I'm forty-five! I know women who've had babies at forty, forty-one, forty-two, forty-three . . . but forty-five? This is crazy, right?

Also, there's history. A few years ago, I got pregnant with what the medical establishment, in its not-at-all gendered or judgmental language, called a "blighted ovum." Basically, it was a bad egg, and my body realized it was no good and shut down the proceedings almost before the pregnancy began. My doctor gave me misoprostol, a drug designed to soften the cervical opening and start the process of the uterus emptying, and sent me home with minimal instructions—if I was bleeding so much that it scared me, go to the ER. Basically, it sounded like I'd take the pill and get my period. "You might have some cramping," my doctor said, and I shrugged. Cramps I could handle. No big deal.

As it turns out, the process was a little more involved than that. I was bleeding a frightening amount, except I wasn't sure it was enough to justify a trip to the hospital . . . and it hurt, a lot more than I'd thought ("bad cramps" made it sound like the miscarriage would be like the first day of my period, not the worst day of my reproductive life).

I do not want to go through that again. I'm afraid to get my hopes up, certain that, at my age, this will just be the same nightmare. I'll go in, there won't be a heartbeat, I'll hear all kinds of fun language about blighted eggs and incompetent cervixes and "advanced maternal age" thrown around, and the whole thing will end in blood and sorrow.

Not only that, but the timing is rotten. Given the way the holidays fell, not to mention my beloved ob/gyn decamping for the suburbs the year before, the earliest I could get to see a doctor is three days after the New Year. I spend ten days holding my breath, taking daily pregnancy tests to confirm that I'm still expecting, swinging between delight and terror, avoiding alcohol and saunas, wanting to tell my friends, not being able to tell anyone, because, at forty-five, you wait until basically the baby's crowning before you announce the joyous news.

Finally, we make it to the doctor's office. Bill sits in the corner, and I lie on my back, babbling, as the technician slathers gel on a wand. "So, I was pregnant before, but I had a miscarriage, and it was a blighted ovum . . ."

The doctor inserts the probe and tilts the screen on the monitor.

"Well, this isn't that," he says, and points, so that we can see the tiny, insistent flicker of the heartbeat. Bill, who's never been through this before, who has no children of his own, starts to cry. Not a few sniffles or a discreet tear or two. Full-on, silent, tears-streaming-down-his-face, shoulders-shaking man-tears. On the table, I roll my eyes at the doctor. "Want to look at another pussy?" I ask.

Bill and I both know the risks. When you're forty-five, half of all pregnancies end in miscarriage . . . and of the ones that don't, the rates for complications from stillbirth to autism are much higher than they are for younger women. But we also know how real it felt, once we'd seen that little flicker. My doctor is cautiously optimistic, telling us that a visible heartbeat means that the risk of a miscarriage has decreased significantly.

"But I'm so old," I moan.

"Not really," the doctor says. "Come back when you're fifty-two. Then we'll talk about old."

I was ready for him to tell me to go home, report directly to bed, and spend the next eight months holding still with my legs crossed and my midsection swaddled in bubble wrap. Instead, he tells me to take prenatal vitamins, avoid tuna, and come back in a month. Yes, I can exercise. Yes, I can travel. "Just go and live your life," he says.

We try not to get too excited as we begin to make plans. First, we have to get married. "You need to give this baby a name!" was, I think, how I put it. Bill and I have had desultory conversations about a wedding at some point down the road, but the pregnancy lends a new urgency to the endeavor. In ten days we've compared calendars, selected a suitable Saturday, sent out save-the-date e-mails, ordered invitations, drafted a prenup, hired a rabbi and a caterer and a florist and a violinist. Bill buys me a beautiful ring and basically shoves it at me over the dinner table.

"Aren't you going to say anything?" I ask, shaking my head at the total and complete absence of sentiment.

"Jennifer Agnes Weiner, will you marry me?"

Good enough. I glare at him a little longer, which gives him time to explain that he's so anxious about having something that expensive in his care that he wanted to make it my responsibility as soon as he could. I put on the ring, buy an adorable little bridal hat, a fascinator with a birdcage veil, and a dress with a forgiving waistline. January goes by at a crawl. We talk about names—Ruby or Josie for a girl, Archie for a boy—and when, exactly, is the right time to tell my daughters. I go for acupuncture once a week and stay away from sushi. Every night that I don't start bleeding feels like a victory. After ten weeks, we'll go for the genetic testing that will tell us whether things are chromosomally normal. I book an appointment with the counselor for a Monday, and, on the Thursday before the ten-week mark, I fly up to the Berkshires to spend a relaxing, take-my-mind-off-things weekend with a friend at Canyon Ranch.

I haven't told anyone but a few of my best friends about the pregnancy. I hadn't planned on telling anyone at all, but my mom and Molly had both figured it out after we'd announced the wedding. ("That's wonderful!" said my mom. "That's crazy!" said Molly. "You're, like, Halle Berry old!") But at Canyon Ranch, I have to come clean. "You're glowing," says Juliana, and I'm so thrilled to tell her why. I schedule a prenatal massage and a mom-to-be facial, and I book a personal trainer to help me devise an exercise routine that I can keep up until the baby comes.

On Friday night, I go for my massage. Afterward, smelling like lavender oil, floating on a cloud of bliss, I amble to the bathroom . . . and, when I wipe, there's a swipe of light brown on the toilet paper.

I think, in my heart, I know what's happening, even as I Google for encouragement—as if blood is ever good news—and pray for the best. Little Ruby. Little Archie. I want so much for this to be real, to have a baby, my last baby, with Bill. I will be a good mother; I'll use everything I've learned; I'll have all kinds of help, a village to raise this last little one, and maybe I won't be the youngest or the most energetic mom in the breastfeeding class or at the playgroup, but there won't be a mother who will love her baby more.

By Saturday the spotting has turned into bleeding. Reluctantly I go to the local hospital, where I wait for hours alone in an exam room, until a nurse comes to hook me up to an IV. The plan is to pump me full of fluids, filling up my bladder, which will help with the ultrasound. "Are you Jennifer Weener the writer?" she asks, putting the needle in the crook of my arm, and I say that yes, I am, and she starts to tell me how much she loves my books. I'm trying not to cry as I ask her for her address and tell her I'll send her a signed copy of my latest. The first rule of womanhood is that you never yell when you feel like yelling, or throw things when you feel like throwing them. You want people to like you, so you behave, even when what you want to do is scream and pull your hair and say, instead of *Thanks for reading*, *This isn't fair* and *Fix it* and *Tell me it'll be okay*.

It takes forever to be wheeled down for the ultrasound, and once I'm there, the technician isn't allowed to tell me what she's seeing. "You need to talk to the doctor" is all she'll say. But I know, from her silence, from the stillness of her face, that the news is not good.

"I'm sorry," says the doctor. "I am not seeing a heartbeat."

"Yeah," I say. "I'm sorry, too." Calling up Bill, telling him what had happened, is the hardest part, one of the worst things I've ever had to do. "Oh," he says, and starts to cry, which makes me cry harder. I've been a mother; he's never been, will never be, the biological father of children. We've tried not to get ahead of ourselves, tried not to let ourselves hope, but how can you not hope? How can you see a tiny flicker of a heartbeat on a screen and not imagine holding a baby in your arms?

My mother and Clair drive up from Connecticut to get me. They feed me dinner and drive me to their house. Bill meets me there and holds me while I cry. On Sunday we drive back to Philadelphia and spend the afternoon in numb silence, walking the dog, reading the paper. We eat. We watch *The Unbreakable Kimmy Schmidt*, and I sing, in my head, "'cause females are strong as hell." We push through the hours until it's Monday morning, and we are back at the office where the pregnancy was confirmed, in a waiting room in another doctor's office, a waiting room full of rosy, glowing, hugely pregnant women. There's another ultra-sound; another confirmation that there will be no baby. "Except there's still a pregnancy in there," says the technician.

I nod, and think about how quickly a *baby* becomes a *pregnancy*, and how much I just want this over with. While I sit in a harshly lit office and try not to cry, the doctor outlines my choices. I can let things happen naturally, which would mean that I'd basically go into labor—"a little labor," I think she says—and that "the contents of my womb would empty." I can take misoprostol, the drug that had given me such a rough ride the last time. Or I can go in for a simple surgical procedure called a manual vacuum extraction—a quick, risk-free, new-age D&C that wouldn't even require anesthesia.

I don't even have to think about it. No way am I going through the waiting and the pain and the should-I-even-be-at-home uncertainty of the drugs. I want the MVE. Get it done, let me go home and get on with it.

I explain this all to the doctor, who says she completely understands. Except—oh dear—there's a big maternal/fetal medicine conference in town, and all the practitioners are at that, and they do MVEs only on Fridays. Too bad, so sad . . . because by then the chances are pretty good that this will have resolved itself.

I tell the doctor that I do not want to sit around with a dead fetus inside of me for the next five days. Friday's no good anyhow—I'm supposed to be in New York and then in Michigan for a speech next week. Things to do! Places to be! And I know that if I keep moving, this won't hurt me as much. I can outrun the sorrow, take a train past it, fly over it, stay so busy that I won't have time to think, and then it will be one week later, then two weeks, then a month, and there will be a wedding, and Lucy's bat mitzvah, and this will just be a thing that happened in the winter, a few weeks where I was happy and hopeful, a few days when I was sad.

My doctor calls around. No luck. "I'm sorry," she says, "but no one can do this before Friday."

At that point, I am pissed. The doctor tells me I am welcome to try other places. I tell her politely but forcefully that it's sad enough to lose a pregnancy, but to then find out that you have to wait five days for a procedure, and get treated like you're trying to jump the line at the hot new nightclub when you object, or that you have to call around, like you're checking other dealerships because they don't have the car you ordered in the color you want, is not improving the experience. Eventually I take the prescription for misoprostol and high-test Tylenol. Bill and I go to a coffee shop, where I start making calls. Clair says she can get me in at Yale on Wednesday, if I come up to New Haven. Susan's husband knows someone at Temple who might be able to help. I call my old ob/gyn's practice out in the burbs, and I call the obstetrician who belongs to my synagogue, and I say, "I need this to happen TODAY." Just as I'm dialing the last number that I have, my midsection spasms. I bend over, eyes squeezed shut. Bill looks alarmed. "Cramps," I manage to say. *Here we go*, I think.

I stagger five blocks to the pharmacy, thinking I can at least get the Tylenol, for all the good that's going to do. I try to breathe through the pain and try to remember the distraction techniques that they taught me in Bradley Method classes, which only makes me sadder. I stand in line, teary and frustrated, stuck behind some idiot who is arguing with the pharmacist because her insurance company won't pay for her nongeneric blood-pressure medication, and poor Bill has no idea what to say or how to help.

I finally collect my meds. The walk home takes me past the pet store, where they keep rescue dogs in the front window so that people see them and maybe adopt them. The little dog wags his tail at me. MY NAME IS MITTENS. LOOKING FOR A FOREVER HOME, his information sheet reads, and I think about how much I'd wanted this baby; how much I'd wanted to be its forever home, and I start to sob; great, heaving, wrenching noises that make it sound like I'm trying to expel an organ. Which, ha-ha, I sort of am.

At home, I change into pajamas and crawl into bed with my heating pad. The cramps have me feeling like I'm in *Alien*, and there's something trying to claw its way out of me. Every ten minutes I get up, go to the bathroom, change my soaked pad, lie down again, or get into the shower, leaning against the wall or squatting over the tiles, letting the blood wash down the drain.

The doctor has sent me home with an illustrated instruction sheet that says to call if I'm soaking through more than two pads in an hour for more than two consecutive hours. After I have soaked through six pads in an hour, I'm debating whether to call, or wait to see if it continues, when I stand up to change my pad again and feel a slithery sensation, a sickening feeling of emptying. When I look down, there's what appears to be half a pound of raw liver sliding down my pajama pant leg, to land on the bath mat with a wet plop. I think I shriek. Moochie, who's been curled on top of the quilt with her bottom jammed up against me, hops off the bed and trots to the bathroom to investigate. "Moochie!" I say as she sniffs at the mess. I shoo her away and pull down my pajama bottoms to change my pad. My vagina appears to be dispensing Campbell's Chunky soup. There is blood pouring out of me—not trickling, not dribbling, pouring, as if someone's turned on a faucet—and there are clumps of tissue along with it, red, gooey, liverish, lumpy things. *You might pass large clots*, says my sheet. *Some of them may be as large as a lemon*. Are these as large as a lemon? I see a few tangerine-size lumps, and one that's at least half a grapefruit. Oh, and also, according to the sheet, I'm supposed to be saving this mess to show the doctors.

I shove a towel between my legs—at this point, I realize, my body is laughing at the pads. I scoop up the mess on the floor, and I call downstairs to Bill that I need some kind of container. A few minutes later, he sticks his hand through the opened bathroom door. "Don't look!" I say, and grab what he's given me, which turns out to be the fancy new Tupperware, not the quart-size containers from the Whole Foods olive bar that you reuse once or twice before tossing, which were what I'd been hoping for.

"Goddamnit!" I yell. "NOT THE GOOD TUPPER-WARE! I MIGHT WANT TO REUSE IT!" In the end, I sacrifice the container to the cause, and then I climb in the shower and stay there until the hot water runs out. For the next three hours, that's how it goes. Cramps. Clumps. Blood, blood, blood. All normal, according to my sheet . . . and, the weird thing is, it feels normal. It feels like my body doing what it is supposed to do—however gross and weird and painful the task. I'm proud of myself for not needing medication, for not having surgery, for having a pioneer-style miscarriage, the kind my ancestors had as they plowed the potato fields of Krychyl's'k. Maybe I didn't have natural childbirth, I think, as I spray Shout on my towels and mop the bathroom floor with Clorox wipes (just like my Ukrainian ancestors in the potato fields). Maybe I never went all the way through labor, but, goddamnit, I had a natural miscarriage. Suck it, Naomi Wolf!

Five hours, three pairs of pajama bottoms, two towels, a box of maxi pads, and a bath mat later, and it's all over.

I tuck the Tupperware full of placental gunk underneath the sink the instant before my twelve-year-old strolls into my bathroom, but forgot to grab the information sheet from the counter. "I'm not even going to ask," Lucy says coolly. "Female trouble," I manage, realizing that I've just given her a 2016 version of the childbirth scene in *The Women's Room*, which had convinced me that I was never having children.

I know, from my Googling, that it's possible that somewhere in the mess was the fetus. According to the Babycenter e-mails that I optimistically signed up for (and from which I would need to remember to unsubscribe), it would have been the size of a walnut, or a prune. It would have had a head and a body; little limbs. The doctors can do testing, they can tell me, more specifically, what went wrong. I can find out if this would have been a boy or a girl. But I don't want to think about it. I don't want to look, to mourn, more specifically, what might have been. I think, instead, about how in both the hospital and the doctor's office, as soon as there was no heartbeat, I never heard the word "baby" again, or even "fetus" . . . it was just "the pregnancy" or "the products of conception" or "the contents of your uterus." The magic of language; the unmaking of a life, not by biology but by words. It was okay. What I've lost, I think, is a possibility, not a person. And because it's just me, in my bathroom, with my Tupperware and my ruined towels, I can frame it any way I want. My voice, my words, are what matter here. No court or politician or outside-the-clinic shouter can tell me what happened or how I have to feel or what I need to believe. My daughters are children. This was a chance, a lottery ticket without the winning numbers; a dream that's dissolved in the morning sunshine, something that could have been real but wasn't. I am sad. I am grieving. But this isn't the same as losing a baby.

The truth is that there's also a part of me that's happy; guiltily relieved that I won't have to rock Lucy's life with news of a new half brother or half sister and see her disgust and listen to her complaints and absorb her horror at what the baby signifies—a mother who's still having sex. I like sleeping through the night; I like being able to have conversations with my kids; I love breezing through an airport, unhampered by a stroller or a car seat or a diaper bag, with my girls beside me, chattering about what they see. I've never been one of those women enamored by infants, intoxicated by the smell of the backs of their heads or the heft and folds of their little limbs. But this would have been my baby; our baby, an entirely new person that Bill and I had made together. I am mourning the loss of the possibility, the non-winning ticket; the door I won't get to unlock, the dream that didn't come true.

I think, at least it's over now. At least it can't get any worse. Then I go to the obstetrician for a follow-up visit, to make sure everything's out. There should be a separate day when doctors see women who've lost their pregnancies, or at least a separate place to wait, but there's nothing like that, and as I walk into a waiting room full of happy, hopeful pregnant ladies, I try not to think about how I sat here not that long ago, how I'd been one of them and how happy I'd been.

Waiting in line, a young woman in sweatpants and a T-shirt straining over her belly scowls at me and asks, in a taffy-thick Philadelphia accent, "Are you in line?"

I nod, because I can't talk. At the woman's side is a little girl, in sparkly sequined shoes, with a pink bow in her hair.

"Did you put your name in?" she demands.

I shake my head. I don't understand. I'm waiting to give my name to the receptionist, who is busy with someone else, all of which she can clearly see, so why is she asking . . .

The woman jerks her arm in the direction of a computer keyboard in the corner.

PLEASE ENTER NAME AND WAIT TO BE CALLED. Head down, I proceed to the machine.

"Could've just gone right ahead of you," the sweatsuited lady mutters. Later, in the waiting room, she'll snap at her little daughter for spilling a paper cone of water on her dress. I will hear her hissing, *Cut that shit out!* I'll see her yank her daughter to her feet when the doctor calls her name, pulling her down the hall as her little feet, in their sparkly shoes, stumble over the linoleum.

I don't curse at my children. I don't yank their arms. I hardly ever yell. I give them only organic milk and antibiotic-free meat. I know their friends and their teachers; I go to conferences and concerts; I monitor their television time and check their homework. I want to tell this to someone, to explain that there's been a mistake, that someone has screwed up. This isn't fair. I should be the one having another baby, not her.

"Jennifer?" A friendly-looking woman in scrubs is calling my name. I get to my feet and cross the room quickly. The technician smiles. "We have some doctors visiting from Turkey," she says as she walks me toward the ultrasound room. "Is it okay if they sit in, and we can show them how to find the heartbeat?"

I stop walking. "There's no heartbeat. I had a miscarriage. I'm here to make sure . . ."

The woman's face is stricken. "Oh my God, I'm so sorry." Glancing at her clipboard, she realizes that she's got the wrong Jennifer. I slink back to my seat. I wish my parents had given me a less common name. I wish I were anywhere but here. I wish this story had a different ending. I wish that it was summer, and this was something that had happened half a year ago, and I wouldn't feel this fishhook in my heart.

Eventually there's more gel. Another ultrasound wand. "It looks like it's all over," says the doctor, a guy this time. He's younger than I am, with a calm demeanor and gentle hands. "Are you doing okay?"

"Sure," I say. I make my head nod. I make the corners of my mouth curve upward, an approximation of a smile, because this is what women do. We don't want to scare anyone. We don't want to be upset or cause concern. We don't ever want to show how much it hurts. "Everything's fine."

One Good Thing

In March 2008, my life was in a good place. I'd wanted to grow up and be a writer and that's what I had done, and now, in an unbelievable development, a television network was paying me to come up with ideas for shows. I'd packed up little Phoebe, just three months old, and we'd flown to California, where I'd spend the next few days having meetings, brainstorming and trading life stories and jokes with potential writing partners.

Because good fortune is best enjoyed with company—and because I'd had a baby twelve weeks earlier—I was rolling with an entourage. My assistant, Meghan, was in a room down the hall in our hotel in Burbank, and my sister, Molly, was on the pullout couch in the living room of my suite. The first day of my trip, I woke up at five in the morning because the baby and I were both still on East Coast time. My phone was plugged into an outlet in the bathroom. Washing my hands, I glanced at its screen and saw that I had three missed calls from a number with a Connecticut area code that I didn't recognize, plus six calls from my mom.

I called Fran first. "Dad died," she said without preamble, her voice uncharacteristically quiet and low. "The police called and told me but they won't give me any information because I'm not the next of kin."

The tiles were cool underneath my feet, and I could see my reflection in the mirror, the circles under my eyes, my hair in tangles, my face looking tired and pale and old. I could hear Phoebe stirring, and my sister breathing, and the silence all around us as the hotel and the city slept. The sky outside the windows was still dark. There was no name for what I was feeling. There was relief that he'd never hurt me again, never scare me; never have a chance to hurt or scare my daughters. Sorrow that there would never be a reckoning or an apology, a day when my father would come back to himself and be the man who'd tucked me into bed and read me poetry when I was a little girl. He would never regain his perspective, or come to his senses, or look at what he had done and be able to tell us he was sorry. Deep down, I think I knew that would never happen. My mother had denied the possibility frequently enough. *If your father ever had any idea of what he'd done, he'd kill himself*, she would say.

I'd had Phoebe in the bed with me, and when she started to fuss, I picked her up and nursed her, sitting up against the headboard, cradling her body with one arm, holding the phone with my free hand, tucking it against my shoulder when I needed to readjust. I dialed the first number, for the Rocky Hill Police Department. The detective told me my dad's body had been found a few hours before, at six in the morning, in the bathroom of an apartment in Rocky Hill—his girlfriend's place, she said. She couldn't tell me much more. She said that it must have been a shock, and that if I called later the detectives who'd been on the scene would be able to give me more information.

I hadn't spoken to or seen my father since 2001, after a reappearance that began when he'd called me on Father's Day in 2000, asking for money. "I need to start over," he told me. "I'm homeless," he said. I was engaged to Adam then, living in an apartment with my husband-to-be, and had just sold my first book, a bit of news that had been reported both at the paper where I worked and in the one I'd grown up reading. He'd seen the news; hence the call. Feeling very responsible and adult, I asked if he was getting help, if he was in therapy, and offered to speak to whoever was treating him, to see if they could confirm what he was telling me, help come up with a plan. But, I said, "it would be irresponsible" to just hand him a check. He understood that, didn't he?

For a moment he didn't answer. The silence stretched just long enough for me to imagine that he would agree to my terms and would tell me that they made sense, and thank me. Then I heard him inhale, and heard him begin, "You stupid bitch." I put the phone down on the bed. I didn't hang up, which would have been answering aggression with aggression. I just put it down on the comforter, so that his voice turned into a blur of sound, and I walked away and left the apartment. When I came back there was a dial tone.

He's lost his mind, my mom would say, and that was what I thought had happened. In the years after the divorce, he'd been inconsistent with his presence and his child support, but he was, at least sometimes, still the same smart, darkly funny father I'd had for the first decade or so of my life. He'd crack mean jokes about my mother's lawyer, whose name was Barry Armata, chuckling every time he blew off a court date or got away with not paying his alimony, "I sunk Armata." He'd dictate letters to his secretary and send them to my mom, missives that began, "Dear Frances, In light of our recent conversation, it is clear that negotiations with Muammar Khaddafi would have proceeded more smoothly." When I'd spoken to him when I lived in Lexington, when I'd seen him at his second wife's house and heard about what he'd done, he'd sounded weird and unhinged. I knew he'd lost jobs and had been arrested for assaulting a girlfriend. Mental illness plus booze equals a life in ruins. Also, there had been a whole mess in 1998. My father's ex-girlfriend had found him in bed with another woman and had attacked him, ripping his scrotum open, tearing it so badly it took more than sixty stitches to repair. The new girlfriend, who'd hidden in the closet during the attack, called an ambulance, which arrived with the police, and the story was in the papers—the *Hartford Courant*, the *Middletown Press*, even the student paper at the University of Connecticut, where my brother went to school. The last name, of course, didn't help.

Everyone laughed. I know, objectively, that it wasn't true—Howard Stern laughed. Jay Leno laughed. Not *everyone*. But it felt that way. I wondered, later, if any of those people, the DJs and the late-night joke writers, ever thought to ask whether the person they were mocking had kids, and how those kids might have felt, hearing the jokes.

As hard as it had been to start the conversation, as little as I enjoyed using the phrases "my father" and "scrotum" in the same sentence, I felt like I had to tell Adam what the situation was and try to explain how far down my father's life had spiraled. Before we got married, I had to try to make him understand the truth of where I had come from, but in spite of my best efforts I wasn't sure he ever really got it. *So he's difficult*, Adam would say, and I'd say, *No, it's a little worse than that.*

Good in Bed came out in May 2001. Three days after its release, I was driving myself home from a bookstore event when my publicist called. "I got a phone call from someone who said he was a friend of your father's. He asked you to call him right away."

By then, it had been a year since the Father's Day phone call. This couldn't be good. I called my mother first. "Are you driving? Pull over," she said. Then she told me that she and my dad had been in court again, and he had finally run into the wrong judge, a woman who looked at his bank statement, then looked at him, resplendent in his suit and his gold pinkie ring, and said, "You have enough money to fulfill your obligations," and sent him to jail for violating the court's orders to pay my mom.

"So he's in jail?" I asked. I couldn't quite believe it. There was still a father who lived in my head, and he was handsome and thoughtful and kind. He wasn't the man who'd yelled at me, who'd slammed himself into my bedroom door, who'd called me fat and said no man would love me. He was the man in suits and ties, whose beard tickled my cheeks when he kissed me, the man who read to me at night. When I gave my mother the name of the person who'd called Simon & Schuster, she said he was a fellow physician, either a friend or someone who'd been treating my father or both, and that my dad was probably looking for money. I didn't call, and I spent my book tour holding my breath, waiting for someone—some reporter or blogger—to find out this piece of my story. No one did— no one would write about it until years later, when the *Inquirer* put it in a profile—but it left me feeling like my first book's publication, all that joy, was just another occasion my father had ruined.

After Adam and I got engaged and had set our date, I was determined to get our wedding announcement into the *New York Times*. If they printed the news of my nuptials, my father would see it or someone would show him, and he would know that I was successful—that I'd published a book, that a man loved me and wanted to be with me forever.

I wanted him to know how wrong he'd been, that I wasn't a secretary, wasn't a failure, wasn't unlovable—but I was terrified of him finding out any details about the wedding. I thought he might try to show up and do or say something to embarrass me, that he would ruin it the way he'd ruined high school graduation and college graduation and a hundred days in between. On our wedding night we had an off-duty policeman in the crowd, watching for him. Something old, something new, I joked, as I gave the man a picture of my dad. Something borrowed, someone in blue.

My father didn't come to Philadelphia. The announcement ran in the *Times* the next morning. It said that I was a daughter of Frances Frumin Weiner. It didn't mention his name. *My father is not in my life*, I told the paper's fact-checker when he called, who was kind when he asked me about it, and didn't push, just inquired whether I was "the" daughter or "a" daughter. Did my father notice? Was he hurt? Was it what he'd expected from me?

A year and a half later, married and pregnant, I was back in Connecticut, giving a reading at a local bookstore. "There's someone very special here to see you!" one of the staffers trilled as she led me from the offices in the back to the stage, and I wondered if it was a high school teacher or an old boyfriend. The first thing I saw was my mother at the back of the room, holding her tote bag with both hands, pressing it against her chest, looking pale and dismayed. In the front row, in a white suit, was a man with horn-rimmed glasses and a gray beard that fell to the middle of his chest. Next to him was a woman in her thirties, with tanned skin and dark hair, wearing cutoffs and a denim shirt tied at her midriff. She was dressed like she was ready to mow a lawn or go line dancing at a strip club, and she kept fidgeting in her seat, bouncing up and down, like she couldn't hold still. She looked like an overgrown six-year-old. He looked deranged.

Numb and scared, I stumbled through my reading, hearing my voice like it was coming out of speakers, not my mouth, and then I made myself look into the audience. "Any questions?"

My father's hand shot into the air. Without waiting to be called on, he jumped to his feet and, in a creaky, gravelly voice, launched into a screed about the nature of art. Didn't I agree that great art came from pain and suffering? Wouldn't I say that every artist owed a debt—of gratitude, at least, but possibly extending into the realm of the financial—to the people or person who had caused them to suffer and had, essentially, turned them into a painter or sculptor or poet or novelist?

I forced my frozen lips into a semblance of a smile. "Ladies and gentlemen, my dad," I said. An uncomfortable murmur ran through the crowd—by then, some people had read *Good in Bed*, and knew about the awful father in that book, not-so-loosely based on my life. I was shooting Fran desperate, do-something looks, knowing that she wouldn't be able to help. I couldn't believe that the bookstore was letting this happen. Did the manager think this was some kind of stunt or part of the show? "And, for the record, I don't think children are topiaries that you get to shape and clip and prune and cut . . ." I swallowed hard. I wanted to grab my book, turn around, and run. Except that wasn't true. I wanted to throw the book, as hard as I could, right in his face, and then run. I didn't want him hurting my baby, my still mostly theoretical baby. I wanted to hurt him before he had a chance, hurt him so that he'd know to stay away from me, from us.

Again, I made myself smile. "Anyone else?"

The cutoff lady bounced in her seat, waving her arm in the air. I ignored her. Someone asked me where I got my ideas. Someone else asked how I'd found my agent. I ignored my father's hand in the air, ignored the woman beside him, wondered how many questions I'd have to get through before I could leave.

Then I had to sign books. My father and the woman stood at the end of the line, hanging back, clearly hoping to corner me. And do what? Ask more questions? Tell me that he'd hurt me on purpose, that he'd achieved what he'd set out to do, because look at me now? Would he ask for money again? Would he hand me a bill?

I don't remember how I got out of there or what else he said to me before I left. I remember sitting in the passenger seat of Fran's car, listening to my mother talk about how she hadn't known what to do, or how to explain to the bookstore people what was going on, or if she should have called the cops. "He keeps guns in his car," she said, and I laced my fingers across my belly and thought, *He will never see this child. I will keep this baby safe.*

In Los Angeles, with Phoebe in my arm, the second of my babies he would never see, the phone against my ear, I listened to the detective explain that an autopsy would be conducted to determine how my father had died, how that was standard procedure "in deaths of this nature." She gave me the name of the girlfriend in whose apartment he'd been found. Her name was familiar. I remembered she was a middle-aged woman who'd shown up, years later, at a different reading in Connecticut, sitting in the front row with an odd, zealous glow in her eyes. Raising her hand and waving it until I'd called on her, she'd talked about how much *In Her Shoes*, with its message of forgiveness, had meant to her. Didn't I think forgiveness was so beautiful? Shouldn't we all forgive the people who had wronged us? Later, she sent me a long e-mail. She said that she knew that my father and I had "fallen out of touch." She said that she was his friend, and that she knew that he loved me, and how he needed my help and support—which, given that she hadn't reached out to my siblings, I suspected meant money. I didn't answer. I deleted her e-mail and tried to forget it. By then, all I wanted was for him to stay away.

In my hotel bedroom, I held Phoebe against my shoulder, patting her back until she burped. "Your grandfather died," I whispered. I wasn't sure I'd ever thought of my father as their grandfather, whether I'd ever used that word in connection to him before.

Then I left the bedroom and began to open the living-room shades. "Are you awake?" I called to Molly, a lump on the pullout couch. Before she could answer, I blurted, "Dad died."

Molly rolled over, opening one eye. "You are the worst," she said. "You have, like, the worst bedside manner ever. 'Dad died,'" she repeated, deepening her voice to sound somber, the way I must have. "Well done, Jenny."

We called Jake and Joe, and they came over—unshaven, wearing sunglasses, with Starbucks cups in a cardboard carrier. Molly grabbed a latte and began making fun of me—"Jenny has a terrible bedside manner. 'Oh, are you awake? Dad died.'" It was funny and awful. It was all funny and awful until it was just awful, but on that first day, I remember the four of us laughing all the time, even if the laughter had an unpleasantly shrill edge, and the jokes weren't all that funny.

I e-mailed my assistant, still asleep down the hall, and told her what had happened, and asked her to let the ABC people know when she woke up. I called my agent, who said, over and over, how sorry she was and asked, over and over, what she could do. I asked if she could start looking at flights to Connecticut for all of us. Then, on little squares of hotel stationery, I started making a list of what I'd have to do next.

I remembered—all four of us did—that our dad wanted to be buried in a veterans' cemetery. The veterans' hospital just over the Connecticut border in Holyoke, Massachusetts, had hedges out front that had been trimmed to spell the words SOLDIERS' HOME. We would drive by it, on our way to or from skiing, or to Mount Tom and its famous alpine slide, and my dad would say, "That's where I'm going to wind up." But how did you go about getting someone buried there? Had my father made, what, a reservation?

I called Fran. She gave me my dad's social security number, and then said to be sure that whoever I spoke to knew that she—not his second ex-wife, but his first—was entitled to the Social Security survivor benefits. "You make sure when you call the VA you tell them that I'm the widow."

God bless Google, and the website it led me to, that spelled out the steps. Call the Department of Veteran Affairs. Call the police back to find out where the body was and when it might be released. Call the funeral home close to the veterans' cemetery in Middletown, the closest one to where he'd died.

That last call didn't go well. The woman who answered the phone was all sweet, sugary sympathy at first. Also, she kept calling my father "Dad." "When did Dad die? Where is Dad now?" When I explained that Dad had died in his girlfriend's apartment's bathroom that morning, and that Dad was currently being held at the state medical examiner's office, pending an autopsy, her voice got chilly. "We're probably not equipped to handle a situation like this."

I called another funeral home, a Jewish one in West Hartford. The man who answered talked in low-pitched, speedy bursts, like he'd been told to sell a certain number of coffins by the end of the day. Yes, his home would accept the body when it was released; yes, they'd do the traditional rituals. There would be someone to sit with the body the night before the service. The VA would pay for soldiers to play "Taps," and a flag and a headstone. We had to pay for the plot, and the funeral home's service, and the coffin.

I scribbled down notes, trying to ask the right questions and answer the ones he asked me. Would the family bring mementos for the casket? Who will get the flag that will drape the coffin? Who will get the shell casings, from after the twenty-one-gun salute?

I could figure all of that out, but the conversation came unpleasantly to a halt when he asked how many copies of the death certificate I'd need.

"I don't know," I said. "How many do people usually ask for?"

"He was a doctor, right? So he'll have a business to close. Creditors to notify. He probably had bank accounts, investments . . ." This poor guy thought that this was a normal story; that he was burying a doctor with adult children, a responsible, professional citizen. I didn't want to explain that he was burying a mentally ill, probably unemployed, completely unreliable, scary man who'd been in jail and in the newspapers, and had not lived a happy life and probably no longer had a 401(k).

We agreed on fifteen copies.

"At most Jewish funerals, Psalm Twenty-Three is traditional. 'The Lord is my shepherd, I shall not want.'"

Green pastures, I thought. Quiet water. I could get behind that.

"It asks for forgiveness and compassion for a soul that's about to ascend."

"That sounds fine."

"So he had, what, four kids?"

"Five. And four grandchildren, except he never met them."

The director permitted the tiniest pause.

"You could say, that he shared life. That he nurtured life."

And that he helped people, I said. Because he was a doctor, and, at one point, it was true.

We discussed the sound system, who would speak, and how many ex-wives would attend. He reminded me to bring a check the day of the funeral and then asked where he could fax the obituary form.

"No obituary," I said. I could hear from his indrawn breath that he was surprised, but I didn't know what I'd write, or if an obituary might occasion someone at a local paper to do a quick Internet search on my father's name and add gossip or news coverage or unwanted guests to our woes.

The last thing needed in order to arrange for a veteran's funeral was something called an unredacted DD-2 form. My mom had no idea where it was.

I wrote out a request for the Veteran Affairs form, explaining that my father is—had been—Jewish, and that we wanted to do the funeral as quickly as possible. "I am his daughter and next of kin," I wrote, and my sister took it down to the front desk, for a clerk to fax.

I nursed Phoebe. I answered the phone. Before leaving for meetings on the ABC lot, I gave Molly my American Express card. "If anyone asks for a deposit, use this," I said. "If I have to pay for this, I want to get the points."

That afternoon I accepted condolences, feeling like a fraud. I hadn't seen him in a while, I told the writers and executives I was meeting, trying to keep the conversations short. Everyone was kind, sometimes offering their own stories of estrangement and mental illness, their own tales of sad endings.

Back in the hotel room after dinner, my siblings and I decided to call the girlfriend. I was in the bedroom, on one extension; Molly and my brothers were in the living room, on speakerphone. Carol was in Connecticut, sounding hysterical, miserable, manicky. She said over and over, "There was a body in my bathroom this morning." She rambled through the story of what had happened, how she'd fallen asleep the night before with my father still awake, on the couch, and how when she'd woken up he'd been facedown on the bathroom floor.

"So what was going on?" I asked. "When you e-mailed me, you said he hadn't been well."

She sighed, then started to talk about how my dad had brittle diabetes and was treating himself because he thought he was a better doctor than any doctor he could see. "He was in poor health. He wasn't working." She said he'd closed his medical office the year before and was no longer treating patients, but had been looking for jobs, at spaces to rent, trying to get back on his feet.

Strange and stranger. Why had he been off his feet, exactly? People lived with diabetes. My grandparents had all developed it, late in their lives. You took your medicine or your insulin, you exercised and watched your diet, and you went on . . . and sixty-six, my father's age, seemed young to be retired, especially considering how, in every court transcript I'd read, he'd complained about how he'd be working forever, about how he was like a hamster on a wheel, and how he'd never be able to stop.

"Were you a couple?" my sister asked, not even trying to hide her skepticism. Carol sounded huffy as she said, "I gave your father a home, and he gave me a great deal of love." That was a line that got a lot of play with my siblings that week. "He gave me a great deal of love."

"Can I have the salt?"

"No, but you can have a great deal of love."

That was Tuesday. I made the arrangements, paid for the tickets; went online and found little black dresses for Lucy and Phoebe to wear, and on Thursday, we all flew back home.

"Everyone, use the bathroom before we go," I instructed my siblings before we climbed into my minivan and drove to see where my father had died.

Carol lived in a sprawling apartment complex, three concrete buildings set around a vast parking lot that looked like prisons and were full of families getting Section 8 subsidies. There was an empty fountain ringed with plastic plants in her building's lobby, and a kid in a football helmet sitting on its edge, rocking and drooling.

The apartment wasn't awful, but it was seriously overcrowded, as if the contents of a home, the furniture and knickknacks and lamps, had been crammed into small rooms with low ceilings, green wall-to-wall carpeting, and dingy white walls. All of the furniture was too big and there was too much of it, which left armchairs pushed right up against tables, and framed pictures and papers and magazines spread thickly on every free surface. In a bookshelf I saw copies of my books and DVDs of some of the movies my brother had produced. On top of the TV was a framed picture of my father at the beach, kneeling down so that he was eye level with a little boy I didn't recognize, a bare-foot toddler in a bathing suit, with a diaper sagging toward his chubby knees. Carol didn't know who the boy was, but she said that she'd always liked that picture, and I could see why. The little boy looked solemn and trusting; my father looked patient and kind, as if he had nothing better to do than to stay hunkered in the sand, listening to whatever the boy had to say. I wondered whether this was the son my father had had with his second wife.

The apartment looked clean, but the air was thick with a strange, unfamiliar chemical scent. There were magnifying glasses on the table. Carol said my father's eyesight had degenerated; that he couldn't drive anymore and could barely read.

For years, I'd been afraid of him. I'd been angry about how he'd left us, the bills he'd never paid, scared of what he'd say or do to me or my family or my children if he ever showed up at our door. Now I just felt sad and sorry for him, for dying in such a shabby place, with so little to show for his life—so few possessions, so few relationships, so few people left who'd loved him.

I was the former reporter, but it was Molly, sharp-eyed and staccato-voiced, who took the lead, drilling Carol with question after question. "How long had you known my dad?" she asked. "How did you meet each other?"

Carol put her best spin on a shady situation. My father, it emerged, had been her son's therapist. Then he'd started treating Carol. Then they'd "developed feelings" for each other. "And when I saw how he was struggling, I offered him a home."

"Tell me about how he was struggling," Molly said.

Carol launched into her story about brittle diabetes and poor health and how he'd been depressed ever since he'd been in jail, in 2001.

"Did he . . . I mean, do you think . . ."

Before I could figure out how to ask the question—did he kill himself?—Carol was shaking her head. "He told me repeatedly. Repeatedly, repeatedly, repeatedly, that he would never harm himself. Last week, he answered a want ad. He was looking for an office to rent. He was very excited . . ." Her voice trailed off. "You know, his father was fifty-three when he died. Your dad thought that every day past his father's age that he got was a gift."

My sister was not impressed with this analysis. "What was really going on here?" Molly asked. "Was it drugs?"

I heard Carol pull in a breath. I was holding my own breath, my body braced, some part of me waiting for her answer, some part of me knowing it already.

Finally, Carol sighed. "Your father was working with addicts, in state hospitals and in his private practice. He was curious about crack—about the hold it had on people, about what it was that they couldn't resist. So he tried it."

Bullshit, I thought. *Bullshit, bullshit, bullshit.* I was so angry. I could feel fury surging inside of me, pushing itself toward my fingertips and toes with each heartbeat. That's not why people use drugs, because they're curious. You try sweetbreads or spinning class because you're curious. You take crack because you're weak, because you're running away from your problems, because you can't handle the pain in your life and you don't care who you hurt.

"Your father struggled. He fought very hard. But he became addicted to heroin and crack."

I felt like a cape of ice was falling, from my neck to my shoulders to my legs, trapping me, freezing me. The words rattled around in my head, like Ping-Pong balls in the lottery drawing's hopper. *Heroin. Crack.* My father? My father, who'd read to me from the *Aeneid* and Shakespeare, who'd made French toast for breakfast, who'd once made me feel so special, so smart, so loved? It was like imagining a dog smoking a cigarette; an upside-down house—something didn't fit. I couldn't make it fit.

The apartment felt like it was squeezing in on me, like the walls of the trash compactor in *Star Wars*. Alcohol wouldn't have surprised me. In hindsight, I could see that he'd probably been drunk at that reading, and I'd seen him drunk before— weeping and slurring insults at my mom the afternoon of my college graduation, passed out naked on my dorm-room futon that night . . . but I don't think I would ever have guessed he was using street drugs.

When I made myself listen to the conversation again, it was like I'd tuned in to an episode of *Cops*. Carol was explaining how she'd cleverly gotten rid of my dad's cell phone before the ambulance had shown up—"his phone had all of his dealers' numbers." *Dealers.* My father had dealers. Then I remembered her saying that his eyesight had deteriorated, that he had given up his car. Was he so addicted that he needed drugs every day? Did dealers make house calls? Or did Carol drive him to meet these people? Did she pay them, too? And with whose money?

I started to shiver. "You should know that your father thought of all of you, at least fleetingly, once a day." *At least fleetingly.* I knew that would soon join *And I gave him a great deal of love* in the Weiner kids' lexicon.

Carol's language was very passive, very careful, very George Bush saying "mistakes were made." She didn't blame my dad for leaving us. She blamed my mom for being vindictive, relentless in her pursuit of all that money he owed her. She blamed the woman who'd slashed him—"All the shame," she said, "was very hard for him." She blamed his second wife, for getting pregnant when she knew my dad didn't really want another child.

On the last day of his life, Carol said, they'd gone swimming and visited a gym my dad wanted to join. He'd been reading newspaper ads, looking for office space. She told us these things, I think, because she did not want us to think that he'd killed himself. She wanted us to think that he'd died accidentally, not because he didn't want to be alive anymore. She said that she'd told the police that she had been planning to leave him over his drug use. I can't remember if she told us that she was lying, so that she wouldn't be suspected of doing anything illegal, but that was what I thought.

Then she led us down to the building's basement, where the storage units were. It was cold and damp down there, moldy-smelling and cobwebby. "Your father was a hoarder, and it got a little crazy," she said, and unlocked the door. There were boxes and boxes, stacked floor to ceiling, crammed with papers—tax returns, junk mail, unpaid bills and copies of patients' records, computer printouts of nutty letters that Carol had written to him, and sad, yearning diary entries she'd written about him. There were maps to my house. Copies of articles I'd written, and, later, articles that had been written about me. Back issues of the *New Yorker* and the *Journal of the American Medical Association*. Old license plates. Holiday cards from his newspaper carrier. A bicycle tire pump. Shoeboxes full of photographs.

We dug through the boxes, standing in the musty air, with the cold from the concrete floors seeping up through our feet, and it was like every layer of his belongings that we uncovered took us down deeper into the wreck, from who he'd been in the 1970s and the 1980s to who he'd become by 2008.

I found his old doctor's bag, black leather with a gold LGW monogram, and, inside of it, an otoscope and a stethoscope and a rubber mallet. When I was five and six and seven, I had ear infections all the time, and they always seemed to start at night. He would pull out that bag when I would wake him up to say my ear was hurting. He'd sit me on the couch and wrap me up in his old army jacket, with WEINER sewn over the breast pocket, and he'd go to the all-night pharmacy to get my medicine, tell-ing me to be brave and not cry. His diplomas were there, in their frames, the glass cracked. I found his discharge papers from the army, including that unredacted DD-2 form it had taken me so long to track down.

There were hundreds of photographs—some of women I recognized, more of women I didn't. Some of them showed my father and these women on vacations—New Mexico, Saratoga,

Cape Cod. Then there were pictures of him in different apartments, at holiday dinners, with families I didn't recognize. Different women, in the same pose, on his blue-and-tan striped couch. Then Polaroids of women, alone or with him, posing naked, touching themselves or him. ("How'd he even get this shot?" I asked my brother, feigning indifference. "Tripod," said Joe, after one swift glance down.)

Molly pocketed a few of the shots. "I'm bringing these home to Fran," she said.

"Don't do that," said Jake.

"Hey, Carol said we could take whatever we wanted to remember him by. I'm taking these!"

I kept digging. There were dozens of letters and cards, signed Betsy, signed Abby, signed Vicky, signed Raquel, signed Laurie, all of them saying how much they loved him, some asking why he'd hurt them, why he'd left.

I found newspaper clippings about his assault ("Girlfriend Arrested in Vicious Assault"). "He kept this?" I asked. "He kept everything," said Joe. It seemed to be true. Letters from bankruptcy lawyers. Letters from creditors. A letter a neighbor had written, after my father left, telling him to reconsider, to look at his beautiful family and everything he was throwing away.

Carol stood at the doorway, watching us, occasionally pointing out something that wasn't junk or ruined. There was a leather firewood carrier, a photo of my father with Molly and Jake and Joe, at Butterfly, the Chinese restaurant in West Hartford where we'd meet him after he moved out. "You should keep that," she'd say. I found letters that I'd written from college, copies of my report cards, or articles I'd written. "Dear Dad, I won the Academy of American Poets prize. I got $100 and a certificate. Be sure to congratulate me at Joe's bar mitzvah." "I wrote this for the *Nassau Weekly*. Tell me if you like it." "I got all As again this semester. See you soon." He'd never written back, but he'd kept every letter I'd sent him. I found copies of short stories I'd written in college and the clipped-out wedding announcement that I had wanted so badly for him to see. I'd gotten my wish . . . but all I could feel was numb.

Down and down we went. Joe reached into a box and came up holding a bulbous glass pipe wrapped in duct tape, discolored from smoke.

"Is that . . ."

"Crack pipe," Molly confirmed.

Jake found a can of garbanzo beans, one of my father's particular favorites. I found the intake form from jail, when he'd been sent there, listing his cell phone, his wallet, his checkbook, his ring. Then there was porn. So much porn. Printouts from websites. DVDs and videocassettes. Magazines. Links to friend-finder websites, profiles of women, handwritten reminders of password for the different sites. Sometimes he'd use our initials—JMJJ. Sometimes he'd use my mother's maiden name or the date of their anniversary.

At some point during the Great X-Rated Excavation, we all started singing "Memories" from *Cats*. Molly kept her promise and brought home some of the Polaroids and handed them to Fran, who didn't have her glasses on. "What am I looking at? What am I looking at?" she asked, turning the photos upside down, then sideways. Molly was very happy to tell her. "That's Dad with his noodle out," she said.

I felt bruised and numb, but safe. The pornography was awful, and the maps and the printouts were scary, and it was all so sad, sad beyond reckoning. I couldn't stop thinking about why he'd kept it all, why he'd kept everything, reminders of the worst, most humiliating moments of his life. I'd think about it in snatches, for five or ten seconds, taking tiny glimpses, like I was looking straight into the sun and didn't want to look for too long. I remembered what my Nanna said when I'd called to tell her—"Well, now you know." Now we knew how his story ended.

Now he'd never hurt any of us again, never scare us or embarrass us. There was no more waiting for the next bad thing; no hope of better days to come. This was it; this was all.

It was sunny and windy as we drove to the cemetery on Saturday. The funeral was anticlimactic—the kids, our spouses, my mom and her partner, and Carol. "Could we see the body?" I asked. "I wouldn't recommend it," the funeral director said hastily, taking my elbow and steering me away from the plain pine casket. "You don't need to remember him this way."

I gave him a photograph of me and Lucy and Phoebe to put inside, and Jake gave him a picture of his son and daughter, Ben and Olivia. A soldier in uniform played "Taps," and we sat on folding chairs, bundled in our coats. The sky was blue, but it felt like winter, the ground still hard, the tree branches bare. There was a microphone, attached to a squat square speaker in front of the grave, and Jake talked about how my father had special rituals with all of us, how he'd take us to get bagels, how he had come to watch our soccer games, how he'd loved us.

Back at my mother's house, ten miles from where my father had died, I tried to put together some semblance of shiva. We ordered deli platters from the Crown supermarket, and some of my parents' old friends—my mom's old book-club buddies; Judith and Brewster, the couple they'd befriended on their honeymoon in 1967—came over to pay their respects.

The next day, we went back to Carol's and continued the excavation. We got out photo albums and looked at pictures of him, back when we'd been a family. It can't get worse, I told myself bleakly as the minivan swung into the parking lot. I'd seen the doctor's bag and the diplomas; I'd seen the crack pipe and the porn, and the boxes and boxes of typed transcripts and depositions from the dozens of times my mother had taken him to court. All the promise, then the sordid denouement. At least we know the story, and it can't get worse.

Here's the truth—it can always get worse.

At the bottom of a box of flyers from insurance companies and unpaid Verizon bills, I found a stack of unopened letters from the Department of Children and Families. I thought they had to do with the child support that he owed my mother, back in the 1980s, when all of us were minors.

I opened one of the letters and it said, "In the matter of the minor child D.H." I read on. D.H. had been born on November 24, 2004. His father was listed as Dr. Lawrence Weiner.

Carol was upstairs in her apartment, and we all went trooping inside, me holding the letters, that cloak of ice wrapping itself around me again.

Yes, she told us calmly, our father had fathered another child, with a woman who'd been a patient in one of his drug-treatment groups. "But he never intended to be a father to that child. He signed his rights away so the baby could be adopted."

It doesn't work that way; that's not the way it works. You can't make a kid and then try to play take-backs, I thought. But the anger felt faint and dim, a lit match flickering behind a triple-reenforced brick wall. It felt like a movie I was watching, a story I was reading, something happening to characters, not real people, not my father, whom I'd known and loved.

Back down in the storage area, I sat on a box and began to read. I found Probate Court documents from May 22, 2006, where the biological mother's stepsister petitioned to adopt the baby boy, charging that his birth mother was unfit. She wrote that my father's name was Larry and that his last known address was in Newington, Connecticut. The documents were handwritten. They "alleged the following specific actions that place the health or welfare of the minor child in danger," all the things the baby's biological mother had done.

Drug usage

Suiside threats

Disappearing for 24 hrs without whereabouts.

Not changing habits.

Misleading program by providing fake urine for tests

Baby was removed after we could not wake her. Police was
   called for her leaving with neighbors vehical 6 hrs and
   brother had baby.

I read and learned that DCF had placed the baby temporarily
with his mother's stepsister and her stepsister's husband, on July
22, 2005. According to a report from D.H.'s guardian *ad litem*, the
plan was for his grandparents to take care of him during the day
and return him to the stepsister at night. "Mr. Weiner, the Re-
spondent, is alleged to have had no recent contact with the child
and it is reported that there is a support enforcement action pending against him."

The birth mother's attorney wrote and said that D.H.'s biological mother was "devoted to him and is actively pursuing steps
to allow her to take care of him." She was in an inpatient program
for addiction when the hearing took place. The attorney also
wrote, "D.H.'s father, Dr. Laurence Weiner, has shown no willingness at all to have any emotional or financial connection with
the child. Since the father has an ongoing psychiatric practice, it
is presumed that he would have the financial resources to provide
child support." *Ha*, I thought bleakly. How wrong you are.

The court found that "the minor child has been abandoned
by his father in the sense that the parent had failed to maintain
a reasonable degree of interest, concern or responsibility for the
minor's welfare." There was an order in place, where my father
was supposed to pay the adoptive parents $160 a month for the
baby's support.

Which he hadn't done . . . at least that's what the stack of letters from the DCF suggested. Most of them had never even been opened. One of the court documents was stained and crumpled, with a footprint on the front page, as if the court had sent my father his copy and he'd stomped on it.

Back in Philadelphia, I carried the boxes from my minivan into my basement. Every night after Phoebe was down I'd bring one box up, sit in front of the TV with a garbage bag by my side, sorting through the mess he'd left. Court transcripts, depositions, more letters from the state, more evidence of how chaotic his life had become. A Family Violence Protection Order that my father had filed against one of his ex-girlfriends in 2003. Creditors' letters and letters from lawyers demanding payment. Dozens of pages of photocopies of checks that Carol had written to him, tens of thousands of dollars' worth of checks. She must have lost her house because of him; must have moved into that crappy apartment because she'd given him, literally, everything.

A few weeks after the funeral, Carol sent us all letters. Mine said, "Your dad loved you all very dearly and told me that he thought of each of you every day. I know he wanted to see you and your children, but I'm not sure he wanted you to see him. His health had deteriorated profoundly, and he could not bear your seeing him so weakened and broken. Diabetes is a terrible disease. He fought against it every day, with determination and grace, and stayed optimistic in the face of it.

"I am terribly sad that you all had to learn the details of how your dad actually died. He would never have wanted you to know how he struggled. He could not bear the reality that something so powerful as addiction had control over him. He felt that his willpower should have enabled him to conquer this demon. He was certain that once I learned this last of his secrets, I would abandon him. It was very difficult for both of us, but because within my own family I've already struggled with alcoholism and mental illness, I did the best I could to remember that addiction is also an illness. I could not bear becoming a cop or a judge. I found a very supportive twelve-step group for families affected by drug addiction, and have leaned on them since May."

My ice-cloak kept me from feeling sorry for Carol. It kept me from feeling much of anything. I didn't care that she'd found a group of like-minded sufferers to commiserate with, didn't care that she'd decided that addiction was an illness and not just my father's mental illness and selfishness destroying everything and everyone, taking everything from her. I didn't care about much of anything, really, except this last awful thing he'd done.

> *you are going to do things*
> *you cannot imagine you would ever do,*
> *you are going to do bad things to children*
> *you are going to suffer in ways you have not heard of,*
> *you are going to want to die.*

In Philadelphia I made contact with the little boy's adoptive mother, and a few weeks later, my sister and I went back to Connecticut to meet him. By then, I had heard the whole story—how my father's last son, David, had been born addicted to crack and crystal meth, six weeks premature and with only one kidney, a common birth defect, I learned, for babies whose mothers abuse cocaine. How DCF had first taken the baby away after his birth mother had given him half a bottle of infant Tylenol and left him alone for twenty-four hours so she could get drugs.

I learned that my father had beaten David's birth mother when he found out she was pregnant and been arrested for domestic violence. She said that his birth mother had tried to kill herself, but that it wasn't a serious attempt, just a cry for help.

She said she'd seen my father just once, in court. "He was a tiny little man, and he had an oxygen tank."

By then I was angry; so furious that I couldn't sleep. My rage melted the ice, heated my skin, had me kicking the blankets and sheets to the floor. I couldn't stop thinking about a little baby, a baby like my baby, and how my dad had brought a child into the world and decided not to love him or care for him or support him or even see him, how he had put that child at risk. If he had wanted to hurt himself, make a fool of himself, scare and threaten people, harm other women, damage me, that would have been one thing. But he had hurt a child, a little boy who'd done nothing wrong, and I was so angry I didn't know what to do with myself. I joked to my friends that I wanted to dig his body up so I could kill him again.

The week after, the autopsy report finally came. "The examination pertaining to the death of your father has been completed and an amended certificate of death filed with the Registrar of Vital Statistics in Rocky Hill. The cause of death has been determined to be 'Heroin Intoxication.' The manner of death has been classified as 'Accident.'"

David is eleven now, smart and stubborn and funny, with one of the most gregarious, winning personalities of any kid I've ever seen. He charms adults, makes friends wherever he goes, slips in easily when he's with my girls or my niece and nephew, and is Phoebe's idol. ("I loves him," she said dreamily, late one night when she was two and a half and almost asleep. "He bes nice to me.") He spends summers with us and some vacations. My girls treat him like a brother and my mom helped him learn to ride a bike in the parking lot of the Corn Hill beach, down the road from our summer house. "I bet you never thought you'd be hanging out with Dad's love child," Molly teases, and Fran says, "It isn't his fault."

When he is old enough to understand exactly how we're related, and what my father did, I will tell him that he didn't deserve to be abandoned, to have parents who wanted nothing to do with him. No kid deserves that. I tell myself that I didn't deserve my father's treatment, either, and wonder which is worse—to have parents who reject you from the minute you exist, or to have a father who loves you, then doesn't.

If my father was a character in a novel I was writing, I would find a way to redeem him, or at least make sense of him, to craft a backstory that explained his descent into addiction (abusive parents? molested as a child? some terrible secret from medical school?). I would make sure that the people he hurt got a happy ending. I'd have Carol meet a charming widower at her twelve-step group; I'd have my half brother grow up confident and strong.

But this isn't a novel. This is life, messy and imperfect and sad. This is what my father left me, the good—the enduring closeness with my siblings, how we're a team now and have one another's backs—and the bad, which is everything else.

Sometimes I think about the reading where my father harangued me, how he called on Father's Day to ask for money. Maybe I should have cut him a check; written a thank-you note. Thank you for hurting me, thank you for leaving me, thank you for breaking me, because the broken places healed and got stronger, because now I can understand everyone who's been left, been hurt, been abandoned. Thank you for making me able to see that, thank you for letting me grow up and tell stories.

But the truth is, I'd trade that ability, and everything it's brought me—all the money, all the fame, all the people who feel less lonely because of something I wrote—to have my dad back as he was, to have him not have done this final, terrible thing.

In the days after my father's death, I talk to everyone I can find who knew him, or saw him, during those last years, which includes his second wife. "He'd get a gleam in his eyes when he talked about the four of you. He had a black-and-white picture of you on a slide that he loved and looked at," she said. "He'd talk about making you sandwiches, and how he was the one who'd cut the nails."

I don't remember sandwiches, but I remember him cutting our nails—that one good thing. I remember sitting on his lap, the tiny metal scissors with their curved blades, his big hand warm on my little one, each careful snip. I hated cutting my own daughters' nails when they were babies. They'd squirm or flinch or pull away, and I'd feel so clumsy, like I had a giant's fingers, and a few times I'd end up cutting past the quick, leaving them bleeding and wailing and looking up at me with wet, accusatory eyes. My father's fingers were steady, even though the scissors looked like something from a doll's house in his hands. I would lean against his chest, be enveloped by the warmth of his body, his smell of starch and soap and cologne. I would hear his heart beat and feel his beard, coarse and ticklish against the top of my head. *Be careful*, I can hear myself saying in my high, little voice, and he would tell me, with his deep baritone rumbling through his chest, *Don't worry. I would never hurt you.*

Men and Dogs: A Love Story

And so, as any good chick-lit writer must, I end my story with the happy news: dear reader, I married him.

"Him" is Bill Syken, and he is tall and dark, with a deep voice and a slow, measured way of speaking that reflects his slow, measured manner of looking at the world.

I met Bill when I was twenty-three and married him when I was forty-five. It took us considerable time to make it to the chuppah, but I was not lacking for love along the way. My whole life, I've had boyfriends and I've had dogs, and sometimes I think that the dogs were the important ones, the faithful companions who watched over me, who taught me how to be a grown-up and how to get along in the world.

My first boy/dog combo was Marcus and Mort. Marcus was an older guy, the twenty-three-year-old, college-graduate brother of one of my best friends, the guy I dated from the time I was sixteen until I was twenty-three. It was not, in retrospect, one of the world's healthiest relationships, and I hung on to it long after I should have let go. But, again in retrospect, I can see why I clung so hard. Being with him when my parents were getting divorced allowed me to re-create some semblance of a family, the structure and support and love that my mom and dad couldn't provide.

The entire time Marcus and I dated, we were chaperoned by the family bulldog, Mort.

My father would go through phases of brief, intense infatuations—with foods (homemade yogurt, a seed-and-grain mixture he called "birdseed"), with beverages (homemade seltzer, made with specially purchased cartridges of gas; Grolsch beer, which came in heavy green glass bottles with white ceramic stoppers and which my father bought, I suspect, mostly because he liked saying the name), and with dogs. In 1982, a few years after our last poodle died, he and my mother purchased a pedigreed English bulldog that my father named Ramona Lisa. Ramona was fawn-colored and, at about twenty-five pounds, smallish for a bulldog, with an L-shaped tail and a deeply underslung jaw. She was bad-tempered and mostly indifferent or hostile toward people, which made her an anomaly in her breed.

Bulldogs are, in general, sweet, lazy dogs who want nothing more than to loll around in the sunshine, collecting pats and treats and compliments. They also, unfortunately, have all kinds of health issues that range from breathing problems (the result of faces that look like they've been flattened by frying pans) to hip troubles to an inability to reproduce without human assistance.

I was not there the day my father introduced Ramona to her swain, a champion bulldog named Hartford, but the union was productive. Ramona had six puppies, six hamster-size light brown, doe-eyed miniature bulldogs with floppy skin and needle-like teeth. We sold five and kept Mort. His ears flopped forward in a way that precluded his ever becoming a show dog, and he lacked the kind of regal mien, the lordly nonchalance, that characterizes champions.* He was a sweet and needy puppy,

---

* And a certain class of literary male writers.

with a mostly white face, oversize white paws, and an enormous head, stumbling around in his droopy skin like a little boy in his father's suit. His flews, the fleshy bits in front of his mouth, were plump and white-furred and pink on the inside, and they'd flap and buzz when he snored, which was frequently. Mort might not have been a champion bulldog, but he was a champion sleeper.

Ramona was short-tempered and snappish. Mort was easygoing and affectionate. The two of them together reminded me of a sour, widowed mother and her kindhearted, not entirely bright bachelor son. Ramona would snarl at Mort when he'd nose up to the food dish before she was done, and he'd slink away, head hanging in apology. On the rare occasions when he'd forget himself and try to hump her, rather than one of our legs, she'd turn on him with *Fatal Attraction*–level wrath.

Ramona died young, after her intestines looped around each other, another common bulldog mishap. For weeks, Mort would wander the house bereft, his droopy, wrinkled face looking even more wrinkled and droopy, sniffing every corner, snuffling at every closed door as if he could find her, waiting in the basement or accidentally closed up in a closet. Gradually he came out of his funk and settled into his reign as the sole dog of the house, a dog who would wag cheerfully when you unleashed him, then stroll halfway around the block before deciding that he'd had enough and collapsing with a sigh, belly down, into a convenient puddle.

My sense is that Mort had very little in the way of longterm memory. Every time we left the house, it was as if we were abandoning him forever, and he'd crowd our legs as we made our escape, or huddle, brokenhearted, by the door. When you came home, though, it was an unbelievably happy ending. Mort would wag! He would twirl! He would heave his chunky body into the heavens, tail-stump whirling, every flap and wrinkle proclaiming boundless joy.

It was the summer before my senior year in high school when I met Marcus. With long blond hair; round, gold-rimmed glasses;

an English degree; and no job (and hence free time), Marcus could not have been more appealing to pretentious, insecure, sixteen-year-old me. He struck me as smart and thoughtful and mature, a man who, unlike the boy I'd dated my junior year, would not lead me on, professing affection for six weeks before dumping me for one of my teammates, a man who wouldn't mind that I was bigger than girls were supposed to be, who would see past my thick thighs and my stretch marks and appreciate my wit and my intellect and the beauty of my soul.

Marcus introduced me to the Talking Heads and the Smiths and Laurie Anderson and, one night when his mother was out of town, to sex.* I lost my virginity on the pullout couch in Marcus's family's den, with a fire in the fireplace and my itchy red-and-black-plaid wool pants on the floor. After months of heavy petting and, more important, years of reading about it, I was eager to have sex, but I was just as eager to shuck those itchy pants that I couldn't quite button. I was sixteen; we were responsible; and even though the act itself left me wondering what all the fuss was about (had Judith Krantz lied to me? I'd had much more fun by myself!), I thought I was in love. Marcus talked about books and poetry, Verlaine and Rimbaud, not just who'd done what to whom at the party on Saturday night. He took me to movies at Hartford's one art-house theater, so while my classmates were watching *Top Gun* and *Karate Kid* sequels, I was bettering myself with films like *Mona Lisa*, *A Room with a View*, and *Hannah and Her Sisters* (I watched *Top Gun* on the sly, on my own, and listened to Meat Loaf and Eddie Money cassettes in private, playing R.E.M. in the car when I drove anywhere with Marcus).

I wasn't supposed to be dating a guy that old. My parents forbade me to see him. They asked me why I thought a man his age was interested in a teenager. "Because I'm advanced," I moaned . . . which, in retrospect, explains why a teenager would

* FRAN, STOP READING HERE.

want to date an older guy but does not say much about the guy, and why he'd be courting a girl just three scant years past her bat mitzvah. But I was a high school senior, with a strong will and a driver's license. There wasn't a lot they could do.

When they told me no I ignored them, tearfully declaring that I was in love, that I needed him, that I would die without him. My parents were unmoved . . . so I snuck out of the house and went to see him anyhow. At which point, they gave up. My father had moved out by then and was no longer there to enforce the rules, and my mom was, I think, doing a kind of triage, deciding which problems she had to cope with and which she could safely let slide. She was trying so hard to keep herself together, to keep the family from cracking. Everything she'd expected, everything she'd been told to want had exploded in her face, in the most embarrassing manner possible—I learned this later, but my father's first affair, the one that made my mother tell him "You're either in this marriage or out of it," was with one of Fran's colleagues at the alternative school where she taught social studies and history. She was alone, and, I am guessing, the subject of gossip; she was, quite suddenly, broke; she had four children, three of them in the throes of adolescence; she had endless demands on her time and her money—soccer games and crew meets, college applications and the application fees, property taxes and federal taxes. She had two boys who'd gulp down a gallon of milk and gobble loaves of bread and pounds of cold cuts when they came home from school, then wipe their lips and ask what was for dinner, and a not-quite-ex-husband who'd sometimes show up at the back door, crying and saying he was sorry and who would sometimes arrive at that same door brandishing a shovel, telling her that that was HIS car, HIS Audi, HIS house that HE had paid for, and if she didn't give him the keys right now, he'd smash the door down.

Marcus wasn't there for that particular shit-show, the night before my high school graduation. My mother locked herself in the bathroom and Mort cowered under the kitchen table, whining, and Nanna whispered, "Do we call the police?" as my father shouted and ranted and wept outside the back door, on the deck where we'd once gathered, as a family, for corn on the cob and grilled chicken. We ended up turning off the lights and waiting until he roared off in his beloved Corvette. The next day, I was one of my class's graduation speakers. I delivered my remarks while my father, in a Tom Wolfe–ian white suit and panama hat, lurked outside the chain-link fence around the football field and drove off without congratulating me. After that, I wanted Marcus with me when I was home at night. He made me feel both loved and safe. As did Mort.

"Mort, come up!" I would say, patting the couch where Marcus and I would be sitting, watching the foreign film we'd selected (Marcus, I think, was secretly delighted when the teenagers at Blockbuster would mangle the titles on the boxes. "*Santa Sangria?*" "*Santa Sangre,*" Marcus would correct, with a flourish, as if all suburban seventeen-year-olds should be intimately familiar with the names of Mexican-Italian avant-garde horror films).

"Come!" Mort would crouch at my feet, eyes shining, tail-stump rotating vigorously on his bottom. He'd want to do it, but, clearly, he'd forgotten how to move himself from the floor to the couch since the last time he'd accomplished that feat, probably the night before.

"Mort! Up! Come on!" I would urge, patting the couch, and he'd whine and wriggle and put his front paws on the cushion and then, typically with a boost from me, heave himself up into position and lick my face in a way suggesting he could barely contain his joy.

After everyone had gone to bed, Marcus and I would pull the pillows off the living-room couch, gather blankets, and make a nest. Mort became our duenna, our chaperone. While we lay entwined on the floor, Mort would stroll into the room.

We would freeze, holding our breath, trying to be so still that he'd ignore us and go away, but usually I'd start to giggle, and then my entire body would be convulsing, shaking in silent mirth. Mort would approach, tail wagging, clearly hoping to join in the fun. First he'd nudge at my head with his nose. He'd sniff and lick at my neck and cheek, a move I called Mort's snaffle. Then he would try to wedge himself between us.

"Mort, go away!" I'd whisper, and give his bottom a gentle push, urging him toward the couch. Mort would not be moved. He would, instead, give me a look of heartrending sorrow, his eyes liquid, his entire face sagging. *You have betrayed me*, his expression said. *You have broken the covenant that requires you to love me more than anything else in the world.* Eventually he would stake out a spot at the top of our heads. He would scratch at the carpet and then, with a grunt, he'd start turning in circles near the pillows by my head until finally, with a weary sigh, he'd settle himself on the floor. Marcus and I would start kissing. Mort would start farting. For years, I associated arousal with the smell of bulldog flatulence. (I'm over it now. Thanks for asking.)

As the year went on, my mother was preoccupied and frequently absent, visiting friends for the weekend, once taking a prophetic vacation, a weeklong sailing stint with an outfit called—wait for it—Womanship. Womanship was, as its name implies, a female-only sailing school that ran trips all over the world and sent its participants home with pink T-shirts that read WOMANSHIP: WHERE NO ONE YELLS . . .

Oh, the jokes we made about "Womanship" after my mother came out of the closet! "Where's Fran?" "You know. Sailing the 'Womanship.'" Years later, we described that sojourn on the Womanship stretching from ten days to two weeks to a month, until we'd convinced ourselves that Fran had ditched us for an entire summer aboard the Womanship. It wasn't true . . . but that year it felt like she was sailing away from us for real, like she was indifferent or overwhelmed or just too sad to cope.

During my last year of high school, I was a mostly responsible big sister. I threw only one party. It ended with only one of my siblings in the hospital, after someone slipped something into the beer said sibling should not have been drinking. The most distressing part of that awful night wasn't the ambulance ride, or Marcus squabbling with the EMTs, or one of my brothers guarding my mother's bedroom, hockey stick in hand, to make sure that no amorous Simsbury seniors made use of her bed . . . it was that when the nurses and the doctors asked if there was an adult responsible for us, no one could find my father, whose job it was to be, if not physically present, at least reachable by phone while my mom was out of town.

Most of the time, I did better. I drove carpools; I looked up recipes and cooked, or tried to cook, dinners; I piled my brothers and sister into the Vanagon and took us all skiing for the day at the little mountain where we had a membership, after Fran would hand me a credit card and the keys. A lot of the time, I had Marcus by my side.

Marcus and I were a couple all through my last year of high school, through four years of college, through infidelity (his) and a few college crushes that never went beyond a few stolen kisses (mine). I hung on to Marcus like a drowning woman clutching a waterlogged piece of driftwood, hoping it would be sturdy enough to sustain her.

I wanted love. I wanted to believe that I was worthy of love, that I was pretty and desirable. I especially wanted that affirmation on a college campus where everyone else seemed so beautiful, where the crew coach had told me I was fat, where everyone seemed so sleek and smart and assured all the time. And so I stayed with him, squeezing every last drop of possibility out of the relationship, wringing it like a tea bag that has long since stopped yielding anything tasty, denying myself all kinds of fun—and, probably, heartbreak—that I look back now and wish I'd experienced. It was like eating low-calorie chocolate fro-yo when you really want gelato, like trying to content yourself with plain grilled fish when you suspect there's steak to be had.

Marcus and I dated until a year into my first job. Then I met Bill. I was, by then, a veteran reporter, with almost an entire year's worth of experience. Marcus was in Connecticut, working as a forest ranger, and it had become abundantly clear that our goals didn't match. He was happy with a day job, one that gave him enough money for food and rent and books and movies, happy to stay in Connecticut. He liked to cook and tend to his garden and chop wood for the woodstove, and he didn't want a life any larger than that.

I did. After my father left, I set goals for myself: a job at a big, national newspaper by twenty-five. A column by twenty-eight. And, by thirty, I wanted to have sold a piece of writing, either a novel or a screenplay, something that would let me bank enough money that I felt secure enough to get married and have children, knowing that whatever their father did, whatever happened, they'd be provided for.

Bill had gotten his English degree at Columbia, and had gone to graduate school for journalism at the University of Missouri afterward. He'd arrived at the *CDT* right after getting his master's. At the *Centre Daily Times*, job candidates spent a day meeting with the editors, taking tests, reporting and writing a story. Then, as a reward, they'd be treated to dinner with one of the reporters, who would presumably fill them in on the details about what the job, and life in central Pennsylvania, would be like.

I had been dieting at the time, seeing the nutritionist I paid to weigh me once a week and hand me Xeroxed pages from a Yale doctor's weight-loss workbook. I was subsisting on cans of tuna fish with lemon juice squeezed on top, lunches of takeout salad and dinners of turkey meatloaf and fifty-calorie packets of artificially sweetened cocoa with sugar-free Cool Whip for dessert. Most days, by four o'clock, when I'd stand up from my desk and feel the world waver, and have to hold on to the back of my chair until it righted itself, I would end up at the vending machine in the break room, gobbling down a bag of pretzels, but I'd lost . . . ten pounds? Twelve? Enough to make me believe that if I just kept at it I could lose the weight, the percentage of myself, that would finally make my body acceptable. Enough to make me believe that a man could like me, could look past my current incarnation and see the beauty that would be revealed when I dropped another thirty pounds.

At six o'clock, after Bill had finished his tests and filed his story, he approached my desk.

"Are you ready?" he asked, in his deep, Barry White–level rumble.

"No, I'm not!" I snapped. I was still waiting for a call back from a source, and who was this newbie who dared to disrupt my concentration?

Finally, my story was finished and filed, and we drove, in separate cars, to Mario and Luigi's, State College's finest Italian restaurant. Bill had worn a blue suit to his interview. He was so skinny that the pants flapped around his legs, and the jacket hung loosely from his shoulders. His eyes were big and brown and regarding me with thoughtful intent. There's no nice way to tell a man you've just met that he reminds you of your pet, especially when the animal in question is a not-very-bright, flatulent bulldog, so I didn't bring it up. We sat down at the table, and I think I asked him, "Where are you from?" And then we were off, talking about school, about friends, about our families, and the books we'd loved, and what we wanted to do with our lives, and, for three hours, I ignored angel-hair pasta with vodka sauce, which I'd been looking forward to for days. At the end of the night we walked out of the restaurant together. "Well. This was nice," he said. Then he looked thoughtful. "If I got one of those X-rated movies at the hotel, do you think the paper would give me a hard time?"

This, I knew, was the guy for me.

The next day, I confronted-slash-accosted the city editor at his desk. "You have to hire him!" I said.

"Why?" the editor asked. "Do you think he's a really good reporter?"

"I have no idea!" I said. "But I'm lonely!"

Bill got the job. He had a girlfriend back in Missouri, and I, of course, had Marcus. I wrote Marcus a letter, then I called him and listened to him cry, and told him that I was sorry but I'd met someone else, and it was time to say goodbye. All those years together, all that history, and all I felt was exhilaration, like I'd slipped out of a too-tight jacket. I was excited about the new guy at the paper, and the short story I'd sold to *Seventeen*, and the other one the *Redbook* editor had asked me to rewrite. I saw open roads, flowers blooming, life as an ocean, deep and scary and thrilling, just waiting for me to dive in.

When Bill had been at the paper for two weeks and both of us were free of our entanglements, I sent him a message, via the brand-new system at the *CDT* that allowed reporters to send texts to one another's computers. "What are you doing this weekend?" I inquired.

"Why do you ask?" he wrote back.

I rolled my eyes. "BECAUSE I'M TAKING A SURVEY," I typed.

On our first date we went to a greenhouse in Centre Hall and he bought a tiny spider plant, small enough to slip into his pocket. The first time we kissed was in my car, in the parking lot of a local bar. We started in the front seat, then moved to the back. The next time I drove, I noticed something strange. Close examination revealed a footprint—mine—on the rear passenger-side window.

When my mother called me at work to tell me that Mort had died at age ten—"he went into his doghouse for a nap, and he didn't come out"—I cried in the newsroom. For the next few days and weeks I'd cry at odd intervals, at movies that made me think about him, or when I'd see other people walking their dogs. I felt abandoned and then childish, like a little kid kicking her heels into the sand, a kid who couldn't be coaxed off the beach when the day was over, and who refused to understand the eternal bargain between pets and people: the pets almost always go first.

Losing Mort had been like losing the last piece of my childhood; the last hope that we could go back to being the family in the pictures when I was twelve—Mom and Dad in the back row; the kids, combed and groomed, in the front; and Mort lolling on the lawn at our feet. He had been my protector and my last link to that particular past, and I missed him so much. I mourned him fiercely.

And then there was Bill, who held me and listened to me talk—about Mort, about Marcus, about my father; about the relationships I'd hung on to for too long, relationships I'd never wanted to let go of.

When my roommate, a colleague at the paper, said she wanted a dog, I was dubious. I wasn't sure either one of us had the time to devote to an animal's care. But we were grown-ups, with jobs and responsibilities, bills that we paid, ambitions that we nurtured, and caring for a pet sounded like another step forward.

My roommate was the one who found Wendell in the *CDT* classified ads: "Dog, small, spotted, free to a good home." When we went to visit, Wendell, who was then going by the name Gambit, spent the entire visit jumping, bounding higher and higher with each leap, advancing from knee to waist to shoulder height. He was ten pounds of nervy energy, with a black-and-brown head, delicate markings, like kohl, around his eyes, and oversize, pointed ears. His body was speckled gray and black, a completely different color from his head, and looked like it belonged to another dog, like a distracted God had simply slapped the wrong top and bottom together. His paws were also black and brown, his nails were black, his tail was a clipped, spotted stump, and his upper lip was curled in a permanent, Elvis-like sneer, scarred by a bite his mother had given him when he was a pup.

Rat terriers, I learned, were a mixture of just about every kind of terrier and whippet there was—a little fox terrier, a little Italian greyhound, some Jack Russell, too. They were prized for their feisty temperament, bred to catch rats on long ship voyages and, once they got to America, on farms. I never saw Wendell anywhere near a rat, nor did he evince the slightest interest in keeping my apartment mouse-free. "Sorry," I imagined him saying with a shrug, "my union only lets me do rats."

We brought him back to Boalsburg, tried to get him used to his new name, then left him alone for ten minutes, during which he snuck off to pee in the corner of our living room and eat the corner of a couch cushion. On his second night with us, Bill, whom I'd just started dating, sat on the couch for an episode of *NYPD Blue* (one of the ones where they either showed a naked butt or said a swear word). Wendell settled himself on Bill's lap. Bill hadn't spent much time around dogs, but didn't want to complain, and so he sat in stoic silence as Wendell ate his way through the loose end of Bill's leather belt.

That was Wendell as a puppy. He was a chewer. A destroyer of purses. A furtive corner-pooper, a devourer of socks and a scritch-scratcher of couches, a lover of forbidden people food. On Chanukah that first year, I prepared a festive holiday meal. My roommate and her boyfriend and Bill and I were in the living room, opening gifts, when Wendell climbed up on the table, inserted the entire upper half of his body into the gravy boat, and slurped his weight in chicken gravy. The next few days were not pleasant for any of us.

My roommate and I were haphazard pet owners, inconsistent with our discipline and our attention. We'd walk Wendell, sometimes, and we'd throw a ball for him, when we thought of it. When he was six months old, we did manage to bring him to the vet to be neutered ("Tell him he's getting his nails clipped!" Bill called as we drove away).

Wendell came home later that afternoon, with a large plastic cone around his neck, and an expression of wounded dignity on his face (which is to his credit, as it must be hard to look dignified while wearing the Giant Cone o' Shame). We were instructed to leave the cone in place for three days, to prevent him from biting his stitches. After three days, the stitches dissolved and the cone came off. I put it in a corner, gave Wendell his kibble, and went to work.

When I came home, there was Wendell, waiting at the door, wagging his tail and looking a little sheepish . . . and there was his cone, around his neck again, only instead of facing out, it faced in, trapping his paws against his body, forcing him to move in tiny, mincing hops. I couldn't figure it out. Either someone had broken into our house and made us the victims of the strangest crime in the world, or . . .

I took off the cone, put it back in the corner where I'd left it, and left Wendell alone. A few minutes later, I stuck my head around the corner . . . and there he was, lying on his side, attempting to slide his head back into the cone that he'd pulled out of the corner.

My roommate speculated that maybe it smelled familiar. I thought that Wendell had decided that it was stylish—a statement piece!—and that he wanted his look back.

After six months, my roommate got another job, at a bigger paper. Wendell and I were alone in State College, where I was miserable, convinced that I would be stuck there forever. A few months later, though, I was hired by the *Lexington Herald-Leader*. My mother reluctantly agreed to keep Wendell while I got settled in Kentucky. "That dog is the weirdest-looking thing I've ever seen" was her less-than-impressed assessment the first time I took him home. By then, she had a sheltie named Boomer, and Wendell, who disdained most other dogs, tolerated Boomer's company, so much so that, for years, anywhere we went, if we came across any kind of dog with a collie-like ruff, Wendell would trot over to give the other dog a friendly sniff and allow himself to be sniffed in return.

After my first week in Kentucky, Wendell arrived at Blue Grass Airport, on the baggage carousel, in between suitcases, looking deeply aggrieved inside of the green plastic carrying case that I had festooned with hand-crayoned signs that read MY NAME IS WENDELL. THIS IS MY FIRST FLIGHT.

A few days later, he got sick. First he had diarrhea, then he started vomiting. In the middle of the night, it got so bad that I found an all-night veterinary hospital, where he was admitted and diagnosed with hemorrhagic gastroenteritis. They shaved his skinny forepaw to insert an IV, hooked him up to a bag of fluids, and put him in a wire cage, where he lay on his side with his eyes glazed, his sides heaving rapidly up and down as he panted. It was touch and go over the night . . . but the next morning, when I was allowed to go see him, he stood up, wobbled to the front of the cage, and pushed his dry nose through the slots to brush against my fingers. "That's a very good sign," said the vet.

That was, I think, the moment that we bonded, the instant that I recognized Wendell not just as a pet or a companion but as a kindred spirit. We were survivors . . . and I would do whatever I could to protect him, to keep him safe, to make him mine.

First, I signed us up for obedience school. There were eight other people, all of them with bigger dogs—golden retrievers, black labs, German shepherds, and collies, one doleful-looking basset hound. And Wendell. All the other dogs were amiable, or at least reasonable, as we taught them to sit and to come and to heel and walk politely on a leash. Not Wendell. He resisted every step of the way, showing his teeth and snarling at the instructor when she tried to teach him the command for "down," refusing to listen when I called for him or made the clicking noise that meant that he should walk beside me. Not even bribing him with the little chunks of dehydrated hot dog that the instructor had taught us to make did the trick.

We trained for hours, walking back and forth in the parking lot of the Adolph Rupp Arena, which was near my apartment on West Maxwell Street. After twelve weeks of class, Wendell could heel and sit, even if his "come" was iffy and his "down" was nonexistent. We scored a diploma, and Wendell was practically placid, walking calmly beside me when we went to the front of the class to collect it. "Can we take intermediate obedience?" I asked the instructor, who winced and said, "Maybe you should just take this class again."

In Kentucky, Wendell and I had a routine. I'd let him out for a quick wee after we woke up. Then I'd get dressed and get into the car. With Wendell settled in my lap—his preferred spot during drives—we'd go to the University of Kentucky's arboretum. There was a group of half a dozen people, middle-aged and older, people with children and houses and insights into life that I didn't have and wasn't hearing from my cynical, transient, mostly young colleagues at the paper. We'd let our dogs off their leashes—tiny, scrappy Wendell, a loose-limbed Dalmatian named Pepper, and a collie called Chief were the three regulars. The dogs would run, and we'd walk and talk for half an hour, and then I'd drive back home to shower and dress for work. Wendell would lie on my bed, his paws crossed and eyes narrowed, watching me as I pulled on my stirrup pants and vests, looking for all the world like he had something to say about my choices, and that something was not complimentary. At some point most afternoons I would make the ten-minute trip from my office to the apartment to let him out. After work, I would go to the gym. Then there'd be another turn around the neighborhood, and we would settle in for the night, with me either in front of my computer, working on a column or a short story or a freelance assignment with Wendell curled on the floor beside me, or lying on the couch, in front of the TV, with Wendell stretched out on the couch cushion above my head. He liked to have his fur brushed, and he liked to have his ears scratched. He wasn't snuggly, but he'd kiss me, taking neat little licks at my mouth or my nose to express his gratitude.

Bill and I made up an elaborate backstory for Wendell—how he'd grown up wealthy on an English estate until he was caught disgracing himself with a stableboy. How he'd been exiled to America, and how his father had disowned him, but his mother sent him money, ten- and twenty-dollar bills tucked into the cookie tin she'd mail him every month. How he'd gone to New York City and designed window displays for Barneys before deciding to lower himself and become a companion for a good-hearted but fashion-challenged young lady. On sunny days, Wendell would perch on top of the concrete retaining wall near my door, head erect, ears up, paws stretched out in front of him like Anubis, or a very small sphinx.

When I got my job at the *Inquirer*, Wendell was not pleased. He was used to quiet and being close to forests and meadows. In Philadelphia, the streets were paved with pizza crust and chicken wing bones, and they were also loud and crowded with pedestrians and cyclists and skateboarders, whom Wendell regarded as his mortal enemies. Instead of a stroll through a grassy arboretum, our morning walks took us to the narrow strip of grass that ran down Front Street, which paralleled I-95. While the rush-hour traffic hummed and honked and screeched along, we would walk north on Front Street, loop around the Society Hill Towers on Spruce

Street, then head back on Second Street, along the cobblestone streets, past the coffee shop and the bank and the Wawa and the homeless guys who came to greet Wendell by name.

Sometimes we'd venture to the dog park a few blocks south on Catharine Street. Released from his leash, Wendell would huddle by my ankles, alternately trembling and snarling at any dog that dared to approach. He could never resist a tennis ball, but when I threw it in the dog park he would race off after it, snatch it in his jaws, zip back to me, drop it at my feet, then hide behind me again, letting me know he wasn't happy. Eventually, though, he met other dogs and I made friends with their owners, including my BFF for life, Susan.

Wendell did not much enjoy the companionship of his canine fellows. Nor, really, was he a fan of other people, including the guy I dated after Bill, the inspiration for Bruce Guberman in *Good in Bed.* That guy lived in a high-rise that did not permit pets. When I went to visit I would put Wendell in a black nylon duffel bag. I'd zip it up so that just his head stuck out as I approached the building and then, as soon as I got to the door, I would zip it completely shut, and hope he wouldn't move around too much or, God forbid, bark. We'd spend the weekend in the reporter's efficiency on the eighth floor, me reading books, my gentleman friend smoking pot from an oversize blue glass bong and Wendell curled up on the bed with a look of disapproval on his face.

Sometimes, Wendell's antipathy was useful. When Susan broke up with an OCD doctor, a miserable fellow who hated his job and yelled at her for putting onion skins down his garbage disposal, we joked that we could make her ex lose his mind by putting a trail of rose petals in his house, leading from the front door to the bedroom . . . only, instead of Susan, he'd open the door and see a small, trembling, sneering rat terrier in his bed.

Susan and Wendell had an interesting relationship. Wendell

ignored Daisy, Susan's sweet mutt, who had white fur and black eyes and a black nose, who was about four times his size, but he liked Susan. When we visited, Wendell would growl at Daisy, then claim his spot on top of Susan's couch. When I traveled for work, Susan would let him stay over, and once I came to pick him up and noticed that he looked different. "I clipped his whiskers," Susan confessed (Wendell had long, quivering whiskers, black on one side of his muzzle, white on the other). "Jen, I had to do it. He's not a looker. He needs all the help he can get."

Our second year in Philadelphia, Wendell was attacked by a stranger's dog when we were out for our evening walk. Wendell was, as always, on his leash. The other dog was not. One minute Wendell was sniffing the mulch, ignoring the other pets and people, and the next minute, a giant dun-colored dog streaked across the open space, snatching up Wendell in his mouth, clamping him in his jaws and shaking him back and forth while Wendell made a horrible screaming noise. The dog's owner grabbed the dog's collar and pulled; I tried to pry the dog's jaws open, my fingers slick with saliva, shouting "DROP!" at the top of my lungs, not even thinking that the dog might decide to clamp those teeth down on me.

Finally, Wendell was free. The other dog's owner called apologies—"he's never done anything like that before!"—as I scooped Wendell up. He was bleeding and whimpering and making that terrible shrieking sound when I jostled him. I cradled him against my chest and ran two blocks to the Queen Village Animal Hospital. The dog had torn a long strip of skin and fur from Wendell's back. He had gouges in his neck that had to be cleaned out and disinfected, wounds on his belly that required stitches and surgical drains. The vet shaved his side, which was how I found out that Wendell's skin was as speckled as his fur. Hairless, he looked even skinnier than normal, a tiny, wounded, spotty scrap of a thing.

I took three days off work and sat with him in my apartment, holding him in my lap, petting him wherever I could between the bandages and the bits of plastic tubing the vet had left protruding from his sides so that his wounds could drain. He would curl in his basket with a pained sigh and look at me with what I thought was betrayal. *How could you let this happen?* Then he'd clamber slowly onto the couch and he'd sigh again and shut his eyes, and I'd feel his body go limp on my lap as I petted him and promised to do better.

Wendell was there when I broke up with the high-rise guy. He was there when Bill and I reconnected, briefly, when I was twenty-eight. Bill had moved from Augusta, Georgia, to New York City, had gotten a job at a magazine covering arts and antiques. He was living on Sackett Street in Carroll Gardens, Brooklyn, paying what I found to be a shockingly high amount for a dismayingly tiny apartment, a place where the kitchen was so small that the refrigerator was in the living room.

I had never stopped caring for Bill. At twenty-eight, I wanted so badly to get married, to have children, to buy a house, to get on with it, to move into the next stage of grown-up life. Bill wasn't ready. We broke up again, and I met Adam, who was funny and smart and plugged into pop culture with the same fervor as me. Unlike the rest of my post-Marcus beaus, who'd been tall, with dark hair and dark eyes, Adam was exactly my height. He had curly blond hair that would spring into a full-on 'fro if he didn't keep it cropped short, and long, curly blond lashes that I thought were wasted on a guy. We made each other laugh, and we had the same level of ambition, the same dreams of a house and a family and enough money for great food and nice vacations. Best of all, Adam was ready. He wanted to get married. He wanted to get married to *me*.

Wendell tolerated Adam when we were dating, but he didn't like it when Adam moved in, and he found ways to make his displeasure known. At night, he would growl at Adam, then grumpily fall asleep in his usual spot, on a pillow above my head. When Adam would put on his suit and go to work in the morning, Wendell would chase him down the length of the second-floor hall, growling and barking. Then he'd stand at the top of the stairs, watching, as Adam let himself out the front door, his posture and the bristle of fur on his back all communicating, "And STAY OUT!"

Wendell, of course, was the inspiration for Nifkin, Cannie's little rat terrier. That's his picture on the back of *Good in Bed*. When I sold the book and my advance check arrived, I took myself to Target with the intention of finally being able to buy absolutely anything there that I wanted. I loaded up a shopping cart with name-brand dish towels and scented candles, then headed to the pet aisle, thinking that I'd upgrade Wendell from his generic kibble to the fancy Iams that came in the bright yellow bag and cost twice as much as his usual fare. When I got there, I found Adam, holding his own bag. "I was going to surprise you," he said.

Wendell saw me grow up, from a single girl to a more responsible, older single girl, to a married lady to a mother, moving from an apartment to a starter house to a bigger house, and eventually acquiring a summer place on the Cape, where we spend most of July and August, and which Fran enjoys from May to October. (Wendell's collar had our Philadelphia address on the front, and the back said "Summer residence," with our Truro address and phone number—the canine equivalent of those snooty author biographies that announce the writer "divides his time between Berkeley and the Hamptons").

Wendell would grudgingly accommodate himself to every shift in my life, but I think that he was meant to be a single girl's dog. By the time that love and marriage led to the baby carriage—the eight-hundred-dollar Bugaboo I'd pilot around Queen Village—he was a senior citizen, grumpy and prickly and set in his ways, miserable every time he had to go to the vet and endure the indignity of being weighed on the cat scale, or when he had to cede my lap or my time or my attention to a newborn. He tolerated the girls but never warmed to them, although they both adored him, and knew his place in my heart. Lucy's first word was "mama," but her first sentence was "Wen-gell! Come, come!" complete with a tap on the bed.

As Wendell got older, his vet noticed the heart murmur he'd always had became an enlarged heart. His cardiologist—yes, my dog had a cardiologist—prescribed diuretics, which made him pee all the time and taxed his kidneys, so then he had to take medication to keep them working. I told myself, every time we made a thousand-dollar visit to the Penn Veterinary Hospital, that by paying for treatments that other, possibly more sane pet owners would have balked at, I was allowing students to get the hands-on experience they needed, so that when the procedures became more commonplace, they'd be ready . . . but the truth is, I couldn't bear to let him go. "As long as he's not in pain," I told the doctors as they reconfigured his medications and performed ultrasounds, trying to find the delicate balance between keeping his compromised heart beating and not sending him into renal failure. When he lost his appetite and I began finding his medication on the floor, I started crushing his pills and mixing them with pâté, which he'd then lick off my fingers. Fran would watch in bemusement and disgust, then announce, "In my next life, I want to come back as your dog."

Wendell died in the early springtime, in 2009. I was devastated, cracked open and exposed in my grief. My dad had died a year before, and I'd gotten through that just fine, handling my business, doing what needed to be done, trying to assimilate my new three-year-old half brother into my life, brightly insisting that it was no big deal, that I was okay, that, honestly, I'd already lost my father a long time ago.

I was not fine. I was not okay. My father had not been in my life, but until he died, I never stopped hoping that he'd straighten himself out, that he'd see the wreckage that he'd left and feel sorry, that he would be, once more, the father I'd loved so much when I was little, or that at least I'd get some answers, that I'd understand what had happened and why he'd left. But it wasn't until I lost Wendell, too, at the very advanced age of eighteen, that I let myself feel anything. I barely shed a tear at my dad's funeral, but when I had to go to the Penn Veterinary Center and say goodbye to Wendell—when I touched his stiffened body, stroked his gray head, and whispered, "Good boy," for the last time, I cried like my heart was breaking. Wendell had been with me for everything, through everything, and now my marriage was ending—a fact I had barely been able to admit to myself—and Wendell wouldn't be there to see me through it. Adam was, and is, a wonderful man—funny and smart and accomplished—but we'd gone into our marriage expecting one version of things, and we hadn't done well at navigating our personal or professional changes.

I should have told Adam what I'd come to realize—that something important had been irreparably broken after Lucy's birth, that I wouldn't be able to trust him with my heart. Instead I went looking for the guy who'd never let me down. Bill and I hadn't spoken since 9/11. Now, here it was, almost nine years later. I didn't have his phone number, hadn't friended him on Facebook or tried to find him on Twitter. I didn't want to be that girl, the one who, late at night, would look up old loves on social media, scroll through the pictures of their vacations and cookouts and adorable children and wonder how it could have turned out differently . . . but I did have his old AOL e-mail address. I wrote him a short note, with a memo line reading "Is this still you?" thinking that if he read it, if he answered, it was meant to be. Thinking, too, that he'd probably never see it, because who still had an AOL address?

Thirty seconds later, my in-box pinged. "Still me," he'd written, "what's up?"

I told him Wendell had died. I told him my father had died. I said that I was married, but unhappy and not optimistic. Bill invited me to have dinner with him in New York in a few weeks, when I'd be there for business. I was sitting in the restaurant bar when he came up behind me and touched my shoulder. He was wearing a suit again, the same way he was the first time we'd met—and, except for some gray in his hair and more fashionable glasses, he looked almost the same as he had when he was twenty-four and I was twenty-three. He'd never been married. I joked that he'd been waiting for me . . . and he didn't tell me I was wrong. "It feels like you just went away for a long weekend," he said at the end of another three-hour dinner, where we talked until everyone else in the restaurant went home and the waiter blew out the candle at our table and finally told us they were closing when we didn't take the hint. We were, we discovered, still each other's favorite people to talk to . . . and finally, all those years after our first conversation, he was ready to commit, to sign up for "forever," and take on a life that included a novelist in the house and two little girls.

The next few years brought a slow untangling—the end of the marriage, Adam moving out, the two of us working through the best way to parent our daughters. I didn't want to add a pet to the drama of Adam's departure and Bill's gradual introduction. I was—we all were—focused on the girls and getting them through it.

After Wendell, I knew it would be a while before I was ready to have another dog. But when Phoebe was three and Lucy was seven, they were both lobbying for a pet. "What kind?" I said, expecting them to ask for a poodle or a pug, or one of the cunning, bat-eared French bulldogs that had started popping up in our neighborhood.

"A dog like Wendell," Phoebe decreed.

"Seriously?" I asked. "Wendell was kind of grouchy."

But Lucy googled rat terriers, and showed me Internet evidence that they are, in fact, known as a breed that's good with families and young children. Then she found RatRescue.com. We told the administrator that we'd be interested in puppies but would prefer an adult, then scrolled through the pictures of available dogs until we came to a shot of a very stout, extremely pregnant female, standing on a deck and staring off into the distance with an expression of resignation on her face. Her name was Moochie. She'd been left at a kill shelter, pregnant. "Seduced and abandoned," I said. The rat rescue people had placed her in a foster home. She'd given birth, and all five of her puppies had swiftly found homes . . . but no one was in a hurry to take on what the site's administrators described as a "teen mom."

I filled out the application, which was more comprehensive than the one I'd completed to get into college. I described the homes where Moochie would live. I wrote an essay about my day-to-day life, explaining that the house was rarely empty, that any dog I adopted would hardly ever be alone. I cited my time with Wendell as proof that I was capable of providing a rat terrier with companionship as well as excellent health care.

Finally, we were approved. On a brilliantly sunny January Sunday, Bill and Phoebe and I drove down to Baltimore. We parked in front of the designated house and out came a young woman with a blue-and-yellow leash attached to a dog that could have been Wendell's significantly more substantial sister. Instead of Wendell's speckles, Moochie's fur is mostly white, with large black spots and brown highlights and a sweet pink triangle on her nose. One of her pointy ears stands straight up, like Wendell's did, while the other one flops down, drooping toward her forehead. Unlike Wendell, she had a long, curved tail. Her belly was soft and pink, with loose folds of skin, evidence of her recent pregnancy, and she was solidly built, a contrast to Wendell's narrow frame and spindly legs. She sniffed my hand, then Phoebe's, and gave Bill a suspicious look, and squatted down for a quick wee. Then I scooped her up and put her in the carrier we'd purchased, and drove her to Philadelphia.

At home, Moochie inspected every inch of the house, sniffing at the carpets and in the corners. In my imagination, she was communing with Wendell's spirit, getting the lowdown on me and the girls and Bill. Upstairs, she wriggled underneath my bed, and would not come out, no matter how we pleaded and wheedled. For the first week of her new life, she stayed under the bed, coming out only for walks and to gobble her bowl of kibble, never making a sound—not a bark, not a whimper. She was, we quickly realized, afraid of almost everything. On our jaunts through the neighborhood, a slammed car door, a gust of wind in the trees, a motorcycle, another dog, or the sight of a man, of any age or size, would make Moochie stiffen, or do a startled jump, or run behind my legs, cringing. Construction crews, which abound in our neighborhood, were terrifying menaces. She'd plant her four feet on the sidewalk, refusing to walk by a cement mixer or the jackhammer, even if they were all the way across the street, forcing me to pick her up and carry her.

"She might have been abused," said the trainer I brought in to help me figure out this strange, un-Wendell-like dog.

In the days and weeks that followed, we started to learn Moochie's ways. We discovered that she hated confinement after we put her in a metal crate during a weekend in Connecticut, and came home to discover that she'd Hulked her way out, pushing two of the bars apart and wriggling through the opening.

We bought a plastic crate. Moochie chewed her way through it. What she wanted, it emerged, was to be with me. On my lap, or against my chest, or, when I was sleeping on my side, wedged under my leg, between my thighs and my knees. She was bigger than Wendell, and heavier, and bossier. She'd hop onto the bed, drop her bottom down against me, shove and wedge and wriggle until we were both where she wanted us, and only then fall into a doze, during which she'd snore and twitch and whimper, paws paddling the air as she ran in her sleep. She found her voice and

started barking—at visitors, at the doorbell, at other dogs walking on the sidewalk by our—her—house. The UPS truck was
her nemesis, prompting a frenzy of barking with every approach.

It soon became clear that whatever had happened to Moochie
had involved men, judging by the way she'd either cringe and hide,
or lunge and bark, whenever a strange man came to the house . . .
but she learned to like Bill. When he'd read on the couch, she'd
sidle up to him, then hop up onto his chest, or settle herself between his legs, napping with her chin resting on his thigh.

On Valentine's Day, when she'd been in residence for six
weeks, Moochie managed to clamber onto a barstool, then
onto the breakfast bar, where she devoured a two-pound box of
chocolates and a dozen chocolate-chip cookies I'd baked. My
assistant, Meghan, and I rushed her to the vet, where she was
weighed—"You might want to watch the treats," said the vet,
noting that Moochie had put on a pound and a half since her
arrival six weeks previously—and then given a shot of what was
described as doggy Pepto-Bismol in her bottom.

"I think she's eating her feelings," Meghan said as we walked
the disgraced and belching Moochie back home. "Valentine's
Day is probably hard for her. She was pregnant, she was abandoned, and now it's a holiday that celebrates love . . ."

"Also, RatRescue.com was like online dating, and she knows
she's not on the market anymore," I said. "So it's not like she has
to maintain her girlish figure to find a home."

The pattern was set. Moochie would eat anything she could
reach and steal, including but not limited to things that were
not, technically, food. She'll gnaw on FedEx envelopes and book
spines and magazine pages. One memorable night she swiped
an entire roast turkey breast that had been placed on the cutting
board to rest before we carved it. Again, Moochie hoisted herself
onto the breakfast bar. She snagged the turkey, dragged it across
the counter, then towed it into the dining room (where all the

finest dogs eat). We found her underneath the table, having her way with the turkey breast, an act that inspired Phoebe, in first grade at the time, to write a story entitled "My Noddy Dog." ("My dog shur is noddy," the first sentence read.)

If Wendell was a stylish and cynical gay man trapped in the body of a rat terrier, Moochie is more like a sweet, plump, slightly bewildered 1950s housewife. I imagined Wendell in three-piece suits and ties and matching pocket squares, looking haughtily down his snout at a world whose vagaries and messiness displeased him. Moochie, I picture in shirtdresses and aprons, wringing her hands and cringing at a car door's slam and eventually ending up with a Valium prescription. "A loyal companion animal," my mother will say as Moochie trails me up the stairs in the house on Cape Cod, rarely straying from my heel. Bill and I learned that she could swim that first summer after I went out in a kayak. I was paddling away from the shore when I heard Bill call my name. I turned around and saw a small black-and-white head, eyes wide, flailing valiantly after me. I rowed back to meet her and lifted her into the kayak, where Moochie gave herself a brisk shake, looked around, and then positioned herself on the bow like a ship's figurehead, bravely scanning the waters for danger.

Moochie might love me the best . . . but if Wendell was my dog, then Moochie is our dog, Bill's dog as much as she is mine. He makes up stories for her, giving her the lines of an insult comic. Sometimes she'll snap at him when he tries to kiss me. I think it's because she's momentarily forgotten herself, and him, and he's just one of those men in her past. He thinks she just wants to remind him who's the boss.

Four years after Moochie's arrival, Bill and I were, at long last, planning our wedding.

Getting married at forty-five is, I discovered, different from getting hitched in your early thirties. I was less worried about inviting everyone or proving anything. I knew who I was, my strengths and insecurities, how I can be thin-skinned and argumentative, how I hold grudges and look brave online while IRL I'm in my closet crying over my hurt feelings. I know who he is, how his stoicism can look like indifference, how his love is more in his actions than his words, how he'll always be my voice of reason, whether it's about art I want to buy or a tweet I want to send.

We knew what we wanted—a ceremony at home, close friends and family, gorgeous flowers, delicious food.

Our first impulse was to have Moochie attend, in an attractive floral garland, possibly carrying the rings. Then we learned that our rabbi is afraid of dogs . . . and we remembered Moochie's tendency to get snarly and defensive whenever there are strange men in the house.

"I'm not going to allow Moochie to be treated like Rosemary Kennedy," Susan said when we explained that, regrettably, Moochie wouldn't be part of the big day. The afternoon of our nuptials, we dropped her off at Fran and Clair's hotel room . . . and, when it was over, I took off my wedding dress, put on jeans and a sweater, and went to retrieve her. When I opened the door, she flew over, wagging and whining ecstatically. She planted herself in my lap and looked up at me, her big brown eyes as trusting as Mort's ever were . . . and then, with Wendell's hauteur, she permitted me to leash her, and strolled down the hotel hallway, nails clicking, snout held high. Past the room where Lucy and Phoebe and David were sleeping with Aunt Molly, who was already planning on marching them back to me in their wedding finery ("Now, children, this is called the walk of shame"). Past my brothers' rooms and out the door, down South Second Street, past Adam's apartment, then around the corner, and home, where the caterers were packing up and Bill was waiting. We sat on the couch, just the three of us. Moochie sighed contentedly, then wriggled herself into position, sprawling across us, her head in Bill's lap and her bottom in mine. "Who's my good girl?" I heard Bill ask in his deep voice, and I shut my eyes, took his hand, and thought, *I have come home.*

Coda

Letter to Lucy and Phoebe
Time, May 2015

I get it. I know that, to you, I am just "Lady Who Can't Work the TiVo." Or "Woman Who Needs Emojis Explained to Her." I know how annoyed you get when I chase you around with the hairbrush/toothbrush/sunscreen/good shoes and insist that you make your bed, clear your dishes, and wear underpants when leaving the house. I see how you cringe when I car-dance every time "Baby Got Back" comes on the radio, especially when the people on the street watch me lip-synch. To you, I am pretty much a large lump of ignorance who exists only to make you eat your vegetables, finish your homework, and write your thank-you notes.

But I do know a few things. Having passed through the vale of tears that is adolescence, I can peek around the corner into your future, and tell you what's coming next.

Within the next few years, some people—not all, but some—will stop seeing you as you and start seeing just your surface: your face, your hair, your body. These people won't care that you're both stars at math or that you both love to swim. They won't want to hear about the time that you, Phoebe, got lost in the supermarket when you were three and how you marched yourself up to the service desk with perfect aplomb and told them that your mom's name was Jennifer Pearl because your name is Phoebe Pearl, so why wouldn't it be? . . . and how, when I found you, you were sitting on the counter, chatting with the manager, with a balloon in one hand, a giant cookie in the other, and a stuffed bunny in your lap. They won't care that you, Lucy, built a spaceship out of a bunch of cardboard boxes, with a ball chute on the outside and holders for an iPad and some lip balm in the shadowy interior, and that you love show tunes and sailing and *MythBusters* and can sing all the words to "It's the End of the World as We Know It."

These people will care mostly—sometimes only—about how you look. They'll reduce you to a body, instead of seeing you as a person. This will persist for the next forty or fifty years or so, at which point you will become essentially invisible, and they will stop seeing you at all.

They'll think that your body is public property. They'll think they can catcall you on the street or grope you on the subway or tell you you'd be prettier if you smiled. If you insist on expressing your opinions—and I hope you will—they'll hide behind their screens and call you ugly, or a slut, or a fat, ugly slut, which always confused me. How can you be fat and ugly and sell sex for a living? How is that a workable business model? If you succeed, they will whisper, or write, that you must have slept with someone important to have gotten whatever you got. If you speak up, they will try to shame you into silence, because—and it breaks my heart to write these words—that's the way some people still think women ought to be.

My prayer is that you'll never lose sight of yourselves—all of yourselves. You are so much more than just your looks. Your bodies are perfect, perfectly made and perfectly sized. You don't have to waste years of your life fighting against them or trying to fit someone else's idea of beautiful (especially if that person is taking your money and whispering snake-oil promises about how if you only stick to this diet/cleanse/fitness plan, if you only get this injection/operation/painful piece of shapewear, you'll look the way you should).

Love your bodies for what they can do. Remember that you've climbed mountains, swum across ponds, collected bucketsful of clams, balanced on bicycles and paddleboards, and danced around in your bedrooms with complete abandon. Remember how great it feels to solve a tough math problem, or cook something delicious, or fall into a really great book, and how none of that has anything to do with your appearance.

Keep swimming. Keep talking. If something's wrong, speak up. I will always love you, and I will always see you, all of you, inside and out. And every single part of you is perfect.

Acknowledgments

I am grateful beyond telling to my family and loved ones for letting me tell my version of this story: my Nanna, Faye Frumin; my mom, Frances Frumin Weiner; her partner, Clair Kaplan; my sister, Molly Beth; my brothers, Jake and Joe and David; and Adam Bonin, the father of my girls.

Thanks to my agent, Joanna Pulcini, who read that very first hot mess of a five-hundred-page manuscript for *Good in Bed* and said, "This is a book." Thanks to everyone at Atria for letting me tell that story, and every story since then, and for handling my work with such care: Carolyn Reidy, Judith Curr, and Lisa Sciambra. Special thanks to Sarah Cantin—may this be the first of many books together! Thank you, Marcy Engelman, for your loyalty and your skills.

My assistant, Meghan Burnett, was a rock star, as always.

To Lucy and Phoebe and Bill—you are my happy ending.